THE FIRST KING OF ENGLAND

The First King of England

ÆTHELSTAN AND THE BIRTH
OF A KINGDOM

DAVID WOODMAN

PRINCETON UNIVERSITY PRESS

PRINCETON & OXFORD

Published by Princeton University Press
41 William Street, Princeton, New Jersey 08540
99 Banbury Road, Oxford OX2 6JX

press.princeton.edu

GPSR Authorized Representative: Easy Access System Europe - Mustamäe tee 50, 10621 Tallinn, Estonia, gpsr.requests@easproject.com

All Rights Reserved

Library of Congress Control Number: 2025930848

ISBN 9780691249490
ISBN (e-book) 9780691249674

British Library Cataloging-in-Publication Data is available

Editorial: Ben Tate, Josh Drake
Production Editorial: Elizabeth Byrd
Jacket: Chris Ferrante
Production: Danielle Amatucci
Publicity: Alyssa Sanford (US), Charlotte Coyne (UK)
Copyeditor: Brian Bendlin

Jacket illustration by Joanna Lisowiec

Printed in the United States of America

10 9 8 7 6 5 4 3 2 1

*In memory of my wonderful mother, Dorothy Woodman,
who, in the study of Latin and Greek, did so much
to elucidate the past*

CONTENTS

Color plates follow pages 124 and 180

ILLUSTRATIONS

Figure

Maps

Plates

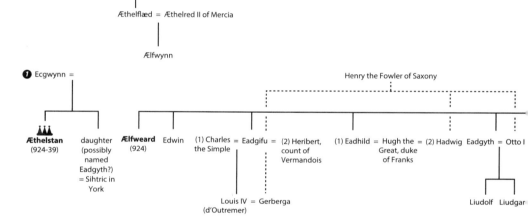

FIGURE 1. Simplified genealogy of the West Saxon royal house and its connections to Europe.[1]

1. Names in bold type are kings of the West Saxon royal house. Note that the genealogy is not intended to be comprehensive nor does it necessarily list people in their correct order of birth.

2. On the difficulty of identifying the name and mother of this daughter of Edward the Elder, and the identity of her husband, see Appendix II.

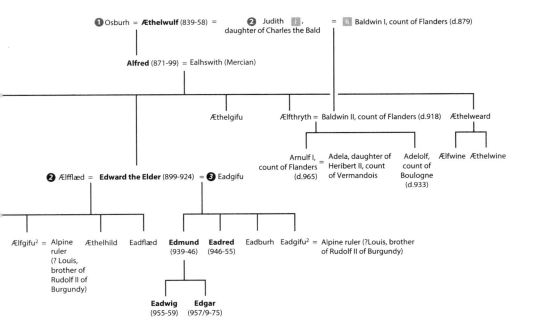

A NOTE ON SPELLING, PRONUNCIATION, DATES, AND FORMS OF REFERENCE

THE NAMES of the people and places that we will encounter in Æthelstan's life were recorded in sources originally written in a variety of places and languages. The modern English Óláf, for example, is a version of the Old Norse name Óláfr, and can be found rendered as Amlaíb in Irish sources, Anlaf in English texts, and Anlavus in Latin. As far as possible, both personal and place names are here given in the most familiar modern English equivalents. For English personal names, the practice of the second edition of *The Wiley Blackwell Encyclopaedia of Anglo-Saxon England* is replicated; for Brittonic names the example of T. Charles-Edwards's *Wales and the Britons, 350–1064* is followed; and, for the majority of Scandinavian names, the usage and spelling follow that in the *Oxford Dictionary of National Biography*. Where it is important to provide the original spelling of a personal or a place name, or where the modern equivalent of a place is not certainly known and the original place name of the source is produced in the text, it is given in italics.

The Old English language contains a number of letter forms not used in modern English. These include ash (Æ, æ); eth (Ð, ð); thorn (Þ, þ) and wynn (Ƿ, ƿ). For the most part, these letter forms have been silently converted to their modern English equivalents, but it has seemed sensible when providing names to retain the ash (Æ, æ), not least because it forms the beginning of Æthelstan's own name. The letter form is pronounced in a similar way to the letter *a* in 'cat'.

Some of the names can at first sight seem very alien, particularly if it is unclear how they should be pronounced. Readers will find at the end of the book a list, 'Dramatis Personae', which contains the names of the vast majority of people mentioned and includes suggested phonetic spellings of the names of the principal individuals as a guide for pronunciation. Some names terminate with the Old English element *-flæd*, where the nearest equivalent in modern English for the pronunciation of *æ* is the *are* in 'stare', but which is rendered simply as 'flad' in the 'Dramatis Personae'. Similarly, the *y* in the names Eadgyth (long) and Ecgwynn (short), is most similar to the modern French *tu*, but the names are pronounced in the 'Dramatis Personnae' as 'Ay-ahd-geeth' and 'Edge-win', respectively.

When citing ranges of dates, readers will find two forms: either '900 × 927' or '900–927'. The use of an '×' indicates that the event in question happened at a specific unknown moment within the span cited, whereas the use of '–' indicates that the event happened continuously throughout the years cited.

When referring to primary sources I often add the pagination of the standard editions in parentheses. For the way in which charters are cited, see the entry 'S' in 'Frequently Cited Sources and Abbreviations' in the bibliography and Appendix I.

ACKNOWLEDGMENTS

IN MY fourth week as an undergraduate student at Cambridge University my then supervisor, Professor Simon Keynes, set me an essay question: 'If you were to write a biography of King Æthelstan, what would its main themes be?' At that stage I was only dimly aware of the name Æthelstan, and no modern biography of him had been written. What I discovered in that week of research led to an enduring fascination with the first king of England. I am very grateful to Ben Tate and Josh Drake of Princeton University Press and Doug Young of PEW Literary for all that they have done to make the book possible. My colleagues Professor Rory Naismith and Professor Levi Roach, with whom I was an undergraduate at Trinity College, Cambridge, very kindly read and commented on the book in advance of its publication and have improved it in numerous respects. A number of other scholars were generous in offering help of various kinds: Dr Fraser McNair shared his translation of Folcuin's work in advance of publication, as did Dr David Pelteret on manumissions; Professor Richard Dance offered advice about the pronunciation of Old English names; Dr Irving Finkel provided guidance about early medieval board games; Dr Ben Guy advised me about Welsh chronology; and Dr Fran Colman and Dr Oliver Padel helped me to interpret the etymons of various early medieval names. Professor Catherine Cubitt very generously provided advice about different aspects of Æthelstan's life and style of kingship from which I have greatly profited. I would also like to record my great gratitude to Elizabeth Byrd, Dimitri Karetnikov, and Michelle Scott for all of their help in the production of the book, including its maps and images.

The writing of the book would not have been possible without a significant period of research leave, which was very generously supported by a grant from the Arts and Humanities Research Fund of Robinson College, Cambridge. The majority of the book was written in the most blissful of circumstances: in the Elmer Holmes Bobst Library at New York University and the Harry Elkins Widener Library at Harvard University. I am indebted to Professor Adam Kosto of Columbia University and Professor David Levene of New York University for their enabling of my time in New York, and to Professor Sean Gilsdorf for his ongoing support in Cambridge, Massachusetts. Were it not for my partner, Dr Sasha Haco, none of my work on Æthelstan would have been possible: she makes life incomparably better.

The idea for the book came especially to the fore during a drive with my father along the Roman road known as the Stanegate, a route taken by vikings as they made their way across England from west to east. As with most of my work, my father has read every word of the book and improved its prose throughout. I cannot thank him enough—for everything. Discussion about Æthelstan—in the car on the Stanegate, and subsequently—offered a small degree of relief from an otherwise unbearable loss from our family. My mother did not live to see any part of the project: her sudden death on 23 October 2020, deprived us of what we had anticipated would be many more years of happiness together. I hope she would have enjoyed reading about Æthelstan.

David Woodman
City Road, Cambridge

THE FIRST KING OF ENGLAND

Introduction

BY 12 JULY 927, Æthelstan had made his way to the vicinity of Eamont Bridge, today a small village just over a mile south from the centre of Penrith, to receive the formal submission of two kings of the Welsh people, Hywel Dda ('the Good') and Owain; of the Scottish king, Constantine II; and of Ealdred, a powerful Northumbrian from the house of Bamburgh.[1] It is possible that another king, Owain of Strathclyde, also recognised Æthelstan's supremacy that day. Earlier in 927 Æthelstan had become the first ever person who could legitimately be titled 'King of the English', having brought the previously independent kingdom of Northumbria within his dominion. It is likely that the occasion at Eamont Bridge constituted formal recognition that Æthelstan was at that moment the premier king in the British Isles.

The site chosen was rich with symbolism. The Old English place-name for Eamont, *æt Eamotum*, means literally 'at the meeting of the rivers', indicative of Eamont Bridge's position at the place where the Rivers Eamont and Lowther flow together. It was also, in the early tenth century, the boundary between the early medieval kingdoms of Northumbria and Strathclyde. Meetings between rulers of roughly equal power were often deliberately held on borders in the early medieval period. That the ceremony was held in a border territory far from the heart of Æthelstan's power in Wessex was a recognition of the way in which he had managed to extend his authority so far to the north; but it was also, perhaps, an indication of the limitations of that authority, inasmuch as he could not compel the kings present to attend him further south. Quite what the kings discussed that day, and whether or not they were moved by the symbolism of the area—which was reinforced by the presence nearby of three ancient sites of significance, the Roman fort Brocavum, King Arthur's Round Table Henge, and Mayburgh Henge—is impossible to know. But the event, recorded in only one of the seven principal extant versions of the *Anglo-Saxon Chronicle*, was the most significant that had yet been set down in English historical texts. The moment was not lost on one member of Æthelstan's retinue. A man of continental origin, possibly named Peter, had journeyed north with Æthelstan and witnessed his political successes of 927.[2] To commemorate the occasion he composed a poem which he directed south to the royal palace in Winchester and in which he records that the 'Saxon-land' (*Saxonia*), by which he means England, had now been 'made whole' (*perfecta*). Eamont Bridge was more than a coming together of rivers and of kings; it represented the beginnings of a newly constituted kingdom of the English, and a growing awareness that all of the peoples within England, who had diverse backgrounds that were variously Welsh, Scottish, Irish, Breton, and Scandinavian, could look towards Æthelstan as their king, and perhaps—if they chose to—could begin to think of themselves as members of the 'English', the *Angelcynn* in Old English.

———

The meeting near Eamont Bridge highlights the political complexity of early medieval Britain. The 'kingdom of the English' forged by Æthelstan comprised territories that had, until relatively recently, been independent kingdoms in their own right, with their own sequences of kings, who minted coins in their name and issued royal documents such as diplomas and laws. Æthelstan belonged to a line of West Saxon kings that traced their descent from a mythical founding figure called Cerdic, from whom descendants in the main line became known as Cerdicings. Their kingdom, Wessex, was located in the south and west. Abutting Wessex to the north was the kingdom of Mercia, situated in the midlands area. Its name derives from the Old English word *mierce*, which

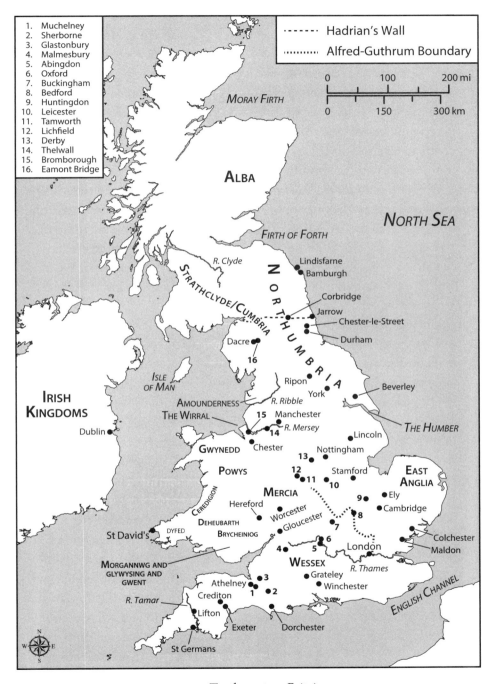

1. Muchelney
2. Sherborne
3. Glastonbury
4. Malmesbury
5. Abingdon
6. Oxford
7. Buckingham
8. Bedford
9. Huntingdon
10. Leicester
11. Tamworth
12. Lichfield
13. Derby
14. Thelwall
15. Bromborough
16. Eamont Bridge

- - - - - Hadrian's Wall
·········· Alfred-Guthrum Boundary

0   100   200 mi
0   150   300 km

MORAY FIRTH

ALBA

NORTH SEA

FIRTH OF FORTH

R. Clyde

STRATHCLYDE/CUMBRIA

N O R T H U M B R I A

Lindisfarne
Bamburgh

Corbridge
Jarrow
Chester-le-Street
Durham

Dacre
16

Ripon
York

Beverley

ISLE
OF MAN

IRISH
KINGDOMS

Dublin

AMOUNDERNESS
THE WIRRAL

15

Manchester
R. Ribble

R. Mersey

THE HUMBER

14

Lincoln

GWYNEDD   Chester

Nottingham

POWYS

13

12
11

Stamford
10

EAST
ANGLIA

MERCIA

Hereford

Worcester

Gloucester

9
8

7

Ely
Cambridge

CEREDIGION

DEHEUBARTH
BRYCHEINIOG

St David's   DYFED

6

London

Colchester
Maldon

MORGANNWG AND
GLYWYSING AND
GWENT

4   5

WESSEX

Grateley

R. Thames

R. Tamar

Athelney

Crediton

3

1   2

Winchester

ENGLISH CHANNEL

Lifton

Exeter   Dorchester

St Germans

N
W   E
S

MAP 1. Tenth-century Britain.

means a 'boundary', and which may have been intended to convey the sense that it was on the boundary, either with Wales to the west, Wessex to its south, or Northumbria to its north, depending on one's perspective. North of the River Humber lay Northumbria itself, which in its earliest manifestation had been divided by the River Tees into two kingdoms, that of Deira to the south and Bernicia to the north, which were latterly joined together into Northumbria proper in the mid-seventh century. A period of viking settlement in and around York from the late ninth century onwards, with which Æthelstan would have to contend, in effect served to reemphasise this old division between the two constituent parts of Northumbria, since vikings did not penetrate north of the Tees in any significant way. To the east of Wessex, the kingdom of East Anglia had also fallen under viking control in the late ninth century, as had parts of the east midlands; Æthelstan's father, Edward the Elder, whom we will soon meet, undertook concerted efforts to bring these areas under West Saxon control.

Owing to a paucity of documentation and narrative accounts, the history of the north-west, in what today we would think of as Cumbria, is relatively obscure for the late ninth and early tenth centuries. From what we can gather, it seems to have been part of a Brittonic-speaking kingdom known as Strathclyde. The origins of Strathclyde itself lay with a series of kings who had as their base Dumbarton Rock (*Alt Clut*, 'Rock of the Clyde') but who, following a viking attack in 870, were forced to relocate their centre further east and inland, to the 'valley' (*strath*) of the River Clyde. According to one recent interpretation, the Strathclyde kingdom, sometimes termed the 'land of the Cumbrians' (*Cumbraland*) by early English sources, expanded its territory southwards in the late ninth and early tenth centuries, beyond the Solway Firth, and it was bounded ultimately by the River Eamont. The kingdom of Strathclyde/Cumbria (as it will be referred to here), whose history is obscure, endured until the eleventh century.[3]

From about 900 we begin to see references to a kingdom in northern Britain called 'Alba', which appears in some ways to be a successor to the northern kingdoms known as Dál Riata and Pictland, and a precursor to modern Scotland.[4] Alba's heartlands were in the region between the

Firth of Forth and the Moray Firth. The kings of Alba traced their descent back to a man named Kenneth MacAlpine (d. 858). Early kings in this line are referred to by the title 'king of the Picts', and it is only from the reign of Donald (d. 900) that the title 'king of Alba' is invoked. From the year 920, the *Anglo-Saxon Chronicle* refers to people of this area as 'Scots' rather than 'Picts', as they had previously been known. Constantine II, who was present that day at Eamont Bridge, ruled Alba for over forty years at this crucial period of its formation. Æthelstan would have multiple dealings with him.[5]

Wales in the tenth century was itself politically fragmented and composed of a number of separate kingdoms which included Gwynedd in the north-west; Dyfed in the south-west (which was incorporated within a southern area known as Deheubarth); Brycheiniog, Gwent, and Glywysing (the latter two would later be joined and known as Morgannwg) in the south-east; the southern kingdom of Ystrad Tywi; the kingdom of Powys in the east; and the western kingdom of Ceredigion. The most influential Welsh king to emerge in the early tenth century was Hywel Dda, with whom Æthelstan would have regular contact.[6]

It might be expected that in the tenth century Ireland, an island less than half the area of Great Britain, would lend itself to being one political unit. But nothing could be further from the truth: in Æthelstan's day there were a number of provincial overlordships, which included Munster in the south-west, Connacht in the west, the Northern and Southern Uí Neill in the north and into the midlands area, Ulster in the north-east, and Leinster in the east. And, according to one recent reckoning, there were in excess of some 150 separate kingdoms (known by the Old Irish word *túath*), whose kings had varying degrees of power and authority.[7]

The term Viking—regularly applied to those Scandinavians who came from regions of Denmark, Norway, and Sweden—is in some ways misleading. Its use not only disguises the diverse origins of the individuals concerned but also suggests a degree of cultural, ethnic, and linguistic uniformity which is inappropriate when describing the Scandinavians we will meet. The derivation of the word Viking has been much debated and is not certainly known. In Scandinavian texts the Old Norse word *víkingr* referred to a man who was part of a military expedition. The term Viking was rarely used in the early medieval period itself. English sources, for example, tend to refer to members of the viking army as Danes (even if they did not come from Denmark) or as pagans. Because the word Viking has become so well ingrained in the modern consciousness, however, it has been used throughout the book, specifically for those involved in military acts. The neutral term Scandinavian (or Hiberno-Scandinavian, to denote those from Ireland) is preferred when no such activity is suggested. Historians have also come to refer to vikings, with a lowercase *v*, and, where possible, without the definite article, to make it clear that the word embraces peoples from many different backgrounds. The same practice is adopted here.

It was not just in the eastern, midland, and northern parts of England that vikings were active and creating settlements of their own. By this stage they had also settled parts of the so-called kingdom of the Isles (the Isle of Man, the Hebrides, and the islands of the Clyde); the Orkney and Shetland Islands, and the Isle of Anglesey. Viking naval camps were also created on the east coast of Ireland in Dublin, Wexford, Waterford, and Cork, and in the west at Limerick. One especially powerful dynasty of vikings, all descended from a certain Ívarr (d. 873), had based themselves in Dublin and would intermittently assert their rights to rule from York in Northumbria, thus causing serious issues for successive English kings, and for Æthelstan in particular.[8] The area encompassed by the Irish Sea and the west coasts of England and Scotland was thus of crucial strategic importance.

Europe itself in the tenth century, as we will see in chapter 6, was experiencing a high degree of political turbulence. Charles the Great (d. 814), better known as Charlemagne,[9] had created an empire that was the first, broadly speaking, to replicate in geographical extent the former western Roman empire. But by the mid- to late ninth century the empire had become politically fragmented. A series of successor regions emerged whose territories were often ill defined and ever shifting, and in which the power of kings, and of other secular dignitaries such as margraves and counts, fluctuated in extent and nature. Modern historians refer to a number of principal kingdoms and regions in existence by the late ninth and early tenth centuries:

1. The kingdom of **West Francia** (the ancestor of modern France), which had its centre around Laon and Rheims and included territory north of the River Loire, and which sometimes laid claim to areas of Lotharingia but did not incorporate the northern areas of Brittany, Normandy, and Flanders nor the eastern areas of Burgundy and Provence.[10]

2. The kingdom of **Italy**, which incorporated the area of Piedmont in the north-west and Friuli in the north-east, and which extended roughly halfway down the Italian Peninsula, just beyond Rome, and whose territories abutted those belonging to the papal see.

3. **Burgundy**, whose western lands, roughly the area between the Rivers Loire and Saône and north of Mâcon, became the duchy of Burgundy, and whose eastern territories were situated to the east of the River Saône and south of Mâcon. The southerly part of Burgundy (known variously as lower Burgundy, cisjurane Burgundy, or Provence), extended roughly from Lyons and Vienne southwards towards the Mediterranean.

4. **East Francia**, which comprised a variety of regions including Bavaria, Franconia, Swabia, Saxony, and Thuringia, with important cities including Aachen, Cologne, Liège, Mainz, Trier, and Würzburg.

5. The duchy of **Lotharingia**, formerly a kingdom, which was itself divided into Lower (northern) and Upper (southern) Lotharingia, and which was broadly bounded in the west by the territory of West Francia (along the lines of the Rivers Scheldt and Meuse), in the north by the North Sea, in the east by East Frankish lands (along the River Rhine), and in the south by Burgundy.

The tenth century in Europe became a particularly formative period as the different parts of the former empire forged their own new and separate identities and as nobles of non-royal stock sought recognition as

MAP 2. Europe around 933.

kings in their own right.[11] There were opportunities here for the ambitious individual, a fact not lost on Æthelstan, who developed a clear and distinctive foreign policy in ways that his royal predecessors had not before managed.

Even this brief overview highlights something of the complications of Britain's (and Europe's) geo-politics in the late ninth and early tenth centuries. The different English kingdoms all fluctuated in their extent and nature. Their borders could follow the course of major rivers, or of major routeways. Watling Street, for example, an old Roman road which runs from London in a north-westerly direction roughly towards Wroxeter, was frequently invoked as a border between territories. But it is unlikely that these borders were thought of as hard and fast by those in the tenth century, and it is certain that they changed in a variety of ways. Across the British Isles a multiplicity of languages was spoken and written: Old English, Old Irish, Old Norse, Old Welsh, Latin, and Pictish, and society was distinctively cosmopolitan. People must have held a variety of beliefs and customs, as can be gleaned from the substantial archaeological and textual remains of the period. At the level of the average individual person, their outlook on life was likely to have been profoundly local: on the whole, what mattered was what happened within the near vicinity of their settlement and what was required of them by their local lord. Conditions of life must have been hard, life expectancy low (at about twenty-five to thirty years, in one estimation), and levels of competent literacy restricted to those of higher status.[12]

Despite their predominantly local horizons, members of the elite did travel, sometimes quite extensively. Vikings, of course, found their way to Britain, and as far east as the Middle East and as far west as North America. The presence of vikings in the Hagia Sophia in Constantinople (modern Istanbul) is revealed by the remarkable discovery of graffiti which depicts four images of viking ships, etched into the building's fabric. It has been suggested that they were carved by vikings who were amusing themselves during a liturgical ceremony in the church.[13] We have records from Æthelstan's reign of visits by Englishmen to Europe, and vice versa. Numerous European scholars sought out his court as a place where learning was respected and encouraged. By the early tenth century, a pilgrimage to Rome was a well-established custom; it is remarkable that a form of travel diary concerning such a journey survives from the late tenth century, undertaken by the then archbishop of Canterbury.[14] An existing network of Roman (and pre-Roman) roads facilitated travel within Britain itself. These routes were carefully maintained by kings and other landowners. In 934, as we will see, Æthelstan and his entourage journeyed some 150 miles from Winchester to Nottingham in ten days, thus travelling at a rate of about fifteen miles per day. Detailed maps were not available, so travellers must have relied on the particulars of routes passed by word of mouth and local knowledge of the landscape and routeways.[15] Place-names, many of which were coined for the first time in this period, contain elements which reveal much about the topography of the kingdom. By the early tenth century it was expected that royal officials would be able to read written instructions: it was by means of documents whose purpose was essentially ephemeral—when and where the royal assemblies were to be held—that the details of such assemblies were communicated.

When he formed 'England' in 927, Æthelstan was not only the first king to have done so, but he was simultaneously confronted by unprecedented complexities in holding it together. There were various ways in which he could assert his authority and seek to foster a sense of English unity, even if the realities were somewhat different. The England that emerged under his leadership must have looked very different to the person standing on the banks of the River Humber than to the person standing on the River Thames in London, or on the River Tamar in the south-west. In discussing Æthelstan's formation of an English kingdom, we must not think of it as any kind of homogeneous whole. Instead it should be celebrated for its mix of peoples, languages, cultures, and ideas, in just the same way that England is constituted today.

———

In writing a biography of Æthelstan it is not possible to take a strictly chronological approach. Such is the nature of the surviving source material that there are too many holes to be plugged. But, by addressing the main themes of his life and reign, and by comparing his actions to those of his royal predecessors and successors, a very full picture can be constructed of Æthelstan as king and of his approach to kingship. What emerges is a portrait of a quite extraordinary individual who rose from a position of relative weakness, fighting even to confirm his place on the throne, to one of a power so great that it was recognised across contemporary Europe. And he accomplished this all within a reign that would last for a relatively short period of some fourteen years.

In order to reconstruct history of the late ninth and early tenth centuries, we are obliged to rely on a variety of textual and artefactual sources, all of which present their own distinctive challenges. The major narrative source is known by the title *Anglo-Saxon Chronicle*, and it takes the form of a year-by-year account of the major, and some minor, episodes of the period. The allotted title is suggestive of a single text. In fact, the *Anglo-Saxon Chronicle* survives in seven main manuscripts, conventionally labelled 'A' through 'G'. The *Chronicle* seems originally to have been a set of annals developed at the court of King Alfred the Great, Æthelstan's grandfather, which, in the early 890s, were sent out to various parts of the kingdom where copies were subsequently kept up to date in different local centres, and thus contain various elements of local bias.[16] The copy of the *Chronicle* that lies behind versions 'D' and 'E', for example, is thought to have contained a so-called 'northern recension', meaning that details about Northumbrian history are preserved in ways not seen in other surviving copies.[17] For Alfred's reign, and that of his successor, Edward the Elder (Æthelstan's father), the different versions of the *Chronicle* provide a relatively full account of the deeds of the years in question, 871–924. These annals were written in a number of stages and by a number of authors.[18] A major focus is the West Saxon kings' actions in combatting successive viking threats. For some of the annals, notably those for 893–96, the level of detail is such that they may have been written by someone who was close to the action, who perhaps had been involved in meetings of the royal assembly in which tactics were discussed and the outcome of different battles reported. For Edward's reign, in addition to the annals that concentrate on his actions as king, it is fortunate that another set of annals survive embedded in versions 'B', 'C', and 'D' (covering the years 902–24).[19] Given that the focus of this set of annals is on Mercian affairs and on the 'lady of the Mercians', Æthelflæd, the daughter of King Alfred, they are variously referred to as the *Annals of Æthelflæd* or the *Mercian Register*.[20] It is greatly to be regretted that the *Chronicle* falls relatively silent for Æthelstan's reign. Major events are reported, such as the 927 meeting near Eamont Bridge, and a long and celebrated poem is entered in the annal for 937 to commemorate Æthelstan's momentous success at the Battle of *Brunanburh*, but we would have hoped for more.[21]

By far the fullest account of Æthelstan's life can be found in a text written by the greatest of the Anglo-Norman historians, William of Malmesbury. Originally composed around 1125–26, and subsequently revised at various points up to 1134, William's *Gesta Regum Anglorum* (Deeds of the English Kings) provides, as its title suggests, a monumental history of England up to the author's own day. As a monk at Malmesbury, it was natural that William took an interest in Æthelstan, who, as we will see, is said to have favoured the religious community there with gifts and donations of land during his lifetime and who would request to be buried there on his death. William was formidably learned and wrote in a range of different genres, in addition to his history. As a companion piece, he also constructed a major history of the English church, the *Gesta Pontificum Anglorum* (Deeds of the English Bishops). He was steeped in classical literature, so much so that his writing is instinctively suffused with learned allusions to authors such as Virgil and Lucan. While he was rigorous in the research for his historical writings, he was not above embellishing his works and paying more attention to style than content, while also, at times, trusting too much in popular opinion.

When it comes to William's treatment of Æthelstan, we are immediately on our guard because of the approximately two-hundred-year gap between William's time of writing and when his subject had lived. Some of the details William provides are clearly anachronistic and say more about the early twelfth century than they do about the early tenth. For part of his information about Æthelstan, William states that he derived it from 'an ancient volume' (*uolumine uetusto*) written by an author whose language was 'bombastic' (*suffultum*) and therefore difficult to follow, and whose 'manner is excused by the practice of that time, and the excess of panegyric is countenanced by his enthusiasm for Æthelstan, who was then still living'.[22] For a subsequent part of his information about Æthelstan, William states that what he has so far written concerning Æthelstan is 'perfectly trustworthy' (*fide integra*) but that what follows has been derived 'more from popular songs which have suffered in transmission than from scholarly books written for the information of posterity'.[23] On the face of it, therefore, William seems to be signalling to the reader when he is drawing from an 'ancient' written (and therefore more reliable) source and when he is deploying information that he found in less reliable oral sources.

There are, however, possible difficulties with William's account. His citing of 'an ancient volume' written in 'bombastic' style is at first sight encouraging: because tenth-century Latin was renowned for its complexity and use of mannered vocabulary, the description 'bombastic' would be appropriate if William did have a tenth-century text in front of him.[24] But modern historians have argued about the substance of what follows in William's narrative, some seeing kernels of tenth-century detail embedded in his work, while others are more sceptical and suggest that most of the relevant text belongs to the late eleventh or early twelfth centuries.[25] The matter is very important because, as we will discover, some details about Æthelstan's life can only be found in the pages of William's work. A comparison of William's information about Æthelstan with established features and trends of early tenth-century history allows us to make progress. But caution is needed.

The best category of evidence for Æthelstan's reign is provided by two classes of royal documents, his diplomas and his law codes. In essence a diploma is a document which, in its original state, comprises a single-sheet record of (most usually) a grant of land and associated privileges by the king to an individual or institution. By the early tenth century, diplomas were highly formulaic and followed certain conventions that had been established since their introduction at some point in the seventh century. A diploma is thought to have been the product of a royal assembly, the occasion when the king called together all of his most senior lay and ecclesiastical advisers to discuss royal business and official promotions and to promulgate his laws. The royal assembly met at certain points during the years, often coinciding with major religious festivals.[26] Those who were present at the meetings of the royal assembly at which the various grants of land were made are listed as witnesses at the end of each diploma. These lists are set out hierarchically, beginning with the name of the king himself, from the form of whose title (known as his 'royal style') various kinds of important information can be gleaned; then there follow, most often, the names of the archbishops of Canterbury and York, then the bishops of the kingdom, then the ealdormen and thegns (both types of royal officials). Because of this hierarchical structure, and because the diplomas themselves are dated, they provide crucial detail for the realpolitik of tenth-century England, of the peaks and troughs of individuals' careers.[27]

On the basis of their style and content, diplomas issued by Æthelstan can be placed into three main groups according to the period: the years 925–26, 928–35, and 935–39.[28] The middle group, as we will see, are the most extraordinary documents of their kind to survive from the whole of the early medieval period. Nothing like them had been produced before, and nothing like them would appear again. Issued in the wake of Æthelstan's making of 'England' in 927, they were clearly designed to proclaim as loudly as possible the king's successes. Historians have attempted to identify the scribe responsible for these diplomas, but the matter has not reached resolution, which means that he continues to be known by the anonymous title 'Æthelstan A'. What is more certain is that he was acting as Æthelstan's royal scribe and had a monopoly on diploma production in the period 928–35. His documents are some of the earliest conclusive evidence we have for the existence of a sort of royal writing office, termed a 'chancery' by historians. Given the expansion of his authority and remit across a newly formed England, Æthelstan certainly had need of such a centralised administrative department. The majority of Æthelstan's diplomas survive only as copies made after the early medieval period and are thus susceptible to having been tampered with by forgers. But a core of authentic documents can be discerned and mined for what they can tell us about his reign, in addition to the remarkable testimony provided by those few diplomas that have happened to survive in their original, tenth-century form.

It is extremely fortunate that, in the realms of law, a relatively large body of written law (known as law codes) survives from Æthelstan's reign. These laws present difficult questions of interpretation: although one might naturally assume that the laws were intended to be used and implemented in everyday life, some scholars have argued that they are rather to be seen as statements of aspiration on the part of the king, perhaps less connected to the realities of tenth-century life than might at first be expected. Because a greater number of Æthelstan's law codes survive than for other tenth-century kings, we are permitted unusual access to his legislative activity and expectations. A number of concerns are clear in the extant documentation, particularly the issue of theft and how it should be punished. The repetitive way in which this crime is dealt with arguably underlines that it must have been a real contemporary issue, one that was proving difficult to eradicate. Æthelstan and his advisers begin by suggesting the harshest possible punishment (execution) for offenders of above a certain age; then they offer a period in which criminals were pardoned, before—once more, presumably in response to a lack of change—returning to the harshest possible position. Some of the law codes of Æthelstan's reign, as we will see, are not statements of royal law at all but rather reports from different parts of the kingdom to Æthelstan about the reception of his laws, the difficulties in implementing them, and sensible changes that have been made in their operation. Collectively they reveal just how sophisticated governance of the early tenth century had become and how dependent it was on the written word.[29]

Although we lack a major contemporary narrative source, the evidence of royal diplomas and law codes, when scrutinised closely, provides crucial access to the heart of Æthelstan's royal assemblies and his ambitions as king. It reveals not just his policies but the realities of his attempts to govern England as a whole. We will find a king who could at once be ruthless and cunning, but also deeply concerned about his own—and his kingdom's—intellectual and spiritual welfare.

Artefactual evidence provides further vital detail about early tenth-century England. And, thanks to the ongoing work of archaeologists and metal detectorists, the corpus of material is ever-expanding. As recently as 2009, for example, our understanding of the kinds of objects that were produced in the seventh century was transformed by the discovery in that year of the Staffordshire Hoard, which contained in the region of forty-five hundred items, many of them crafted in gold, and many of them martial in character. For Æthelstan's reign, we will encounter precious silks, relics, and archaeological details, all of which supplement the written record. Coins, of which a few thousand survive from the early tenth century, constitute a particularly important type of evidence and sometimes offer a corrective to surviving texts. At one level, coins—which were stamped with the king's name and title, sometimes an image of his bust, and sometimes with other details, such as the place of minting and/or the name of the moneyer—provide information about the way in which the king wished to be seen by his subjects. Æthelstan tried to keep tight control over his coinage, and the royal titles that he employed on his diplomas following his achievements of 927 were echoed in the inscriptions used on coins. It was a concerted campaign of propaganda, designed to leave no uncertainty about his status. At another level, coins provide details about the socio-economic conditions of early tenth-century England. The mapping of coins found on their own ('single-finds') reveals much about the extent and currency of a particular coin type and how widely it circulated across different parts of England. The survival of large numbers of coins in hoards can help in dating successive coin types and in an assessment of the levels of productivity of different mint places. During Æthelstan's reign there were at least thirty-seven mints in action, which extended from Lydford in the south-west as far north as York.[30] Their distribution was not even: the majority are clustered in Wessex, while York is the only mint known to have operated for the whole of Northumbria. At the time of this writing, a collection of some twenty English coins has recently been found as part of excavations at the Palazzo della Rovere in Rome, in an area recognised in the tenth century as the English quarter (the *Schola Saxonum*, 'School of the Saxons' (i.e., English), in early sources), some of which include specimens from Æthelstan's reign. It is too early to know what further light they may shed on Æthelstan's monetary system, or on trips taken by English travellers to Rome. But they serve as a reminder that there is always the potential for new tenth-century sources to emerge.

Most of the evidence so far mentioned provides an Anglocentric view of matters. It is, of course, important that these texts are compared and contrasted with sources written by outside observers.[31] These are not as plentiful or as straightforward to access as we might like. Numerous annalistic texts survive from Wales, Ireland, and Scotland, for example, but some only as very late recensions which have suffered in their transmission and whose details are therefore sometimes difficult to verify. Generations of work on them by modern historians, linguists, and textual critics have nevertheless revealed the kernels of contemporary detail that can be ascertained. From Wales we will meet texts such as the *Annales Cambriae* and from Ireland the *Annals of Ulster*, among many others. Scotland is not as well served by written material for the period: its *Chronicle of the Kings of Alba*, which covers events from the mid-ninth to the late tenth centuries, and which is thought to contain a tenth-century king list to which details were added over time, survives only in a manuscript of the fourteenth century.[32] If we are looking for a counterpoint to the pro-Æthelstan, pro-English panegyric of the famous poem *The Battle of Brunanburh*, we fortunately find it in the remarkable Welsh prophetic poem known as *Armes Prydein Vawr* (Great Prophecy of Britain). Its tenth-century Welsh appeals for the slaughter of the English are chilling—no less so eleven hundred years on. One wonders how widely held such views were.

Connections between England and Europe were long standing and indeed strengthened during Æthelstan's reign. As a result, details relating to Anglo-European relations appear sporadically in a variety of tenth-century continental texts. We will find the names of English men and women recorded in precious books such as *Libri vitae* (Books of life) held by religious communities across north-western Europe: these were people travelling across the Continent and making stops at the communities in question along the way.[33] European chronicles and letters give detail about Æthelstan's actions and status: so powerful did the English king become that he is at times shown intervening at crucial junctures in the evolution of different European kingdoms and able to influence their subsequent history. We will encounter the vivid testimony of contemporary West Frankish authors such as Flodoard of Rheims and Folcuin of Saint Bertin, and of East Frankish authors such as Adalbert of Magdeburg and Widukind of Corvey. Hrotsvitha, a tenth-century canoness of the abbey of Gandersheim in modern Germany, who was perhaps the first ever female historian from East Francia, composed a poetical text which, in recording details about the reign of Otto I, 'the Great', also reveals information about that king's relations with Æthelstan's England.

———

Use of the term 'Anglo-Saxon' has, in recent years, become controversial.[34] Its adoption by far right white supremacists as part of their agenda for racial 'unity' and 'purity' has led to reevaluations about deployment of the term in relation to early medieval England. But any notion that early tenth-century England was homogeneous in racial, ethnic, cultural, linguistic, or religious terms is radically misplaced. Æthelstan knew this better than anyone. From this chronological distance we cannot know his motivations in creating England for the first time. Perhaps it was simply a case of increasing his power and status and of stabilising his position as king. Perhaps it was the most sensible way of galvanising domestic defences against the continued external threat in the form of vikings. In any modern examination of the reign of a man credited as the 'first king of the English', we need to be wary of the dangers of teleology: because we know both that 'England' was formed under Æthelstan and that over subsequent generations it became a lasting reality, we should not assume that historical episodes of the early tenth century led inevitably towards its creation. In fact, events on his death in 939 at first suggested that Æthelstan's England would not survive. But he had provided a potent blueprint, and one from which future kings would build.

As we approach the eleven hundredth anniversary both of Æth-elstan's coronation as king in 925 and of his creation of England in 927, his pioneering actions should be marked. He was a master politician, a warring king, and a keen supporter of the church and of intellectual endeavour. He was England's first king, and seemingly one of its greatest.[35]

1

A Kingdom in Flux

ÆTHELSTAN's illustrious grandfather Alfred, later known as Alfred the Great, became king of the West Saxons in 871. His reign was marked by serious and frequent viking assaults. A viking force, labelled the 'great army' (Old English: *micel here*) by the *Anglo-Saxon Chronicle*, had first landed in 865. Taking advantage of existing networks of roads and rivers, it roamed across English territory and launched attacks in numerous places. The same army, which later splintered, caused problems until the late 870s and affected all four English kingdoms of the time—Wessex, East Anglia, Mercia, and Northumbria, thus transforming the late ninth-century political map.[1] Thanks to Alfred's leadership, as we will see, Wessex was the only English kingdom that did not fall at least partially into viking hands.

East Anglia would be the first to succumb. In 869, viking forces had made their way to Thetford, where they fought a winter battle against the East Anglian king, Edmund. Although Edmund briefly resisted, he was ultimately killed.[2] The *Anglo-Saxon Chronicle* suggests that vikings at this stage 'conquered all the land' in East Anglia. What this means in practice is difficult to know. Two obscure native kings, Æthelred and Oswald, are named on coins of this period, which may suggest that they were established as puppet kings by the vikings. By about 879/80, East Anglia had fallen under the control of a viking king named Guthrum, to whom we will shortly return.[3]

A similar pattern of events unfolded in Mercia. In 868 the 'great army' had already been putting pressure on Mercia, spending the winter in

Nottingham. The Mercian king, Burgred, acutely aware of the threat that they posed, appealed to his West Saxon neighbours for their support. The West Saxons duly obliged and helped drive the vikings from the Mercian kingdom. Alfred was not yet king, but he is said to have assisted his elder brother, King Æthelred, in the military encounter. It was also in 868 that Alfred married the Mercian noblewoman, Ealhswith, an attempt to create a bond between the two kingdoms at a time of trouble. In 873 vikings returned to Mercia, this time to take up 'winter quarters at Torksey in Lindsey', just to the north-west of Lincoln.[4] Recent archaeological work at Torksey has revealed that the viking camp there was of an enormous scale, indicative of an ambition to settle permanently in the area.[5] In 874 the viking army is described as moving to Repton, the old centre of the Mercian kingdom, and then as driving the king of Mercia, Burgred, into an overseas exile before 'they [i.e., the vikings] conquered all that land'.[6] A king named Ceolwulf II was established by the vikings in his place. Ceolwulf II, labelled a 'foolish king's thegn' by the *Anglo-Saxon Chronicle*, did not retain sole control: in 877 renewed viking activity in Mercia led to its being divided between a western portion under Ceolwulf II and an eastern portion directly under viking authority.[7]

In 867 the 'great army', which had spent the winter of 866 in East Anglia, moved 'across the Humber estuary to the city of York'.[8] It is possible that the vikings were seeking to take advantage of a period of civil war that had been ongoing in Northumbria between their king, Osberht, and a rival king, Ælle, who was not of the royal line. A massacre ensued in which large numbers of Northumbrians were killed, as well as their two kings, and the city of York was captured. One of the viking leaders of 866–67 is named as a certain Ívarr, who is probably synonymous with the Ívarr who had come to dominate Dublin in the late 850s and early 860s.[9] In the immediate aftermath of York's fall in 867, an English puppet king named Ecgberht I was installed as ruler by the vikings. In 875 the viking army split its forces, and some of them were taken by Hálfdan, Ívarr's brother, into Northumbria. Hálfdan and his army 'conquered the land' and in 876 are described as dividing up Northumbrian territory among themselves before they 'proceeded to plough and to support themselves'.[10] From the mid-870s until the mid-tenth century a series of Scandinavian kings ruled in York, interspersed with English kings. Many of these Scandinavian kings had risen to power in Dublin before coming to York, and many can be identified as members of the same family, the Uí Ímair (descendants of Ívarr) as they are termed in Irish sources.[11] The evidence of place-names and of styles of sculpture suggests that Scandinavian influence petered out roughly at the line of the River Tees. It is difficult to be precise about the situation further north in Northumbria, but it is possible that a political centre comprised of native Northumbrians endured at Bamburgh, since some of its rulers enter the historical record at various points in the late ninth and early tenth centuries. One of them, Ealdred, would have important interactions with Æthelstan.[12]

But what of Alfred and Wessex? It is evident that Wessex, just like its neighbouring kingdoms, experienced serious challenges to its existence. In late 870 and into 871, before Alfred's accession, the West Saxons fought numerous encounters with vikings at places such as Ashdown, Basing, Reading, and the unidentified *Meretun*. According to the *Anglo-Saxon Chronicle* there were 'nine general engagements' fought against the vikings in 871 alone, as well as numerous other smaller encounters, and viking forces were bolstered by the arrival of a 'great summer army'.[13] And, only a month after his accession in 871, Alfred had to confront the viking army at Wilton—an encounter in which he was unsuccessful.[14] The *Anglo-Saxon Chronicle* concentrates its narrative for the years 873–74 on viking activity in Northumbria and Mercia, but by 875 Alfred can be found taking part in a naval battle against seven viking ships. And, in 876–77, the *Chronicle* describes a viking attack at Wareham, just to the west of Poole, and then another attack by the same force further west, in Exeter. By 878 Alfred was on the brink of defeat. With their taking of Chippenham that year, vikings, led by Guthrum, had managed to infiltrate the heart of Wessex. Some West Saxons were compelled to flee overseas, while others were subjected to viking authority. Alfred himself managed to retain his independence, but his position was greatly diminished and he was forced to take refuge in Athelney in the Somerset marshes with only a small group of followers.[15]

But Alfred fought back. Having ridden to a prominent feature in the landscape known as Egbert's stone, Alfred summoned military support from Somerset, Wiltshire, and Hampshire. Although the precise location of this stone is now lost, an early eighteenth-century monument known as 'King Alfred's Tower', which is situated at the far western edge of Cranborne Chase, just north of Penselwood, may provide as good an approximation as any.[16] With this newly enlarged army, Alfred then marched to Edington, braced for battle. It is hard to imagine that Edington—now a small, rural village of about eight hundred inhabitants in a picturesque part of Wiltshire—formed the location of the most crucial conflict of Alfred's reign. Asser, a Welsh cleric at Alfred's court who wrote a biography of the king, describes how Alfred and his men formed a shield wall, a tactic which permitted them to counter the greater numbers of the viking army and to kill many of them. When the vikings fled back towards their stronghold at Chippenham, some seventeen miles directly north of Edington, Alfred and his followers pursued them, killed those that they could, and then besieged the stronghold itself.[17] After two weeks the vikings surrendered; Alfred had successfully turned the tide of viking aggression. The magnitude of his success is revealed by the terms on which peace was subsequently agreed by both parties. Instead of each side exchanging hostages to guarantee their mutual behaviour, as had happened hitherto, only the vikings were required to hand over hostages. In addition, their leader Guthrum agreed to be baptised at Aller along with thirty of his men and to have Alfred stand as his baptismal sponsor. Guthrum was reborn from the baptismal waters and given a new name of 'Æthelstan'.

By the late 870s, then, Alfred had achieved enormous success, in a way that had eluded native rulers of neighbouring kingdoms. Parts of the north and east of the English kingdom would become so heavily settled by vikings that they developed distinctive Scandinavian characteristics, as reflected in a range of linguistic, legal, and artefactual evidence that displays Scandinavian influence. By the early eleventh century the Scandinavian particularity of this northern and eastern region would be recognised by contemporaries, who began to refer to the area as the 'Danelaw', using the Old English words *Dena* (Danes) and *lagu* (law). The Danelaw's exact boundaries are much debated, but it came broadly to encompass the south of Northumbria, East Anglia, and eastern Mercia and fluctuated in area over time.[18]

With his Mercian wife, Ealhswith, Alfred had five children, who, in order of age, were: their daughter Æthelflæd, their son Edward, their daughters Æthelgifu and Ælfthryth, and their youngest son Æthelweard. Asser, in his biographical *Life of King Alfred*, devotes a chapter to the paths taken by these children. We learn that Æthelflæd would go on to play a key role in Mercia, that Æthelgifu took up a religious life at Shaftesbury abbey, and that Æthelweard, while growing up, was entrusted to a school in which he was taught to read and write in Latin and Old English alongside the children of other nobles. Edward and Ælfthryth are described as being kept close at the royal court, where they, too, received an education. Ælfthryth would later be married to Count Baldwin II of Flanders, thus cementing an alliance with a continental power. Edward, however, would play a pivotal role closer to home.

In the 880s, vikings who had been active in English territory shifted their attention to north-west Europe. From the combined testimony of the *Anglo-Saxon Chronicle*, Asser and contemporary continental historians such as Regino of Prüm and Richer of Rheims, we learn of their activities in particular around the River Loire, in towns such as Nantes, Angers, Poitiers, and Tours. The reaction to their presence may be inferred from Regino's description of the arrival of vikings as the beginnings of a wildfire that needed to be extinguished as quickly as possible. For the years 880–84, a relatively detailed account of the movements of those vikings who had travelled to the Continent is provided by the *Anglo-Saxon Chronicle*, which shows that Alfred's court felt the need to keep close attention to the unfolding of events in Europe. We learn that in these years vikings went to Saucourt, Condé, and Amiens in modern-day France, to Ghent in Belgium; and to Elsloo in the Netherlands.[19]

In general, given the lessening of viking pressure on Alfred and his kingdom, the 880s constituted a period of relative peace and prosperity. Alfred made the most of the respite by strengthening his defences. He refortified various important strongholds and, as we will see, reinvigorated his military resources with changes to his army and to the ways in which ships were designed and constructed. Alfred was also able to turn his attention to matters of religion and scholarship. In a famous passage, he laments that there was no longer a single person south of the River Humber who could translate a word of the divine services from Latin into Old English.[20] The decline seems to have been genuine if the standards of Latinity on display in diplomas of the 870s at Christ Church, Canterbury, are an accurate guide. A diploma of 873, for example, is characterised by words that are spelled incorrectly, by poor grammar, and also by the scribe's inability even to understand where the divisions between words should occur.[21] As a result, Alfred tried to reinvigorate scholarship and learning by importing scholars to his court. He set in motion a major programme of educational reform which placed a particular emphasis on the value of the written word, both in Latin and in Old English. When recruiting scholars to help him, Alfred turned to Mercia, from where he drew a group of individuals that included Wærferth, the bishop of Worcester; Plegmund, who would later become the archbishop of Canterbury; and two 'priests and chaplains' named Æthelstan and Wærwulf.[22] He also looked overseas and engaged men such as Grimbald (a monk of Saint-Bertin in Saint-Omer, Flanders) and John the Old Saxon, as well as gaining the services of Asser himself from south-western Wales. Numerous texts were produced, including the first translation into the vernacular of Bede's famous eighth-century Latin *Ecclesiastical History of the English People*.[23] An Old English translation of Gregory the Great's *Pastoral Care* was also made. A sentence in the preface to that work, written as if in the voice of Alfred himself, declares, 'I intend to send a copy to each bishopric in my kingdom; and in each copy there will be an *æstel*'.[24] It is not entirely clear what an *æstel* was and what function it performed, but the stunning Alfred Jewel, found in the late seventeenth century in Somerset and preserved today in the Ashmolean Museum in Oxford, may be an example of one. It was possibly the decorative end of what originally was a pointer used when reading.[25] Alfred also made it a requirement of his royal officials that they were able to read written instructions. We think that it is from this period that a form of official document known as a royal writ began to be used, to issue commands from the centre of the kingdom to the different regions.[26]

The 880s saw significant political advances, too. Ceolwulf II of Mercia had died ca. 879 and was succeeded by a man named Æthelred. That Mercia was increasingly subordinated to Wessex and losing a degree of its autonomy is indicated by the fact that Æthelred on some occasions issued charters with West Saxon approval, and he seems never to have issued coins in his own name. English sources refer to him by the title 'ealdorman' rather than 'king'.[27] The ealdorman's relationship with Alfred is illustrated by a significant event of 886 as recorded in the *Anglo-Saxon Chronicle*. Alfred had earlier signalled London's importance by minting a special issue of coins in his name, which bore a bust of Alfred depicted as a Roman-style leader on the obverse and a monogram composed of the letters LVNDONIA on the reverse, to represent 'London'.[28] The *Chronicle* reports that in 886 Alfred entrusted London to the control of Æthelred, and it may have been at about this time that Alfred arranged for Æthelred to marry his eldest daughter, Æthelflæd, thus cementing the relationship between the two kingdoms. In the same entry recording details about London, the *Anglo-Saxon Chronicle* states that 'all the English people that were not under subjection to the Danes submitted to him [i.e. Alfred]', which suggests that, at least according to this West Saxon source, Alfred's authority extended beyond Wessex itself.[29] In fact, there seems to have been a growing sense in the mid-880s that Alfred was the king not just of Wessex but of a new and emerging polity known as the 'kingdom of the Anglo-Saxons', which embraced Wessex and parts of Mercia, too. Not everyone would have accepted this novel political concept, but it is clear that Alfred and his advisers, in the face of external viking aggression, saw the advantages in creating a common sense of purpose and identity that included those living outside Wessex. It was in Alfred's court that ideas about what it meant to be a member of the 'English', the *Angelcynn* in Old English, were being discussed in earnest.[30] At the same time that Alfred was increasing the bounds of his own authority, the 880s also saw him codify the terms on which he and the viking leader Guthrum, the man he had defeated at Edington and renamed Æthelstan, coexisted. Thanks to the survival of a remarkable treaty, probably to be dated to the period 886–90, we can see the agreement that the two reached. Guthrum was recognised as the king of East Anglia, and the boundary between their respective territories was set: it was to follow the course of the River Thames, then the Rivers Lea and Ouse, before connecting with Watling Street.[31]

By 892 vikings were once more threatening Alfred's kingdom. Having crossed the Channel from Boulogne, they sailed up the River Lympne and attacked a settlement in Kent. Soon afterwards a second viking fleet led by a certain Hæsten sailed up the Thames. The *Anglo-Saxon Chronicle*'s entry for the year 893 provides a full and vivid account of the movements of Alfred's armies and their viking opponents, together with the encounters that ensued. The high level of detail recorded suggests that the annal was written by someone who was either very close to the action or who had privileged access to royal records. Alfred's forces were stretched on several fronts, with the result that he had to form some of his men into a standing army that could be called upon in an emergency. To strengthen his position further, the king also developed a set of 'long ships' which could out-perform the vikings' own. Battles were fought across the whole of the south at places such as Benfleet, Farnham, Buttington and Exeter, before some vikings eventually made their way to Chester in the north-west. Alfred seems to have concentrated his own attention on the south-west, while various of his ealdormen, including Æthelred, the husband of Alfred's daughter, Æthelflæd, were involved in defending attacks further to the west.

Alfred and his advisers recognised the fundamental importance of internal unity in the face of the external, viking aggression. We have seen that in the 880s the idea of an enlarged 'kingdom of the Anglo-Saxons' had gained ground which embraced both Wessex and parts of Mercia. At just the moment that vikings were once more a threat to Alfred's kingdom, a decision was taken within Wessex to publish for the first time ca. 892 the *Anglo-Saxon Chronicle*, followed in 893 by Asser's *Life of King Alfred*, which, given its draft form, seems to have been distributed in a hurry.[32] Both texts disseminated messages concerning the benefits of Alfred's kingship. The *Chronicle* does not have one single theme, and it would be incorrect simply to view it as a straightforward piece of propaganda. But its annals concerning Alfred provide a deliberately exaggerated view of the success of his actions in combating vikings (no matter the outcome of an individual battle) and of his abilities to prevent Wessex from being overrun in the way that other kingdoms had been.[33] A genealogy that appears alongside the *Chronicle*, which details Alfred's illustrious pedigree, was designed to impress the point further. Asser's *Life* had a different reader in mind. With its explications of English place-names alongside their Welsh equivalents, it anticipated a Welsh audience.[34] By the late 880s, as we will see, a number of Welsh kings had submitted to Alfred's authority either to avoid depredations at the hands of other Welsh kings or to avoid Mercian intrusion. An added complication was the viking raids that the Welsh were also experiencing at the time: because of their proximity to Dublin and the east coast of Ireland, the Welsh kingdoms were just as vulnerable as the English kingdoms and there are indications that they, too, suffered at the hands of Ívarr's viking family.[35] Asser's *Life*, which borrows material from the *Chronicle*, was intended to proclaim Alfred's merits to a Welsh audience and thus to persuade it to remain sympathetic to him. In doing so, Asser turned the conflict into one that he, as a cleric, found the most persuasive: a battle between the Christians (Alfred and his followers) and the pagans (their viking opponents).

The year 893 was also the first year in which we have record of Alfred's first-born son, Edward, being heavily involved in the military action. The detail is supplied by the nobleman Æthelweard, who, in the late tenth century, compiled a Latin translation of the Old English *Anglo-Saxon Chronicle* that differed in some of its details from any surviving copy of that text. Æthelweard describes how Edward himself commanded the forces which countered vikings at Farnham and that he was later the leader in the push against vikings in the east, having connected with forces brought by Ealdorman Æthelred from London.[36] It is likely that Edward, having been born at some point in the mid-870s, was about eighteen years old at this stage.

Edward, who would later succeed his father as king and would become known as Edward the Elder, married three times. It was his first wife, Ecgwynn, whom he married ca. 893, who would be the mother of Æthelstan. Edward and Ecgwynn would also have a daughter together; her name is not provided in any contemporary source.[37] The evidence about Ecgwynn is conflicting. According to the tenth-century East Frankish author, Hrotsvitha, Æthelstan's mother was 'an ignoble consort' (*consors non inclita*) to Edward.[38] There are reasons to be cautious about Hrotsvitha's testimony, since her aim was to expound the deeds of the East Frankish King Otto I who, as we will see, would later marry Æthelstan's half-sister, Eadgyth. Concerned to promote Eadgyth's status, Hrotsvitha sought to depict Ælfflæd, her mother and Edward's second wife, in a more flattering light than Ecgwynn. The later testimony of William of Malmesbury, from whom we first learn Ecgwynn's name, depicts Æthelstan's mother in contradictory ways. When she is first introduced, William describes her in Latin with the phrase *illustri femina*, which can mean a 'noble' or 'illustrious woman'.[39] But later in his account of Æthelstan's life, William offers a rather different view. On Æthelstan's accession to the throne there was, as we will see, a degree of opposition to his rise to power. One reason given by William for this reaction was that Ecgwynn's own status was somehow in doubt, that she was thought to be a concubine. But William himself, in mentioning this suggestion for the first time, then expresses uncertainty about the idea and distances himself from it by saying 'if indeed there is any truth in it'.[40] Perhaps William had been unable to verify a speculative detail, or perhaps he was unwilling to believe it, not least because Malmesbury Abbey, where William lived and wrote, cherished its special connection with Æthelstan.[41]

It is difficult to be precise about Ecgwynn's status, whether she was noble or not.[42] Edward's own marital history means that there were many different individuals who at various points had good cause to impugn the character of Ecgwynn, and therefore that of Æthelstan as well. After Ecgwynn, Edward would have two more marriages: the first was ca. 899, with a certain Ælfflæd, the daughter of Ealdorman Æthelhelm, and the second ca. 919, with a certain Eadgifu, the daughter of Ealdorman Sigehelm. By Ælfflæd he had two sons (Ælfweard and Edwin) and possibly six daughters (Æthelhild, Eadgifu, Eadflæd, Eadhild, Eadgyth, and Ælfgifu), while by Eadgifu he had two sons (Edmund and Eadred) and possibly two daughters (Eadburh and Eadgifu).[43] Each of Edward's successive wives (and their offspring) had good reason to create or simply to favour the story of Ecgwynn's lowly status, both to elevate their own positions but also to discredit Æthelstan, who was a rival to their own sons for status and power.

Whatever Ecgwynn's background, William's account, when it continues, reaches a point where he inserts material taken from 'popular songs', whose factual accuracy, he tells the reader, cannot be verified. It is not certain what these 'popular songs' were but it is has been suggested that they may in origin have been saga-like in form and that they latterly survived beyond the Norman Conquest, into William's day.[44] From them William borrows miraculous details about Æthelstan's birth and therefore about Ecgwynn. The story centres on an unidentified village. One night Ecgwynn, who is described as being of low birth but so beautiful that it compensated for her social standing, is said to have had a dream in which her stomach, as vivid as the moon, brightened England. Although Ecgwynn herself thought nothing of the dream, her friends took it more seriously. The story reached the attention of a local wet-nurse who had served King Alfred (and had therefore looked after Edward himself) and who decided to allow Ecgwynn to live with her. Edward, who happened later to visit the village, took the time to visit his former wet-nurse, and, seeing Ecgwynn, immediately fell in love with her. William's account describes how, after only one night together, Ecgwynn became pregnant, later giving birth to Æthelstan, and thus fulfilling her original dream because Æthelstan 'gave great promise of a kingly nature and won renown by his distinguished record'.[45]

No surviving source provides an exact date for Æthelstan's birth, but, if William of Malmesbury's statement about his being thirty years old when he became king in 924 can be taken literally, then 894 seems approximately correct.[46] His name, a relatively common one for the early medieval period, is composed of the Old English elements *Æthel-*, meaning 'noble', and *-stan*, meaning 'stone', suggesting that his parents hoped he would in the future provide stability and strength for the kingdom. He may have been named after Edward's uncle, who had been king of the south-eastern areas of Kent, Essex, Surrey and Sussex from 839 to 851 × 855, and who is remembered in the *Anglo-Saxon Chronicle* for his role in a naval battle and for defeating a viking army in Kent in 851. If it is correct to link the uncle with a grave found in the nave of the Old Minster, Winchester, then he had clearly been a much respected member of the West Saxon royal house.[47] A more startling possibility is that Æthelstan was named after the viking leader, Guthrum, who, as we have seen, had himself been renamed 'Æthelstan' in the baptismal ceremony that followed his defeat by Alfred at Edington, and who thereafter issued coins as king of East Anglia with the name 'Æthelstan' imprinted on them. Given the emphasis placed by Alfred and his advisers on a sense of common identity and a notion of the 'kingdom of the Anglo-Saxons', is it feasible to suggest that the name of Alfred's first grandson was also chosen with similar ambitions in mind? Were members of the West Saxon royal house seeking to make a connection between their own royal line and Scandinavian rule in East Anglia?[48] The inference must have been made by contemporaries.

If Æthelstan was indeed born in 894, he arrived under the most difficult of circumstances. Only a year earlier his father, Edward, is recorded for the first time as having to lead major military campaigns against vikings. And 894 saw continued viking activity: those vikings who had established themselves in Chester are said to have crossed into Wales before returning to England, where they first travelled to Northumbria and then turned south to East Anglia, eventually coming to Mersea Island in Essex, from where they later launched aggressive forays up the River Thames and its tributary, the River Lea. Meanwhile, those vikings who had moved on Exeter caused destruction in the vicinity of Chichester. Æthelweard, in his chronicle, adds the detail that vikings were also responsible in 894 for ravaging in Mercia, to the west of Stamford.[49]

Almost nothing can be reconstructed about the earliest years of Æthelstan's life.[50] We can imagine that, as Edward's eldest son, he was brought up in relative physical comfort, perhaps in a complex of buildings that included a royal hall. Some idea of the nature of such a royal site, and the buildings that Æthelstan might have inhabited and used, can be gleaned from archaeological excavations at Yeavering in Northumberland, which was active until roughly the mid-seventh century, and Cheddar in Somerset, which may have formed a secondary residence for the West Saxon kings of the tenth century. In both places the royal hall is part of a larger complex of several buildings. The hall is rectangular in shape and over twenty metres in length; it comprises one room and is constructed with massive wooden beams and with two storeys. Excavations have revealed that particular importance was placed on both the doorways and the hearths in such royal halls.[51] The royal hall at Cheddar had three entrances, two of which were centrally located, close to the hearth, which was in the southern half of the building. These physical remains bring to life the literary description of Heorot, the hall of King Hrothgar, one of the legendary characters in the epic Old English poem *Beowulf*, where the king himself was given physical and symbolic prominence in the hall and he and his companions were able to receive visitors. Thanks to the evidence of charters, we know that Cheddar, which was actively developed in the 930s, was used for meetings of the royal assembly on at least three specific occasions in the tenth century, in the years 941, 956, and 968.[52]

Some detail about the young Æthelstan is provided by William of Malmesbury. He describes how Alfred arranged for his grandson to be 'knighted at an early age with the gift of a scarlet cloak, a belt set with gems, and a Saxon sword with a gilded scabbard'.[53] It is important not simply to accept this description at face value. William, writing in full knowledge of Æthelstan's later acquisition of the royal throne, had every reason to say that the young boy had been specially marked for future greatness. William's description of Æthelstan being 'knighted' can certainly be discarded, since knighthoods were not introduced until after the Norman Conquest. But it is possible that Æthelstan received some kind of formal recognition of his special position given that Alfred himself may have had a similar experience. Both the *Anglo-Saxon Chronicle* and Asser's *Life of King Alfred* state that in 853 Alfred had been sent by his father, the then king Æthelwulf, to Rome where, as a four-year-old, he was consecrated a future king by Pope Leo IV. It is difficult to believe that a four-year-old was formally consecrated as a king in 853, and a letter from Pope Leo IV to King Æthelwulf suggests instead that on this occasion Alfred had actually been invested with the insignia of a Roman consul (which included a consular belt and clothes). It is therefore more likely that Leo was formally marking Alfred's high status rather than specifically designating him to be a future king.[54] Perhaps the significance of this early trip to Rome was repeatedly stressed to Alfred as he was growing up, with the result that, when Æthelstan was of a similar age, Alfred felt it important for the young boy to be similarly adorned with markers of secular authority.

On 26 October 899, Æthelstan's grandfather Alfred died and was buried in Winchester.[55] According to one version of the *Anglo-Saxon Chronicle*, Alfred had been 'king over the whole English people except for that part which was under Danish rule'.[56] The passing of one king, and the transition of power to a successor, created a period of political uncertainty and tension. With no strict rule of primogeniture, but the expectation that a successor with royal blood would become king, there could be many challengers for the position. Astonishingly, Alfred's own will still survives, composed at some point in the period 872 to 888. It does not prescribe to whom the throne should pass, but it does describe how, of all Alfred's beneficiaries, his eldest son, Edward, was to receive the most estates in important locations across Wessex, implying that he was viewed as the natural successor. And a royal diploma dated 898, which may survive in its original form and is drawn up under Alfred's name, contains in its list of witnesses the name of Edward, who is described as a 'king' (*rex*) and who is said to be 'making firm' (*stabilito*) the grant made by his father, suggesting both that Edward was already being recognised as king in 898 and that he was assuming various royal responsibilities.

The *Anglo-Saxon Chronicle*, in the same sentence that records Alfred's death, also records the succession of Edward as king. But it goes on to reveal that Edward's succession was challenged by his cousin, a man named Æthelwold. Although Edward tried to confront Æthelwold with an army, Æthelwold engineered his own escape and fled to Northumbria, where he is said to have been recognised as king by the 'Danish army in Northumbria', a statement which may be supported by the survival of Northumbrian coins minted in the name 'Alvvaldus', a rendering of Æthelwold's name.[57] By late 902 Æthelwold had persuaded a Scandinavian contingent in East Anglia to ravage as far west as Cricklade, north-west of Swindon. Edward pursued them as they returned towards East Anglia, but he later abandoned the expedition. A band of Kentish men is said to have continued the fight following Edward's departure and to have defeated the Scandinavians in the Battle of the Holme, the location of which is uncertain. A number of important people were killed on both sides, including Æthelwold himself and a Scandinavian man named Eohric, who had been king of East Anglia.[58]

Edward's accession was, therefore, not without opposition. But he was consecrated king on 8 June 900, at Kingston upon Thames according to a later tradition, in a ceremony which stressed that he was king of both the West Saxons and the English parts of Mercia.[59] Thus the 'kingdom of the Anglo-Saxons' that had been created by Alfred seems to have endured, a situation confirmed by the evidence of Edward's laws, charters (which only provide a partial record, since they do not cover the years 910–24), and coins. Edward was 'king of the Anglo-Saxons' and the parts of Mercia that were then governed by his sister, Æthelflæd, and her husband, Æthelred, recognised his overlordship.[60] At about this time Æthelstan's own fortunes changed quite significantly. A diploma dated 901 contains among its list of witnesses the name 'Ælfflæd', who is described as the *coniunx regis* (king's wife).[61] Edward had taken a new wife for reasons that are nowhere stated. William of Malmesbury suggests that Edward's new wife, Ælfflæd, was the daughter of an ealdorman named Æthelhelm, who is most likely to have been the ealdorman of Wiltshire.[62] It is possible that Ecgwynn had died, or that, in the wake of his becoming king, there were benefits for Edward in securing an alliance with a noble family from Wiltshire which caused him to put Ecgwynn aside. If the latter explanation has any validity, it recalls the doubts cast about Ecgwynn's status that had been made by Hrotsvitha and later by William of Malmesbury. We have seen that, by his new wife, Ælfflæd, Edward had numerous children, including the sons, Ælfweard and Edwin. In diplomas of 901 Ælfweard is already named as the *filius regis* (king's son), which suggests that Edward's second marriage may have taken place at about the time of King Alfred's death, ca. 899. Whether or not Æthelstan had previously been marked out as a future king by his grandfather Alfred, his position after his father's second marriage was considerably weakened. Two diplomas of the year 901 confirm the demotion that had taken place: after the name of Edward as king can be found the names Æthelweard and Ælfweard, both listed before Æthelstan. Æthelstan's status behind his uncle Æthelweard and his newly born half-brother Ælfweard was thus enshrined in royal documentation.[63]

William of Malmesbury's history is the only source to reveal that, as a child, Æthelstan was sent by Alfred to Mercia to be raised and educated at the court of his aunt, Æthelflæd, and her husband, Æthelred.[64] Perhaps Alfred, recognising that his own life was coming to an end, and with arrangements for Edward to marry for a second time under way, felt that the removal of Edward's eldest son by a previous wife made good political sense. Because Æthelstan would later experience a negative reaction from Wessex itself on his initial accession as king, but a warm reception from Mercia, it seems likely that this detail in William's account about Æthelstan's removal to Mercia should be accepted.[65] William's account continues with a poem, which says of Æthelstan's upbringing,

> By his father's orders he was handed over to be taught at school, and feared stern masters and the swish of the cane; there he absorbed into his thirsty veins the honey of instruction, and so he passed his childish years, but as no ordinary child. Then, once clothed with the bloom of adolescence, he practised the pursuit of arms at his father's bidding, and in him too the laws of war did not find a laggard.[66]

If we look beyond the poetical expression, the core message, that Æthelstan, as a child, would have been sent first to school for an education and then afterwards instructed in the art of war and soldiery, seems likely to be true.[67] As we have seen, Alfred himself had placed particular emphasis on the benefits of learning and had implemented a programme of educational reform. In one chapter of his *Life of King Alfred*, Asser remarks how Alfred had sent his youngest son, Æthelweard, Edward's brother, to a 'school' together with other noble children, and indeed children from a less noble background. There, Asser says, Æthelweard studied books in both Old English and Latin and learned how to write.

Edward and his sister Ælfthryth are also described as receiving a 'liberal education', which involved, in addition to reading books in Old English, learning the psalms.[68] The 'school' described by Asser is not a school as we would understand it, but rather the result of arrangements Alfred had made for the education of certain children at his court.[69] Given the importance placed by Alfred on education, it seems likely that Æthelstan would have received a tutelage of some kind, although it is impossible to know whether this was delivered in the court of Æthelflæd and Æthelred or whether Æthelstan was sent elsewhere. It was to Mercia that Alfred had turned when seeking support for his scholarly ambitions, and Mercian diplomas of the late ninth century show a degree of literary accomplishment. Mercia may therefore have been well placed to deliver an education to a young noble. We can be sure that Æthelstan would have studied a variety of texts in Old English. On the basis of his later interests in Latin manuscripts, and in the learned form of Latin that would come to typify his royal diplomas, it is possible that he was also exposed to Latin texts at a young age.[70] When the poem in William's text refers to 'stern masters and the swish of the cane', we can be sure that the description owes something to conventional stereotypes. But the extraordinary survival of a set of *Colloquies* dating to about the year 1000, and attributed to a schoolmaster named Ælfric Bata, provide an intimate portrayal of an early medieval classroom in which teachers were quick to chastise students for mistakes and physical beatings are described as happening frequently.[71] Æthelstan's own education may have been in a more sheltered environment, but it is possible that he, too, suffered at his teachers' hands. By the time that William was writing in the early twelfth century, he could report that 'there is a vigorous tradition in England that he [i.e. Æthelstan] was the most law-abiding and best-educated ruler they have ever had'.[72]

While Æthelstan was being brought up in Mercia, his father, Edward, was faced with a very difficult and complex political situation. We previously saw that parts of Northumbria, East Anglia, and eastern Mercia had fallen in the late ninth century into Scandinavian hands, such that an area known as the Danelaw came into existence. These areas were not exclusively inhabited by Scandinavians, and a degree of integration with existing native populations can be shown to have taken place.[73] In East Anglia the last known Scandinavian king was Eohric, who was killed in the 902 Battle of the Holme. Following his death the political organisation of East Anglia becomes very obscure. The *Anglo-Saxon Chronicle* refers without any more detail to the deeds of an East Anglian army. The political structures in the eastern parts of Mercia, which had also fallen into Scandinavian hands in the late ninth century, are equally opaque, but seem to have involved the division of Mercia into various districts under the control of different armies led by earls and based at various burhs (fortified strongholds). Some of these burhs—including Derby, Leicester, Lincoln, Nottingham, and Stamford—would later be known as the 'Five Boroughs' of the Danelaw. Scandinavian forces were not exclusively tied to those burhs, though, since they can also be found occupying places such as Cambridge, Huntingdon, Northampton, and Tempsford, among others.

With Scandinavian forces to the north and east of his kingdom, Edward's reign, as it is reported in the *Anglo-Saxon Chronicle*, involved a concerted campaign to reclaim different parts of the Danelaw. In 906, presumably as a result of fighting that was not recorded in the *Chronicle*, Edward agreed terms of peace with the East Anglians and Northumbrians. But the peace was later broken, and in 909–10 Edward deployed a force composed of men from both Wessex and Mercia to take on the Northumbrian army. Across the years 912 to 920 Edward oversaw the construction of burhs in a series of strategic locations, supported in his programme of burh building by the actions of his sister, Æthelflæd, and her husband, Æthelred. Between them, they oversaw the construction of burhs on the border with the Welsh kingdoms, in Chester, Chirbury, and Bridgnorth, and also in the eastern Danelaw in places such as Derby and Leicester. One wonders what role the young Æthelstan, who was presumably still in Mercia in these years, would have played in the fighting that was taking place. In 909–10, when the *Anglo-Saxon Chronicle* specifies that Edward's forces had both West Saxons and Mercians in them, Æthelstan would have been about fifteen or sixteen years of age. We can imagine at the least that the young boy would have been impressed by the actions of his aunt, Æthelflæd, who, on the death of her husband in 911, became the 'lady of the Mercians' and stands out as a female ruler of exceptional abilities in a time of largely male-dominated affairs.[74] So brilliant was her leadership that the *Mercian Register* pays her close attention.

The military activity of these years and the creation of a network of burhs, which were strategically located to inhibit viking movements on the kingdom's Roman roads and on rivers and coastal routes, came to a head in the years 917–18. In 917 those under Scandinavian rule in East Anglia and Essex submitted to Edward, as did the East Anglian army and the Cambridge army, while Æthelflæd was able to take Derby for herself.[75] In 918 those occupying the northern Stamford burh also submitted to Edward, and the *Mercian Register* records how Æthelflæd took the burh at Leicester and that 'the people of York . . . promised her . . . that they would be under her direction.'[76] These were very significant gains for Edward and his sister. Not long after those in York had agreed to follow Æthelflæd, the 'lady of the Mercians' died in Tamworth. Edward rushed to secure Tamworth for himself, which led to the Mercians who had been under her power submitting to Edward and also to a number of Welsh kings agreeing to recognise his authority. Edward then proceeded to Nottingham, and, after he had taken the burh there, 'all the people who had settled in Mercia, both Danish and English, submitted to him.'[77] By 918, then, Edward had managed to take control of East Anglia and Mercia. Although the English part of Mercia had always recognised his ultimate authority, Æthelflæd's death in 918 and Edward's capture of Tamworth enabled him to take direct control there in a way that would not previously have been possible. Edward moved also to remove any potential opposition to his rule in Mercia: after its record of Æthelflæd's death, the *Mercian Register* describes how Ælfwynn, the daughter of Æthelflæd and Æthelred, 'was deprived of all authority in Mercia and taken into Wessex.'[78]

The year 918 witnessed another significant event which goes unmentioned in any version of the *Anglo-Saxon Chronicle*: the arrival of Ragnall I, the grandson of Ívarr. Having fought a battle at Corbridge that year against the combined forces of Ealdred of Bamburgh and Constantine II of the Scots, Ragnall proceeded south to York, where he can be found

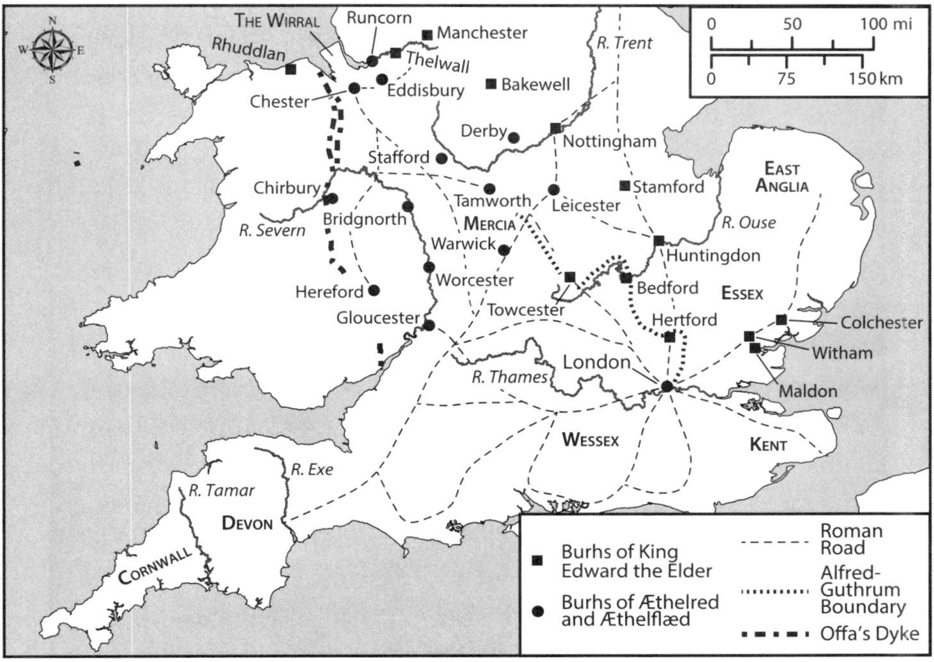

MAP 3. The network of burhs of Edward the Elder and of Æthelflæd and Æthelred of Mercia.

to have taken up rule by 919.[79] Ragnall's presence had profound consequences for the politics of these years. It may have been his appearance
which caused those in York to seek out Æthelflæd's support before her
death in 918. Whatever the case, his position in York reestablished the
link between that northern city and Ireland (and with other areas that
may have been in Ragnall's control, including the Isle of Man) and
threatened Edward's kingdom on numerous fronts once more.[80] It is no
wonder that Edward can be found in the years 918–20 to have concentrated his attention in the north of his kingdom: in 919 he built burhs in
the north-west at Thelwall and Manchester, and in 920 he built a burh
in Nottingham on the River Trent (together with a bridge) and then
proceeded to Bakewell, where another burh was built. Together, these
fortified strongholds created a defensive line that sought to block arrivals
on the west coast from Ireland or inroads through the Peak District from

York. Following Edward's building of a burh at Bakewell, the *Anglo-Saxon Chronicle* records a remarkable event for the year 920: 'the king of the Scots and all the people of the Scots, and Ragnall, and the sons of Eadwulf and all who live in Northumbria, both English and Danish, Norsemen and others, and also the king of the Strathclyde Welsh and all the Strathclyde Welsh, chose him as father and lord'.[81] It is not feasible that Edward, who had so recently managed to take control over Mercia and East Anglia, would have been able to exert any kind of real authority north of the River Humber in the way that his son, Æthelstan, would later do.[82] It is more likely that Ragnall's recent arrival had prompted all of the northern rulers to reassess their options. In Edward's case, for example, Ragnall had the potential to turn his attention south beyond the River Humber to areas that had recently been sympathetic to Scandinavian rule. From Ragnall's perspective, his newly won position in York was threatened by the Northumbrian lords of Bamburgh who had recently joined forces with Constantine II of Alba against him. It therefore made good practical sense to reach an agreement in which the authority of each ruler was formally acknowledged.[83] For the author of the West Saxon *Anglo-Saxon Chronicle*, this resulted in recognition of Edward as the 'father and lord' of these northern potentates.

At some point in the years 917–19, a marriage was arranged for Eadgifu, Edward's daughter by Ælfflæd. She became the second wife of Charles the Simple, who was king of West Francia, and she was granted the status of queen. They would later have a son, Louis, who, as we will see, would spend some time with Æthelstan during a period of political instability on the Continent. Eadgifu's marriage to Charles was significant: it not only suggested that the West Saxon royal house was now of such a standing that it could have influence on a European stage but also set a precedent of Anglo-European interaction that would make an impression on Æthelstan.[84]

It may have been at about this time, ca. 919, that Edward entered into his third and final marriage, with a woman named Eadgifu, who was the daughter of Sigehelm, a Kentish ealdorman. We have seen that, by Eadgifu, Edward had four more children, two boys and two girls. The boys, Edmund and Eadred, would in due course become kings themselves after Æthelstan had died. It is not clear what had happened to Edward's second wife, Ælfflæd. William of Malmesbury describes how she was buried at the nunnery at Wilton, in Wiltshire, which might suggest that she had not died prematurely but had perhaps instead retreated to a religious life.[85] Edward's new wife, Eadgifu, seems not to have played a prominent role in the politics of his reign, or in that of Æthelstan. She would come to the fore when her own sons became kings. Surviving charters indicate that Eadgifu was wealthy and that she had landed interests in the south-east of the kingdom in Kent, thanks in part to bequests made to her by her ealdorman father. Her resources may have been one reason why Edward married her.[86]

The Irish *Annals of Ulster* record that in 920 Ragnall's kinsman, Sihtric, another descendant of Ívarr, departed Dublin 'through the power of God' and left the naval port there in the control of a further kinsman, Guthfrith.[87] Thanks to the later testimony of the *Historia Regum*, we know that Sihtric then landed on the north-west coast, where he attacked Davenport, just to the south-west of Manchester.[88] Sihtric's raid targeted an area of the kingdom that Edward and Æthelflæd had been trying to reinforce, and it contravened the agreement that had been made by Edward and the other rulers in Britain in 920. Either he had come to support Ragnall in Northumbria or, given Ragnall's own death in 921 and Sihtric's succession in York, perhaps Sihtric had anticipated an opportunity to take control.[89] The *Anglo-Saxon Chronicle* falls relatively silent for the years 921–23, just before Edward's death, which makes it difficult to piece together the dynamics between Edward and Sihtric. One striking development was Sihtric's ability to mint coins in his name in Lincoln—in other words, south of the River Humber and thus outside Northumbria's usual area of influence.[90] This raises the possibility that Sihtric had retaken part of the eastern Danelaw from Edward and that Edward's fears of Scandinavian expansion from York, which had prompted the agreement of 920, were to some extent being realised.[91]

No details are recorded about Æthelstan's reactions to Sihtric's position nor concerning his whereabouts in the early 920s. If he were still in Mercia, he would have witnessed first-hand the undoing of some of his father's achievements in the Danelaw. In 921 Æthelstan would have been about twenty-seven years old. He was of an age when he could be king in his own right, and it is possible that he had one eye on his father's throne. If he did, the years 920–23 would have impressed on him the significance of maintaining the power balance between the various rulers to the north and of neutralising the potential threat from the descendants of viking Ívarr at York. These were important lessons from the reign of his father and there are signs that, when Æthelstan did become king, he took them seriously.

2

The Birth of England

ON 17 JULY 924, Æthelstan's father, Edward, died. The *Mercian Register* states that Edward died at Farndon in Mercia, a detail also found in the 'Worcester Chronicle', a text of the mid-twelfth century, and in the work of William of Malmesbury, who adds that Edward had been in the north-west to deal with a rebellion at Chester.[1] He had been king for just shy of twenty-five years and would have been about fifty years old at the time of his death. He was buried in Winchester, Wessex, in an abbey called the New Minster, the construction of which had been initiated by Alfred the Great and was eventually completed in Edward's reign and founded in 901. The New Minster, which was situated near to the north side of the existing Old Minster, became a royal mausoleum, where Edward's parents were laid to rest (Alfred having been moved from his original burial site in the Old Minster).[2]

It is unclear what succession arrangements had been made in advance of Edward's death. Æthelstan was Edward's eldest son by his first wife, but Edward's sons by his second wife, Ælfweard and Edwin, were also potential heirs. Æthelstan's other half-brothers, Edmund and Eadred, were too young to be in the running: we know that Edmund, the eldest, was eighteen in 939, so he may only have been about three when Edward died.[3] Some versions of the *Anglo-Saxon Chronicle* report plainly that, on Edward's death, Æthelstan succeeded without any indication of further complexity.[4] But there is strong evidence that Æthelstan's half-brother, Ælfweard, was recognised (at least for a short time) as king in Wessex. The New Minster *Liber vitae* (Book of life), written in 1031, preserves the detail that Ælfweard had been crowned,[5] while a royal genealogy in the *Textus Roffensis* (Rochester text), a manuscript of the early twelfth century, records in Old English, 'Đa feng Ælfwerd Eadwardes sunu to and heold .iiii. wucan' (Then Ælfweard, Edward's son, succeeded to [the kingdom] and ruled it for four weeks).[6] But the *Mercian Register*, in addition to describing Edward's death at Farndon, proceeds by saying that 'his son Ælfweard died very soon after at Oxford . . . and Æthelstan was chosen by the Mercians as king'.[7] The entry can be interpreted to mean that although Ælfweard may have taken over in Wessex, in Mercia it was Æthelstan that was elected as king, and therefore that the kingdom may have been divided between the two half-brothers. If that explanation is correct, it is unclear whether the division was one that had been planned or whether Æthelstan had seized the opportunity presented to him by Edward's death and used his base of support in Mercia to establish himself as king.[8] Whatever had happened, Ælfweard did not live much longer: the 'D' version of the *Anglo-Saxon Chronicle* reports that he died sixteen days after the death of his father, Edward, which would be 2 August 924. According to the royal genealogy cited above, however, he was king for four weeks.[9]

With Ælfweard deceased, Æthelstan became sole ruler. How Ælfweard's only surviving full brother, Edwin, would have felt about these developments is a good question; there are allusions to a rebellion by Edwin later in Æthelstan's reign. Although Edmund and Eadred, Æthelstan's half-brothers, were too young at this stage to figure as potential successors, as we have seen, William of Malmesbury records the care afforded to them by Æthelstan following Edward's death (and adds that, once they were adults, they were included in the management of the kingdom). On becoming king in 924, Æthelstan was about thirty years of age. A very notable feature of his life is that, as far as we know, he remained unmarried throughout, and no contemporary source mentions that he fathered any children. William of Malmesbury's suggested reason for this is as good as any: in one version of the same passage in which he describes the upbringing of Edmund and Eadred at Æthelstan's court, William comments that Æthelstan did not choose a wife because of the 'respect' he held for his young half-brothers.[10] Although

William does not elaborate further, the implication of his statement is that Æthelstan saw the benefits in remaining unmarried because, without producing his own children who would also be potential heirs, Edmund's and Eadred's future claims to the throne would not be challenged.[11] One twelfth-century text, known as the *Liber Eliensis* (Book of Ely), contains the only surviving reference to a potential child of Æthelstan when it records how a certain 'Edith, the daughter of King Æthelstan', gave a relic to the Ely church.[12] Since no other text refers to a daughter of Æthelstan, it is more likely that this is simply an erroneous reference to Æthelstan's homonymous sister.

The nature of Æthelstan's position on becoming king may be inferred from a diploma issued at an unspecified point in 925. It refers to Æthelstan being king over a region that was 'almost in the whirlpools of cataclysms' (*ferme cataclismatum gurgitibus*). Its list of witnesses, which survives in incomplete form, contains bishops drawn only from Mercian (and not from West Saxon) sees, indicative of the restricted range of Æthelstan's authority at this stage.[13] In fact, royal diplomas issued by Æthelstan in 925–26 show in various ways a focus on Mercia. Of four documents that survive to this day, at least one concerns land in Derbyshire (in Mercia),[14] and two explicitly refer to the fact that the land they mention had originally been bought 'from the pagans at the command of King Edward and Ealdorman Æthelred', an allusion to the campaign of Æthelstan's father and uncle to reclaim parts of Mercia in Scandinavian possession.[15]

It is possible not just that Æthelstan's early power was confined to Mercia but that there was also active opposition to him in Winchester. William of Malmesbury recounts an extraordinary episode in which a certain Alfred was so seriously opposed to Æthelstan becoming king that he hatched a plot to have him blinded in Winchester.[16] The scheme was foiled, and Alfred was sent to Rome to be judged for his actions by the pope. Alfred is said to have died soon afterwards in the *Schola Anglorum*.[17] The details of William's story cannot be straightforwardly accepted, not least because William recounts them in connection with the claims of his own abbey at Malmesbury to the deceased Alfred's landed estates. A forged diploma preserved in the Malmesbury archive shares details and verbal formulation with the story of Alfred in William's text and may have been William's exemplar.[18] But it is possible that William's text preserves the memory of a degree of serious opposition towards Æthelstan that came from Winchester.

Thankfully, we do not have to rely on the later testimony of William alone, since a variety of near-contemporary evidence supports the hypothesis that Winchester opposed Æthelstan. Some sources are striking for what they *do not* say. Æthelstan's diplomas of the years 925–26, including one thought to have been issued on the occasion of Æthelstan's coronation, are conspicuous for the absence of Frithestan, the bishop of Winchester, from their lists of witnesses. In the reigns of previous West Saxon kings, a bishop of Winchester would have occupied a position of some prominence.[19] And, when the very text from Winchester, the New Minster's own *Liber vitae*, describes the crowning of Ælfweard, it is notable that no mention is made of Æthelstan becoming king.[20]

Any argument made from the silence of our sources is problematical and capable of different interpretations. But there is further evidence that demonstrates the nature of the relationship between Æthelstan and Winchester. When St Cuthbert's tomb in Durham was opened in the early nineteenth century, a remarkable set of tenth-century silken religious vestments was found, including a stole, maniple, and girdle.[21] Inscriptions on the vestments reveal that they had originally been commissioned by Ælfflæd, the second wife of Edward the Elder, as a gift for Frithestan. Given that they had been intended for Frithestan at Winchester, how did they end up in the possession of St Cuthbert's community in the north? A text written by St Cuthbert's community, the *Historia de Sancto Cuthberto* (History of St Cuthbert), states that when Æthelstan visited them on his way north in 934 he donated a variety of gifts which included 'two chasubles, and one alb, and one stole with maniple'.[22] Could the clothing found in Cuthbert's tomb be the same as that referred to in the *Historia*? It is difficult to be certain, not least because doubt has been cast on the status of the relevant part of the *Historia*'s account.[23] But if it can be accepted, it would suggest that Æthelstan had somehow come to be the owner of this luxury gift that he

deliberately removed from Frithestan, hinting again at animosity between the two parties.

Additional detail about the hostility between Æthelstan and Winchester can be gleaned from the record of a lease of land produced at a
meeting at the New Minster itself. It describes an irregular level of involvement by Æthelstan. The document can be dated broadly to the
period 924 × 933 and survives in its original form.[24] The lease is said to
have been issued by the New Minster community with the 'consent . . .
of Æthelstan, the most glorious king of the Anglo-Saxons and Danes'
(*consensu . . . Æthelstani Angelsaxonum Denorumque gloriosissimi regi[s]*),
a royal style which may date the document more narrowly to between
4 September 925 (Æthelstan's coronation) and July 927 (when he became king of the English).[25] It grants a thegn named Alfred twenty hides of
land at Chiseldon in Wiltshire in return for a payment of eighty man-
cuses of gold, with the agreement that each year, on the anniversary of
Edward the Elder's death, Alfred would make a further payment to the
community. As was standard practice for a lease of the period, the arrangements were to remain in place for three generations before the
land would revert to the religious community. The lease includes an
unusually long list of witnesses, just over eighty in number. Æthelstan's
attestation comes first, rather than that of the head of the New Minster.
He is followed by Edwin, described as *cliton*, then by a certain priest
named Wærwulf and by a range of others, including those who may
have been of continental origin, one of whom is named Peter. Although
the lease is a product of a meeting in Winchester, and although it concerns lands that belonged to the New Minster, Frithestan is again notable for his absence.[26] The terms of the lease are also unusual. We
would not normally expect a religious community to have to seek the
king's permission to lease out its lands, but here they have explicitly
done so. Given the friction between Æthelstan and Winchester, the
lease may demonstrate Æthelstan's desire to impose his will on a religious community that had been acting in opposition to him.

Some comment should also be made about the appearance of Edwin
cliton in the lease's list of witnesses. This is none other than Edwin, full

brother of Ælfweard and half-brother of Æthelstan. It is his only known attestation of any royal document of the period and may indicate that he was based in Winchester. The Latin word *cliton*, derived from the Greek κλυτός (renowned), perhaps conveyed the notion that Edwin was an *ætheling*, an Old English term used to denote a royal prince.[27] Although Æthelstan may have been trying to impose his authority on the New Minster, he was perhaps not able to have things entirely his own way, with the result that Edwin (a rival) was not only listed as being present and second only to the king, but his status as a prince was also registered.[28]

A record of one of Æthelstan's earliest deeds as king can be found added by a tenth-century scribe onto a page of an eighth-century, possibly Northumbrian, gospel book. The scribe records how, 'very soon after he first became king', Æthelstan freed a slave called Eadhelm (an act known as 'manumission') and that 'Ælfheah the mass-priest and the community/household [Old English: *hired*], Ælfric the reeve, Wulfnoth the White, Eanstan the provost [*prafost*], and Byrnstan the mass-priest were witnesses of this'.[29] Because it is impossible to know when, exactly, the scribe responsible for the record thought that Æthelstan 'first became king'—whether in 924 when he was elected king by the Mercians, or shortly after the death of his brother Ælfweard who was recognised as king in Wessex, or indeed after his formal coronation, an event to which we will return—it has proved difficult to know exactly when Æthelstan carried out this act of manumission. Since other royal documents date the beginning of Æthelstan's reign to some point before his coronation, it is likely that it should belong to this very early phase of his kingship.[30]

The record's details, that Æthelstan freed a slave in connection with his becoming king, are interesting in their own right. But they also provide information about the composition of the king's household early in his reign, if that is the correct meaning of the Old English word *hired* in this instance. The household would have comprised those responsible for different aspects of the king's daily life and for the organisation of all that was needed by the king and his retinue as they travelled round his kingdom. By the late ninth and early tenth centuries we begin to see

details about individual household members who were assigned specific duties and titles, and the emergence of a hierarchy of roles, although the picture is by no means complete and would continue to
develop.[31] The manumission names the ecclesiastics Ælfheah and Byrnstan, who would later become bishops of Wells (acceded 926 × 928)
and Winchester (931), respectively, and who seem therefore to have
formed their early careers in the close service of the king. Ælfric the
reeve is listed, who would have had administrative responsibilities: Æthelstan's laws call on reeves to be involved in a variety of royal business
and required them to act as link between the centre of royal administration and the different localities across the kingdom.[32] Eanstan in the
manumission is described as a 'provost', using an Old English word—
prafost—that can either apply to a person who held a relatively high
status in an ecclesiastical setting or someone who held a similar position
in secular society, perhaps a reeve or 'steward'.[33]

We have seen that the New Minster lease for Ælfred had a long list of
witnesses—over eighty in number. It has been plausibly suggested that
these witnesses must have included the names of people who were members of the New Minster community and also of those who were part of
Æthelstan's household.[34] A lack of other records means it is not possible
to differentiate between these two groups. But it is notable that the list
includes a number of people assigned specific titles, including Wærwulf
sacerdos (priest), who is probably to be identified as the Mercian of that
name who was originally brought to Wessex by Alfred,[35] and two
deacons, Wigferth and Eadhelm. We have noted that there was a man
of possible continental origin there, Peter, and, judging by the form of
their names, those identified as Waltere, Gundlaf and Hildewine may
also have been from Europe.

Diplomas from Æthelstan's reign contain the names of those who
attended the royal assemblies and were designated *ministri*—that is,
'thegns.' Some thegns would have had administrative roles in different
parts of the kingdom, but others, presumably those that attended very
frequently and in high-status positions, would have been members of
Æthelstan's household. For the most part, no more specific titles are
given to these individuals, which makes it impossible to know precisely

what role they played. But in one diploma a man named Wulfhelm is entitled the *discifer regis*—that is, the 'king's dish-bearer,' also known as a seneschal or steward.[36] He would have been responsible for provisioning the royal household. The equivalent term in Old English is either *discthegn* (dish-servant / minister of food) or *hordere* (steward). Æthelstan's second law code reveals that a *hordere* could be involved in overseeing an exchange of goods, and there are stipulations which state what would happen if a *hordere* were found to have stolen anything or to have been an accessory to a theft.[37] Since these passages occur in sections of the law which explicate the roles of local officials, it seems likely that reference is being made to those who had the role of *hordere* in the localities rather than at the royal household.[38] From the will of one of Æthelstan's successors as king, his half-brother Eadred (d. 955), more detail can be gleaned about the structure of the royal household. In addition to a seneschal, it mentions the existence of: a keeper of the wardrobe (Old English: *hrægel-thegn*), who was a chamberlain with responsibility for the rooms of the royal household, for the king's wardrobe and for guarding the king's valuable possessions; and of a butler (Old English: *byrele*), whose duties included serving drinks and the management of the king's cellar.[39] Although officials occupying these roles are not specifically named in documents from Æthelstan's reign, men with those responsibilities may have been included among the *ministri* listed in his diplomas. Evidence from the reign of Edward the Confessor (d. 1066) shows the existence of a *cancellarius* (chancellor), who seems to have taken over responsibility for the royal treasures and relics and additionally to have been in charge of producing and perhaps also archiving royal documents. The *cancellarius* is on occasion described also as a *sigillarius*, a 'keeper of the (royal) seal', which suggests that the holder of the office may additionally have been responsible for the seal that was attached to documents such as royal writs.[40] Again, the title and office of *cancellarius* cannot be found in genuine documentation from Æthelstan's reign, but we will see that there was one royal scribe who was given authority to compose all of the king's diplomas produced in the years 928–35.[41] As a whole, then, the royal household would have constituted an extremely important group of people, their importance to

Æthelstan personally being all the greater because the king remained unmarried. He would have spent most of his time in their company and they would have supported him in his duties as king.[42]

On 4 September 925, over a year since the death of Ælfweard, Æthelstan was crowned king at Kingston upon Thames.[43] A delay of such a length of time is indicative of the problems he had faced in establishing himself as king. If his father, Edward, had been consecrated king at Kingston, the choice of the same location may have been designed to convey a message of continuity and stability.[44] Kingston had previously been chosen as a site of symbolic importance in the year 838, when the then king of Wessex, Ecgberht, managed to bring Kent, Surrey, Sussex and Essex within West Saxon dominion. And its significance for the West Saxon royal house is indicated by its etymology, since it is composed of the Old English elements *cyning* (king) and *tūn* (an enclosure/farmstead/village/estate). Perhaps it held similar importance for Æthelstan, who wanted to stress that Mercia, which bordered Wessex in the area of the River Thames, was now also within his control. The location is also noteworthy for its proximity to London, which, as Alfred's issue of the London monogram coin had shown, was by now a very significant city and emporium for trade.[45]

The survival of a text known as the 'Second Coronation *Ordo*' affords us access to the ritual and ceremony used on the occasion of a coronation, which borrowed from the practices followed in West Francia on the Continent. It is possible that one version of this *Ordo* was used for Æthelstan's coronation in 925.[46] Care was taken in the ceremony both to make Æthelstan's special status clear as having been appointed by God, but also to delineate what was expected of Æthelstan as king. Having been invested with a ring, sword, crown, sceptre, and rod as symbols of his office, the new king is reminded, in a section of the *Ordo* known as the 'three precepts', of the expectation that peace be maintained; that theft and injustice not be permitted; and that judgements be made in merciful and equitable fashion.[47]

After his formal establishment as king, early diplomas of Æthelstan entitle him *Angulsaxonum rex* (king of the Anglo-Saxons): Æthelstan was declaring himself to be the successor to the kingdom created by his grandfather, and perpetuated and extended territorially by his father.[48] The kingdom in 925 would technically have incorporated Wessex and Mercia, including the gains in East Anglia and the east midlands made by his father, perhaps except for the territory of the eastern midlands in which Sihtric was able to issue his own coins.[49] The recent and rapid expansion of the kingdom by Edward, and its incorporation of distinct peoples with their different senses of identity, would have brought significant challenges for Æthelstan. The royal title deployed in the New Minster land lease document, 'most glorious king of the Anglo-Saxons and Danes', represents an acknowledgement of the (probably significant) Scandinavian element that existed in society.

Although Æthelstan seems to have experienced a certain hostility to his rule from Wessex, his upbringing in Mercia may have predisposed the Mercians to be more favourable to a West Saxon king than they might otherwise have been. But it is clear that a potential threat to stability was represented by those living north of the River Humber, particularly Sihtric in York, with his links to Ireland. Once he had secured his position as 'king of the Anglo-Saxons', Æthelstan moved quickly to establish an alliance with Sihtric. Just under five months after his coronation, in January 926, the 'D' version of the *Anglo-Saxon Chronicle* records how: 'King Æthelstan and Sihtric, king of the Northumbrians, met together at Tamworth on 30 January and Æthelstan gave him his sister in marriage'.[50] The occasion marked a settlement of peaceful terms between the two parties and is full of interest. Near-contemporary records of marriages demonstrate that the agreement of conditions between both parties was a public affair: numerous witnesses were involved, in order to guarantee the behaviour of each party, and then the details were published throughout the immediate region in which the marriage had taken place.[51] The sister concerned was Æthelstan's full sister, whose name is not recorded in contemporary accounts.[52] That the agreement had been reached in Tamworth, the old centre of the Mercian kingdom, is itself striking. We have seen that meetings between kings of neighbouring territories were often held in border areas,[53] but Tamworth, even taking into account Sihtric's possible authority in Lincoln, seems to have been firmly within Æthelstan's kingdom.[54] So the location suggests prima facie that Æthelstan held the upper hand in the negotiations that followed. That said, Sihtric is entitled 'king' (Old English: *cyng*) in the annal in 'D', and there is no mention that he formally submitted to Æthelstan (as had been the case when the northern rulers met with Edward in 920), which has led some modern historians to conclude that the meeting was one between rulers of equal status.[55] Nonetheless, it is hard to avoid the conclusion that Æthelstan would have held the upper hand at any meeting held in Tamworth. In addition to its being the capital of the Mercian kingdom, the town also occupied a pivotal place in a ring of burghal defences established by Edward and Æthelflæd. If Æthelstan had been brought up in Mercia, it may have been an area with which he was personally connected.[56] There are various possible routes Sihtric could have taken in a journey from York to Tamworth. The most direct probably involved travelling on Roman roads that went south from York to Doncaster, then in a south-westerly direction to Chesterfield, then on to Derby and Lichfield, before arriving at Tamworth. Whichever way he travelled, Sihtric was not only advancing into the centre of Mercia but he would also have been forced to go past areas that had recently been militarily strengthened by the addition of a burh as part of Edward's and Æthelflæd's campaign against viking raids and settlement. Perhaps, rather than this being a meeting of equals, Æthelstan had choreographed the occasion to display his superior position. Whatever the respective status of the kings that day, the agreement reached was important for both parties. For Æthelstan it at least temporarily removed the threat from York, and possibly also from Ireland. For Sihtric it was an acknowledgment of his own kingship by Æthelstan, who ruled the majority of land south of the River Humber.

The year 926 saw a further marriage alliance. The West Frankish author, Flodoard, in his annal for that year, describes how Eadhild, Æthelstan's half-sister, was married to Hugh the Great, duke of the Franks.[57] More details about the way in which the marriage was arranged survive uniquely in the later testimony of William of Malmesbury. According to William, the count of Boulogne, Adelolf (the name is a continental Germanic rendering of the Old English name Æthelwulf), had travelled to Æthelstan, who was then involved in a meeting of his nobles at Abingdon, in order to suggest the match. Adelolf was the son of Count Baldwin II of Flanders and of Ælfthryth, the daughter of Alfred the Great. He was therefore Æthelstan's cousin, which was presumably why he was selected as Hugh's ambassador. As we will see, Æthelstan would become renowned, both in Britain and on the Continent, for his love of relics. Adelolf was evidently aware of the English king's partiality and is said to have brought with him an impressive array of items, which included the sword of the Roman emperor Constantine, the lance of Charlemagne, the banner of St Maurice, a precious crown, a piece of the Cross, and a small part of the crown of thorns.[58] His tactics seem to have been successful. Æthelstan is recorded as replying 'with gifts that were scarcely less, and comforted the passionate suitor with the hand of his sister'.[59] Although William suggests that the impetus for the marriage between Hugh and Eadhild had come from Hugh, it seems as if Æthelstan had formed a plan early in his reign to deploy his numerous (half-)sisters in strategic marriage alliances in order to develop relationships with contemporary rulers. The example had been set by his father, Edward, when he earlier arranged for the marriage of his daughter, Eadgifu, to Charles the Simple. It has been suggested that Eadgifu may also have been involved in the marriage of Eadhild to Hugh the Great.[60]

The year 927 is one of the most significant dates in British history. Folio 48 verso of British Library, Cotton MS Tiberius B IV, a manuscript which dates to the mid- or late eleventh century, better known as the 'D' version of the *Anglo-Saxon Chronicle*, records how: 'In this year appeared fiery lights in the northern quarter of the sky, and Sihtric died, and King Æthelstan succeeded to the kingdom of the Northumbrians; and he brought under his rule all the kings who were in this island: first Hywel, king of the West Welsh, and Constantine, king of the Scots, and Owain, king of the people of Gwent, and Ealdred, son of Eadwulf from Bamburgh. And they established peace with pledge and oaths in the place which is called Eamont [*æt Eamotum*], on 12 July, and renounced all idolatry [*deofolgeld*] and afterwards departed in peace'.[61] The entry is written in a relatively straightforward way, the portentous allusion to 'fiery lights' being the only concession to the significance of the occasion. As copied in 'D', no presentational distinction is made between the text for the 927 entry or that which comes immediately before it. Its bare details are extraordinary in their own right and require no embellishment. They record how, on the death of Sihtric in 927, Æthelstan succeeded to the Northumbrian kingdom, and subsequently that other kings in Britain also submitted to his rule at a ceremony held in the summer *æt Eamotum*, an Old English place-name which, as we have seen, means literally 'at the meeting of the rivers' (the second word being composed of the vernacular *ea* (river/water) and *motum*, from *mot* (a meeting/court)).[62] There are no details in contemporary sources about the fate of Sihtric's wife (and Æthelstan's sister) following her husband's death, but it is possible that her status in Northumbria provided some justification for Æthelstan's succession there.

The later testimony of William of Malmesbury preserves different details. William states how, after the death of Sihtric, 'Sihtric's son Óláf fled to Ireland and his brother Guthfrith to Scotland'—the latter to the court of Constantine, king of the Scots. Æthelstan threatened both Constantine and Owain, king of Strathclyde/Cumbria, with war unless the men were returned, with the result that the British kings preferred to recognise Æthelstan's superiority, which William says they did at an occasion at Dacre. But Guthfrith, together with a certain 'Turfrith', is described as attacking York and attempting to cajole its citizens—ultimately unsuccessfully—to join their cause against Æthelstan. Irish annals may corroborate William's detail that Guthfrith, who was a grandson of Ívarr and who had previously been in control of Dublin, had launched his own bid for control of York in 927; although they do not provide any information about his intentions, they record that in that year Guthfrith left Dublin 'and returned again within six months'.[63] William states that Guthfrith and Æthelstan reached a settlement, with Guthfrith described as spending some time at Æthelstan's court. Æthelstan then took decisive action by razing York's viking fortress 'in order to leave disloyalty no place of refuge'.[64]

Whatever the circumstances in which Northumbria was added to Æthelstan's domain, this was the year in which an 'England' of a recognisable geographical and political form was born. That the event was

considered important to contemporaries is signalled by the survival of
a remarkable poem, known from its first line as 'Carta, dirige gressus'.
The poem's author, who may have been named Peter, begins by addressing the poem itself, 'Letter, direct your steps' (using the Latin vocative
form, *Carta*), and instructing it to travel over sea and land and bring
news back to members of the king's household, which included the
'queen' (*regina*) and 'prince' (*clito*).[65] The metaphorical address to a
letter takes inspiration ultimately from classical antiquity and the work
of such poets as Horace, Ovid, and Martial. But it owes a more immediate debt to a ninth-century Carolingian poem composed for Charlemagne, from which it borrows various words and phrases and which
seems therefore to have been its model.[66] Because Æthelstan was unmarried, the 'queen' in question may have been his father's third wife,
Eadgifu, who was still alive at this point but seems to have occupied a
relatively obscure position at court; and the 'prince' may have been
Edwin, Æthelstan's oldest brother, who had been recognised as a 'prince'
(*clito*) in the New Minster lease discussed above.[67] Stanzas 3–5 of the
poem tie it very specifically to the moment in 927 when Æthelstan, following the death of Sihtric, was able to create England for the first time.
The poet rejoices about 'The Saxon-land [i.e., England] [now] made
whole' (*perfecta Saxonia*) and declares that Æthelstan is 'glorious
through his deeds!' (*per facta gloriosus!*).[68]

The poem as a whole bears witness to the extraordinary events of 927
and Æthelstan's creation of England. It shows how, in the immediate
aftermath of the expansion of his kingdom, Æthelstan desired to commemorate and publicise his success. The author may have been in the
king's retinue *æt Eamotum*, and, given the Carolingian source used to
compose 'Carta, dirige gressus', it has been suggested that he was of
continental origin.[69] It is possible that the poet, in modelling his poem
on a ninth-century equivalent for Charlemagne, who had created
the most extensive continental realm so far and was the first king of the
Franks to be designated an emperor,[70] was attempting to cast Æthelstan
in a similar light. It is notable that the author felt the medium of poetry
was the right way to mark Æthelstan's political expansion. Literacy in
Latin cannot have been widespread at the time, far less the ability to

understand Latin verse. The use of this genre of writing may have been intended to convey the impression that Æthelstan's court was a place of special learning and culture, a theme that recurs in other ways, as we will see. And the poem was carefully constructed so that it employs, as its opening, the Latin *Carta*, a word that can also refer to a royal diploma. The copy that survives in the bottom margin of Durham Cathedral Library MS A. II. 17, part I, begins with a cross at the left-hand side, which is reminiscent of the way that contemporary original royal diplomas open. Had the original copy of the poem begun with a cross in a similar form? Perhaps the poet, by invoking contemporary diploma terminology (and possibly physical form), sought to convey a legal formality and permanence to the events described in the poem.

Æthelstan's creation of England in 927 meant that he was the first king of the West Saxon line to knit together the formerly independent kingdoms of Wessex, Mercia, East Anglia, and Northumbria. His enhanced authority was publicly marked by the royal styles (titles) inscribed on contemporary coins and diplomas: having been 'king of the Anglo-Saxons', he could now be restyled 'king of the English' (*rex Anglorum*) and even 'king of all Britain' (*rex totius Britanniae*). Significantly, Æthelstan was able to interrupt the type of coins that had previously been minted in York under Scandinavian kings and, by the later part of his reign, align it more firmly with those used elsewhere in England.[71]

Despite his extraordinary achievements in 927, the polity Æthelstan formed must have been precarious, especially at its inception. We should not imagine that, overnight, Æthelstan was able to bring the kingdoms of Mercia, East Anglia and Northumbria fully within his control, even if they were notionally under his authority and even if areas of Mercia and East Anglia had already been part of his father's 'kingdom of the Anglo-Saxons'. These kingdoms must have retained their own sense of identity and independence within the umbrella of the 'kingdom of the English', and in any case they were themselves internally fragmented in various respects. It is notable that, after the death of Æthelstan, later in the tenth and eleventh centuries, moments of political crisis would see the English kingdom fragment: in 957–59, for example,

King Eadwig would become king in Wessex while his brother, Edgar, was king in Mercia, East Anglia, and Northumbria.[72]

There were also severe complications for Æthelstan in the extension of his dominion. Northumbria represented a particular challenge, both because it was situated far away from the base of Æthelstan's government in Winchester and because the region itself was politically complex and fragmented. In its earliest days Northumbria had been divided by the River Tees into two kingdoms, Deira to the south and Bernicia to the north. Although this division had technically disappeared by the seventh century, there are indications that political divisions remained, leaving a fractured kingdom for Æthelstan to contend with. And this disunion had been exacerbated by the settlement of York and its surrounding area by vikings from 867 onwards. Viking influence seems broadly to have stopped at the line of the River Tees, beyond which distribution of power is less clear, with the house of Bamburgh having a degree of secular rule and the community of St Cuthbert holding ecclesiastical authority.

With the incorporation of Northumbria within his control, Æthelstan had deprived the descendants of Ívarr of their power at York. Presumably to prevent any backlash against his territorial expansion, Æthelstan quickly sought acknowledgment of his superior standing from other kings and rulers in Britain in the ceremony æt Eamotum on 12 July 927. As we have seen, the annal in the Anglo-Saxon Chronicle records that the rulers who recognised his authority included: Hywel Dda, king of Deheubarth and latterly of Gwynedd; Constantine II, king of the Scots; Owain, king of Glywysing and Gwent; and Ealdred of Bamburgh. William of Malmesbury states that another Owain, king of Strathclyde/Cumbria, was also involved. Given the meaning of the place-name æt Eamotum—'at the meeting of the rivers'—its probable location is Eamont Bridge, situated slightly south-west of the confluence of the Rivers Eamont and Lowther.[73] A number of ancient sites in the close vicinity—including Mayburgh Henge, King Arthur's Round Table Henge, and the Roman fort of Brocavum—would have endowed the area with topographical significance. While Eamont Bridge is likely to have been the general location, any one of these

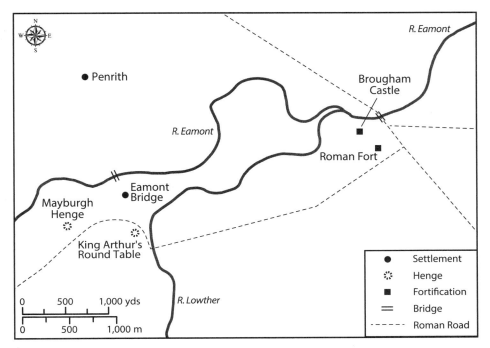

MAP 4. Eamont Bridge and the ancient sites of King Arthur's Round Table
Henge, Mayburgh Henge, and the Roman fort of Brocavum. Adapted from
T. Clarkson, *Strathclyde and the Anglo-Saxons in the Viking Age* (Edinburgh:
John Donald, 2014), 79.

nearby sites could have provided the venue itself, as could the land situated immediately to the west of the rivers' convergence, a liminal zone
created by the initial separation of the two rivers and then by their
flowing close together again further to the west.[74] Dacre, mentioned
by William of Malmesbury, is situated roughly five miles to the west
of Eamont Bridge, close to Dacre Beck, itself a tributary of the River
Eamont. Writing in 731, Bede mentions the existence of a monastery at
Dacre, so it is possible that this site also held importance of some kind
for the events of 927.[75] Significantly, a number of Roman roads, which
would have provided access to those coming from Wales and from York,
and also to those coming from the north in Alba, all meet in the region
near Eamont Bridge.

One phrase in the *Anglo-Saxon Chronicle* entry describing the ceremony in 927 is worth closer scrutiny. It records that those who submitted to Æthelstan also agreed to renounce all 'idolatry' (*deofolgeld*). The rejection of idolatry was presumably a matter that all of those involved could agree on, thus giving moral support to Æthelstan's hegemony.[76] The Old English word *deofolgeld* is composed of *deofol* (devil) and *geld* (tribute), which raises another possibility: that this could be a reference to payments previously made to vikings by the leaders present that day. Æthelstan would have been acutely aware that any one of the Welsh, Scottish, or Northumbrian leaders listed had the ability to form a coalition with vikings against him, something that would become all too real later in his reign. Perhaps in 927, as part of the political settlement negotiated, he had demanded that the leaders cease any dealings with vikings.[77]

According to William of Malmesbury, once Æthelstan had secured the submission of the leaders in the north at Eamont Bridge, which included two Welsh kings, he then proceeded to Hereford, where he met with the 'princes of the Northwalians, that is, the Northern Britons', an expression which implies that Æthelstan was dealing with representatives of all the Welsh people.[78] William narrates that Æthelstan compelled them to submit to his rule and to commit to the payment of an exorbitant annual tax, and he set the boundary between their kingdoms along the River Wye. William adds that Æthelstan then attacked the Cornish people who were in Exeter (described as the 'Western Britons'), drove them from the city, and again fixed the boundary between the English and Cornish along the River Tamar. According to William, Æthelstan had 'purged that city by sweeping out an infected race'.[79] As we will see, there may be a degree of truth in William's claims regarding Æthelstan's subjection of Wales: royal diplomas show that a number of Welsh kings were compelled to attend English royal assemblies during his reign and a Welsh prophetic poem, *Armes Prydein Vawr*, rails against the harsh realities of English rule, with a particular focus on the issue of tax. The poem has proved difficult to date, but many of its concerns could relate to the nature of Æthelstan's rule.[80] As for the claim that Æthelstan drove the Cornish from Exeter, he can certainly be linked with the city. Diplomas show that he held royal assemblies there in mid-April 928 and again in early November 932.[81] And eleventh-century records from Exeter register that he was a generous patron of the Exeter church and remember his gifts of relics. But there is no tenth-century evidence which supports the view that he expelled the Cornish from Exeter. In the early twelfth century a historiographical trend emerged which saw authors characterise British neighbours as somehow 'barbarous' when compared to their English counterparts: William's statements about the Cornish being an 'infected race' who were 'purged' from Exeter speak rather to William's alignment with that historiographical convention than to the realities of Æthelstan's tenth-century actions. By contrast, Æthelstan may well have been responsible for positive changes in the area—for example, the establishment around 930 of an episcopal see for Cornwall at St Germans, as we will see.[82]

By 929 Æthelstan was once more involved in marriage negotiations for one of his half-sisters, this time with Henry the Fowler, king of East Francia (d. 936), who was seeking a suitable bride for his son, Otto. William of Malmesbury suggests that, in answer to Henry's request, Æthelstan sent two of his sisters for the East Frankish royals to choose from.[83] A party of courtiers and others, led by Bishop Cenwald of Worcester, left England and made their way across the Continent towards Henry's court, visiting a number of German monasteries as they went. The sister chosen was Eadgyth, while the other sister, whose identity has proved difficult to determine, was also deployed in a tactical marriage, probably into the ruling house of Burgundy. By 929/30, then, Æthelstan had installed his half-sisters in such a way that England's influence was unusually prominent among many of the major ruling European dynasties. And it is clear that there were also advantages for continental rulers in establishing formal ties with Æthelstan, especially following his creation of the English kingdom. This would have been particularly apparent to the East Frankish Henry and his son, Otto, whose own positions had only quite recently been established.[84]

The relative silence of the *Anglo-Saxon Chronicle* for the years 928–34 obscures our view of this period of Æthelstan's reign. But we do have the testimony of his surviving royal diplomas, law codes, and coins, from which we gain an impression of a king who was indefatigable in matters of governance and who sought to proclaim his own significant political successes as widely as possible. His diplomas for 928–35 are written in Latin that is exceptionally ambitious, while his laws and coins demonstrate his attempts to impose legislative and monetary structures across his newly expanded kingdom, even if these were not, in the end, logistically sustainable.[85] Æthelstan also emerges as a king who supported the church, was a keen proponent and collector of relics, and had interests in scholarship and attracting scholars to his court. One of Æthelstan's successors, Edgar (d. 975), is celebrated for his ecclesiastical reforms and for his sponsorship of learning. But the roots of these innovations are to be found in the reign of Æthelstan. Two of the driving forces of Edgar's reforms, Dunstan and Æthelwold, spent time at Æthelstan's court, and the ambitious form of Latin that was embraced by the late tenth-century reformers, characterised by the use of recondite vocabulary and long, elaborately structured sentences, and which is known as 'hermeneutic' Latin, can actually first be found in Æthelstan's diplomas.[86]

We know that the years 928–34 also brought their problems. Folcuin, a monk of Saint-Bertin in Saint-Omer, in modern France, wrote in 961/2 a history known as the *Gesta Abbatum Sithiensium* (Deeds of the Abbots of Saint-Bertin). It includes an episode involving Æthelstan and his eldest half-brother, Edwin. Folcuin describes how in 933 Edwin, whom he had previously described as a 'king' (*rex*), was driven from his kingdom by some unspecified 'disturbance' (*perturbatione*) and, when fleeing by ship, was drowned at sea. His body was later taken to Saint-Bertin for burial by his kinsman Adelolf, the person who had earlier petitioned Æthelstan concerning a marriage alliance. After the burial, Æthelstan is said to have sent numerous offerings to the monastery and, on account of its duty to Edwin, to have received any monks from Saint-Bertin who sought to visit his court in England.

Folcuin is the earliest author to describe this episode, and it is difficult to know what to make of the details he provides. Should we attach any weight to the fact that Folcuin describes Edwin as a 'king' (*rex*), and perhaps infer from this description that, in circumstances that are now unknown, he had been recognised by some in England as king at some point between 924 and 933? Or was this a misunderstanding on Folcuin's part of Edwin's position as an *ætheling*? Or was it indeed a simple error? We know that Folcuin is not immune to error, as this same passage exhibits other inaccuracies.[87] The exact nature of the 'disturbance' is not revealed by Folcuin. Could it be linked somehow to the title of Edwin as 'king', perhaps suggesting that Edwin had made his own bid for power? From the detail in Folcuin it is impossible to be certain. It is notable that the Latin word for 'disturbance', *perturbatione*, is used later in the same sentence to describe how the winds were swirling such that Edwin was drowned in the waves; Folcuin may either have been trying rhetorically to stress the general turbulence of the time by means of repetition, or his choice of word owed as much to narrative dialectic as to factual detail.[88]

Whatever had happened in 933, texts of the early twelfth century begin to attach a degree of blame to Æthelstan himself, that he was somehow implicated in the death of his half-brother. William of Malmesbury describes how there were informants who led Æthelstan to believe that Edwin was plotting against him, with the result that, according to William, Æthelstan drove him out of the kingdom. William's account is written in such a way that no blame is attached to Edwin himself. Not only is Edwin described as doing his best to convince Æthelstan of his innocence, but William also says that Edwin was someone whom 'even strangers could not choose but [to] pity'. William goes so far as to criticise Æthelstan, saying that, in abandoning Edwin to a boat that was old and not properly equipped with men or oars, 'his cruelty took a form without parallel'.[89] As William narrates, so dire were the conditions Edwin found himself in at sea that he voluntarily left the boat and jumped to his death into the waves. Other twelfth-century texts also contain details about Edwin, including that probably compiled by Symeon of Durham and known as the *Historia Regum* (History of the Kings) and Henry of Huntingdon's *Historia Anglorum* (History of the English). In both of these texts, the death of Edwin at sea is simply noted, with the *Historia Regum* adding that this had taken place at Æthelstan's command. One version of the *Anglo-Saxon Chronicle*, which survives in a twelfth-century copy, records plainly that Edwin had drowned, without any reference to Æthelstan.[90] It is impossible to gain any greater degree of certainty about what may have happened. Since Edwin was the full brother of Ælfweard, the man who had been recognised as king in the immediate aftermath of Edward the Elder's death in 924, and since Edwin was himself recognised as an *ætheling* in a document from early in Æthelstan's reign, it is at least feasible that he had launched a challenge to Æthelstan's position. And it is equally possible that Æthelstan had responded with strength, forcing Edwin into an overseas exile that resulted in his death.

In 934 Æthelstan went to war with the Scots. The *Anglo-Saxon Chronicle* merely reports that Æthelstan took military forces into Scotland and 'ravaged much of it'.[91] Other sources offer more detail, including that Æthelstan advanced far into the kingdom of Constantine II, for reasons to which we will return.[92] As he progressed northwards, Æthelstan took the opportunity to reinforce his rule in the kingdom of Northumbria. It is not always possible to give precise dates to the movements of an Anglo-Saxon king and his followers. But highly innovative documents from Æthelstan's reign, written by the royal scribe 'Æthelstan A', provide information about the exact day and place that they were issued.[93] We therefore know that the king and his entourage departed from Winchester on 28 May 934 and that they had arrived at Nottingham by 7 June. They would later progress to Chester-le-Street, in Northumbria, although the precise date of their arrival there is unknown.

While in Nottingham, Æthelstan summoned a royal assembly, which was attended by an extraordinary group of individuals. Fifty-nine people are listed as having been present, which included the archbishops of Canterbury and York, bishops from a range of sees, some Welsh kings, and important secular officials known as ealdormen and thegns, some of whom had particular power in the north. Gathered together in Nottingham that day were some of the most significant political figures in Britain. The king and others listed would have had their own entourages, whose names are not recorded; the meeting could have involved several hundred people in total. At least four different languages would have been spoken: Old English, Old Welsh, Old Norse, and Latin, with

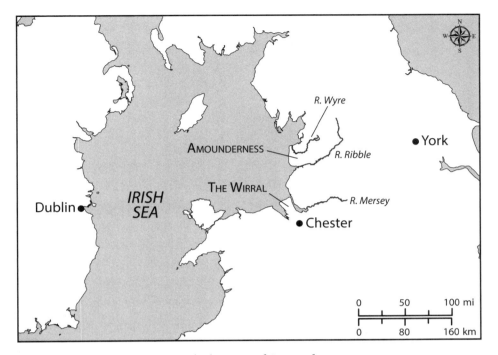

MAP 5. The location of Amounderness.

the last perhaps acting to some degree as a common language.[94] And Nottingham had been chosen as the site of the assembly not only because it lay just to the west of a major Roman road, the Fosse Way, and was therefore easily accessible as Æthelstan made his way north, but also because it was situated in previously Scandinavian territory.

At the meeting, a record of which fortunately survives to this day, Æthelstan made an exceptional gift. He is said to have bought with his own money the land called Amounderness, which he subsequently gave to the York church and its then archbishop, Wulfstan I. The etymology of the place-name Amounderness, comprising the Old Norse personal name, Agmundr/Ǫgmundr, and the Old English word for a district subject to secular authority, *-hērness*, raises the possibility that Æthelstan had purchased the land directly from a viking lord, although the record itself does not specify this detail. This grant of land is unusual for two principal reasons: firstly, because Amounderness constitutes an area on the north-west coast of England, between the Rivers Ribble and Wyre, far distant from the York church itself, and, secondly, because the size of the area granted is thought to have been the largest ever made by an Anglo-Saxon king, embracing a significant portion of modern-day Lancashire.

Why would Æthelstan do this? An examination of the details of the grant reveals his formidable political acumen. The land lay in an area that had been heavily settled by Scandinavians and was therefore a landing ground for vikings travelling to York from Dublin across the Irish Sea. York had been ruled by vikings since about 867, but Æthelstan needed to guarantee the city's support so that it no longer looked towards Dublin for its political leaders. As we have seen, he had attempted in 927 to bring the city on his side by means of a military venture. This gift indicates that, by 934, he was attempting to consolidate the support of the York church and its archbishop, Wulfstan I, by means of a bribe of a significant amount of land.

After the break in his journey at Nottingham, Æthelstan continued further north and eventually arrived at Chester-le-Street, where he met with members of another religious establishment, St Cuthbert's community, which in the late ninth century had relocated inland from its original home on Holy Island (Lindisfarne), off the north-east coast of England. In just the same way that Æthelstan had tried to buy the support of the York church, so he seems also to have attempted to gain the endorsement of the Cuthbertines. The *Historia de Sancto Cuthberto*, written at some point between the mid-tenth and the mid-eleventh centuries, contains a relatively detailed description of various gifts Æthelstan is said to have made to the community. Some of these survive today, including the remarkable silken stole and maniple that were discovered in St Cuthbert's tomb, and a copy of the *Life* of St Cuthbert, which is now housed in the Parker Library of Corpus Christi College, Cambridge. The manuscript in question opens with an extraordinary image, of Æthelstan in front of a church, holding a book with his head bowed out of reverence for St Cuthbert. It is the earliest surviving manuscript portrait of any English ruling king.

Æthelstan's visit to St Cuthbert's community is commemorated in one further manuscript, known as the Durham *Liber vitae*. The manuscript was very important to the local religious community. It had been begun in the early ninth century and was considered so precious that various of its pages had been written in alternating gold and silver letters. Scholars think that it was displayed on the church's high altar so that it could be easily seen by visitors. One of its early folios contains a list of names of those kings and 'leaders' (*duces*) who had some kind of special connection with Cuthbert's church. The list is arranged chronologically, beginning with two seventh-century kings of Northumbria, Edwin and Oswald. But a tenth-century scribe has taken the liberty of inserting Æthelstan's name right at the top of the list, just after the rubricated title. The record is extraordinary for a number of reasons. At one level it recognises Æthelstan's special new status: rather than having his name inserted in its proper chronological place several folios later, it is given prominence right at the start, next to the names of some of the most illustrious early kings of Northumbria. But it may also represent a shrewd political ploy on the part of the Cuthbertine community itself. We know that on subsequent occasions in the tenth and eleventh centuries members of the religious community used the same *Liber vitae* to enter records of land transactions agreed between themselves and various individuals. The deployment of their holy book for such a purpose was a deliberate tactic: it enmeshed the donor of the land in a deal not just with living members of the religious house, but directly with their saint, Cuthbert, himself. It seems likely that the donor would have been involved in some kind of ceremonial occasion, at which their grant was formally acknowledged, and then recorded in the *Liber vitae*. By invoking the otherworldly saint, the community hoped to make the terms of the grant inviolable, both by the donor himself and by any would-be defrauder of their lands. Does the recording of Æthelstan's name in such an unusual way in the *Liber vitae* indicate that he, too, had been involved in a deal done directly with Cuthbert, designed to make sure that he would not in the future withdraw from what he had promised?

The recording of Æthelstan's name in the *Liber vitae* may provide further, admittedly slender, evidence for the nature of his rule over the northern part of Northumbria, beyond the River Tees. When he had earlier given land to the York church in 934, it was recorded in one of the diplomas drafted by Æthelstan's royal scribe, 'Æthelstan A'. The absence of such a record in his dealings with the Cuthbertine community is notable. Perhaps there had been such a diploma at one stage, which has subsequently been lost. Even if that were true, it is striking that the Cuthbertines themselves placed greater value on records drawn up in their own, idiosyncratic ways, that directly involved their saint, Cuthbert, rather than on a diploma produced by Æthelstan's royal writing office. It suggests that the governmental structures, and modes of issuing lands south of the River Tees, did not extend in any authoritative way further north.[95] Æthelstan may notionally have been the king in this area of northern Northumbria, but the realities of rule at the extremities of his new kingdom may have been quite different.[96]

The separatist nature of northern Northumbria is further revealed by the position of Bamburgh (in origin a royal fortress in the Northumbrian kingdom of Bernicia) and its rulers in the tenth century. We have already seen that Ealdred of Bamburgh was listed in 927 in the *Anglo-Saxon Chronicle* as being one of the leaders who submitted to Æthelstan's rule. His precise status is difficult to determine. His father, Eadwulf, can be found described in Irish annals as 'king of the Saxons of the North', while the *Historia de Sancto Cuthberto* allots him the title 'prince' (*princeps*).[97] It is possible, therefore, that Ealdred himself could have had a quasi-royal status in this northern part of Northumbria. If that were the case, it is striking that he is not titled 'king' in the relevant entry of the *Anglo-Saxon Chronicle*. Diplomas of the years 930–33 record the presence of Ealdred (among the ealdormen) at Æthelstan's royal assemblies held in the south of England, which suggests that his recognition of Æthelstan's overlordship was not simply theoretical. His disappearance from the historical record in 933 indicates that he might have died at about this time. Ealdred's successors at Bamburgh, some of whom were entitled 'high-reeve of Bamburgh' in royal diplomas, seem to have been members of the same family, including his son, Osulf, who attests some of Æthelstan's diplomas of the years 934–35. The significant point to note is that the circumstances in which many of these individuals rose to power in Northumbria are obscure, and their positions may have been hereditary rather than selected by subsequent kings of the English. That there was a family of such high status, well entrenched in an ancient royal fortress in the north of Northumbria, one which had links with the Scottish royal line, represented another indication of the challenges facing Æthelstan in extending his rule this far to the north.[98]

By 13 September 934, Æthelstan's northern campaign had finished: he can be found on that date to have returned to the south of his kingdom, where he held a royal assembly in Buckingham. Significantly, it was the first time that Constantine II also attended a meeting of the English witan; the king of the Scots had been forced into submission.[99] Æthelstan's acquisition of Northumbria in 927 is one of the most significant events in English history. It could not have been evident at the time, but it would ultimately lead to the creation of England as we know it today. But Æthelstan's expansion of his power from 927 onwards caused resentment. Matters came to a head in 937 when he was confronted militarily by an alliance of rulers that included Constantine II of the Scots, Óláf Guthfrithson of Dublin (who was asserting his claim to rule in York), and Owain of Strathclyde/Cumbria. There is no indication that the Welsh were involved, but they, too, found ways to express their dissatisfaction with English rule.[100] Modern historians have not reached a consensus about the precise location at which the 937 Battle of *Brunanburh* was fought. But its significance is hard to deny: the anti-Æthelstan alliance threatened not just to topple the English king from power but also to undo all of the political and territorial advances he had made.

3

Wielding the Sceptre

BY THE EARLY tenth century, English kings could depend on systems of governance that were remarkably sophisticated. Grants of land and of privileges could be issued in the form of Latin royal diplomas (which contain some elements in the Old English vernacular, particularly the 'boundary clause', which gives the physical outer limits of the land being granted), which were composed for and ratified by meetings of the royal assembly. The assembly itself was referred to by a variety of contemporary terms, one of which was *witan*, an Old English word meaning, literally, 'wise men'.[1] From the centre of his kingdom, the king could send out less formal instructions via the medium of a 'writ' (Old English: *gewrit*, which means a letter), a small document—both in length and physical format—written primarily in Old English and addressed to members of local courts across the kingdom. No writs survive from the reign of Æthelstan, but it is thought that the origins of this genre of documentation lie with the reforms to learning instituted by his grandfather, Alfred.[2] Æthelstan must have used this mode of communication, even if no examples in his name survive today. Kings were also responsible for the promulgation of laws and for the maintenance of order in society. Law codes survive from as early as the turn of the seventh century, a famous example being that issued by the king of Kent, Æthelberht (d. 616). It is fortunate that, for the reign of Æthelstan, an unusually large body of legal material has survived. One consequence of Æthelstan's expansion of the kingdom in 927 was that he had to find ways to incorporate and govern the novel territories within his jurisdiction (in particular Northumbria). As we have seen in chapter 2, he may have struggled to extend his authority in a uniform way, especially into the extremities of his newly enlarged kingdom. This chapter will investigate how matters operated at the kingdom's core.

Thanks to the evidence of diplomas and of law codes, which were the products of Æthelstan's royal assemblies, we can reconstruct a relatively large amount of detail about the nature of those gatherings. It goes without saying that the surviving sources represent only a fraction of the original material produced in Æthelstan's reign and therefore that we do not have a complete view.[3] But diplomas, in particular, provide details which allow us to approximate how frequently royal assemblies met, the types of day on which they convened, and the areas of the kingdom in which they were predominantly held. Thirty-nine authentic diplomas survive from Æthelstan's reign, which can be divided into three principal groups according to their style and date of issue: (i) 925–26, (ii) 928–35, and (iii) 935–39.[4] As we will see, the diplomas of the second group, produced by the scribe known as 'Æthelstan A', are in various respects revolutionary. They contain unprecedented amounts of information, in particular about the date and place of issue of each diploma, allowing us for the first time to see how tenth-century peripatetic kingship worked.

From the lists of attendees included in royal diplomas (known literally as witness-lists), quite a lot of detail can be reconstructed about the composition of the royal assembly, not least the peaks and troughs of different individuals' careers, since the lists are set out hierarchically according to status. But these lists require a certain circumspection. Most of the diplomas in question survive only as later copies, made long after the original grant of land had been issued. The copyists responsible could make mistakes—for example, in the spelling of the names, in the order in which the names should have been listed, or in the omission of names that should have been recorded. We should also be aware that there may have been individuals present who went unrecorded. A further complication is the unique form of the 'Æthelstan A' diplomas, since their unparalleled detail about witnesses may say more about the peculiar nature of the evidence than about the reality of the people being present.[5] All of that said, Æthelstan's witness-lists are so carefully organised, and at times so comprehensive, that they have given historians broad confidence in the details they contain.[6]

By the time that Æthelstan became king in 924, there were well-established conventions for who should be attending meetings of the royal assembly.[7] Prominent ecclesiastics, including the archbishop, bishops, and sometimes abbots, and lay figures, including ealdormen and thegns, were present. The title 'ealdorman' (*dux*, in Latin) described a person who was both of noble status but also (by the tenth century) an officer of the king. He was responsible for the governance of a local area, where he enacted the king's wishes. Ealdormen were meant to oversee the law and the maintenance of order, the raising of military forces, the collection of tax, and the settling of disputes. The number of ealdormen holding office varied, and the regions over which they held power differed in geographical extent. As agents of the king in the different localities who would have had their own retinues of men, ealdormen held trusted positions which were vital as Æthelstan sought to expand the bounds of his kingdom. Given their rank, they had the power to cause the king serious problems if their loyalty wavered. 'Thegns' (*ministri*), too, were nobles, and landowners. Their status was not as elevated as that of the ealdormen, as indicated by their lower positions in the witness-lists of diplomas. As servants of the king they had administrative and military roles and could achieve the status of ealdorman. Some thegns could hold the administrative office of 'reeves': individuals who, as we will see, were relied on by Æthelstan to maintain oversight of his laws in the different parts of his kingdom.[8]

Æthelstan's England was divided into a variety of administrative zones which enabled certain functions to be completed, including the raising of military forces, the collection of tax, and the issuing and enforcing of law. At the top level were the 'shires', which, having been introduced originally in Wessex and which are referenced in ninth-century parts of the *Anglo-Saxon Chronicle*, were later extended into Mercia and further north in tandem with the expansion of the West Saxon kingdom. By the time of Domesday Book in 1086, the vast majority of England south of the Rivers Tees and Ribble had been organised into shires. It has proved difficult to know when areas outside Wessex were first 'shired'. Some regions may have been shired in the early tenth century under Edward the Elder, but others may have been reorganised in the late tenth or eleventh centuries.[9] Domesday Book, in addition to its details about shires, provides a picture of the shire's administrative subdivisions, known as 'hundreds'. The 'wapentake' of the north was broadly equivalent to the hundred, but with a Scandinavian-influenced name, from Old Norse *vápnatak*, 'a taking of weapons'.[10] But, as with the shires, it is difficult to know exactly when these districts were originally formed; versions of them (or some of the functions performed by them) may have existed in Æthelstan's time, but, if they did, they are not referred to in his laws, and it is likely that they were given clearer form in the mid- to late tenth century.[11]

There was no sharp division between church and state in the tenth century: archbishops and bishops performed functions that we would today regard as 'secular'—for example, in the encoding and enacting of laws.[12] In Durham bishops continued to have secular responsibilities even until the early nineteenth century, which is why visitors arriving in the city are greeted by signs that read 'County Durham: Land of the Prince Bishops'. The high status of ecclesiastics in the early tenth century is recognised by their preeminent rank at meetings of the royal assembly: the archbishop(s) often attest first, after the king himself, and the bishops can take precedence over the ealdormen. Royal assemblies must have involved discussion about both secular and ecclesiastical business.

The witness-lists for Æthelstan's diplomas show profound changes between those that were issued in the years 925–26 and those that were issued in the years 928–35, and then again with those for the years 935–39. The first group conveys the impression of a king whose power and influence was relatively constrained: in terms both of the ecclesiastical and the lay witnesses, the number of those present was comparatively small, and, at least in the case of the bishops, the attestations reveal a dependence on Mercia in a way that corroborates what we have seen about the beginning of his reign and the Mercian roots of his power.[13] Following Æthelstan's elevation as king of the English in 927, the diplomas' witness-lists are transformed. In general, there is a large increase in the number of individuals recorded as attending the royal assemblies in the years 928–35 across all categories of subscription, ecclesiastical and lay—much larger than anything that had so far been recorded and greater than any lists that would ever again be produced in the pre-1066 period. Some of the lists include upwards of fifty thegns alone. It has been estimated that, when due account has been taken for the presence of servants and other such people who would have accompanied members of the *witan* but who would not have been recorded in the witness-lists, the occasions could have involved anywhere between two hundred and six hundred people in total.[14] And there are, in addition, three categories of people listed who had not before been included: important figures from the north, particularly the archbishop of York and the bishop of St Cuthbert's community; various sub-kings from Wales, Alba and Strathclyde/ Cumbria, who would only attest one other set of diplomas in the tenth century, the so-called 'alliterative' diplomas;[15] and a number of bishops who did not belong to any known see.[16]

As noted above, we need to be careful in how we handle these details. The witness-lists of 'Æthelstan A' are so distinctive that they must reflect a degree of 'personal choice' on the part of the scribe responsible. But, seen in the light of the witness-lists of Æthelstan's predecessor, Edward the Elder, and of his successors as kings of the English, it becomes apparent that there was in general a trend for the lists to become more inclusive and thus longer, even if they never again reached the heights of 'Æthelstan A', a trend which suggests a growing number of attendees at the royal assemblies.[17] The augmented lists must in part reflect the expansion of Æthelstan's kingdom in 927 and the subsequent ceremony of submission to Æthelstan involving several kings near Eamont Bridge. For some modern historians, these vast gatherings, when compared to smaller occasions of previous reigns, now resembled 'national assemblies', a sort of 'proto-parliament' that connected all of the major actors in the kingdom directly with the king.[18] Among the lists of Æthelstan's ealdormen are men with names that display Scandinavian influence, individuals such as Guthrum, Grim, Styrcer, Gunner, Fræna and so on.[19] Because of the limited source material for these years, it is difficult to know who these men were and the areas covered by their jurisdiction. The character of their names raises the possibility that at least some of them were drawn from the Anglo-Scandinavian population of the north and east.[20] Perhaps they were men who had held positions of power in the north before Æthelstan's expansion in 927 and who were subsequently required to attend the English king's assemblies. If they were, their presence in diplomas of 928–35 may indicate Æthelstan's dependence on an existing Northumbrian nobility for the implementation of his power there, in the same way that we will find him trying to collaborate with members of the Northumbrian church.[21]

Diplomas for the years 935–39 are again different: in general, they include many fewer witnesses, and the northern dimension also disappears. What this evidence suggests about Æthelstan's assemblies in the latter part of his reign is difficult to ascertain. We know that by 935 'Æthelstan A' had ceased his work, so the changes may also be attributed to the drafting styles of new scribes. Diplomas issued after Æthelstan's death help to understand the documents of 935–39. From the reign of Æthelstan onwards, a so-called 'mainstream' of royal diplomas can be detected up until the Norman Conquest.[22] At times, though, series of diplomas were produced outside of this 'mainstream' by a variety of agencies. Two such distinctive sets of diplomas survive from the 940s and 950s, known as the 'alliterative' and 'Dunstan B' diplomas, which, like their 'Æthelstan A' predecessors, once more show a greater level of inclusivity in their lists of witnesses.[23] Comparison of their witness-lists with those of the 'mainstream' of the same period has revealed two characteristics: first, that there may in general have been more ealdormen and bishops present at meetings of the *witan* than surviving witness-lists allow; and second that, despite the likely presence of a greater number of witnesses than indicated in the extant diploma witness-lists, it was nevertheless the case that the less senior bishops and ealdormen were not as regularly present as they had been in the diplomas of 'Æthelstan A'.[24] We should perhaps allow that diplomas of 935–39, although representative of assemblies that were smaller in scope than those of 928–35, may still have had people in attendance whose names did not make it into the written record.

In 935 it is notable that Archbishop Wulfstan I of York, having been a witness at Æthelstan's assemblies since 931, drops off the lists. When he reappears in historical records thereafter, his allegiance to English authorities was not guaranteed, since he can be found at times to act on the side of Scandinavian kings.[25] Also in 935 those ealdormen with Scandinavian-influenced names disappear from the lists, and that remains the case until 939. Were they present but not listed, or had they genuinely ceased to attend? It is possible that their disappearance reflects a similar reality to that of Archbishop Wulfstan I and the transfer of their allegiance away from Æthelstan. On the other hand, a number of distinctive sets of diplomas from after Æthelstan's reign do display some attestations of ealdormen with Scandinavian-influenced names, suggesting that their inclusion partly depends on the perspective of those responsible for drafting the diplomas.[26] We should allow for the possibility that some of these figures had been present in 935–39 even if their names are not listed, but also recognise that, since their power was established in northern and eastern areas of the kingdom, their attendance at the assemblies may have been less frequently required.[27]

Further analysis of the attestations of the ealdormen in 935–39 reveals that a significant realignment of politics took place, perhaps a coup of some sort. In the years 937–38, only two ealdormen witness Æthelstan's diplomas, a certain Ælfwald and Uhtred.[28] By 939 the pattern has changed: Ælfwald no longer witnesses the king's diplomas, and Uhtred has been demoted in rank below two newcomers, who are named Ælfhere and Wulfgar. A fourth ealdorman also appears, who shares the king's name of Æthelstan and who is the third-ranking ealdorman, thus superior in position to Uhtred but below the rank of Ælfhere and Wulfgar. We know an unusual amount about this ealdorman Æthelstan. As the ealdorman of East Anglia, his tenure in office from 932 to 956 extended beyond that of successive English kings. So powerful did he and his family become that a near-contemporary narrative source referred to him as Æthelstan 'Half-King', indicating his quasi-royal status.[29] In 938 Æthelstan 'Half-King', who had been present at royal assemblies of the years 932–35, but had disappeared by 937–38, had been given some land in Devon by the king.[30] This donation, followed in 939 by the elevation of two new ealdormen, suggests that the years 938–39 may have witnessed a changing of the guard among Æthelstan's ealdormen.[31] The proximity of these changes to the 937 Battle of *Brunanburh*, an event to which we will return, may be more than a coincidence: perhaps there were new opportunities available in the aftermath of that major military episode.[32]

Unfortunately, we have no surviving records which resemble the 'minutes' from the royal assemblies.[33] The diplomas themselves only record what was ultimately decided concerning grants of land. Diplomas from the later reign of King Æthelred the Unready (d. 1016) do preserve some details about the deliberations that took place in advance of a land grant being made. We learn, for example, of the history of various lands that were being granted, and the circumstances in which that land had come into the king's possession. Astonishingly, we are even permitted close access to Æthelred's own voice, since some of his diplomas preserve details about the regrets he had concerning his decisions as a young king.[34] If Æthelstan ever felt concern about his actions, none of the detail found its way into his diplomas. But it is virtually certain that similar discussions about the history of particular estates were held, and that the assemblies were fora in which Æthelstan's leading figures could raise matters that were close to their hearts. They must also have been highly formal and ritual occasions, an opportunity for the king to display his majesty and generosity.[35] Some diplomas from before Æthelstan's reign refer to a sod of earth or to the diploma itself being placed on an altar by a grantor, which endowed it with divine authority, before being handed over to a recipient. The symbolic act, known as a 'ceremony of conveyance', offered a visual representation of what was involved in the writing and donation of a diploma. One early eighth-century text, the *Life of St Wilfrid*, refers to the bounds of land being read out, which would have been one way to impress the details of the transaction on those present.[36] As we will see, royal assemblies were also the places where the king issued his legislation: because Æthelstan's surviving law codes cannot be precisely dated, it is difficult to know whether some assemblies were dedicated simply to the disbursement of land while others were focused on legal matters.[37]

Narrative sources do not preserve details about the length of any given royal assembly. Royal diplomas may have been drawn up at the assembly so that their terms could be discussed and agreed on before the documents were issued at the assembly's conclusion.[38] A number of single-sheet originals show signs of their having been used at the assemblies themselves and of their details being emended, which provides important evidence about the practical value of these documents. Given the length of the documents and the importance of the matters to which they testify, we can imagine that royal assemblies would have occupied several days of business. A record for the year 1085 refers to an assembly that spanned five days.[39] Attendance at a royal assembly must have been an important matter: Æthelstan's second law code contains stipulations designed to regulate attendance at assemblies of a lesser scale, held by reeves, which suggest that if someone were not present on three occasions, that person would be fined.[40] Those requested to attend these smaller-scale meetings were given seven days' notice. One can imagine that punishments would have been more severe if a person failed to attend Æthelstan's royal assembly and that a greater amount of advance warning was provided for these larger gatherings.

From the extant diploma record,[41] it can be seen that Æthelstan convened his royal assembly several times a year (five being the most documented), although this is based on incomplete records. By chance, for the year 956, during the reign of one of Æthelstan's successors, King Eadwig (d. 959), a disproportionately large number of diplomas have survived, over sixty in number, which allows for unusual comparative analysis. It has been demonstrated that these diplomas were the products of four separate meetings of the royal assembly during that year, which means that an approximation of up to five annual meetings under Æthelstan seems broadly correct.[42] When the dates of Æthelstan's assemblies are analysed, it emerges that a high number (but not all) were issued either on a holy day itself, or close to one, or during a period of particular religious importance such as Lent.[43] It is not solely from diplomas that information about the convening of royal assemblies is provided. We may reasonably conclude that an event such as a king's coronation, or another important diplomatic occasion such as the arrangement of the marriage allegiance between Æthelstan and Sihtric of Northumbria, as recorded in narrative texts, may also have involved the gathering of the assembly. The dates of these episodes seem not to align with religious festivals, which suggests that they were pragmatically arranged according to the needs of contemporary politics.[44]

Analysis of the locations of the land granted by Æthelstan, and of the places where the royal meetings were held during his reign, reveals some distinct patterns. From the relatively scant details we have for the early years of his reign (924–26), it seems that the king concentrated his efforts in Mercia.[45] Following his elevation as king of the English, Æthelstan's focus turns to Wessex. The majority of the land granted in the period 928–33 is in the south, in Wessex, as are the locations at which the royal assembly was held. It is interesting that on 16 April 928 the king held a meeting in Exeter, Devon, almost a year after he had received the submission of the Cornish and set the boundary with their territory at the River Tamar.[46] Perhaps the gathering of his royal assembly there was designed to stress the effectiveness of his rule in the south-west. Another meeting in Lifton, Devon, on 12 November 931 would have had a similar effect.[47] The remaining assemblies in 928–33 were concentrated in the heartlands of Wessex.[48] All of the sites chosen were situated close to Roman roads or to rivers, both of which would have facilitated travel for those hoping to attend. The majority of locations used seem also to have been royal vills (townships). Because royal vills collected a tax in kind, the *feorm*, which provided food for the king and his entourage, they were therefore better prepared to receive the assembly and its large number of attendants.[49] In the early summer of 934, for reasons that will be discussed in chapter 5, Æthelstan left the southern centre of his kingdom and progressed north with the ultimate aim of waging war against the Scots. As he did so, he stopped both at Nottingham, where he granted land to the York church (and its archbishop, Wulfstan I), and at Chester-le-Street, where he visited the shrine of St Cuthbert and also dispensed land to that religious community.[50] As far as we know, this was the first time that the royal assembly had been convened so far north since the meeting near Eamont Bridge in 927, suggesting that it was irregular for the king to move his operations outside Wessex.[51]

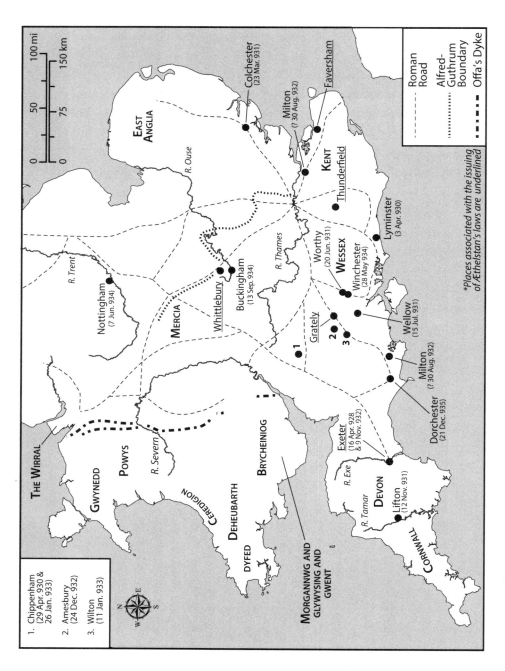

MAP 6. Places of issue for the 'Æthelstan A' diplomas noted in Appendix I, and places associated with the issuing of Æthelstan's laws.

Legend:
- Roman Road
- Alfred-Guthrum Boundary
- Offa's Dyke

*Places associated with the issuing of Æthelstan's laws are underlined

Inset (top left):
1. Chippenham (29 Apr. 930 & 26 Jan. 933)
2. Amesbury (24 Dec. 932)
3. Wilton (11 Jan. 933)

Map labels:
THE WIRRAL
GWYNEDD
POWYS
R. Severn
CREDIGION
DEHEUBARTH
DYFED
BRYCHEINIOG
MORGANNWG AND GLYWYSING AND GWENT
CORNWALL
DEVON
R. Tamar
R. Exe
Lifton (12 Nov. 931)
Exeter (16 Apr. 928 & 9 Nov. 932)
Dorchester (21 Dec. 935)
Milton (? 30 Aug. 932)
Wellow (15 Jul. 931)
Grately
1
2
3
Worthy (20 Jun. 931)
WESSEX
Winchester (28 May 934)
Lyminster (3 Apr. 930)
Thunderfield
KENT
Faversham
Milton (? 30 Aug. 932)
R. Thames
MERCIA
Buckingham (13 Sep. 934)
Whittlebury
R. Trent
Nottingham (7 Jun. 934)
R. Ouse
EAST ANGLIA
Colchester (23 Mar. 931)

Scale:
0   50   100 mi
0   75   150 km

Already by 13 September 934 Æthelstan and the royal assembly had returned to the south, this time convening a meeting in Buckingham, before moving on three months later to Frome in Somerset.[52] Because Æthelstan predominantly held his assemblies in the south, it was expected that those coming from the further reaches of his kingdom, from Northumbria and the south-west, and those sub-kings who were attending from the Welsh kingdoms, from Alba and from Strathclyde/Cumbria, had to make the journey *to* Æthelstan rather than the other way around. This fact alone would have sent a message about the power that he commanded. For the year 936 the West Frankish authors Flodoard and Richer of Rheims, describe how Æthelstan was in York when he was visited by a Frankish embassy who were seeking the return of Louis, a continental prince who had been in exile at Æthelstan's court.[53] Given that Æthelstan had primarily conducted his business in the south of England, this record is striking.[54] It is suggestive of the growing importance of the north in the years after Æthelstan's 934 invasion of Alba, which is demonstrated also by the elevated positions given both to Constantine II of Alba and to Owain of Strathclyde/Cumbria in diplomas of these years.[55]

In addition to information about royal assemblies, diplomas reveal other aspects of Æthelstan's reign. Close scrutiny of a document's 'diplomatic'—that is, the Latin and Old English formulae of which it is composed—offers an indication of standards of learning and of royal ambition, for it contains clauses such as the 'royal style' which indicate how the king and those close to him viewed his power and the extent of his authority. Of the three groups of Æthelstan's diplomas—those of 925–26, those of 928–35, and those of 935–39—the first and third are relatively conventional in form, although they do contain particular points of interest and idiosyncrasies. But the diplomas of the second group, attributed to 'Æthelstan A', are, as we saw with their witness-lists, ground-breaking.

Four diplomas survive from the beginning of Æthelstan's reign, the years 925–26: two of them are preserved in the archive of Burton Abbey, one from Abingdon Abbey, and one in the archive of St Augustine's Abbey, Canterbury; this last was issued on the very day of Æthelstan's coronation and, because it is distinctive in various respects, should be considered separately.[56] The remaining three diplomas exhibit a number of formulaic similarities, and in fact two overlap to such an extent that, as we will see, they may have been written by the same person.[57] After the usual preamble at the start of the diploma, known as the 'proem', which often includes some reflection on the transitory nature of existence, or the importance of a Christian way of life, the king's title in Latin is specified as part of formulae known as the royal style and the royal subscription, which provided the opportunity to proclaim the king's royal status and the extent of his authority (or at least how the drafter of the diploma wished to portray it). The royal style occurs at the moment that the king makes the grant, and the royal subscription is attached to the king's name in the witness-list at the end of the diploma. In these early diplomas of Æthelstan's reign, the most common designation is the Latin *Angulsaxonum rex* (king of the Anglo-Saxons), with each royal subscription using the straightforward *rex* (king), with no further elaboration. On the face of it, this suggests that, in 925–26, Æthelstan laid claim to a polity that was in essence the same as that of his father, Edward the Elder. The diploma dated 925 from the Burton archive constitutes an exception to this pattern, however, with its royal style declaring that Æthelstan was *rex Anglorum* (king of the English).[58] Because this did not reflect a political reality for the year 925, it may be that the word *Anglorum* meant, more narrowly, 'Angles', or, because the diploma survives in a manuscript copy made in the mid-thirteenth century, perhaps the royal style was at some point updated to reflect Æthelstan's later political accomplishments.[59]

Once the king's name and his royal style have been articulated in the body of the diploma, each document continues by providing the details of the actual grant of land being made, known as the dispositive section. Here we are told how much land is being granted (using a measurement of land known as the hide),[60] the name of the beneficiary, the name and location of the land, the conditions on which the land in question was to be held, and, in some cases, the amount of money that was paid by the beneficiary for the land. Only one of these diplomas from 925–26 has a boundary clause, which describes, typically in Old English rather than the Latin of the rest of the diploma, the outer limits of the land being granted. Boundary clauses provide a great deal of important information. They indicate, for example, that the medieval land market was administered in a sophisticated way: it involved both the work of a royal scribe on behalf of Æthelstan as king, tasked with the production of the Latin formulae for the diploma, and also, because the boundary clauses contain minute details about the English landscape, of an official who was situated close to the location of the land being granted.[61] Boundary clauses also demonstrate that a bilingual system was in operation. The fact that the operative part of the diploma, the detail of the actual land being granted, was in Old English rather than Latin suggests that the majority of those interacting with these documents were more likely to be able to read and understand Old English than Latin. The boundary clause usually begins at the northernmost part of the estate in question and follows the circuit clockwise, noting prominent features of the landscape as it goes, until it returns to the same starting point. In the 926 diploma from the Abingdon archive, five hides of land at Chalgrave and Tebworth in Bedforshire are granted to a man named Eadred, who was a royal thegn. Its Old English boundary clause is relatively short and opens by saying, 'Ðær se dic sceot in Þæclinga stræte, anlanges Þæxlinga stræte ðæt on ðane ford' (There the ditch flows quickly into Watling Street, along Watling street then on the ford); it continues by tracing the outer limit of the bounds which follow waterways and ditches of various kinds, before returning to its start at Watling Street, a major Roman road which ran across England and connected Kent in the south-east to Wroxeter further to the north and west.[62]

Following the details of the land being granted and its bounds (if available), the diploma normally continues with a formula known as a 'sanction', which was designed to warn would-be defrauders of the consequences of any action in contravention of the diploma's terms. It is striking that early medieval English diplomas threaten ecclesiastical and spiritual punishments rather than secular and monetary equivalents. These early diplomas of Æthelstan are no different and threaten accountability on the Day of Judgement if anyone should appropriate the lands in question. They then conclude with a relatively short dating clause, giving the date of the transaction concerned and the list of witnesses, which have been discussed above.

As a whole, then, the diplomas issued by Æthelstan in 925–26 were of a form and type that differed little from diplomas of previous and recent generations and would have been readily recognisable to contemporaries. The two diplomas issued in 926 are so similar in content that they may have been composed by the same draftsman.[63] Some parts of their Latin formulation exhibit a small degree of literary pretension. For example, in their royal style, both include the expression 'non modica infulatus sublimatus dignitate' (crowned and elevated by no humble rank), which describes Æthelstan himself and which anticipates a similar phrase later found in the revolutionary diplomas issued in 928–35. Their sanctions, with threats of what would happen on the Day of Judgement, and their use of the Latin phrase *poli cardines* (the heights of heaven), also pre-empt formulations that can be found in diplomas dated 928–35. It has been suggested that these two diplomas may even represent the initial stages of what would become the highly distinctive diplomas of 'Æthelstan A'—perhaps that they were his own creations.[64]

One diploma, of the year 925, preserved in the archive of St Augustine's Abbey, Canterbury, sees Æthelstan restore land in Thanet directly to the abbey itself. It is dated 4 September, and seems to have been issued on the very day that Æthelstan was consecrated as king.[65] Its form is unique among diplomas surviving from 925–26, and the earliest copy we have dates to the beginning of the thirteenth century, factors which make it difficult to judge its authenticity with certainty. The diploma itself is very short: after a perfunctory dating clause, it omits the usual diplomatic preamble and instead plunges straight into the details of the grant, that land had been 'unjustly' (*iniuste*) seized from St Augustine's and was being restored by King Æthelstan. There is no detailed dispositive section, nor is there any sanction. Instead the diploma moves immediately from the statement about Æthelstan restoring the land to a sentence which says that the grant was effected with the agreement of eight bishops and two *principes*, by which 'ealdormen' is probably meant. A list of names of these witnesses is then provided, with spellings of the names that are in highly corrupted form; it then extends beyond the bishops and ealdormen to include also a thegn, an abbot, a priest, and one further man described as being both a priest and a monk. Because this document is so idiosyncratic, it is difficult to judge its genuineness. That it contains the correct date of Æthelstan's coronation, and the list of witnesses is feasible for its purported date of issue, may suggest that it is broadly authentic.[66] If this can be accepted, it raises questions about the status of the document and how it may have been used. In the form in which it survives today, is it a summary of a now lost diploma? Or was it a summary made with the intention of it being turned into a diploma at some subsequent point? Was there something about the circumstances in which it was composed and issued, at the very moment of Æthelstan's consecration, that led to the production of this unique document? These are important questions to pose, even if we cannot today answer them with certainty.

No diplomas survive from 927, the year in which Æthelstan brought Northumbria within his authority and thus created the 'kingdom of the English' for the first time. But from 928 until 935, the form of these documents has drastically changed, in terms of both physical appearance and textual content. All diplomas of this period were written by 'Æthelstan A', who is known by this anonymous title because the drafter's identity has not been certainly proved. So radical and so marked were the changes introduced by 'Æthelstan A' that they were clearly intended to celebrate the political advances that Æthelstan had made in 927. The diplomas of this scribe can be further sub-divided into four groups depending on the type of proem they employ: the first group dates to 928, the second to 930, the third to 931–33, and the fourth to 934–35.[67]

Remarkably, two of 'Æthelstan A's' diplomas survive in their original, tenth-century form rather than as later copies. We are therefore able to handle the very diplomas that would have been produced at Æthelstan's royal assembly, the details of which would have been received and debated by its members. In one, dated 12 November 931, Æthelstan makes a grant of land in Wiltshire to his thegn, Wulfgar. And in the other, of 934, Æthelstan makes a grant of land in a place called *Derantune* (perhaps Durrington in Sussex?) to another thegn, Ælfwald.[68] Both documents are truly monumental in format, the first measuring 48.3 centimetres by

29 centimetres and the second 50.9 centimetres by 27.5 centimetres, roughly similar to, or slightly larger than, an A3 sheet of paper.[69] So substantial in size are these documents that, when ordered to the manuscripts room of the British Library, you are provided with a separate large desk from which to view them. Their size was designed to create a lasting impression on those in the royal assembly. And the way in which they were written was no less striking. Both are copied in the same hand throughout, in a distinctive form of script which is characterised in part by the square-looking *a*, the development of which has been linked in particular to Æthelstan's court.[70] It must have been a very difficult task to plan the layout of the single sheet of parchment and to use it in such a way that it was fully covered by text and a list of witnesses. The resulting diplomas look highly professional. The letter forms are regularly and neatly reproduced, with very few errors in spelling and copying, the occasional mistake being corrected by the insertion, for example, of an interlinear letter where needed.[71]

The text of the diplomas of 'Æthelstan A' is no less impressive than their physical appearance. The generic form of the diploma had been relatively fixed since the seventh century. But under 'Æthelstan A' the rhetorical possibilities of diplomas were exploited to an unprecedented extent. The opening clause (the proem) becomes longer and significantly more elaborate, as do those that threaten punishments for transgressions (the sanction) and those that give the details of the grant being made (the dispositive section). Æthelstan's royal style is changed, so that he is now routinely entitled *rex Anglorum* (king of the English) to reflect the elevation in his kingly power. In the surviving original for the year 934, for example, Æthelstan is recorded as being 'rex Anglorum per omnipatrantis dexteram totius Britannie regni solio sublimatus' (king of the English elevated by the right hand of the Almighty to the throne of the whole kingdom of Britain), which points to his claims to rule over Britain as well.[72] The dating clause also underwent significant change. Hitherto, it had been most common for diplomas to be dated according to their *anno Domini* date or using a chronological marker known as an indiction, which harked back to fourth-century imperial tax cycles.[73] But 'Æthelstan A' gave more detail than ever before. In addition to the *anno Domini* date and the indiction, the scribe provided the date of the month, the phase of the moon, and Æthelstan's regnal year in which the diploma was granted, presumably drawing some of this information from computistical tables that were at hand. As noted above, this level of detail allows us for the first time to follow Æthelstan on his travels around his kingdom.

As well as making changes to the diploma template, 'Æthelstan A' took great care with the way in which the diplomas were written and with the Latin used, to the extent that these documents should be regarded as literary articles in their own right. A close analysis of their Latin reveals that they are shot through with learned allusions to, and evocations of, literature from the sixth century, such as the Irish hymn, 'Altus Prosator' (Great Creator), and of the seventh century, particularly the work of the scholar and monk Aldhelm of Malmesbury and his prose and poetical tracts on the subject of 'Virginity' (known in Latin as *De virginitate*). As well as containing allusions to other texts, the Latin itself is carefully structured. 'Æthelstan A' employs literary devices, such as alliteration and rhyme, and also more complicated features, such as chiasmus (where the elements of an expression are arranged in an ABBA order, as in William Shakespeare's 'Remember March, the ides of March remember'), hyperbaton (which involves in Latin an adjective being separated from the noun it is describing) and word-play or assonance (in which the same word is used with two different meanings or in which the same letters are used in consecutive Latin words but in different orders). So learned and intricate are diplomas that one scholar of the late nineteenth century likened them to a display of fireworks.[74]

The erudition of these diplomas is all the more remarkable given that, as we have seen, the ninth century in general had witnessed a decline in literary output and in standards of literacy across the kingdom. Despite the general picture of a decline, there were, in ninth-century Mercia, a few diplomas which can be shown to contain allusions to the work of Aldhelm, indicative of some appetite for and ability to write in an elevated literary style.[75] Could 'Æthelstan A' have been inspired by these Mercian diplomas? Unfortunately, the identity of 'Æthelstan A' has not been securely established, which hinders questions about the scribe's origins and training. One striking feature of the 'Æthelstan A' corpus of diplomas is the prominence among episcopal witnesses of Ælfwine (also known as Ælle), the bishop of Lichfield, who attests towards the top of the episcopal witnesses in a position usually reserved for the bishop of Winchester. This has led some to suggest that Ælfwine (Ælle) could be one and the same as 'Æthelstan A' himself.[76] If 'Æthelstan A' could be shown to belong to a Mercian see such as Lichfield, it makes it all the more feasible that he had learned his skill in Mercia, perhaps by reference to the ninth-century diplomas available there.

A manuscript copy of Aldhelm's prose *De virginitate* that survives today in the British Library, and which is known by the classmark Royal 7 D. xxiv, provides visual indications for how a reader such as 'Æthelstan A' must have scrutinised earlier texts. The main hand of the manuscript is written in a script dated to the early to mid-tenth century, which is of the same form as that used in writing the two extant original diplomas by 'Æthelstan A'.[77] And a glance at its pages reveals that it was extensively glossed in a near-contemporary hand.[78] The glosses themselves reveal a scribe who was trying to understand and explicate words from Aldhelm's text that were particularly exotic or unusual. The use of glosses in order to decipher meaning from a text was a long-established scholarly technique, and can be attested centuries earlier in classical times.[79] It must have been just this kind of attentive reading that allowed 'Æthelstan A' to perfect his own Latin style.

The impact of the 'Æthelstan A' diplomas on contemporaries would have been significant; they were unprecedented in their size, physical appearance, and Latin style. They were also the products of royal assemblies that were vast in scope, incorporating all of the major secular and ecclesiastical figures from Æthelstan's newly created kingdom of the English, and even those from beyond its bounds, such as the sub-kings of Wales, Alba and Strathclyde/Cumbria. These diplomas had performative potential, and were perhaps designed to be read out at the meetings of the royal assembly.[80] An average royal official of the tenth century would surely not have been able to identify literary allusions to Aldhelm or to 'Altus Prosator', but that same official would have instantly realised that, under King Æthelstan, he was operating in a new environment that was emboldened by its own political successes. These documents formed a fitting way for the king to celebrate and cement his rule over England as a whole.

The diplomas of 'Æthelstan A' hold further significance. For the early Anglo-Saxon period, roughly before the mid-ninth century, diplomas were produced by a variety of different agencies, which included local scribes attached to ecclesiastical scriptoria. By the reign of King Æthelwulf (d. 858) matters seem to have been changing. There are indications in diplomas produced in his name that there may on some occasions have been a royal scribe or scribes in charge of drafting the documents. This is not explicitly acknowledged, so the suggestion depends on careful comparison of extant diplomas: where they share points of formulation, but concern separate grants of land which concern different beneficiaries and were preserved in separate places, it may be safe to suggest that the only point of commonality between them was the king—and therefore that the diplomas had been produced under his auspices.[81] The diplomas of 'Æthelstan A' offer the first unequivocal evidence for the operation of a royal scribe: for the years 928–35 'Æthelstan A' had a monopoly on diploma production no matter where in the kingdom the grant of land was being made and no matter where the royal assembly was convened. 'Æthelstan A' was clearly acting in the service of the king, and it has been suggested that what we are seeing is a central agency, which may be termed a chancery, or royal writing office, that would continue in various ways for the rest of the Anglo-Saxon period (although it was not the only agency responsible for the production of diplomas). One can imagine that the expansion of the kingdom had necessitated a degree of professionalisation and a rethinking of the way in which royal documents were issued.[82]

After 'Æthelstan A' ceases to produce diplomas in 935, those issued in the remainder of Æthelstan's reign until 939 once more take on a new form. Although they continue to have a degree of literary sophistication, including the use of alliteration, Grecisms, and biblical quotations, they are noticeably restrained in form when compared to the 'Æthelstan A' diplomas. The elaborate and lengthy opening (the proem), the detailed dating clauses, and the long witness-lists are all removed and replaced by equivalent diplomatic elements that are marked by their concision. Æthelstan himself continues to be styled in a grandiose way, with the Grecism *basileus* (king) being frequently deployed, and claims to power over Britain are made regularly.[83] In diplomas of these years, their rhetorical possibilities have been jettisoned in favour of a style that is more accessible. A surviving original from 939, written by a scribe known as 'Æthelstan C', in which Æthelstan grants land to his thegn, Ealdwulf, shows that the physical form of these diplomas was also designed in such a way that the principal details of the diploma could be quickly discerned. The main diplomatic elements (particularly the Old English boundary clause) are clearly signposted by the use of spaces and capital letters, and the names of the donor (Æthelstan) and the recipient (Ealdwulf) are written entirely in capitals. The work of 'Æthelstan C' was sufficiently successful that this form of diploma continued to be used in the reign of Æthelstan's successor, Edmund (d. 946).

As noted above, it seems likely that royal diplomas were produced at the royal assembly and there officially conveyed to the relevant beneficiary, in front of the witnesses who came from different parts of the kingdom.[84] The conveyance of the document was probably effected in a ritualised way: the drawing of a cross over the Latin word for 'cross' (*crucis*) at various points in the 'Æthelstan C' original discussed above may suggest that the individuals named signed themselves at that point of the ceremony.

Royal assemblies also offered Æthelstan the opportunity to issue vernacular laws in his name, an important duty for an early medieval king.[85] By the tenth century there was a relatively well-established tradition of laws and law-making. Æthelstan's grandfather, Alfred, had ordered the composition of a major law code, his *domboc*, an Old English term meaning literally the 'book [*boc*] of judgement [*dom*]', which began with a preface that heavily alluded to Mosaic law and which owed a debt to the late eighth- and ninth-century law-making of the Carolingians.[86] A significant question in the study of surviving law codes is the extent to which these documents represented a statement of reality— that is, of laws that should be consulted, abided by, and which were responding to contemporary concerns; or whether they were statements of intent and ideology, composed in the name of kings who thought that it was their duty to be seen as those setting the law and keeping order in society, with the result that the laws themselves were rarely used or consulted.[87] Because a large number of law codes have survived from Æthelstan's reign, this (and related) questions can be explored in relative detail.[88] By modern scholarly convention, law codes are assigned a number. Those from Æthelstan's reign are labelled 'I–VI Æthelstan'.[89] But this system of numbering is highly misleading, for it suggests a stylistic homogeneity and a sequence of issue that cannot be applied to the law codes themselves. Three of the law codes (his first, second, and fifth) were issued in Æthelstan's name and are thus 'royal' in nature. But the remaining codes (the third, fourth, and sixth) take a different form altogether. None of the law codes bears specific dates of issue, but a likely sequence of composition, based on cross-references between the codes, is: the first code, the second, the fifth, the third, the fourth, and the sixth (and then the twelfth clause of the sixth).[90] In addition, three further texts with a legal form are thought to belong to Æthelstan's reign: the so-called 'Ordinance relating to charities', which is explicitly in Æthelstan's name, and two anonymous texts, *Be blaserum* and *Ordal*, both of which deal with the early medieval method for determining the guilt or innocence of someone charged with a crime, known as the ordeal.[91]

Of the law codes that are explicitly 'royal' in nature, Æthelstan's first is relatively short and contains some clauses that may have been added at a date after the end of his reign.[92] It is composed in the first person singular, as if Æthelstan himself is legislating directly to his people. This has the rather startling effect of making it seem as if Æthelstan's own voice can still be heard today. It opens, for example, by stating, 'I, King Æthelstan, with the advice of my Archbishop, Wulfhelm, and my other bishops also, inform the reeve in every borough, and pray you in the name of God and of all His saints, and command you also by my friendship, that in the first place you render tithes of my own property'.[93] The use of the first person singular in this way constituted a powerful means of conveying the authority of the code's injunctions, presumably as an attempt to make sure that people adhered to its terms. The code is almost entirely concerned with the payment of taxes to the church, in the form of a tenth (tithe) of livestock and crops. It has recently been argued that the way in which the code discusses tithes suggests that the Old English version (there is also a twelfth-century Latin version) was significantly altered in the early eleventh century by a man named Archbishop Wulfstan II (d. 1023), who was famous for his work on the legislation of the kings Æthelred II (d. 1016) and Cnut (d. 1035), in order to create the impression that the regular payment of tithes, enforced by fines for non-payment, had been required already by the early tenth century.[94] The Latin version of Æthelstan's first code, which may actually be closer to the original version, indicates that there may have been the requirement by Æthelstan for a one-off payment of alms, although not in the form of a regular tax, as the Old English version implies. There was precedent for such a one-off charitable payment: Æthelwulf, the mid-ninth-century king of Wessex already mentioned, seems to have made a similar donation of a tenth of all land to the church, perhaps in connection with his pilgrimage to Rome in 855.[95] As we will see in chapter 4, Æthelstan was a major patron of the church and so any such focus on one-off support for the church in his laws is in keeping with his desire to foster religion around his kingdom.

Æthelstan's second code constitutes *the* major statement of royal law to survive from his reign. From the body of the code itself, we learn that the laws were agreed at a 'great assembly' (Old English: *miclan synoþ*) that had been convened by Æthelstan at Grately in Hampshire and at which all of Æthelstan's principal advisers had gathered, including the archbishop of Canterbury, Wulfhelm. The code seems therefore to have had the direct oversight of Æthelstan and of his supporters. Grately is situated in Wessex, close to Winchester, and near to numerous locations that were used as meeting places for the royal assembly during the tenth and eleventh centuries. It was also located close to a Roman road, which would have made it a convenient location at which to convene dignitaries from around the kingdom.[96]

As it survives today, Æthelstan's second code cannot represent the output of one meeting of the royal assembly alone. For, having already provided twelve injunctions, the code then inserts injunctions concerning burhs which are given their own, discrete numerical sequence which begins with a clause describing itself as 'secondly' and ends with that described as 'seventhly'. This suggests that these injunctions originally belonged elsewhere, perhaps that they had been agreed as part of a separate law-making session and then incorporated into the code drawn up and agreed to at Grately.[97] The predominant concern of Æthelstan's second code is that of theft and the actions of thieves, perhaps suggesting that stealing was a major and recurrent issue in his reign and therefore needed extended attention.[98] The severity of the punishment recommended for a thief caught in the act is beyond modern comprehension: anyone aged twelve or older, and caught stealing property worth more than eight pence, would be killed. In cases where a thief had not been immediately executed, the laws allowed for the person to be sent to prison for a period of time, for fines to be paid instead, or for the taking of an oath in order for that person to exculpate themselves. The laws composed in Æthelstan's second code were so thorough that they also stipulated what should happen if a lord, or a royal official such as a reeve, was an accessory to theft committed by their slaves. There were also clauses drawn up to deal with occasions where a thief had not been caught in the act of stealing but had been accused on multiple occasions and found guilty. A further injunction aimed to deal with situations where a thief was killed in mistaken circumstances and their family sought compensation for such a wrongful killing.[99]

As a whole, Æthelstan's second code does not seem to have been set out in any particularly logical way. Clauses dealing with theft, for example, occur randomly at different points, interspersed with other concerns. The impression is of laws being composed in response to a number of queries being raised by and for the king and his officials. Other notable areas of focus relate to the behaviour of a 'lord' (Old English: *hlaford*), and the plotting against a lord; the punishments for forcing entry into a church; claims to ownership of farm animals; and the consequences if someone is convicted of 'witchcrafts and sorceries and deadly spells'.[100]

One broad subject discussed in some detail concerns expectations of people's behaviour in various different scenarios. For Æthelstan himself, as a king who had recently extended his kingdom into Northumbria, such issues would have been at the forefront of his mind.[101] It was imperative that he was able to enforce good systems of governance, and that a legal structure was put in place so that, if it were ever necessary, people could be held accountable for their actions—even if the enforcement of the law turned out to be impossible in practice.[102] In Æthelstan's second code, there are clauses that deal specifically with attendance at assemblies. The code does not explicitly specify which type of assembly was being described, and it has been suggested that these injunctions refer to local assemblies held every four weeks by reeves (rather than Æthelstan's royal assemblies).[103] The code indicates that there would be seven days' warning before an assembly was held by a reeve and that if a person failed on three occasions to attend an assembly, they would be fined.[104] Quite a high degree of detail follows concerning expectations of behaviour and the ways in which the king's laws should be respected. In a situation where someone did not 'comply with the law, and pay the fine for insubordination', the 'chief men' (*yldestan men*) were to deprive the person concerned of all of their property and force them into 'surety', which meant finding a certain number of trusted individuals who would swear and give witness for the person's good behaviour. So concerned were Æthelstan and his advisers about non-compliance that the law code anticipates a situation where those tasked with enforcing Æthelstan's will choose not to do so, and stipulates what should happen in that situation. Even in these clauses concerning the operation of the assembly, theft is again a concern: 'and it shall be proclaimed in the assembly, that men shall respect everything which the king wishes to be respected, and refrain from theft on pain of death'.[105]

For Æthelstan's laws to stand any chance of being effective, he needed a range of officials who could be trusted to transmit his laws throughout the kingdom, and to act on any infringements of those laws. Æthelstan's second code (among others) calls on just such a body of people, the reeves, to oversee the enacting of his laws. As we have seen, reeves were men in positions of power, who owned land, but whether they were exclusively responsible for the role mentioned in the code is disputed.[106] Whatever the truth, Æthelstan's second code carefully stipulates what should happen if a reeve does not attend to his duties. At first a fine of five pounds would be expected, which would increase to the reeve's wergeld for the second offence,[107] and finally, if the reeve were found deficient for a third time, he would be deprived of all of his possessions, and of the support of the king, thus in effect making him an outlaw. It is interesting to note that it was an ecclesiastical figure, the local bishop, who was made responsible for collecting the fines owed by reeves who were not fulfilling their roles.[108] Bishops and archbishops figured prominently in the world of royal administration, including in law codes, as we will see.

One particularly difficult aspect of early medieval law involved the proving of a suspect's innocence or guilt. Æthelstan's law codes make various stipulations in this connection: an accused person could be invited to swear an oath and/or to gather a group of trusted individuals who would attest to that person's innocence and probity (the process of standing 'surety' referred to above). We can imagine that the use of such oaths and witnesses would have taken place as part of a highly ritualised occasion which would have made the seriousness of the situation apparent to the person concerned and imbued it with authority. Those in charge of enforcing Æthelstan's laws could invoke another method for determining guilt known as the ordeal. The ordeal itself involved some sort of physical test. In the ordeal of water, for example, the accused person was asked to plunge their hand into a vat of boiling water to retrieve an object. If the hand were found to have festered after a certain amount of time, then the person was thought to be guilty. In the ordeal involving iron, a bar of iron heated to a very high temperature was grasped by the accused: again, if the hand were found to have been damaged after a set time, then the person was pronounced guilty. Ordeals could be 'simple' or 'threefold'. If 'threefold', the person had to submerge three times the amount of their arm into the boiling water compared to a 'simple' ordeal. Æthelstan's second code contains numerous references to the ordeal and situations where it should be used, including some detail about how it should be conducted. But the fullest statement of process can be found in the anonymous text *Ordal* which, on the grounds of its contents, language, and phrasing, has also been dated to Æthelstan's reign. From it we learn that there were strict regulations governing its procedure, that the ordeal was loaded with Christian ritual and symbolism of various kinds, and that the whole episode was overseen by a priest in a church. In any convening of the ordeal procedure, *Ordal* calls for it to be rendered null and void if any of the terms it contains are not properly observed, and for a fine of 120 shillings to be paid to the king by the person who caused the issue.[109]

As it survives today, Æthelstan's fifth code—another code written in the first person singular, as if Æthelstan were speaking directly to his audience—does not offer such an extended treatment of law as had his second code. Written at Exeter in midwinter and the result of deliberations between Æthelstan and his advisers, the fifth code touches on a variety of issues including (once again) theft, the movement and ownership of cattle, and a stipulation for fifty psalms to be sung for the king every Friday in every minster, a request that can be paralleled in some of the diplomas of 'Æthelstan A'.[110] The fifth code also touches on the proper behaviour of royal officials, this time not just reeves but also thegns, making it clear that they should not be open to bribery.[111] But the most important aspect of Æthelstan's fifth code occurs in its opening lines, which state, 'I, King Æthelstan, declare that I have learned that the public peace has not been kept to the extent, either of my wishes, or of the provisions laid down at Grately. And my councillors say that I have suffered this too long'.[112]

By itself this brief sentence inadvertently reveals a great deal about Æthelstan's legal aspirations. Firstly, it suggests that Æthelstan and his royal officials had every expectation both that the laws they had previously issued at Grately would be consulted and that they would be adhered to throughout his kingdom. Secondly, it shows that the issuing of laws by the king was an ongoing process—that, having issued a set of laws, the king would later be updated about the manner in which they had been received, any issues that might be forthcoming and any ways in which they should adapt their procedures and punishments.[113] Such a process is highlighted by the remaining laws from Æthelstan's reign—specifically, his third, fourth, and sixth codes.

Æthelstan's third code, which survives in Latin rather than Old English, cannot be regarded as a statement of royal law. In fact, it constitutes a report back from a meeting of the bishops and secular officials in Kent about the implementation of Æthelstan's laws, what had been working and what had been impractical.[114] It opens by addressing Æthelstan as 'dearest' (Latin: *karissime*), a salutation that is repeated at various points during the code. Æthelstan is thanked for having provided a set of laws 'concerning the peace of our land' and for having investigated ways in which people's lives could be improved. Those in Kent report that they have done their best to implement the king's laws, and they specifically refer to the laws enacted at Grately (i.e. Æthelstan's second law code) which were subsequently promulgated again in a separate meeting at Faversham (in Kent). In those laws Æthelstan had called for punishments of various kinds, with a focus on the actions of thieves. From the third code we learn that, from the time when the Grately code had been issued up until the meeting at Faversham, the king had had a change of mind, that he had offered pardon to all criminals as long as they would no longer participate in criminal activity and would make good the damage they had previously inflicted.[115] From the time of the Faversham meeting onwards, where infringements of different kinds are uncovered, Æthelstan's third code refers back to the penalties recommended in his second code, showing the central position that that code still held in legal thought, and the expectation that such codes would be kept and consulted as appropriate. Nevertheless, the very end of the third code reveals that, in the minds of those in Kent, there were times when they could only do so much in the enforcement of law: 'and we are zealously prepared to carry out everything you are willing to order us, in so far as it lies within our power to do so'.[116]

It is difficult to be certain about the exact nature of Æthelstan's fourth law code, and the circumstances in which it was written.[117] It opens by referring back to the laws that had been issued at Exeter (the fifth code) and Faversham, and by saying that its own injunctions were written up at Thunderfield, a place located directly south of London which was close to the modern airport at Gatwick in Surrey. As a whole, the fourth code comprises a restatement of the laws as they were then established. Perhaps it was written by someone who was involved in the operation of the law, or in the writing and codification of laws as they developed.

The second clause recognises the centrality of the Grately code (the second code), as Æthelstan's third code had done, but also suggests that matters had moved on and that the law had changed concerning trading in towns and on Sundays.[118] As with previous law codes, the fourth code reveals that certain laws had not been kept as Æthelstan had hoped.[119] Thieves are again an area of focus. The problem of theft must not have abated since Grately, because the fourth code states that the punishment for those caught was death. There was no longer any ability to pay a fine in certain situations, as the second code had previously allowed. The fourth code also emphasises that the laws with regard to thieves applied to all, specifying for the first time in Æthelstan's legislation that it also embraced women.[120] Alleged thieves had the ability to claim sanctuary of various periods of time if they sought out certain secular and ecclesiastical figures (such as the king and archbishop) or a church. But, if shown to be guilty, there was no mercy, and the fourth code is even specific in detailing the different ways that thieves of various social status should be killed, which included being thrown from a cliff, drowned, burned to death, or stoned.[121] A male slave would be stoned by twenty-six of his fellow slaves, and the law code includes punishments for those slaves who failed on three occasions to strike their fellow slave with a stone. Finally, royal reeves and thegns are reminded of the importance of completing the duties assigned to them in enforcing the law, on pain of monetary fines and social dishonour.

In the same way that the third code provided evidence for the reaction to Æthelstan's laws from those in Kent, the sixth code also contains a set of injunctions which comprise the view of the so-called London peace-gilds (Old English: *friðgegyldum*) towards Æthelstan's laws.[122] It also has details about the operation of the London peace-gilds themselves. Already from the seventh century, it was clear that there were in England a number of gilds of different types. These were groupings of people who had banded together because membership of the gild offered a degree of collective protection both spiritually and in the event that something negative were to happen in everyday life—for example, if a member were to be harmed in some way or have their property stolen.[123] In the case of the London peace-gilds, their membership seems to have included not just those of relatively high status, the bishops and reeves of London, but also those who were described as 'commoners' (*ceorlisce*), and both men and women. A main priority of the London peace-gilds was to offer their members protection against theft, the same concern that had been voiced in many of Æthelstan's laws. The sixth code reveals that each person paid an annual subscription (unless they were too poor) and that there were certain responsibilities expected of them, that they would stand together 'both in friendship and in feud'.[124] Penalties could be enforced if members of the gilds did not comply with what was expected of them. And, on the death of a gild member, the remaining members were expected to sing psalms and also to arrange for the donation of a loaf of bread each, presumably as an offering of alms.[125]

The twelfth clause of the code reveals that Æthelstan had convened a further royal assembly at Whittlebury, just north of Buckingham, at which legal matters were again discussed. We are told that the king had had a change of heart, that he now felt that previous injunctions concerning theft had been too harsh. As the law code itself puts it, 'he thinks it cruel to put to death such young people and for such slight offences, as he has learnt is the practice everywhere'.[126] Æthelstan decreed that, henceforth, nobody younger than fifteen would be put to death for theft, nor if they had stolen property of a value less than twelve pence.

Overall, then, the sixth law code is interesting for showing the ways in which Æthelstan continued to revisit the legal injunctions he had issued throughout his reign, and also for revealing the existence of gilds—in this case, the peace-gilds of London. Seventh-century gilds must originally have been founded owing to a lack of public security (London's Metropolitan Police force was not formed until 1829), which suggests that kings of that period did not have the ability to enforce law and order in the way that they might have wished.[127] That gilds still existed in Æthelstan's time demonstrates that conditions were such that people still felt they were needed. Nevertheless, one part of the sixth code calls for Æthelstan to inspect the London peace-gilds' regulations and to suggest emendations, which, they say, they will 'accept . . . gladly'.[128] The same clause makes it clear that members of the gild saw the real advantages in adhering to the king's laws and they declare their intention to follow his commands, suggesting that, at least in London, Æthelstan's ultimate authority was recognised.

There is another notable feature of the sixth code: the prominence afforded to the archbishop of Canterbury, Wulfhelm, in matters to do with law. The code's tenth clause stipulates that, when laws were issued previously at Thunderfield, pledges had been made particularly to the archbishop. And, at the end of the code, when Æthelstan is said to have changed his mind about the strictness of punishments for young thieves, it is striking that one of the king's first actions is said to have been to inform the archbishop of this shifted position. This tallies with the impression given of Wulfhelm in other codes: the preamble to both the first code and the 'Ordinance relating to charities' take care to say that the laws that follow had been issued with Wulfhelm's 'advice' (*geþehte/geþeahte*), and Æthelstan's second code, the fullest statement of royal law to have survived from his reign, ends by making it clear that Archbishop Wulfhelm (along with other, unnamed dignitaries) had been present at Grately when the laws had been agreed on and issued. It is very unusual for an individual to be named in this way in the context of early medieval English laws. There is the strong suspicion that Wulfhelm was the author of some of Æthelstan's laws, or that he was closely involved in the oversight of their composition.[129]

By the early tenth century there was a sophisticated system of money in operation, with a large stock of silver coins—known to contemporaries as pennies (*penningas*)—in circulation.[130] Already in the eighth century the coinage was so well developed that, in order to facilitate trade between southern England and the Continent, the coins of King Offa of Mercia (d. 796) and Charlemagne (d. 814), king of the Franks and emperor, were designed so that their silver content and weight were comparable.[131] The tenth-century economy was by no means *fully* monetized, in that goods could be bought and sold in exchanges of property in kind, but it is likely that coins were widely used—as shown, for example, by the monetary fines stipulated in Æthelstan's law codes. A very few 'halfpennies' survive from Æthelstan's reign, which indicate that there had been at least some need for money of a smaller denomination.[132] Control of the coinage brought practical benefits to a king, who could thereby raise money and regulate trade. And, because coins were relatively commonplace, they also became a vehicle for the assertion of royal messages in their use of inscriptions and stylised busts. The apogee of the early medieval English coinage can be found in the early to mid-970s in the reign of King Edgar. By that stage the king was able to impose a coinage of one design, with strict standards of weight and silver content (known as fineness) across the entirety of the English kingdom. Kings of the late tenth century and afterwards in fact had so much control that they were able to institute regular recoinages, where one style of coin would be recalled and taken out of circulation so that a new one could be issued.

How did the coinage operate in Æthelstan's reign? Was he able to exert similar authority over the financial system as found later in the tenth century? Given his recent political incorporation of Northumbria, and the changes made to royal diplomas, which were now issued across the majority (but not all) of the kingdom, we might expect Æthelstan to have kept tight control over the monetary system, and to have demanded that only one type of coin be in use. And certainly that is what his laws seem to imply. His second law code, issued at Grately, contains the earliest surviving legal stipulations about the kingdom's money, and they are important for a variety of reasons that we will return to. In the code, the laws about money are found within a set of injunctions which concern the business of the burh and which, as we have seen, may have formed a discrete whole that once had a separate existence before being incorporated into the second law code as a block of text.[133]

One part of Æthelstan's second law code states, 'We declare that there shall be one coinage throughout the king's realm, and no man shall mint money except in a town'.[134] At first glance, Æthelstan's laws anticipate that there would only be one type of coin in circulation and that manufacture of the coinage would be closely regulated and could only happen in a 'town' (port).[135] Those making coins, known as moneyers, were threatened with severe sanctions for the minting of counterfeit or base coins. If found guilty of such misdeeds, for example, the moneyer's hand would be struck off and nailed to the mint itself. Despite the stipulation for there to be only 'one coinage' (*an mynet*), surviving coins in Æthelstan's name show that different designs were in circulation in different parts of the kingdom; that these different coins could be used simultaneously; and that the introduction of a new design did not automatically mean that coins of the previous type lost their value as money, with the result that coins could remain in circulation for a long time.

Broadly speaking, there were three main types of coin used during Æthelstan's reign: the Horizontal/Two-Line type, which carried the king's name and title in an inscription around the edge of the obverse and the name of the moneyer in two lines on the reverse; the Circumscription type, which had the name of the king and his title on the obverse again around the edge surrounding a cross, and this time the name of the moneyer and often also of the mint on the reverse, also in circumscription; and the Bust type, which, as its name suggests, now carried the king's bust on the obverse and retained the circumscription of the moneyer's name on the reverse, although it did not provide details of the mint place as often as the Circumscription type. There were in addition different regional variations of these main types and indeed other types that were wholly distinct in design, as we will see. Study of the dies, designs, and inscriptions has revealed that there were five distinct numismatic zones: southern England (that is, Wessex together with the south-east, and some parts of what had been southern Mercia); the west midlands (stretching from Gloucester and Hereford on the Welsh border to Chester in the north); East Anglia; the east midlands (what had been formerly viking territory); and Northumbria, where there was only ever one mint, at York.[136]

Two types of coin can be discerned from the beginning of Æthelstan's reign, the main being the so-called Horizontal Trefoil type, a slight variant of the Horizontal/Two-Line type, which, in addition to having the name of the moneyer responsible for producing the coin written across two lines on the reverse, also had two groups of three pellets (hence 'Trefoil') at the top and bottom for decoration. This type of coin was used throughout Æthelstan's kingdom with the exception of East Anglia. The other early type, which does not seem to have been produced in as great a volume as the Horizontal Trefoil coins, has a bust portrait of Æthelstan on the obverse in which the king is shown wearing a diadem, and an inscription (sometimes written around the outer edge rather than in two lines) on the reverse that again bears the name of the moneyer responsible. Before Æthelstan's acquisition of York in 927, the city had seen a huge variety of styles of coin being produced, some in the names of different viking kings. Following 927 a design that incorporated an image of a church on the reverse was the first to appear and was employed for a short period of time.[137] It is possible that this distinctive design influenced an Italian style of coin minted in the name of Pope John XI (931–36).[138]

With the Circumscription type came important developments in the inscriptions used on both the obverse and reverse of the coins. Some variation of the royal style REX TO[TIUS] BRIT[ANNIAE] (king of all Britain) was now employed on the obverse, suggesting that this coin type must have been introduced at some point following events of 927 when Æthelstan had both incorporated Northumbria within his kingdom and had his status recognised by various kings of Britain in the ceremony near Eamont Bridge.[139] That these inscriptions are so similar to the statements of royal power found in the contemporary diplomas of 'Æthelstan A' suggests that the changes were being driven by those at the centre of the royal administration. Meanwhile, on the reverse can be found details of the mint at which the coin in question had originated and sometimes also whether or not that mint was a *civitas* (city / major town, which tended to apply to former Roman cities) or an *urbs* (also city / large town, but which seems to have been used for more recent settlements). This information would have helped the king and his officials to keep control of the standards of the coinage, and it also provides important detail for us about the growth in minting during Æthelstan's reign, as will be seen further below. Circumscription coins were in use across southern England, the west midlands (where local variations were introduced, including the use of the incorrectly spelled royal title, REX SAXORUM (king of the Saxons)) and Northumbria, but do not seem to have been employed in either East Anglia or the east midlands.[140]

The so-called Bust Crowned type of coin seems chronologically to have followed the Circumscription type. Unlike coins of the early years of Æthelstan's reign, which displayed his bust with a diadem, this new type shows Æthelstan wearing a very distinctive form of crown which is similar to that found in the tenth-century portrait of the king at the front of the manuscript housed at Corpus Christi College, Cambridge, which was given by Æthelstan to St Cuthbert's community.[141] The Bust Crowned type circulated in southern England, East Anglia, the east midlands (in a variant form discussed below), and Northumbria, but, unlike the other (Horizontal / Two-Line and Circumscription) coin types, it was not used in the west midlands.

It is worth noting that the east midlands, covering an area that had formerly been in viking control, seems to have remained in some sense separate in monetary terms during Æthelstan's reign.[142] Numismatists have identified three main types to have been in circulation in the east midlands, one of which is a variant of the Horizontal / Two-Line type with distinctive lettering, while the other two are inscribed with busts and carry various differences in design.

Given the numerous stylistic varieties of coins in use across the kingdom at different times, and the deployment in some but not all areas of the kingdom of these different designs, it has been difficult to know how to interpret the clause in Æthelstan's second law code that calls for there to be 'one coinage' throughout the kingdom. Some historians have suggested that the favouring of different designs in different parts of the kingdom indicates that Æthelstan did not exert as much control over his coinage as he did over his issuing of diplomas, for example, and therefore that his authority over his newly extended kingdom was not as uniform as he might have liked.[143] But it is perhaps easy to misunderstand what was intended by Æthelstan's legislators when they referred to 'one coinage'. For, despite these typological differences, all of the coins issued and used across Æthelstan's kingdom shared on their obverse a reference to Æthelstan as king, and, on their reverse, details of the moneyers' names. In an important sense, then, all of these coins did form 'one coinage'—that of the king.[144] Furthermore, we know from the evidence of hoards and single finds that, while different types of

English coin circulated throughout England no matter where they had originally been minted, viking and continental coins were not permitted in circulation in the same way and seem instead to have been melted down and reminted into English coins.[145] It seems, therefore, that English coins, no matter their design and origin, were accepted throughout the kingdom.

Between the end of Alfred's reign (on his death in 899) and the latter part of Æthelstan's, the number of mints across the kingdom grew significantly, from around eight or nine in total in Alfred's kingdom (excluding viking-held territories) to at least thirty-eight in Æthelstan's newly extended English kingdom.[146] Æthelstan's second law code, in addition to stipulating that there should be one coinage throughout the kingdom, also legislated that 'no man shall mint money except in a town', and that 'in Canterbury there shall be seven moneyers: four for the king, two for the archbishop, one for the abbot. In Rochester, two for the king and one for the bishop. In London eight; in Winchester six; in Lewes two; in Hastings one; another in Chichester two in Southampton; two in Wareham; [one in Dorchester]; two in Exeter; two at Shaftesbury, and one in [each of] the other boroughs'.[147] These extracts reveal that mints were closely tied to burhs, which in origin had been fortified settlements and which latterly evolved to be centres with administrative and organisational functions and then also as urban centres involved in commerce.[148] According to the second code, a mint could only be established in a burh, presumably so that the king could keep tight control over its moneyers and their products (although not every burh possessed a mint). Æthelstan's second law code then lists how many moneyers there were to be in twelve different places. The list of mint locations is evidently incomplete, for it stops with mints located on and to the south of the River Thames, does not name all mints south of the Thames, and does not take account of any mints further north in the kingdom. From the evidence of surviving coins, all of the mints noted in the law code can be shown to have been active in Æthelstan's reign, apart from Hastings and Dorchester, for which there are no extant coins. It is impossible to know why the list of mints in Æthelstan's law code is incomplete. As we have already discussed, this part of the Grately code may well have been already in existence by the time that the Grately decrees were codified and it may have had a separate circulation as a discrete set of laws perhaps associated with an area south of the Thames. What we *can* say is that, from the evidence of numbers of moneyers at each place, mints could vary quite drastically in their size and therefore in the volume of coins they produced. A small mint such as that of Maldon, for example, operated with just one moneyer, while the Chester mint proved to be especially large, with some twenty-five moneyers named on types of Æthelstan's coins. There were also places named on coins, such as *Smrierl* or *Weardburh*, which have not so far been precisely located.[149]

The study of moneyers' names found on Æthelstan's coins has revealed a mix of name types, including those in Old English, of course, but also those influenced by Old Norse or continental Germanic. Because a name incorporates Old Norse elements, it cannot simply be assumed that the person so named is of Scandinavian ethnicity; perhaps their parents were of mixed ethnicity, for example, or perhaps those who gave the person the name simply favoured Scandinavian naming patterns. But Æthelstan's coins do reveal some interesting evidence in this regard. As we might expect, given the extensive Scandinavian settlement that had occurred between the 870s and the 920s, Scandinavian names can be found on coins connected principally with areas of the Danelaw and with the north-west of the kingdom. One particularly prominent example is a certain Regnald who seems to have had a monopoly on coin production at York in this period.[150] Continental names, too, appear in significant numbers, a trend which can already be seen in the later phases of Edward the Elder's coins. Men with names such as Abonel (a French version of Abbo, a continental Germanic name), Barbe (derived from Old French), and Eofermund (derived ultimately from the continental Germanic name Evermund) can be found inscribed on the reverse of the king's coins.[151] With the growing infrastructure of mints under Æthelstan, and the close links that the king fostered with Europe in general,[152] it is possible that these individuals had arrived from the Continent seeking new opportunities.

With the expansion of his authority in 927, Æthelstan had an even greater need for a stable and uniform system of governance that embraced the formal gifting of land and associated privileges, the issuing of laws, and the use of money. His innovations in and emphasis on all three of these aspects of kingship show his determination to foster one 'England' (even if that was not always possible, especially at the limits of his power). In doing so, similarities between Æthelstan's actions and aspects of Carolingian kingship in the late eighth and ninth centuries can be identified: the use of public assemblies in which the king's authority was buttressed by the agreement of the leading figures of his kingdom, or in the issuing of laws which recall the composition by the Franks of legal texts known as capitularies. Officials at Æthelstan's royal assembly, such as his ealdormen, can be paralleled by their Frankish counterparts known as dukes or counts. At a time in the tenth century when the Carolingian empire was largely disaggregating, it has been argued that England, although of course never part of that empire, was 'Carolingian in its aspirations'.[153] These echoes of Carolingian-style rule in England were not new in Æthelstan's time. They can be clearly identified, for example, in the reign of his grandfather, Alfred, and must have made an impression on Æthelstan.[154] So important was continental Europe in his thinking that Æthelstan, as we will see, would develop a policy to connect England to the Continent more closely than ever before.

This chapter began by stating that Æthelstan's systems of governance were sophisticated—a description which, as we have seen, is appropriate in various respects. In fact, the mechanics of early medieval governance—particularly from the late tenth century onwards, but beginning with some aspects of Æthelstan's reign—became so sophisticated that some commentators have argued that we are witnessing the origins of a medieval 'state'. In the view of one modern historian, 'late Anglo-Saxon England was a nation state. It was an entity with an effective central authority, uniformly organised institutions, a national language, a national church, defined frontiers (admittedly with considerable fluidity in the north), and, above all, a strong sense of national identity'.[155] There are difficulties here, not least in how a 'state' is defined.[156] It has been highlighted that, while those in early medieval England did discuss issues of ethnic identity and secular authority, they seem not to have formed for themselves the model of the 'state', a fact which may in itself be telling.[157] In the early eleventh century Archbishop Wulfstan II of York (d. 1023), a man we have already met in connection with his role as an editor of Æthelstan's laws, wrote a text entitled the *Institutes of Polity*. In it he discusses the roles expected of different members of society, including that of the king. For Wulfstan II, 'seven things befit a righteous king: first that he have a very great awe of God; and second that he always cherish righteousness; and third that he be humble before God; and fourth that he be resolute against evil; and fifth that he comfort and feed God's poor; and sixth that he advance and protect the Church of God; and seventh that he order correct judgement for friend and stranger alike'.[158] In terms of his approach to the practicalities of early medieval governance, Æthelstan certainly lived up to these ideals. It remains to be seen how he managed his relations with the church.

4

Steward of the Christian Citizenry

BY THE TIME that Æthelstan came to power, Christianity had long
been established in England. Already by the late sixth century St Augustine, having been dispatched by Pope Gregory the Great, had arrived in
England, intent on spreading the Christian message. Remarkably, a
manuscript extant today at Corpus Christi College, Cambridge, and
recently used in the coronation of King Charles III, has a good claim to
be the very copy of the Bible that Augustine brought with him to aid his
work. The Christian mission came not just from Italy: a degree of pre-
existing native British Christian influence remained from before the
arrival of the Anglo-Saxons in the fifth century, and further stimulus
latterly came from contemporary Ireland and Francia. Writing in the
early eighth century, Bede, the great Northumbrian historian, outlined
Gregory's original blueprint for the infrastructure of the English church.
The pope envisaged there being two archbishoprics, one in London and
one in York, each served by a network of twelve bishoprics.[1] In the end
Gregory's plans did not fully materialise: the northern archdiocese
never amassed the intended number of bishoprics and was not firmly
established until 735, and the southern archbishopric was ultimately
situated in Canterbury rather than in London.

Christianity took hold relatively rapidly (although precision about
the extent to which it had fully permeated society at all levels is unob-
tainable) and churches of different sizes and institutional character were

established across the English kingdoms.[2] But from the late eighth to the late ninth centuries the church became the target for viking depredations. An entry for 793 in the *Anglo-Saxon Chronicle* describes in shocked terms how vikings arrived off the north-east coast and proceeded to ransack the holy site of Lindisfarne, killing and looting as they went.[3] By the mid-ninth century, vikings, in addition to launching periodic raids, had graduated from pillaging and now settled in various parts of the kingdom. The effects of the Scandinavian settlement in parts of eastern and north-eastern England, particularly its impact on the church, have been much debated. Traditionally, historians viewed the period as one of unending disaster, with churches in certain areas being destroyed, episcopal succession in different places halted, and a resulting cessation in Christian worship. But recent research has suggested a more nuanced view. There was certainly destruction and plundering of churches, but perhaps not the wholesale devastation that has previously been suggested. In fact, in cities such as viking-held York, there is evidence for Scandinavians themselves converting to Christianity and even founding churches in their own names.[4]

Despite some reasons for optimism, King Alfred in the late ninth century saw the need for reform and renewal. In the 880s, during a period relatively free of viking attacks, he set in motion a programme of religious and moral reform from his base in Wessex and assembled a number of ecclesiastics from the Continent (Grimbald and John the Old Saxon); from Mercia (Bishop Wærferth of Worcester; Plegmund, who became archbishop of Canterbury; and the priests and chaplains Æthelstan and Wærwulf) and from Wales (Asser). The West Saxon king also founded new religious houses, in Athelney and Shaftesbury, the latter a nunnery given over to the control of Alfred's daughter, Æthelgifu. Alfred, who famously lamented that very few people either side of the River Humber could understand 'their divine services in English', also instituted a revival of education and learning.[5] He placed special emphasis on the translation of Latin works into Old English, to make sure that they were accessible to all. Bede's *Ecclesiastical History*, which provided an overview of the success of the early church in England, received special attention in Alfred's reign and was itself translated into the vernacular. Other works that were translated included the *Regula pastoralis* (Pastoral care) and *Dialogi* (Dialogues) of Gregory the Great (d. 604), the *De consolatione philosophiae* (Consolation of philosophy) by Boethius (d. 525), and the *Soliloquia* (Soliloquies) of St Augustine (d. 430). As part of an attempt to train the next generation, Alfred made sure that there was a school at the royal household where works in both Latin and Old English were studied, and which helped not only members of Alfred's own family but also those of other noble families.[6]

The most notable ecclesiastical achievement of Edward, Alfred's son and successor, was his completion of the building of the New Minster at Winchester, which stood next to, and was larger than, the existing cathedral church there, which became known as the Old Minster. Edward and his family clearly intended the New Minster to be a place of some importance, both a centre to serve the spiritual needs of those living in Winchester and a royal mausoleum for kings of the West Saxon line. It was completed by 901, and into it were translated the relics of the Breton saint, Judoc, and then also of Grimbald, who had helped and guided Alfred during his programme of reform. The remains of Edward's mother, Ealhswith, were also placed in the New Minster following her death in 902, as were those of his father, Alfred, which were translated from their original resting place in the Old Minster. Edward himself would later be buried there. But despite the building of a major new ecclesiastical site at the political centre of his kingdom, Edward seems not to have been remembered as a generous ecclesiastical benefactor.[7] Those at the Old Minster recalled him negatively. Because the New Minster's endowment was in part created from the Old Minster's existing resources, the latter community referred to him as *rex avidus* (greedy king). A further source of resentment may have been caused by Edward's handling of the episcopal sees of Winchester and Sherborne: the early tenth century saw Winchester's area of responsibility reduced when the new see of Ramsbury was created; and Sherborne also had its responsibilities curtailed, when sees at Wells and Crediton were established. The changes seem to have been part of a strategy that linked bishops more clearly with the shires—that is, the secular districts of administrative responsibility—but the effect was to diminish the reach of two West Saxon sees.[8]

To a greater extent than his father, and even than his grandfather, Æthelstan was an enthusiastic supporter of the church. As we will see, he was generous in his donations of land, manuscripts, and relics, and indeed he collected relics for his own purposes. He was also intent on the fostering of learning throughout his kingdom, and created strong bonds with churches in the new, northern part of his jurisdiction. Part of the inspiration must have come from Edward's actions in building the New Minster, and from Alfred's programme of ecclesiastical revival. But it is striking that Æthelstan seems, in some respects, actively to have turned away from West Saxon example, not least by abandoning the New Minster as a site of royal burial. Following the deaths of his cousins Ælfwine and Æthelwine in 937, he requested that they be interred instead in the abbey of Malmesbury, which is where he himself too would later be laid to rest. It is possible that Æthelstan's upbringing in Mercia had also provided him with important examples of the ways in which rulers should interact with and support the church. His aunt and uncle, Æthelflæd and Æthelred, had not only created a new foundation at Gloucester into which were translated the relics of the Northumbrian saint, Oswald, but they also sponsored Mercian royal cults at Chester and Shrewsbury.[9]

The liturgical rite used for Æthelstan's coronation in 925, which is known as the second English coronation *Ordo* and borrows from West Frankish rites of a similar kind, highlighted at least in theory the close cooperation of church and king. Not only was the ritual overseen by ecclesiastics, but it began with bishops entreating the king to protect the church and all of its bishops, something which Æthelstan subsequently promised to do.[10] Such sentiments pervade the *Ordo*, which is replete with invocations of God for His protection in various ways, enhanced by allusions to prominent biblical figures like Abraham, Moses, David and Solomon; the ritual itself involved the anointing of the king with holy oil and his acceptance of Holy Communion from the archbishop at the end of the ceremony. Æthelstan's obligations towards the church could not have been made more evident.

That the king himself took his responsibilities seriously and did not view his coronation ceremony as empty ritual is revealed by some of the diplomas issued early in his reign. In one, dated 925, in which Æthelstan grants land in Derbyshire to his thegn Eadric, he is described both as 'king of the English' (*rex Anglorum*) and as 'steward of the Christian citizenry' (*Cristiane patrigene preuisor*), indicative of how he viewed himself.[11] A surviving poem, known as 'Rex Pius Æthelstan' ('Holy King Æthelstan'), was entered on folio 15 recto of a British Library manuscript with the classmark Cotton Tiberius A. ii. The manuscript itself, thought to have been written on the Continent in the late ninth or early tenth century, is a beautifully ornamented copy of the four Gospels, with gold lettering, portrait pages, and enlarged and decorated initial letters for each of the Gospels. Thanks to the poem, which was added by a continental scribe, and to an accompanying prose inscription, which formed the original opening to the manuscript, we know that this copy of the Gospels later came into Æthelstan's possession, whereupon he donated the manuscript to the religious community of Christ Church, Canterbury. Because the poem was added to the manuscript to commemorate the occasion of its donation, we can presume that it was written by someone close to the king himself, and it is interesting to find that it is copied in the hand of a scribe from the Continent.[12] The poem provides a view of how the king and his entourage wished him to be portrayed to this religious community. His military credentials are stressed, but most prominent are the notions that he was established as king by God and that he was a keen supporter of religion, of churches and of learning—not least in the donation of precious manuscripts, such as Cotton Tiberius A. ii.

The diploma record shows the care with which, across the entirety of his reign, Æthelstan sought to foster good relations with churches. A diploma issued on the very day of Æthelstan's coronation on 4 September 925, and which employs formulae not found in any other Æthelstan diploma, demonstrates how the king was already favouring St

Augustine's abbey, Canterbury, with a gift of land in Thanet, Kent. The exact land granted is referred to in the diploma by the name *Werburgin-land*, which cannot be precisely identified today.[13] The contents of the diploma claim that, many years prior to 925, the land had been 'unjustly' (*iniuste*) seized from St Augustine's, and that Æthelstan was here return-ing it to the rightful owner. The St Augustine's community seem to have begun developing their landed interests in the Thanet area already by the early ninth century.[14] Other diplomas show Æthelstan aiding epis-copal sees in the accumulation of their endowment. So in April 930 the king granted land in Sandford, Devon, to the then bishop of Crediton, Eadulf, while in September of the same year he granted land in Med-merry on the Sussex coast to the bishop of Selsey, Beornheah.[15] The other ecclesiastical establishments favoured by Æthelstan in surviving authentic diplomas include Athelney, Shaftesbury, Sherborne, and the church of St Mary, Wilton.[16] We have already seen that Æthelstan, by looking to Malmesbury as a burial site for members of his family, seems in some ways to have departed from the pattern established by his father of favouring the New Minster in Winchester. But this list of land grants by Æthelstan indicates that he was nevertheless keen to bolster the pos-sessions of religious communities intimately connected to the West Saxon royal house, since both Athelney and Shaftesbury had been founded by Alfred.

It is very difficult to determine the nature of the religious communi-ties that had responsibility for churches across the kingdom. Although there would have been variation from place to place, it has been sug-gested that in the early tenth century many churches would have been staffed by so-called secular clergy—that is, priests who were not re-quired to share communal property or live in a shared dormitory and who were entitled to marry.[17] If this was so, it is striking to find that under Æthelstan there is a new emphasis on the monastic way of life which prefigures the celebrated monastic reform movement of the later tenth century in the reign of King Edgar (d. 975). In Æthelstan's diplo-mas, for example, prominence is given to abbots: they are not only re-cipients of grants of land but are named as attestors in the witness-lists which conclude each diploma, although in the majority of cases it is not possible to know over which abbeys they presided. In 931 Æthelstan gave land in Hampshire to a certain Abbot Ælfric, and in the following year he gave more land, this time in Essex, to an abbot named Beorht-sige.[18] Both of these men, as well as being the direct beneficiaries of royal diplomas, also formed part of a group of some nine abbots who can be found listed as witnesses in diplomas of Æthelstan that date principally to the period 931–34, at the time when the royal scribe 'Æthelstan A' had a monopoly over the writing of diplomas. A certain Abbot Cynath, to whom we will return below, was already present at Æthelstan's royal assembly in 925, before 'Æthelstan A' was in charge of producing diplomas. Two diplomas dated 930 describe abbots as having been present at the relevant meeting of the royal assembly, but do not list their names individually.[19] In the diplomas of 931–34, the abbots are placed quite high in the witness-lists, with their names either being listed immediately after the bishops and before the ealdormen, or occurring after those of the ealdormen and before those of the royal thegns.[20] And, within the group of abbots themselves, there seems to have been a relatively clear hierarchy: Ælfric always attests as the leading abbot, followed by a certain Eadwine, and then by either Æthelnoth or Beorhtsige.[21] Before this period, abbots had not routinely been named in diploma witness-lists. As we have previously seen, we need to be cautious in our handling of witness-lists, especially those of 'Æthelstan A', which were deliberately idiosyncratic.[22] But it seems likely that, with their attendance at the royal assemblies of the years 930–34 now routinely recorded, the status of abbots had increased under Æthelstan.

Mention should be made of an abbot who attests two diplomas of Æthelstan dated 925 and who on one occasion is named as Cened and on another occasion as Cynaht, both of which are renderings of the name 'Cynath'.[23] The name form Cynath has proved problematic. Its first element, *Cyn-*, is well attested in Old English. But its second element, *-ath*, is less common, and the combination of the two parts is unique in the Old English corpus of personal names. Could this have been an authentic but otherwise unattested Old English name, or does its peculiarity suggest external influence of some kind? Comparison with names elsewhere in early medieval Britain has suggested the possibility that Cynath could actually have been a Pictish (Ciniod/Cin-ioth) or a Gaelic (Cinaed) name. If that is the case, Abbot Cynath, whose name first appears in diplomas in 899 at the end of King Alfred's reign, could be another example of a member of the British clergy who came to Alfred's court as part of the king's programme of educational and spiritual revival (in the same manner as men like Asser, from St David's in south-west Wales).[24] When Cynath attests diplomas of 899, he is a member of the Worcester religious community, where, by 904, he has the title of deacon. By 915 he has become an abbot (as we find him in Æthelstan's reign) and, thanks to records from Evesham abbey, he can be connected at this point to Evesham rather than to Worcester.[25] It seems that Cynath, whatever the exact origins of his name, was highly trusted by Æthelstan. As we will see, his name can also be found listed in the St Gall confraternity book, which suggests that he may have been a member of the party that journeyed with Bishop Cenwald of Worcester to Germany in 929; and a diploma dated 930 may indicate that Æthelstan gifted Cynath with land in Gloucestershire and Worcester, although the surviving text has suspicious features.[26]

In 939, the last year of his reign, Æthelstan made three grants of land to women. In one he donates land in Berkshire to a certain Eadwulfu, who is described in the diploma as a 'religious woman' (*religiose femine*); in another he gives land at Droxford in Hampshire to his half-sister, Eadburh, who is described as a 'venerable Christian' (*uenerabilis Christicola*); and in the third he disposes of land at East Overton in Wiltshire to a certain Wulfswith, a 'maiden of Christ' (*ancilla Christi*).[27] The favouring of nunneries with land was not uncommon, but the dona-tion to individuals in this manner is unusual before the late 930s. And, according to the surviving diploma record, the trend for grants to reli-gious women continued beyond Æthelstan's reign into those of his two successors, Edmund and Eadred, to the year 955. It is difficult to know how to interpret these details and how to understand the circumstances that led to religious women being beneficiaries of diplomas in seemingly new ways. Perhaps there was a fresh zeal for religious observance that resulted in land being set aside for the purpose, either solely for the individuals mentioned to follow their own holy lives or so that they could found communities on the land in question.[28] Or perhaps some of the women mentioned had been widowed, and one practical solution to their new situation involved their seeking out a religious life.[29] As we will see, Æthelstan deployed his numerous half-sisters in marriage alliances across Europe, putting them to diplomatic use. But his half-sister Eadburh, who was the daughter of Edward the Elder by his third wife, Eadgifu, is said by William of Malmesbury to have been marked out by her religious tendencies already from an early age. William tells a story in which Edward the Elder offers a three-year-old Eadburh the choice between secular objects (bracelets and necklaces) and religious objects (a chalice and gospel book). Eadburh chose the latter and, so William tells us, subsequently became a nun in Nunnaminster, Winchester, in keeping with the way in which she is described in the grant of land to her by Æthelstan.[30] Eadburh was later remembered as a saint and is listed as such in the text known as 'On the Resting-Places of the Saints'.[31]

The evidence of diplomas suggests that Æthelstan was motivated by a high level of personal piety when making grants of land and associated privileges. By the early tenth century it had become conventional for a royal diploma to declare that the grantor in question was in part motivated to make the grant for religious reasons, even though the land could subsequently be used as the beneficiary desired: phraseology such as 'for the [benefit of] my soul' (*pro anima mea*) became formulaic. But Æthelstan's diplomas indicate religious motivations in ways which make it seem that the formulae in question are more than standard legalese and in fact reflect his genuine concerns. Several documents include the stipulation that the grant of land is only made on the condition that prayers are said for Æthelstan himself and for members of his family. In a diploma dated 937, for example, land in Somerset is granted to the church at Athelney on the understanding that prayers would be said both for Æthelstan and for his grandfather, Alfred the Great, who had founded the Athelney church.[32] The pattern of a request for prayers for the king is continued with a diploma from the last year of Æthelstan's reign, discussed above, in which Æthelstan grants land at East Overton in Wiltshire to Wulfswith, who is described as a 'maiden of God' (*ancilla Dei*).[33]

A cluster of five documents drafted by 'Æthelstan A' in December 932 and January 933 stand out for the religious stipulations they expect in return for the grant of land being made. Æthelstan's requirements concerning the religious duty vary quite widely: in those of January 933 he asks that annually on All Saints' Day (1 November) prayers should be said on his own behalf, and for the feeding of ten 'poor people' (*pauperes*), again on All Saints' Day.[34] But in the diplomas of December 932, both dated to Christmas Eve and both issued at the same meeting of the royal assembly at Amesbury in Wiltshire, the expectations are higher. In one, land is granted to Shaftesbury abbey on the understanding that prayers would be said daily (rather than annually) for the king.[35] In the other, the demand is more onerous still: a royal thegn named Ælfred is given an estate at North Stoneham in Hampshire on the condition that no fewer than 120 'poor' (*pauperes*) are fed daily until 'Doomsday'—in other words, in perpetuity.[36] Clearly the burden of feeding 120 needy souls on a daily basis was a significant one. It may reveal an expectation that Ælfred, rather than using the land at North Stoneham for his own benefit, was expected by Æthelstan to maintain it for charitable purposes, perhaps in conjunction with a religious community (*familia*) mentioned in the diploma. Such a view is certainly compatible with the legal text known as the 'Ordinance Relating to Charities', in which Æthelstan, with the help of Archbishop Wulfhelm, calls for a 'destitute Englishman' (*an earm Engliscmon*) to be provided with sustenance if needed.[37] The content of diplomas and law codes would have been discussed at meetings of Æthelstan's royal assemblies, and it seems likely that a decision had been taken to promote charitable causes.[38]

The unusual stipulations in Æthelstan's diplomas confirm the impression that he was an especially devout king. But was there something in particular that prompted him to make donations—some of them very significant in scope—on Christmas Eve 932, and into late January 933? It was in 933 that Edwin, Æthelstan's half-brother, who had been driven out of England on account of an unspecified 'disturbance' (according to the near-contemporary account of Folcuin), died in a shipwreck at sea.[39] As we have seen, later writers, including William of Malmesbury, provide a slightly amplified and altered interpretation, that Æthelstan was somehow implicated in the death of his half-brother.[40] In his text, William states that Æthelstan was distraught on account of Edwin's death and recognised that he should not have listened to those who had spread rumours in the first place. In order to make amends, William narrates that Æthelstan then undertook a period of seven years' penance.[41] If these events can be believed,[42] and if they had been unfolding for a while and culminated in Edwin's death in 933, is it possible that the religious stipulations in diplomas of December 932 and January 933 were made with Edwin's fate in mind? Edwin may not have been dead by January 933, but perhaps Æthelstan recognised that any action against his own kin required a considered programme of penance in recompense.[43]

It is possible that Æthelstan took other actions to atone for having had Edwin cast out to sea. This was certainly the view of William of Malmesbury, who, in his *History of the English Bishops*, states that Æthelstan had founded two religious communities, Milton Abbas in Dorset, and Muchelney abbey in Somerset, for this very reason.[44] William also records that Milton was used as a repository by Æthelstan for relics that he had acquired from Brittany, including the bones of St Samson, who had been archbishop of Dol. Milton was itself dedicated to the Breton saints Samson and Branawaltr.[45] A famous letter from Radbod, prior of Dol, which gives detail of some of the relics sent to Æthelstan, appears to have been stored at Milton in the archive there. Later house traditions from Milton itself carefully preserve and elaborate its association with Æthelstan: to have been founded by the first king of England would have conferred a degree of status on the community.[46] Unfortunately, the only diploma to have survived in the name of Æthelstan, which claims to grant a large sequence of lands to the abbey, is a later forgery, drawn up to overcome a gap in the abbey's records, meaning that we have no contemporary documentation connecting Æthelstan to the community.[47]

The history of Muchelney abbey was greatly clarified in the late nineteenth century when a manuscript known as the 'cartulary of Muchelney Abbey' was discovered among the collection of the Marquis of Ailesbury at Savernake Park in Wiltshire. The manuscript, which has been dated to the early fourteenth century, was later acquired by the British Library, where it is now housed.[48] Towards its beginning can be found a series of copies of diplomas that claim to have been granted by various Anglo-Saxon kings, starting with one in the name of Ine, king of Wessex (d. 726). (Remarkably, the cartulary was also found to contain an original single-sheet diploma of King Æthelred the Unready [d. 1016], which had survived by being tucked into the volume.)[49] There is much work still to be done on the early medieval documents copied into the cartulary, and great need for a modern edition of and commentary on each document. If taken at face value, the documents themselves suggest that King Ine had been responsible for the initial foundation of the religious community at Muchelney. The one surviving document in the name of King Æthelstan, dated to 934 × 939, has been judged to be spurious in its received form.[50] It claims to benefit the Muchelney community by a grant of land at Curry Rivel, at Stowey in Fivehead, Somerset, and by a further parcel of land that had been held by a layman named 'Muda'. There are certainly features of the document that are doubtful. It lacks many of the diplomatic elements we would expect to see in a diploma of Æthelstan of the mid- to late 930s, and it makes claims that immediately arouse suspicion. But some parts of it, which tally with other known features of Æthelstan's diplomas, are more reassuring: they read almost as if there could at one stage have been a document in the name of Æthelstan in the background. Two aspects stand out. The first is its statement that a note of the grant of land had been inserted into a copy of the holy gospels, a practice with which Æthelstan can be associated and which is known to have been employed by various Anglo-Saxon communities.[51] The second is the phrase in the boundary clause in which Æthelstan states that he has made the grant of land 'for the souls of his forefathers, and for his soul, and for the souls of all the kings that should come after him',[52] a penitential statement not unlike those we have already encountered. The document is in addition furnished with an Old English boundary clause, and with a witness-list that is credible for its purported date. The document in its received form cannot be wholly authentic. It is just possible, though, that an original record provided some of its details. Whatever its status, it is of further interest for its claim that Æthelstan had constructed the church in honour of St Peter. If it is true that a church at Muchelney had first been founded by Ine of Wessex, then perhaps Æthelstan had had to refound it following a period of decay and neglect.

It is important to remember that the religious and secular worlds were not so distinct in the early medieval period. As we have noted,[53] the significance afforded to religious figures in secular contexts can clearly be seen in the meetings of the royal assembly, the attendance at which is set out in the hierarchical witness-lists found at the end of royal diplomas. Given their high rank at meetings of the royal assembly, and their status at the top of the church in England, it was important for Æthelstan to ensure that he had the support of the archbishops of Canterbury and York. Following the death of Æthelhelm in 926, Wulfhelm, who had been the bishop of Wells, was appointed as his successor at Canterbury. It was probably deliberate that an appointment from an existing West Saxon see was made, in the hope that the appointee would be the more likely to be sympathetic to a king of the West Saxon line. A year later, in 927, one version of the *Anglo-Saxon Chronicle* records that Wulfhelm journeyed to Rome, possibly to collect the pallium, the papal symbol for the authority invested in the archiepiscopal position.[54] It is likely that under Æthelstan, international in outlook and pious, Wulfhelm saw the importance of official papal recognition of his new position.[55] Wulfhelm would go on to play a major part in the governance of Æthelstan's kingdom, with a special role in the area of legislation.[56] His attestations feature at the top of all the diplomas issued by Æthelstan from 926 until 939. As we will see, Æthelstan can be found giving manuscripts to the religious community at Christ Church in a further bid to secure their favour.

After his conquest of Northumbria in 927, one of Æthelstan's main priorities must have been to secure the support of the incumbent of the York see. At first this was a man named Hrothweard, who witnesses Æthelstan's diplomas of 928–30. Not much is known about Hrothweard's time as archbishop, but one of his predecessors, Wulfhere, seems at times to have sided with viking kings in York, with the result that Æthelstan must have been wary of the archbishopric's loyalties.[57]

By 20 June 931 Hrothweard has been replaced as archbishop by Wulfstan I, who subsequently attests all of Æthelstan's diplomas until 935, at which point he disappears from both the diploma record and, for a time, from narrative texts. In Wulfstan I's time, Æthelstan attempted to win over the archbishop and the York church. As we have seen, a large area of land on the north-west coast called Amounderness, which is situated in a zone of Scandinavian settlement and where vikings travelling from Dublin to York are known to have landed, was granted directly to the York church in a diploma in Æthelstan's name. The grant is unusual in various respects and seems to constitute a shrewd bargain effected by Æthelstan with the York church: he was willing to be excessively generous, but only on the condition that church members abandoned any previously held viking sympathies. Because he disappears from records, we know nothing more about Wulfstan I's actions during Æthelstan's reign. When he does reappear, in the *Anglo-Saxon Chronicle*'s entry for 943, he can be found acting in alliance with the then viking king, Óláf Sihtricson, and against Æthelstan's successor, Edmund. Unfortunately, it is impossible to know whether Wulfstan had turned against Æthelstan at some point in the years 935–39, when he disappears from our records. But, as one might expect of a Northumbrian archbishop who lived at a time when viking kings in York were of recent memory, he seems to have been politically pragmatic, willing to shift his and his church's position when necessary.[58]

In the same way that it was important for Æthelstan to secure the support of the two archbishops in his kingdom, there is also evidence that he strategically selected individuals from his close entourage for promotion to the level of bishop, as and when episcopal sees became vacant. Ælfheah and Beornstan, for example, the two ecclesiastics who had witnessed Æthelstan's freeing of the slave Eadhelm soon after becoming king, were themselves elevated as bishops of Wells (acceded 926 × 928) and Winchester (consecrated 29 May 931), respectively.[59] A list of names can be found entered by a scribe of the early twelfth century on one page of the Durham *Liber vitae*. The list seems to represent the names of those who were in attendance on Æthelstan as he went north, perhaps in connection with the occasion in 927 when he ultimately received the submission of various rulers near Eamont Bridge. The names may have been derived from the witness-list of a royal diploma. Towards the end of the list, it is interesting to find, in addition to an abbot (Ælfric) and two dish bearers (*disciferi*), the presence of a certain Cenwald *monachus* (monk) and Oda *presbiter* (priest).[60] If it is correct to identify these men as the Cenwald who would later become bishop of Worcester (acceded 928 × 929) and Oda, who became bishop of Ramsbury at some point in the period ca. 909 × 927, then it appears that they, too, had been close to Æthelstan before being promoted to the rank of bishop.[61] When Beornstan died on 1 November 934, he was replaced as bishop by another person with the name of Ælfheah, known by the cognomen *Calvus*—that, is 'the Bald'. Before he became bishop, Ælfheah is described as *sacerdos et monachus* (priest and monk) when he attests the diploma issued on the day of Æthelstan's coronation, again suggesting that he may have been one of the king's royal priests.[62] We know that this Ælfheah was related to Dunstan (to whom we will return), who is also known to have spent time at the court of King Æthelstan.[63]

From the witness-lists of Æthelstan's various diplomas we can see that, within the archdiocese of Canterbury, there were the following episcopal sees: Rochester, Selsey, London, Winchester, Ramsbury, Sherborne, Crediton, Wells, Cornwall, Lichfield, Hereford, Worcester and Dorchester. In the northern part of the kingdom, the York archbishopric is known to have had only one episcopal see, the community of St Cuthbert, which by the tenth century had relocated from Lindisfarne and, according to later Durham traditions, had moved to Chester-le-Street.[64] (It is possible that a number of further bishops discussed below, whose sees are not explicitly identified, may also have been Northumbrian.) The order in which the bishops from these different sees attest Æthelstan's diplomas reveals interesting dynamics and royal priorities. If we are to analyse the witness-lists properly, the diplomas need to be divided into their three chronological groups: those of 925–26, those of 928–35, when 'Æthelstan A' had a monopoly on their production; and those of 936–39, after 'Æthelstan A' had stopped his work. The most striking feature of the first group of diplomas is the complete absence of Frithestan, the bishop of Winchester, indicative both of Winchester hostility towards Æthelstan and of Æthelstan's Mercian upbringing.[65] The antipathy between Æthelstan and Frithestan shows why it was so important that, when the Winchester see became available in 931, the king selected a priest from his own household to take up the role. At the same time that Winchester was omitted from the scene, the sees of Lichfield and London,[66] from former Mercian territory, are noticeably prominent in certain diplomas, suggestive of the geographical base of Æthelstan's power in the opening years of his reign.

The diplomas by 'Æthelstan A', across the years 928–35, provide new patterns of episcopal attestations. Although there does not appear to be a regular order in which the bishops attest, some priority is afforded to bishops from western Wessex and southern Mercia.[67] As we might expect given his role in negotiations of a marriage alliance in 929, Bishop Cenwald of Worcester has an elevated status at the royal assembly, although not consistently so. When Beornstan takes over from Frithestan at Winchester, he attests in quite a high position, most often in fifth, sixth, or seventh place, and this is presumably indicative of the faith Æthelstan had in him. The most obvious characteristic of the episcopal witness-lists of 928–35 is their comprehensiveness, covering all episcopal sees in the kingdom.[68] For diplomas dated 925–26 only a sub-set of bishops had attested, whereas, for the 'Æthelstan A' diplomas, bishops from practically all of the sees are regularly listed (in the same way that the witness-lists also contained many more laymen). And this includes the two episcopal sees at the very limits of Æthelstan's authority, Cornwall and St Cuthbert's community (which are not present in diplomas of 925–26 or 936–39). There is difficulty in interpreting this evidence: as we have seen, the absence of a name from a witness-list does not necessarily imply that someone had not been present. But after extending his authority into Northumbria in 927 and thus creating 'England' for the first time, it would have been important in practical and symbolic terms for Æthelstan to bring together all of the bishops under his jurisdiction, and for that gathering to be formally recorded in his royal diplomas, in ways that had not hitherto happened.

PLATE 1. The Alfred Jewel, preserved in the Ashmolean Museum in Oxford, bearing an inscription in Old English, AELFRED MEC HEHT GEWYRCAN ('Alfred ordered me to be made'). Image reproduced by kind permission of the Ashmolean Museum, Oxford.

PLATE 2. Coin of Alfred the Great with the monogram LVNDONIA inscribed on its reverse. Image reproduced by kind permission of the Classical Numismatic Group, LLC: https://www.cngcoins.com.

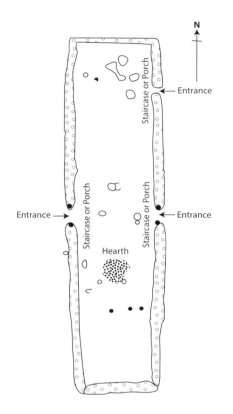

PLATE 3. Plan of the Cheddar
royal hall. Adapted from H. Hamerow, 'Anglo-Saxon Timber Buildings and Their Social Context', in
*The Oxford Handbook of Anglo-
Saxon Archaeology*, ed. D. A. Hinton, S. Crawford, and H. Hamerow
(Oxford: Oxford University Press,
2011), 140.

PLATE 4. Top image: A royal diploma in the name of Alfred, dated 898, and
with the attestation of Edward the Elder as *rex* (king); S 350, CCA-DCc/
ChAnt/F/150. Bottom image: a close-up of the attestations of Alfred and Edward. Reproduced courtesy of the Dean and Chapter of Canterbury Cathedral.

PLATE 5. St Cuthbert's stole and maniple, with the inscriptions detailing the commissioning of the vestments by Ælfflæd for Frithestan, bishop of Winchester. Reproduced by kind permission of the Chapter of Durham Cathedral.

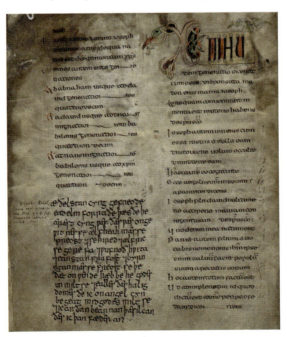

PLATE 6. Fol. 15v of London, British Library, Royal 1. B. vii, a (possibly) Northumbrian gospel book of the first half of the eighth century with a tenth-century record of a manumission carried out by Æthelstan early in his reign. From the British Library Archive / Bridgeman Images.

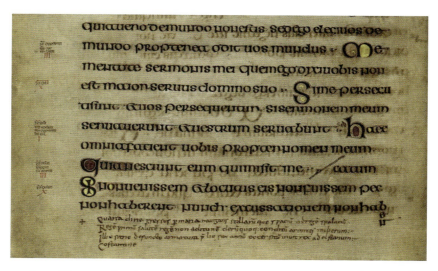

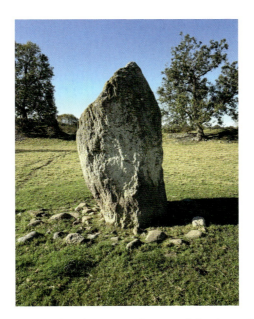

PLATE 9. Mayburgh Henge. Photograph by the author.

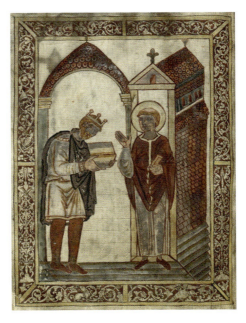

PLATE 10. Fol. 1v of Cambridge, Corpus Christi College, MS 183, a portrait of King Æthelstan and St Cuthbert. Reproduced by kind permission of the Parker Library, Corpus Christi College, Cambridge.

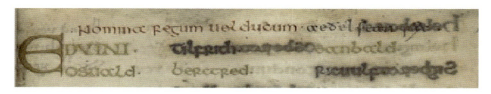

PLATE 11. Fol. 15r of the Durham *Liber vitae*, London, British Library, Cotton MS Domitian A. vii, where the words 'aeðelstan rex' can be seen added after the rubrics 'Nomina regum uel ducum'. From the British Library Archive / Bridgeman Images.

PLATE 12. Bamburgh Castle as it stands today. Photograph by Matthew Hartley, "Bamburgh Castle, Beautiful Day," Wikimedia Commons, https://commons .wikimedia.org/wiki/File:Bamburgh_Castle,_beautiful_day.jpg.

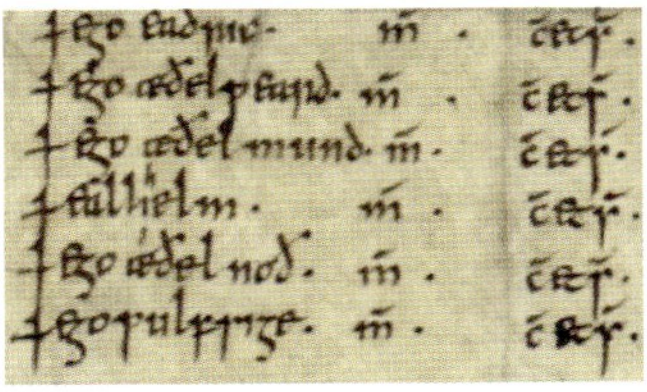

PLATE 13. Top image: An 'Æthelstan A' diploma in which nine hides of land at Ham, Wiltshire, are granted to the thegn, Wulfgar; S 416, British Library, Cotton Charters viii. 16. From the British Library Archive / Bridgeman Images. Bottom image: Enlarged detail from the witness-list of S 416, which shows the interlinear correction of the name Ealhhelm with the addition of a second *h*.

PLATE 14. Fol. 87v of London, British Library, Royal 7. D. xxiv, a copy of Aldhelm's prose *De virginitate*, his treatise on virginity. From the British Library Archive / Bridgeman Images.

PLATE 15. S 447, a diploma of 939 written by 'Æthelstan C' in which King Æthelstan grants land in Kent to his thegn, Ealdwulf; British Library, Cotton MS Augustus II. 23. From the British Library Archive / Bridgeman Images.

PLATE 16.

a) Æthelstan's Horizontal 'Trefoil' type. This coin was made from a north-western die by the moneyer, Eadmund.

b) Æthelstan's 'Diademed Bust' type. This coin was made by the moneyer, Arnulf.

c) Æthelstan's 'Bust Crowned' type. This coin was made at the Norwich mint by the moneyer, Hrodgar.

d) Æthelstan's 'Tower' or 'Reliquary' type (from York). This coin was made by the moneyer, Froteger. All images reproduced by kind permission of Classical Numismatic Group, LLC: https://www.cngcoins.com.

Another striking feature is the prominence afforded to the bishop of Lichfield, a man named Ælfwine (also known in contemporary sources as Ælle). In diplomas of the reign of Æthelstan's father, Edward the Elder, the bishop of Winchester (first a man named Denewulf and then Frithestan, who remained in post into Æthelstan's reign) is usually accorded the highest-ranking position in the list of witnesses after the archbishop of Canterbury, as one might expect in documents in the name of a king from the West Saxon line. But in the diplomas of 'Æthelstan A' this position is given instead to Ælfwine as bishop of the Mercian see of Lichfield. Two reasons for this exalted rank have already been discussed: that Æthelstan himself had been raised at the Mercian rather than West Saxon court, and that Æthelstan's relationship with Frithestan was fraught with difficulties.[69] There is also a third possible explanation. Could Bishop Ælfwine have been the very person responsible for the drafting of these diplomas? In other words, should he be identified with the anonymous 'Æthelstan A'? If so, it could explain why Ælfwine occurs as the highest-ranking bishop in the royal assemblies of the years 928–35. But the arguments put forward in favour of this identification have so far fallen short of being definitive.[70]

In the diplomas of 'Æthelstan A' there are about twelve further bishops who do not appear in the diplomas of 925–26 or 936–39 and who, unlike the majority of bishops attesting, cannot be assigned to any known episcopal see. It is impossible to be certain about the precise status and function of these bishops. In a diploma dated 929 and preserved in the Worcester archive, land is said to have been given by Æthelstan to the church of Worcester.[71] The diploma itself is thought to have been forged, but its list of witnesses is not incompatible with its purported date of issue; and nor is it dissimilar to others of about the same date, suggesting that that element at least may derive from a genuine diploma of Æthelstan. It is interesting, therefore, to find that Hrothweard, the then archbishop of York, is said to have attested the document together with four further bishops who are described as 'the suffragans of York'. One of these four is Wigred, the bishop of St Cuthbert's community, but the remaining three (Æscberht, Earnulf and Columban) are from sees that are not otherwise recorded. Perhaps these three bishops had been appointed by Æthelstan to rejuvenate the church in areas of the kingdom that were overseen by the archdiocese of York, or perhaps they were bishops of old Northumbrian sees (such as Hexham and Whithorn) that otherwise, owing to scanty documentation, disappear from view in the late ninth and early tenth centuries.[72] We are not given any further detail about the nine other bishops whose names are recorded without known sees. Some may have been employed as 'auxiliary bishops'—known by the Latin term *chorepiscopi*—to help those in post across Æthelstan's kingdom.[73] It is notable that some of these extra bishops possess distinctive and/or rare names, including one we have already met, Columban, which is Irish; the monastic name Benedict; and the name 'Mancant', which may ultimately derive from the Brittonic form Maucant.[74] In the diplomas in which Mancant is listed, he appears adjacent to the Cornish bishop, Conan, and higher up in the witness-lists can be found the names of various Welsh kings. Could Mancant have been an otherwise unattested Welsh bishop brought to Æthelstan's royal assemblies by one of the Welsh kings?[75]

The diplomas of 'Æthelstan A' cease to be produced by the year 935, and from 936, diplomas of a wholly new kind begin to appear. There are profound changes with regard to the attestations of bishops in the period 936–39. Perhaps most notably, Ælfwine, the bishop of Lichfield, disappears, and the bishop of Winchester, a role which by 934 had passed from Beornstan to Ælfheah *Calvus* ('the Bald'), becomes the leading bishop to attest the king's diplomas. As we have seen, Ælfheah may previously have been a royal priest in close service to Æthelstan before his promotion. Likewise, the bishop of London, Theodred, also increases in importance, consistently attesting immediately after Ælfheah in diplomas of these years, as does Cenwald, the bishop of Worcester, who now reliably attests in fourth place.[76] The comprehensive nature of the 'Æthelstan A' diplomas, which deliberately embraced all the bishops in England, certainly ceases in this last group. In addition to the disappearance of the bishop of Lichfield, the bishops of Sherborne, Cornwall, Hereford, Dorchester and Chester-le-Street, and the archbishop of York, are either entirely absent or only attest on occasion. The group of twelve bishops for whom there is no recorded see also cease to attest diplomas. If taken at face value, there seems to have been a major shift in the ecclesiastical composition of the royal assembly, with fewer bishops in attendance from 936 to 939. If this did represent reality, and there were fewer bishops present, perhaps it had become impractical and unnecessary to expect all of these individuals to be present at each of Æthelstan's assemblies.[77] It is possible that the bishops concerned were grateful to be spared this extra burden. Although, given the importance of contact with the king, what German scholars term *königsnähe* (proximity to the king), it is more likely that they felt insulted by having been excluded.

No matter who was present, the royal assembly would have provided an important opportunity for Æthelstan and his bishops to discuss matters related to ecclesiastical business, including the granting of land and privileges to churches around the kingdom and the appointing of different individuals to ecclesiastical offices. Æthelstan's acquisition of new territories would have necessitated discussion about how to incorporate those areas within existing church structures.[78] We have seen that, earlier in the tenth century, under the aegis of Plegmund, archbishop of Canterbury, and King Edward the Elder, and perhaps because of directions from Rome, the large West Saxon diocese had undergone a degree of reorganisation when the two existing sees of Winchester and Sherborne were divided to create five sees in total: Winchester (Hampshire), Sherborne (Dorset), Ramsbury (Wiltshire), Wells (Somerset) and Crediton (Devon).[79] Further to the south-west, the kingdom of Cornwall, which had long remained independent but which from the ninth century was being drawn within the orbit of West Saxon control, received particular attention in Æthelstan's reign as he took steps to increase his authority there (even if Cornwall continued to retain its distinctiveness and independence in various respects).[80] Records from Canterbury indicate that, already by the ninth century, a bishop of Cornwall, named Kenstec (d. before *c.* 890), who had his base in Bodmin, viewed the Canterbury church as his spiritual superior.[81] And, in a letter of the period 981 × 988—probably written by Dunstan, then archbishop of Canterbury, and concerning the history of episcopal estates in

Cornwall—reference is made to the fact that earlier in the tenth century
Æthelstan 'gave to Conan the bishopric as far as the Tamar flowed'.[82] In
other words, Æthelstan had set up Conan (whose name implies that he
was a Cornishman) as its bishop. Rather than being based at Bodmin, as
Kenstec had been, a number of sources associate Conan's episcopal see
instead with St Germans in Cornwall, where there had been a Cornish
religious establishment before the time of Æthelstan.[83] One can imagine
that—in trying to understand how to incorporate Cornwall within existing English diocesan structures, identifying the right person to be bishop
of Cornwall who would be accepted by the local population but also
loyal to the king, and identifying the right place to house the episcopal
seat—Æthelstan would have relied on the ecclesiastical members of his
royal assembly for guidance. Diplomas of the years 931–34 indicate that
Conan joined the assembly and would then have been able to lend his
Cornish view of matters directly to Æthelstan.

Two diplomas, the contents of which make it impossible to date
them more narrowly than to the reign of Æthelstan (i.e., 924–39), provide further detail about Æthelstan's dealings with the Cornish church.
In the first, which is preserved in the archive of Exeter Cathedral, Æthelstan is said to have granted land in seven places to the church of St
Buryan in the far west of Cornwall.[84] The style of the document is problematic. Parts of its formulation recall contemporary diplomas in the
name of Æthelstan, but parts do not, and there are in addition clear
errors of formulation, with the result that historians have been divided
about the diploma's authenticity. Nevertheless, there seems to be consensus that the diploma, although suspicious in various respects, may
have been based ultimately on a genuine record of a gift by Æthelstan
and perhaps that its idiosyncratic formulation in some ways reflects
Cornish diplomatic practice of the tenth century.[85] If this interpretation
can be accepted, it shows both that Æthelstan had the authority to be
granting land in the far west of Cornwall, far distant from his own centres of power, and that he was inclined to be generous to Cornish religious communities.

The second diploma, which survives only in a very late copy of the
eighteenth century from the archive of Athelney, is in various ways more

extraordinary than the first.[86] It takes the form of a grant of land in Lan-
lawren, in Cornwall, by a certain 'Maenchi *comes*', the son of Pretignor,
to one 'St Heldenus', which is to be identified as St Hyldren. Maenchi is
said to have made this grant 'in the land of the Saxons in the island of
Adalne [i.e., Athelney], in the reign of King Æthelstan on the festival of
All Saints, before the altar of SS. Peter and Paul, in the sight of God and
all His saints, in the presence of Seignus the abbot'. The first point of
interest is that this grant of land is not in the name of the king himself
but rather a private individual, the *comes* Maenchi. It is rare to have a
private (rather than royal) charter of this nature from the early tenth
century. The name Maenchi is Brittonic and means 'stone-hound'.[87] The
name's similarity to Menki, a common Breton name, has led to the suggestion that Maenchi may have been from Brittany.[88] His title in the
diploma is given as *comes*, which, when used of the pre-Conquest period, normally means 'ealdorman' or 'earl'.[89] Short in length and idiosyncratic in form, there is nothing else like it in the corpus of Æthelstan's
diplomas. Despite this, it has mostly been accepted as genuine by historians, not least because there is no discernible motive for it to have
been forged by the Athelney community where it has been preserved.
If genuine, it casts light on what must have been a Cornish diplomatic
practice that was in use at the same time as Æthelstan was granting land
by means of the more 'standard' royal diplomas. But why did Maenchi
travel to Athelney in Somerset to make a grant of land in Cornwall to a
Cornish church, and why does the diploma carefully record that it had
been granted 'in the reign of King Æthelstan'? Perhaps Maenchi, like
other important secular and ecclesiastical figures from around the British kingdom, was on his way to attend one of Æthelstan's royal assemblies and made a grant of land while he did so. Or perhaps Æthelstan's
expansion into Cornwall necessitated such private grants of land being
confirmed by reference to the king.[90] It is interesting to note that the
charter itself is said to have been 'executed' on All Saints' Day (1 November), the very date when a number of 'Æthelstan A' diplomas stipulate
that various religious duties are carried out by the recipients of the
grants of land in question. This may have been a further manifestation
of Æthelstan's generosity to the church and of his concern for his own

soul, that he encouraged powerful individuals to make grants of land to the church on the same day that other penitential acts were being carried out in his name.

In the same way that Æthelstan took steps to incorporate the Cornish church within English infrastructures, so, too, did the king make a concerted effort to win over St Cuthbert's community in the north of his kingdom. By the early tenth century, St Cuthbert's community had had a long and distinguished, although not untroubled, existence. Founded at Lindisfarne off the north-east coast of England in the early seventh century by St Aidan, the community had engineered its survival and success across some three hundred years. If we can believe sources written by the Cuthbertines, particularly the *Historia de Sancto Cuthberto* (History of St Cuthbert), the community had acquired a number of estates, making it significant and powerful. In 793 the Cuthbertines were attacked by vikings, and in the mid-870s, again according to Cuthbertine tradition, the situation was such that members of the community took the decision to move from their original home on Lindisfarne further inland and take the body of Cuthbert with them. Cuthbertine texts suggest that, following a period known as the 'seven years' wandering', the community finally settled at Chester-le-Street in the early 880s (and would later move to Durham in the 990s). If it can be accepted that, by the late ninth century, the Cuthbertines had moved further inland and south, it is probable that one motivation for their relocation was the desire to bring themselves closer to the growing power of the West Saxon kings rather than being isolated on an island in the North Sea.[91] Another was to move themselves to a site less vulnerable to viking attack. On his journey north towards Scotland in 934, Æthelstan visited the community. This may have been the occasion on which his name was entered into the Durham *Liber vitae* with unusual prominence.[92] The *Historia de Sancto* remembers Æthelstan as being particularly generous to the Cuthbertines, giving them a variety of gifts that included precious manuscripts; valuable objects connected with religious observance (such as liturgical vestments, chasubles, tapestries, and candelabra); money; and a series of estates in the northeast.[93] According to the same text, the connection between the West Saxon royal house and the Cuthbertines could be traced back to the time of Æthelstan's grand-father, Alfred.[94] Written by the Cuthbertine community itself, the *Historia* needs to be considered with care. But it seems clear both that Æthelstan made a special effort to bring them under his influence, and that the Cuthbertines were keen to cultivate his support. Given that this part of Northumbria had been relatively isolated from contact with Wessex following the settlement of a Scandinavian population in and around York, and that Æthelstan had only recently formally acquired Northumbria, his approaches to St Cuthbert's community would have formed a vitally important part of his tactics in securing his grip on England as a whole.[95]

In his dealings with St Cuthbert's community, it is possible that Æthelstan had learned from the example set in Mercia by his aunt and uncle, Æthelflæd and Æthelred. We have seen that they supervised the translation of St Oswald's relics into a new minster at Gloucester, an event which the *Mercian Register* dates to 909. The relics had been relocated from Bardney, in Lincolnshire, which would at that stage have been in Scandinavian-held territory.[96] St Oswald was a Northumbrian king of the seventh century who in 642 died in battle against the pagan Mercian king Penda at an unidentified place called *Maserfelth*. Oswald is one of the heroes of Bede's *Ecclesiastical History*, in which he is celebrated for his saintly rule and for his establishment, together with Aidan, of an episcopal see at Lindisfarne. Following Oswald's death, Bede narrates that Oswald's niece, Osthryth, who had married the then king of Mercia, Æthelred, had taken some of Oswald's bones to the 'famous monastery' (*monasterium nobile*) of Bardney. His head and hands, which had been cut off by Penda and placed on stakes, were later taken by Oswiu (Oswald's brother and successor in Northumbria) back to Northumbria, where the head was given to Lindisfarne and the hands and arms to Bamburgh.[97] The 909 translation of Oswald's relics by Æthelflæd and Æthelred from eastern Mercia to their new ecclesiastical foundation at Gloucester represented the beginnings of their—and of Edward the Elder's—campaign to reclaim the areas of eastern Mercia from Scandinavian possession. Their acquisition of the remains of Oswald, a seventh-century Northumbrian saint venerated in Mercia, therefore made a political statement about their territorial aspirations in wider Mercia.[98]

There is some evidence that Oswald remained important during Æthelstan's time. When the East Frankish author Hrotsvitha describes the marriage between Otto the Great and Æthelstan's half-sister, Eadgyth, she takes care to stress Eadgyth's noble lineage. Hrotsvitha remarks that Eadgyth 'was descended from a family of sainted ancestors. For they say . . . that she was descended from the blessed stock of King Oswald'.[99] Sarah Foot has shown that Eadgyth was not related to Oswald in the way that Hrotsvitha suggests. But a link between the Northumbrian royal dynasty and that of Wessex was provided by Oswald when he sponsored the baptism of the West Saxon king, Cynegils (d. ca. 642), and subsequently married Cynegils' daughter.[100] It is possible that Hrotsvitha, in recording the detail of Eadgyth's ultimate relationship to Oswald, was preserving a tradition about her that was being promoted by Æthelstan himself.[101] That said, Oswald's fame had, by the tenth century, already spread to the Continent, meaning that Hrotsvitha could independently have seen the value in making a link between Eadgyth and the Northumbrian saint.[102]

Another feature of Æthelstan's reign was the influence exerted by Brittany on the English church. Connections with Brittany were relatively long-standing and can certainly be traced back to the time of King Alfred.[103] In Æthelstan's reign we see an importation of Breton ecclesiastics, manuscripts, and sacred objects. Brittany itself was a complex area in terms of its identity, politics, and outlook: on the one hand, it was part of a linguistically and culturally distinct zone that embraced Cornwall, Wales and Strathclyde/Cumbria; on the other hand, it was linked with its closest geographical neighbours, the Frankish empire, and, after 888, its successor states.[104] In the early tenth century Brittany was coming under political pressure from the Franks and suffered from viking raids, with the result that various Bretons sought refuge overseas. Some political exiles ended up at the court of King Æthelstan, who offered them support.[105]

Embedded within the writings of William of Malmesbury is a letter addressed directly to Æthelstan. William tells us that it was found in the archives of Æthelstan's foundation at Milton Abbas and that it was writ-ten by a man named Radbod, who was the prior of the church of St Samson in Dol, Brittany.[106] In it, Radbod first reminds Æthelstan that his father, Edward the Elder, had been connected to the Breton com-munity at Dol via a bond of confraternity, and then also takes the op-portunity of sending and commending the relics of various Breton saints (to which we will return) to Æthelstan, in the hope that he 'may not forget us'. It is possible that the Dol community were appealing to Æthelstan as a king of evident power and authority at a time when the political situation in Brittany was deeply uncertain. Whatever the rea-son for the contact, the letter reveals the close connection between Breton and English religious communities in the early tenth century.

Further evidence of links with Brittany are to be found in another letter, preserved in the British Library. The letter itself is in parts difficult to interpret and its author is unknown. It takes the form of a general recommendation of an unnamed Breton soldier who had laid aside his arms to become instead a religious man and who subsequently travelled to England. Thanks to Æthelstan's permission, the religious convert is said to have lived as an anchorite at a place in England called *Cen* (which cannot be identified). The anchorite seems to have been encouraged by Æthelstan to undertake a religious pilgrimage, and one purpose of the letter was to ensure the safe passage of the Breton pilgrim on his jour-neys.[107] The chance survival of this letter reveals that in the early tenth century people from different sections of society were quite regularly crossing the channel, in both directions.

The influence of the Breton church—in the form of its people, manu-scripts, and religious objects—left its mark on Æthelstan's England. A large number of Breton manuscripts found their way into English librar-ies, which would in turn have influenced the everyday liturgical routines and practice of the English church.[108] Breton saints were also sup-ported: William of Malmesbury describes how Æthelstan had overseen the purchase of saintly relics from Brittany, including the bones of St Samson, so that they could be deposited in Milton Abbas. Later rec-ords from Milton Abbas itself also indicate that, thanks to Æthelstan's generosity, the community had charge of the arm of the Breton saint

Branwalatr.[109] Further detail of Æthelstan's donation of the relics of Breton saints, this time to the Exeter church, is provided by a list of relics which is written in Old English almost as if in the form of a sermon and in the second half of the eleventh century was added to a ninth- or tenth-century Breton gospel book then housed at Exeter.[110] So strong had been the influence from the Breton church during Æthelstan's reign that, later in the Anglo-Saxon period, the feasts of various Breton saints were commemorated in calendar entries.[111]

During Æthelstan's reign, closer relations with East Francia were fostered. In response to a request from Henry the Fowler for a marriage alliance between the kingdoms, Æthelstan enlisted the help of Bishop Cenwald for escorting to East Francia a group which included two of his half-sisters, from whom Henry's son, Otto, was to choose a bride. Cenwald's origins as a royal priest closely connected to the king may have meant that he had a good relationship with the sisters and was therefore well placed to lead the mission. As we will see, Cenwald set off in 929. Some details of the journey can be recreated from entries that were made in continental manuscripts as Cenwald and those accompanying him stopped at different religious establishments en route, including that they had visited 'all the monasteries throughout Germany', as recorded in a manuscript from St Gallen.[112] We can imagine that Cenwald made the most of the journey to learn about continental modes of religious observance. The same entry of the St Gallen manuscript states that Æthelstan had entrusted Cenwald with a quantity of silver, some of which he donated to the monastery there. Cenwald's visit, and his donation of silver, would have fostered good relations between the English and German Churches. Cenwald may also have been carrying silver in order to acquire relics and manuscripts to bring back to Æthelstan. The formal alliance between the two kingdoms may also have resulted in a movement of people, because moneyers with German names can be found inscribed on coins, and the New Minster lease, already mentioned, contains the names of various individuals from the Continent.[113] Records from Abingdon suggest the presence of another continental ecclesiastic during Æthelstan's reign, a man named Godescealc.[114] And the bishop of London, Theodred, bore a

German name, as did some of those named in his will who were closely associated with him.[115]

We know from Radbod's letter to Æthelstan (and from other sources) that the king had a particular penchant for saintly relics, which Radbod says were 'dearer to you [i.e., Æthelstan] than any earthly property'. Together with the letter, Radbod himself had sent as a gift to the king relics of some of the saints of Avranches: Senator, Paternus and Scubilio.[116] In the preface to the Old English list of relics added to the Breton gospel book at Exeter, we are told that representatives, described as 'honest, discerning men', had been sent abroad by Æthelstan to seek out new relics and to acquire them on his behalf, using riches that Æthelstan had provided for the purpose.[117] Sources from the Continent suggest that these same representatives may not have been as 'honest' as the Exeter account states, and perhaps that they resorted to theft in order to satisfy their king's wishes.[118] If the testimony of William of Malmesbury can be believed, Æthelstan's desire for relics was so well known across Europe that Hugh the Great, duke of the Franks, in seeking one of Æthelstan's half-sisters as a bride in 926, had sent an envoy to Æthelstan who took with him impressive gifts and relics. The relics included Constantine the Great's sword, Charlemagne's lance (which William says was the one 'driven by the centurion's hand into our Lord's side'), the banner of Maurice (which had been owned by Charlemagne), a magnificent crown, a piece of the cross on which Christ had been crucified, and a piece of his crown of thorns.[119] The items had been carefully selected to flatter Æthelstan's sensibilities as a Christian, military, and imperial leader. Constantine was the first Roman emperor to convert to Christianity; Maurice was likewise an early convert, and he led the Theban legion of Rome. Charlemagne represented the greatest example in more recent times of a king who had extended his rule over nearly all of continental Europe, had been crowned emperor in a ceremony at Rome in 800, and who was peculiarly dedicated to the health of his empire's church.[120] Given Æthelstan's own imperial claims to rule over Britain, not just England, the comparison with Charlemagne (if William's account of the 926 gift itself can be accepted) would have fuelled Æthelstan's ambitions the year before he brought Northumbria under his control and received the submission of a number of British rulers near Eamont Bridge.[121]

Relics would have been important to Æthelstan for a variety of reasons. At one level they supported his own religious beliefs and pious outlook. They also provided a powerful demonstration and validation of the sanctity of his rule, that he was ordained by God to be the legitimate king of the English. Once in his possession, relics could be used as part of Æthelstan's own creation of networks of patronage and favour. If gifted to an English religious community, the relics provided the opportunity for the growth of a cult connected to the saint in question and thereby for the spiritual and financial health of those that possessed them, since relics attracted pilgrims who, in turn, had spending power. In a variety of records written by English religious communities, Æthelstan is remembered as a generous donor of such artefacts. Some of the relics that had been given to him by Hugh the Great, for example, were, according to William of Malmesbury, latterly donated to Malmesbury abbey, with which Æthelstan had a special connection.[122] Such was Æthelstan's reputation as both a collector and donor of holy relics that many different religious communities, including those at Abingdon, Exeter, Malmesbury, Milton, and Winchester, claimed to have received gifts of relics from him, and sometimes different institutions laid claim to what seem to be the same relics.[123]

Manuscripts could be put to the same use as relics. Thanks to a sequence of dedication inscriptions added to various manuscripts, we can trace numerous occasions on which Æthelstan came into possession of a manuscript and then donated it to a religious community. The inscriptions reveal that Æthelstan gave manuscripts to Christ Church and St Augustine's, Canterbury; to Bath abbey; and to the community of St Cuthbert. Many of the manuscripts donated by Æthelstan were gospel books which had originally been written on the Continent and subsequently come into Æthelstan's possession in a variety of circumstances. By having an inscription inserted into each manuscript to mark the occasion of its donation, Æthelstan sought to have his generosity and piety remembered through the ages, creating a record that subsequent members of each religious community would be able to consult and on the basis of which they might then offer prayers in his memory. And the texts of the dedication inscriptions themselves are further revealing. Their vocabulary and style reveals that they were written by some of the same draftsmen who were responsible for the production of contemporary royal diplomas, and for diplomas from after Æthelstan's time. The evidence suggests that Æthelstan had created a vibrant literary hub at the centre of his court and that he had brought together a team of expert scribes who at one moment could be called on to write a royal diploma of enormous ambition in a recondite style and at another point could be asked to turn their hands to the writing of a dedication inscription.[124] And the use of Latin and Old English text was not their only expertise. We have seen that in one manuscript commissioned by Æthelstan—housed today at Corpus Christi College, Cambridge— there is the most extraordinary portrait of the king himself, with his head bowed, giving a manuscript to St Cuthbert.[125] The image has been interpreted in a variety of ways, either as a presentation portrait of a form ultimately derived from similar images in late antiquity and found in Carolingian manuscripts,[126] or as a depiction of Æthelstan's personal devotion to Cuthbert.[127] Æthelstan is the picture of a pious king, and his crown bears a striking resemblance to that found depicted on some of the coins issued in his name.[128]

Taken straightforwardly, the gift of the Corpus Christi manuscript to St Cuthbert's community signalled that Æthelstan was a generous and pious donor. But an examination of its contents suggests that Æthelstan may have had ulterior motives in making this particular donation. Among other things, it contains a copy of the prose and verse *Lives* of St Cuthbert, texts that were written ultimately by Bede in the early eighth century. Given that Æthelstan had only recently extended his own royal authority northwards, beyond the River Humber, the inclusion of texts that demonstrated his own veneration for this major northern saint was a masterstroke of diplomacy. But at the same time, the manuscript's insertion of a set of episcopal lists and royal genealogies that spanned the English kingdom conveyed the message that Northumbria was now naturally part of a kingdom that was subject to kings of the West Saxon line.[129]

A manuscript preserved today in the archbishop of Canterbury's magnificent library at Lambeth Palace, close to London Bridge, and known as the MacDurnan Gospels, was written originally in the latter part of the ninth century, perhaps at Armagh in Ireland.[130] It was one of the manuscripts that came into Æthelstan's possession, after which he gave it to Christ Church, Canterbury. The inscription recording Æthelstan's gift reads, in its original Latin (with modern English translation):

+ MÆIELBRIÐVS·MAC
DVRNANI·ISTVM·TEXTVM
PER·TRIQVADRVM·DEO·
DIGNE·DOGMATIZAT·
+ AST·AETHELSTANVS·
ANGLOSÆXANA·REX·ET·
RECTOR·DORVVERNENSI·
METROPOLI·DAT·PER ÆVVM.

Mael Brigte mac Tornain propounds this gospel-book throughout the world, in a manner worthy of God; but Æthelstan, king and ruler of the Anglo-Saxons, gives it forever to the metropolitan see of Canterbury.[131]

The inscription itself, written in lines of verse that alliterate, reveals a connection between the manuscript and an Irish ecclesiastic named Mael Brigte mac Tornain. From the evidence of Irish chronicles, Mael Brigte (d. 927) was a *coarb* (a term which broadly equates to 'abbot') of Armagh and Raphoe in the north of Ireland, and of Iona in modern-day Scotland. He was therefore a figure of no little importance, also revealed by the fact that in 913 he was able to offer support to a British pilgrim in Munster, an area in the south-west of Ireland beyond his usual orbit of influence.[132] The inscription preserves the tradition that Mael Brigte was somehow connected with the manuscript, but it falls short of saying that the *coarb* himself had presented it as a gift to Æthelstan. The linguistic and metrical form of the inscription are of further interest because of the similarities they share with a set of royal diplomas produced after the reign of Æthelstan, in the 940s and 950s, known as the

alliterative charters, and which have been associated with Bishop Cenwald of Worcester. It appears, therefore, that when Æthelstan wished to
have an inscription composed for insertion into this gospel book, he
turned to Cenwald for assistance.[133] The king's ownership and subsequent donation of this ninth-century Irish copy of the gospels to the
Canterbury church, in whose possession it remains today, demonstrates
a connection between England and Ireland that added to the cosmopolitan nature of his court. And there may have been other Irishmen in
England. The lease from the New Minster, Winchester, contains a very
distinctive name form among its list of witnesses, of a certain 'Dupliter',
which may actually be a rendering of an Old Irish name, Dub-litir (Black
letter).[134] When Æthelstan proceeded north in 934 on his way to campaign in Scotland, we have seen that he made a visit to St Cuthbert's
community, where he presented gifts of various kinds, including manuscripts. One of the manuscripts given by Æthelstan—British Library,
Cotton Otho B. ix—was badly burnt in a fire of the early eighteenth
century. But on one of its surviving folios a prayer and associated colo-
phon have been inserted which were written, so the text declares, by a
certain Benedictus Evernensicus—that is, Benedict the Irishman. The
script of the addition suggests it belongs to Æthelstan's reign, and therefore that another Irishman was working closely with Æthelstan. It is
possible that this Benedict might be one and the same as the Benedict
who attests a royal diploma of 20 June 931 as a bishop.[135]

Irish (and Breton) ecclesiastical links can be further evidenced.
Towards the front of a twelfth-century manuscript, housed today at
Corpus Christi College, Oxford, and known as the 'Corpus Irish Gos-
pels', a very striking image can be found. The image itself depicts a board
game of some sort. It is preceded by various Latin inscriptions, one of
which, when translated into English, reads: 'Here begins the *alea* of the
Gospel, which Dub Innse, bishop of Bangor, brought from the king of
the English, that is, from the household of Æthelstan, king of the
English, drawn up by a certain Frank [*or* by a certain Franco] and by a
Roman scholar, that is, Israel'.[136] The inscription thus reveals the cosmopolitan nature of Æthelstan's entourage, which included an Irish
bishop (Dub Innse), a Breton scholar (Israel, to whom we will return)

and a certain man from Francia, or a man named Franco.[137] (From the inscription it is unclear whether the original Latin *Francone* means 'a Frank'—i.e., someone from Francia on the Continent—or whether it refers to a specific individual named Franco.) And what is the game depicted? Because of the format of the board, and the way in which the pieces seem to have been laid out, with a group defending a central piece (the 'king') and an attacking group placed on the outside, it has been related to a class of early medieval board games known as *tafl/tæfl*, or by the Latin term *alea*.[138] But, in fact, this particular image does not represent a real game. An accompanying text reveals that it is an allegorical game intended to explicate the canon tables included in manuscript copies of the gospels. Canon tables were a device to aid a reader in navigating the gospels' contents and in comparing between similar passages of biblical text.[139]

The 'Israel' of the inscription has been identified as Israel the Grammarian, a Breton scholar of some distinction, learned in both Latin and Greek, and responsible for the composition of a range of texts including the poems *De arte metrica*, *Rubisca* and the 'Saint-Omer Hymn'. Israel was well travelled: as the inscription suggests, he had spent time in Rome, and he is known to have been closely connected to Otto the Great and his brother, Bruno. Israel saw out his life as a monk in Trier, in modern-day Germany.[140] Israel's time in England left a lasting impression. Various idiosyncratic Latin words, used only in texts of his authorship, found their way into the diplomas of 'Æthelstan A', suggesting that some of his work was being read and digested by Æthelstan's royal scribes so that it could be utilised when forming diplomas of a new kind.[141] The image of the board game may provide a further indication of the advances taking place at Æthelstan's court. It is true that it represents an allegorical game, but the text which accompanies the image, and which explains how the game works, refers to a hierarchy of pieces used on the board in ways that are not dissimilar to chess. It has therefore been suggested that the image of the *alea* of the Gospel may represent one of the earliest examples of English interactions with chess, itself a game of Indian origins.[142]

Israel was one poet who found favour at Æthelstan's court. Others included the continental author of 'Carta, dirige gressus' (possibly named Peter), and the author of 'Rex pius Æthelstan', texts which we have already encountered.[143] A further learned poem has survived by being copied into the back of a manuscript preserved today in the Bodleian Library in Oxford. As can be seen, the first letters of each line spell out the name 'Adalstan' (making it an acrostic), while the last letters of each line render 'Iohannes' (which means it is also a telestich):

Archalis clamare triumuir nomine sax I
Diue tuo fors prognosim feliciter aeu O
Augustae · samu · cernentis rupis eris · el · H
Laruales forti beliales robure contr A
Saepe seges messem faecunda praenotat altam i N   5
Tutis solandum petrinum solibus agme N
Amplius amplificare sacra sophismatis arc E
Nomina orto petas donet precor inclita doxu S

You, leader, are proclaimed by the name of 'sovereign stone'
Divine one, may this prophecy happily happen for your age
You will be of the 'eminent rock' of discerning Samuel
With mighty strength against the devilish demons
Often an abundant field foretells a rich harvest   5
In peaceful days the stone army will be smoothed
You are exalted more greatly in the holy citadel of wisdom
I pray, glorious one, that you may seek and He may provide illustrious names.[144]

Because the poem is copied in a script that can be linked to Æthelstan's court, and because the manuscript as a whole contains texts studied by scholars associated with Æthelstan, it has been accepted that the 'Adalstan' addressed in the acrostic is Æthelstan himself. The unusual spelling of the name's first element, *Adal-*, has further suggested that the poem's author may not have been English, and may have been from the Continent.[145] Only eight lines in length, the poem is highly skillful.

Its references to 'sovereign stone', 'eminent rock', and 'stone army' provide puns on the meaning of Æthelstan's name, 'noble' (Æthel-) 'stone' (-stan), while in the third line the name 'Samuel' is divided into two parts, as is the word *ortodoxus* in the eighth line (a literary device known as tmesis) in order to fit the poem's metrical form.[146] The poem constitutes a prophecy, in which the poet expounds the future greatness of Æthelstan—for example, with the wish that 'you [i.e., Æthelstan] will be of the "eminent rock" of discerning Samuel / With mighty strength against the devilish monsters'. It has been suggested that, because the poet predicts Æthelstan's prospects as ruler, it is likely to have been written early in his life, and that the 'Iohannes' named was the poet himself, who may have been John the Old Saxon, the man who had been brought to the English kingdom by Alfred the Great. According to this view, John composed the poem in honour of the occasion organised by Æthelstan's grandfather, Alfred, in which Æthelstan's future status as ruler was formally observed.[147] More recent interpretation has called this reading into question. Arguments have been made that the poem should belong to a later part of Æthelstan's life, partly because its penultimate line celebrates Æthelstan's learning, which would be an inappropriate observation if he were a child. It has also been suggested that 'Iohannes'—rather than being John the Old Saxon—could either be a baptismal name for Æthelstan or that it is an allusion to John the Baptist, and therefore that Æthelstan is being depicted as Christ-like.[148] Clearly we need to be careful in handling the evidence of an early medieval poem, which can be interpreted in a variety of ways. But its connection with Æthelstan is undeniable and helps build a picture of a king who was peculiarly devoted to the fostering of religion and learning within his kingdom.

Another poet who may have been at Æthelstan's court was the viking Egill Skalla-Grímsson, whose deeds are recounted in *Egils saga*.[149] The saga is an Icelandic text first copied in the thirteenth century, but which purports to relate events of the tenth century: it contains a number of passages involving Æthelstan.[150] Egill and his brother, Thorolf, in search of financial gain, are said to have sought out opportunities offered by Æthelstan. The saga narrates how the king of Scots, whom it erroneously calls Óláf, gathered a large force in order to invade England; the details recorded suggest that the saga's author was alluding to the Battle of *Brunanburh*, which it refers to as the Battle of Vinheiðr.[151] Egill and Thorolf fought on the king's side and helped Æthelstan overcome his enemies, although Thorolf was killed in the process. In the wake of the battle, Egill was rewarded by Æthelstan for his support, and the saga suggests that Egill remained with the English king for the following winter.[152] The late date and legendary nature of *Egils saga* deprive it of credibility as a historical source. But the saga also contains stanzas of skaldic verse (that is, poetry composed by Scandinavian poets, known as skalds) which are composed with complex form and metre, the accuracy of which has encouraged the view that they constitute verses originally composed by Egill himself.[153] One of the poems is a praise piece—a *drápa*—in which Egill exults in Æthelstan's successes and in his generosity. The way in which the poem is written, with its direct appeal to Æthelstan, has suggested that it may once have been recited directly to the English king.[154] Egill, in attempting to highlight Æthelstan's prowess, concluded his *drápa* with a refrain that reads, 'Now the highest reindeer road lies under bold Æthelstan'.[155] The expression 'reindeer road' is a kenning, a technique common to skaldic poetry in which a metaphorical phrase is used in the place of a noun—in this case, a mountain. Egill's purpose was to demonstrate the great victory that Æthelstan had won in his battle against the Scots. If Egill's poetry can be accepted as authentic tenth-century material, his skilled verses, replete with Old Norse poetical techniques such as kennings, also demonstrate the intellectual vibrancy of Æthelstan's court.[156] Æthelstan had assembled scholars from contemporary Europe and Scandinavia who worked in a number of languages and genres of text and whose interests extended to include innovative board games. It is no wonder that those in the direct service of Æthelstan himself, figures such as 'Æthelstan A', felt emboldened to explore their own literary abilities.

During the reign of King Edgar (d. 975), one of Æthelstan's successors, a major reform of the English church began, influenced in part by previous ecclesiastical reforms on the Continent, and which adhered to the Benedictine Rule.[157] Three ecclesiastics—Æthelwold (d. 984),

Dunstan (d. 988), and Oswald (d. 992)—are credited with spearhead-
ing the English reform. Of these three, Æthelwold can certainly be
linked to the court of King Æthelstan, and Dunstan may have had
connections to the king as well (perhaps being distantly related to him).
Details of Æthelwold's career are provided by the *Life of St Æthelwold*,
composed by Wulfstan of Winchester ca. 996.[158] As with any hagiographical text, it is written in such a way as to expound the (saintly)
virtues of its subject. For Wulfstan, Æthelwold's peculiar holiness meant
that word had reached Æthelstan about him quite early in his life, with
the result that he became a member of the king's court and the 'king's
inseparable companion'.[159] Æthelwold is said to have gained experience
from the king's *witan*, and it is possible that his name can be found in
some witness-lists of Æthelstan's diplomas.[160] Æthelstan subsequently
ordered that Æthelwold be tonsured by Bishop Ælfheah of Winchester,
before a few years later he became a priest (which is said to have happened on the same day that Dunstan was made a priest).[161] For whatever
reason, Æthelstan required Æthelwold to remain with Bishop Ælfheah
to receive instruction, and it may only have been once Æthelstan died
in 939 that Æthelwold then sought out Dunstan's guidance at Glastonbury, where he subsequently became a monk.[162]

It is more difficult to determine what happened to Dunstan during
King Æthelstan's reign owing to the complexity of interpreting and rec-
onciling the hagiographical material for his life. This includes a text written between 995 and 1004 by an author known only by his first initial,
B., and a second set of materials by the continental author Adelard of
Ghent, who was writing at some point in the years 1006–12 at the request of the then archbishop of Canterbury.[163] According to B., Dunstan began his ecclesiastical career at Glastonbury before then coming
under the influence of Bishop Ælfheah of Winchester who persuaded
him not to marry and latterly consecrated him a monk. Adelard offers a
different account which connects Dunstan more particularly to Æthelstan: that Dunstan, having left Glastonbury, went to join the household
of 'his uncle' (*patruo . . . suo*), Æthelhelm, archbishop of Canterbury
(923 × 925–8 January 926), who in turn brought him to Æthelstan's
court, where Dunstan 'became great in the eyes of the king and his

nobles'. Adelard suggests that Dunstan then became a monk and abbot of Glastonbury during the reign of Æthelstan's successor, Edmund.[164] Doubt has been cast on the account by Adelard on the basis that, because he was writing on commission from the Canterbury church, he had good reason to insert the material about Æthelhelm and thereby to bolster Canterbury's reputation. It is unclear, therefore, whether or not Adelard's suggestion that Dunstan was related to Æthelhelm and introduced by him to Æthelstan's court can be accepted. Diplomas of Æthelstan's reign do not appear to register Dunstan's presence among members of the *witan*, although that in itself does not provide conclusive evidence that he was *not* present.[165] B. also suggests that Dunstan was related to several other people of influence: to Ælfheah, the bishop of Winchester, who has already been mentioned; to Cynesige, who later became bishop of Lichfield (946×949–963×964); and to a wealthy *matrona*, who is possibly to be identified with a woman subsequently named by B. as Æthelflæd, who herself is designated a kinswoman of King Æthelstan.[166] If these relationships can be accepted, they place Dunstan in high circles and may even suggest that he was of royal stock himself and thus a plausible member of Æthelstan's court.[167] Again, though, caution is needed. It suited B.'s aims of extolling the virtues of his subject to stress Dunstan's illustrious family. For one modern commentator, the possibility remains that B., in describing Dunstan's connections to Bishop Ælfheah and Æthelflæd, was actually referring to an 'adoptive kinship' rather than to real family ties.[168]

The importance of establishing Æthelwold's certain ties to Æthelstan's court, and Dunstan's possible links to Æthelstan's circle, resides in showing that the origins of their views about monasticism, which would later shape the trajectory of the English church, may have been formed during Æthelstan's reign. They are both said to have come under the influence of Bishop Ælfheah of Winchester, who was himself a bishop of importance under Æthelstan. As we have seen above, Ælfheah bore the cognomen *Calvus*, 'the Bald', which was possibly an allusion to his tonsure as a monk. He would presumably have had much knowledge about monastic practice to impart to Æthelwold and Dunstan.[169] In addition, people such as Bishop Cenwald of Worcester, who had visited

German monasteries in his journey to the East Frankish court in 929, could have relayed their experiences to Æthelwold and Dunstan, as could any one of the continental figures who have been identified as also being at Æthelstan's court. Those around the king were scholars of distinction and ecclesiastics who had been exposed to the most recent ideas about religion from the Continent. Æthelstan's entourage therefore offered an environment in which the future leaders of tenth-century ecclesiastical reform would have acquired foundational experience.[170]

Æthelstan, then, certainly lived up to the moniker 'steward of the Christian citizenry'. Even by early medieval standards he seems to have been a particularly devout king, who developed a keen interest in religious objects such as manuscripts and relics which he enthusiastically collected and also distributed as gifts. And with his support of religion came also his patronage of scholarship. Poets and other scholars were favoured who subsequently contributed to major advances in Latin learning including the development of new forms of ambitious and abstruse Latin. Such was Æthelstan's reputation that ecclesiastics from across Europe came to his court, where they would have been able to discuss the most recent developments in ecclesiastical doctrine and exchanged literary texts that were in fashion. We can be sure that Æthelstan would have been motivated by a degree of personal piety in his actions, but there were political advantages here too. When it came to his interactions with St Germans in Cornwall and St Cuthbert's community in the north he attempted to win them over to his cause. In the extremities of his newly extended kingdom the good will of these powerful local institutions would have significantly enhanced his standing, and, crucially, the chances of his royal authority being long-lasting.

5

British *Imperium*

WHEN VERSION 'D' of the *Anglo-Saxon Chronicle* records Æthelstan's annexing of Northumbria in 927, it notes, 'He brought under his rule all the kings who were in this island: first Hywel, king of the West Welsh (*Westwala cyning*), and Constantine, king of the Scots (*Scotta cyning*), and Owain, king of the people of Gwent (*Wenta cyning*), and Ealdred, son of Eadwulf from Bamburgh. And they established peace with pledge and oaths in the place which is called Eamont (*æt Eamotum*), on 12 July, and renounced all idolatry (*deofolgeld*) and afterwards departed in peace'.[1] Taken at face value, the entry is extraordinary for its suggestion that Æthelstan wielded authority not just in his newly formed England but more widely in Britain as well. Two Welsh kings are named, Hywel and Owain. There is in addition Constantine II, king of the Scots; and Ealdred, a member of the powerful noble family from Bamburgh. It is difficult to determine the extent to which these details can straightforwardly be accepted. For this entry, version 'D' of the *Anglo-Saxon Chronicle* is thought to represent the viewpoint of a northern author, which means that the writer's support for Æthelstan was not automatic (as it might have been for someone writing from the centre of Æthelstan's kingdom). This in turn lends a degree of credibility to the record.

Claims that Æthelstan's rule stretched beyond England and into Britain are mirrored in the diplomas and coins produced by his royal administration. In diplomas from 931 until the end of his reign, Æthelstan is regularly said not only to be 'king of the English' but also 'king of all

Britain' (*rex totius Britanniae*) or 'elevated to the throne of the kingdom of all Britain' (*totius Britanniae regni solio sublimatus*). The descriptions of Æthelstan's position regarding Britain vary. Some diplomas entitle him king with a Greek term, *basileus*, that has imperial connotations.[2] In others, the Latin name for Britain, *Britannia*, is substituted for *Albion*, a name that appeared in the pages of Bede to mean 'Britain', and which came to be used in a more consistent way in the reign of King Edgar (d. 975), one of Æthelstan's successors, who placed a special emphasis on his own pan-British authority.[3] On his coins, too, Æthelstan proclaimed his rule over Britain: on its obverse, the Circumscription type employs variants of the royal style, +ÆÐELSTAN REX TO[TIUS] BRIT[ANNIAE] (+Æthelstan, king of all Britain).[4]

Whatever the accuracy of these statements, many of which would have been bitterly resented by his British neighbours, it was vitally important that Æthelstan paid close attention to developments in the Welsh kingdoms and in the northern kingdoms of Strathclyde/Cumbria and Alba.[5] Not only did members of these different regions have the ability to cause problems for Æthelstan in their own right, but they had the potential to join forces with each other, or with disaffected parties in England: those Scandinavians who had previously settled in the east midlands and in York and its surrounding territory constituted the most obvious potential allies in any coalition against the English king. A further challenge came in the form of distinct groups of vikings, some of whom were members of the dynasty of Ívarr (d. 873). From bases in Ireland they patrolled the Irish Sea zone and opportunistically raided and settled parts of Wales (including the island of Anglesey), Strathclyde/Cumbria, Alba and England from the late ninth to the early tenth centuries. The so-called 'kingdom of the Isles', which comprised the Isle of Man, the Hebrides and the islands of the Clyde, were Hiberno-Scandinavian in character and formed an intrinsic part of this area of viking influence. The greatest external threat to Æthelstan's England therefore came from the west and north: any of the kings of the Welsh kingdoms, of Strathclyde/Cumbria and of Alba, together with the descendants of Ívarr, had the potential to collaborate in order to threaten the English king. Æthelstan's worst fears were realised in the

937 Battle of *Brunanburh*, in which an attempt to destroy him and his newly forged kingdom was made by an alliance that comprised vikings from Dublin acting in collaboration with Constantine II, king of the Scots (the very man who had submitted to Æthelstan in 927), and probably also with a certain Owain, king of Strathclyde/Cumbria, whom we will soon meet again and who is not to be confused with the Owain mentioned above. So momentous was the occasion that chroniclers from all parts of Britain and Ireland, and later saga writers from Scandinavia, registered the magnitude of the encounter.

Æthelstan and the Welsh Kingdoms

For a long time before Æthelstan's accession, the political dynamics between the English and Welsh kingdoms had been complex and in a state of flux. The late eighth century had witnessed a number of aggressive forays by Offa, the king of Mercia, into Welsh territory. Offa's construction of a now famous dyke stands as lasting testimony to the animosity that had existed. Mercian claims to the overlordship of various parts of Wales persisted into the ninth century, a period when West Saxon power within England was itself increasing, sometimes at the expense of Mercia. The West Saxons began to assert their own claims to control over Wales, as demonstrated by King Egbert in 830, who is said to have 'reduced them all [i.e. the Welsh] to humble submission to him'.[6] On occasion Mercia and Wessex seem even to have collaborated in their ambitions concerning the Welsh kingdoms, as can be shown by the joint actions in 853 of the Mercian king, Burgred, and the West Saxon king, Æthelwulf, to bring the Welsh under their control.[7] But Mercian and West Saxon positions were not static, and over the years that followed they can be found pursuing a variety of policies both between themselves and in their approaches to Wales.

By 853 in Wales a celebrated king had come to power in the northwestern kingdom of Gwynedd and in Anglesey: Rhodri Mawr ('the Great'), the son of Merfyn Frych. His numerous sons and grandsons—known as the 'Merfynion' dynasty—would dominate Welsh politics of the late ninth and early tenth centuries. At the same time that Mercian and West Saxon rulers were intruding into Wales, so, too, were vikings, some of whom are labelled the 'dark heathens' by Welsh (and Irish) annalists and some of whom were members of the family of Ívarr that had established itself in Ireland. A laconic entry for 877 in Irish annals states plainly that Rhodri Mawr had been forced by the 'dark foreigners' to flee north-western Wales and head to Ireland. One feasible explanation for the attack on Rhodri is that the vikings were trying to open a path from England (where they were also active, having taken control of York in 867 and parts of Mercia by ca. 874) back to Ireland across Gwynedd and Anglesey, which provided one of the most direct routes available.[8]

Thanks to the work of the Welsh cleric Asser, we are unusually well informed about Anglo-Welsh politics of the mid-880s. Asser tells us that he himself had previously left his ecclesiastical community of St David's, situated in the south-western kingdom of Dyfed, to seek out the court of Alfred the Great in Wessex. Asser had hoped to persuade Alfred to protect his Welsh brethren against the predatory king of Dyfed, Hyfaidd ap Bleddri (d. ca. 892). Asser also reveals that, from the mid- to late 880s, a series of Welsh kings likewise submitted themselves to Alfred's protection. Some, like Hyfaidd himself and the then king of Brycheiniog, Elise ap Tewdwr, did so in the face of aggression from the sons of Rhodri Mawr, who had died in 878. Others, like Brochfael and Ffernfael in Gwent, and Hywel ap Rhys in Glywysing, requested Alfred's support because of the tyrannical behaviour of Æthelred of Mercia. Anarawd, the son and successor of Rhodri in Gwynedd, had at first established an alliance with the Scandinavians at York. But when this faltered he, too, turned to Alfred.[9] The internal politics of Wales had therefore resulted in the West Saxon Alfred's securing of an unusual amount of power over the Welsh kings by the late 880s. But already by 892 events were undermining Alfred's dominant position: the death of Hyfaidd in that year prompted Anarawd, perhaps acting with the support of Mercia, to ravage parts of both Ceredigion and Ystrad Tywi in the west, showing how ephemeral political alliances of the period could be.[10]

Our sources do not provide as much detail about Anglo-Welsh relations in the reign of Alfred's successor, Edward the Elder. A major event of 902 seems to have been the expulsion of vikings from Dublin by the native Irish, which caused the vikings to seek out new areas to inhabit, in Anglesey and the north-west of Wales (and, as we will see, in the north-west of England and in the Strathclyde/Cumbria area). By 913–14 the vikings were once more active in the Irish Sea region, in the latter year in a naval encounter off the coast of the Isle of Man which involved Ragnall, a descendant of Ívarr.[11] Also in 914 a separate viking force is known to have come from Brittany: it arrived in the River Severn estuary and reached as far inland as Archenfield, to the west of Hereford. In doing so they took captive a Welsh bishop named Cyfeilliog.[12] By 917 Ragnall was in Ireland, and his kinsman, Sihtric, had established himself in Dublin.[13] Anxious about the threat from the west, Æthelflæd, the 'lady of the Mercians', ensured in 914–15 that burhs had been built in the north-west at Eddisbury and Runcorn, and on the Welsh border at Chirbury in 915.[14] All three sites were located close to Roman roads which, if accessed by vikings, would provide them with routes into the Mercian and West Saxon kingdoms.

When Æthelflæd of Mercia died in 918, the *Anglo-Saxon Chronicle* inserts an entry of great importance for our understanding of Anglo-Welsh politics. It states that 'all the nations in the land of the Mercians which had been subject to Æthelflæd submitted to him [i.e., Edward]; and the kings in Wales, Hywel, Clydog, and Idwal, and all the race of the Welsh, sought to have him as lord'.[15] Because the *Chronicle*'s detail concerning the submission of the three Welsh kings is not written in a eulogistic way (as are its other annals concerning Edward's reign), historians have accepted its bare details—that the three kings named, all of whom were of the Merfynion line, submitted to Edward after Æthelflæd's death.[16] The origins of power of the first, Hywel Dda (d. 949 or 950), lay in a part of southern Wales that, in combining the kingdoms of Seisyllwg and Dyfed, came to be called Deheubarth; he later expanded his authority into much of northern Wales. Clydog, the second named, shared power with Hywel (his brother) in part of the south. And Idwal Foel ab Anarawd (d. ca. 942), the final king—and Hywel's cousin—ruled in Gwynedd. The implication of the annal is that the named kings had previously recognised the Mercian Æthelflæd as their ruler, and that, once she had died and Edward had taken over in Mercia, he naturally also became their lord. The latter part of the entry, which claims that 'all the race of the Welsh' submitted to Edward, was hyperbole on the *Chronicler*'s part. Edward may have had a degree of authority in Gwent (where he intervened to free the Welsh bishop, Cyfeilliog, from viking captivity in 914), but Gwent itself, and the kingdom of Brycheiniog, can be shown to have had their own kings at this time who were not part of the Merfynion dynasty.[17]

When Æthelstan became king in 924 he therefore inherited a complex set of relationships and expectations in connection with Wales, which had intermittently been subject to English rule (whether by the Mercians or the West Saxons) and which had the potential to offer support to those (particularly vikings) seeking to win power in English territory. It was important that, by whatever means, he bring the Welsh on side. Following his success in becoming king of the English in 927, Æthelstan is said—in the annal with which this chapter began—to have taken two Welsh kings under his control. One of them, Hywel, is the Hywel Dda we have already met who submitted to Æthelstan's father, Edward, in 918. That Hywel is explicitly identified as being king of the 'West Welsh' in the 927 annal may be a reference to the south-western kingdom of Dyfed, which was increasingly dominant in Welsh politics of the early tenth century.[18] The other Welsh king listed, Owain, was the son of Hywel ap Rhys of Glywysing. Owain ruled in the south-eastern Welsh kingdoms of Glywysing and Gwent, which would later be joined as one and become known as Morgannwg. He died in about 930. It is notable that Idwal, the king of Gwynedd who had recognised the overlordship of Edward in 918, and who continued to rule until 942, is not included in the list of those submitting to Æthelstan in 927.

In his account of events in 927 following Sihtric's death, William of Malmesbury, perhaps relying on a different source, provides some alternative details to the *Anglo-Saxon Chronicle* entry, one of which is that a certain Owain, king of Strathclyde/Cumbria, rather than Owain, king of Gwent, submitted to Æthelstan. As we will see, it is likely that both men named Owain had been involved. William adds further information about Æthelstan's dealings with the Welsh (and with the Scots)

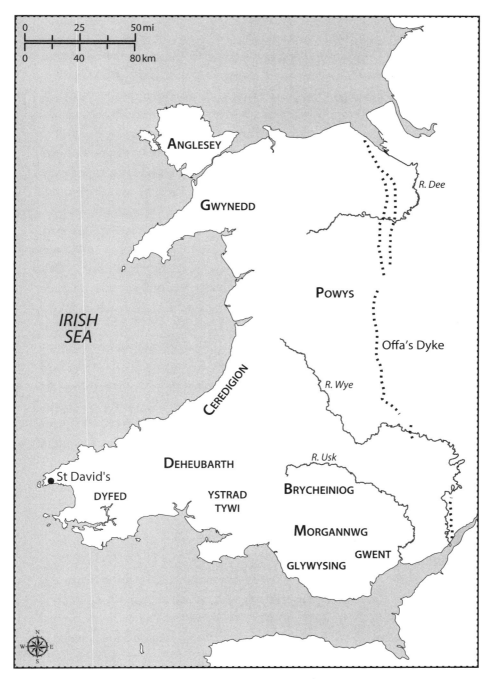

MAP 7. The political configuration of Wales during the reign of Æthelstan.

when he notes how, after his conquest of Northumbria, Æthelstan at first forced both Idwal of Gwynedd (who is described as 'king of all the Welsh') and Constantine, king of the Scots, to relinquish their positions as kings, although he later had a change of heart and permitted them to rule once more, on the condition that they recognised his ultimate authority.[19] Later in his account, William relates that Æthelstan had forced the 'princes' (*regulos*) of Wales to meet him at Hereford and to submit to his rule and that he was afterwards able to impose a hefty annual tribute on them which 'no king before him had presumed even to contemplate'. The English king then set the River Wye as the boundary between their kingdoms.[20]

As we saw in chapter 3, Æthelstan's political successes in 927 were soon afterwards followed by the introduction of a highly ambitious form of diploma, drawn up by the king's royal scribe, 'Æthelstan A'. One innovation of these diplomas is that, from 928 until 935, they include among their lists of witnesses a number of 'sub-kings' (each termed a *subregulus* in Latin). Welsh sub-kings are listed as attesting in the period 928–35, while a sub-king from Strathclyde/Cumbria attests one diploma of 931 and two of 935, and a sub-king from Alba attests two diplomas of 934–35. It is difficult to interpret the evidence of witness-lists, especially from diplomas like those of 'Æthelstan A', which are so radical in form, but analysis of the diplomas issued in the period 928–35 has inspired confidence in the details they provide.[21] Of the Welsh kings listed in Æthelstan's diplomas, the three most frequently present are Hywel Dda; Hywel's cousin, Idwal Foel; and Morgan ab Owain, of Glywysing and Gwent (d. 974). Other Welsh kings listed, but on a less regular basis, include a certain *Wurgeat*, a name which is probably a rendering of the Welsh 'Gwriad', but who is otherwise difficult to identify with certainty,[22] and Tewdwr ab Elise of Brycheiniog. The other sub-kings represented in Æthelstan's diplomas are Constantine II of the Scots and Owain of Strathclyde/Cumbria. The order in which the Welsh kings are listed shows that, most frequently, Hywel was placed in the principal position, with Idwal second and Morgan third. Gwriad only appears in two diplomas, while Tewdwr is listed in one document dated 934. By means of his royal assemblies, Æthelstan was able to demonstrate to the gathered participants his superiority over the Welsh kings named (and those of Alba and Strathclyde/Cumbria, when they were present), a power dynamic that was reinforced by the requirement for these kings to travel long distances to be present. But what this meant in terms of Æthelstan's real power in Wales itself is less clear, and it only represents the English side of the story. For one modern commentator, the Welsh kings present at Æthelstan's assemblies 'must have been seething with suppressed indignation'.[23]

The Welsh sub-kings Hywel, Idwal, and Gwriad appear (in that order) in a diploma issued on 16 April 928 in Exeter, Devon; Hywel is known to have travelled to Rome in the same year, presumably after this meeting in the south of England.[24] At that stage, Æthelstan is still described by 'Æthelstan A' as 'king of the English' (*rex Anglorum*) and without claims to rule over Britain. No Welsh kings are listed as being present at meetings in April 930 in Lyminster, Sussex, and in Chippenham, Wiltshire, nor in a March 931 diploma from Colchester in Essex. Despite the absence of the sub-kings, it is from the year 930 that Æthelstan's diplomas begin to declare that he was king not just of the English but more widely of Britain too. A group of four sub-kings enter the record once more in June 931 at an assembly held in Worthy, Hampshire. This includes Hywel and Idwal once again, but this time Gwriad is not listed and instead we have the attestations of Morgan of Glywysing and Gwent, and Owain of Strathclyde/Cumbria. The sub-kings seem not to have been present at an assembly held in July 931, in Wellow, Hampshire, but Hywel and Idwal return in September of that year for a meeting in Lifton, Devon. Of four diplomas surviving from 932 (one issued in August, one in November, and two in December), Welsh sub-kings are named in the August and November diplomas—the first issued in Milton, in Kent or Dorset, and the second issued in Exeter. No sub-kings are present in diplomas spanning the period December 932–January 933. In a diploma issued on 16 December 933 in Kingston, Surrey, Hywel is once more listed, this time on his own.

By the summer of 934, as we will see, Æthelstan was preparing for war with the Scots. In an assembly at Winchester on 28 May, 934, the Welsh kings Hywel, Idwal, Morgan, and Tewdwr seem all to have been present. Shortly afterwards Æthelstan and his entourage had made it as far north as Nottingham, where, on 7 June, they issued a diploma in favour of the York church at which Hywel, Morgan, and Idwal were present, but not Tewdwr. Perhaps he had returned to Brycheiniog in Wales, or perhaps, for some now unknown reason, he was present but was simply not listed in the version of the diploma that survives.[25] Æthelstan continued his march north towards Scotland with a view to invasion. Had the Welsh kings gone with him beyond Nottingham, and provided support to him in his fight in the north? Surviving records do not permit a definite answer.[26] From a diploma dated 13 September 934, we know that Æthelstan was once more in the south of England, in Buckingham. Two diplomas from 935 provide very interesting evidence concerning the relative status of Wales and Strathclyde/Cumbria in that year. In his one previous attestation in 931 Owain, king of Strathclyde/Cumbria, had been listed at the end of the sub-king section, after the names of the Welsh sub-kings. But in these two 935 documents he is given priority over the Welsh sub-kings, for reasons to which we will return.[27] One of the diplomas issued in 935 survives only in truncated form. But its Latin tells us that it was issued 'in the city formerly constructed by the Romans which is called Cirencester' (*in civitate a Romanis olim constructa que Cirnecester dicitur*) and that the sub-kings present were, in order, Constantine of the Scots, Owain of Strathclyde/Cumbria, Hywel of Deheubarth, Idwal of Gwynedd, and Morgan of Glywysing and Gwent.[28] In other words, it was an impressive array of people, drawn from the major kingdoms on England's borders. It is interesting that the diploma draws attention to Cirencester's Roman roots; perhaps Æthelstan and his advisers had carefully choreographed the assembly in order to reflect imperial glory.[29]

From 935 'Æthelstan A' ceased to compose royal diplomas, and, as a result, documents of the period 935–39 are radically different in form. The very long and elaborate lists of witnesses found in the period 928–35, which included Welsh kings, disappear, replaced by more concise lists which have different emphases. In the same way that groups of bishops, abbots, ealdormen, and some thegns no longer appear, so too the Welsh kings cannot be found listed in Æthelstan's 935–39 documents.

Given that the nature of the evidence changes so significantly, it is hard to know what conclusions to draw from the absence of Welsh attestations and whether or not it represents a change in the dynamics between Æthelstan and Wales. Despite the absence of the sub-kings in general from witness-lists of 935–39, Æthelstan continues to claim that he is the king of Britain, not just of England. Some Welsh kings, including Hywel and Morgan, would attest a distinctive set of 'alliterative' diplomas that were issued after Æthelstan's death, in the 940s and 950s, at a time when the political situation had radically changed.[30]

The evidence of witness-lists in Æthelstan's diplomas therefore demonstrates that, in the years 928–35, various Welsh kings attended the English king's court in different parts of his kingdom, even that they marched north with him as he began his preparations for war with the Scots in 934. While they were not in attendance at every assembly for which we possess records, they were present for about half of the occasions, which took them away from their everyday affairs in Wales.[31] But, despite having these detailed records of attendance, it is difficult to be more precise about the nature of Anglo-Welsh interactions in this period. Some historians have seen in Hywel Dda a Welsh king who had English sympathies and perhaps even modelled aspects of his own kingship on English precedent (although others have not found this assessment compelling).[32] It is striking, for example, that Hywel's pilgrimage to Rome occurred after his first recorded presence at Æthelstan's royal assembly on Wednesday, 16 April 928. Was there something discussed at the assembly that inspired him to set out across Europe? Easter Sunday that year had taken place only three days prior to this meeting, on 13 April, raising the possibility that the timing of Hywel's decision was connected to the rhythm of the Christian year.[33] Or was it the death of his wife, Elen, in the same year that had prompted him to embark on a pilgrimage?[34] Inevitably, we cannot be sure about his exact motivations. Ninth-century English kings seem to have undertaken journeys to Rome in order to affirm their own positions of political power by receiving papal approval. Perhaps, at the meeting in Exeter in April 928— when Hywel would have rubbed shoulders with his fellow Welsh kings, Gwriad and Idwal, but also with Æthelstan himself and the leading

English magnates—he thought of strengthening his own position in the minds both of Æthelstan and the other Welsh kings by travelling to and from Rome.[35]

Another distinctive feature of Hywel's reign is his naming of his son Etguin, which appears to be an Old Welsh spelling of the English name, Edwin—the name of Æthelstan's half-brother who had died by drowning in circumstances that are now obscure.[36] Hywel's choice of the name is certainly notable. But it is again unfortunate that his motivation for its selection is unknowable. The choice could have been made positively to flatter the English royal family, or to lend credibility to his own family line, or as a clear political statement of his English loyalties. On the other hand, because Æthelstan himself had been implicated in Edwin's death, it could be interpreted as a means of casting aspersions on the English king.[37]

When Hywel attended Æthelstan's royal assemblies he would have witnessed, in addition to Æthelstan's granting of land via the diplomas drafted by 'Æthelstan A', the king's promulgation of his laws, a feature of his kingship that Æthelstan himself had perhaps particularly inherited from his grandfather, Alfred. In Wales a body of legal material was not set down in writing until the period from the early thirteenth to the early sixteenth centuries. The prologues in this later codification credit Hywel with having organised an assembly involving representatives from across Wales that then oversaw the composition of Welsh law in the tenth century.[38] These statements, written so long after Hywel's reign itself, are to be interpreted with care, not least because contemporary chronicles do not characterise Hywel as a legislator.[39] Nevertheless, the routine accrediting of Hywel with the establishment of law, and the use in Old Welsh of some technical terms which may have been borrowed from their equivalent Old English versions, may suggest that Hywel and his advisers had been influenced by what they witnessed at Æthelstan's assemblies.[40]

Another aspect of tenth-century English governance to which Hywel would have been exposed was its system of coinage. There does not seem to have been an equivalent monetary framework in Wales in the tenth century and, in fact, only one coin in the name of Hywel survives.

Inscribed in Latin with the words HOWÆL REX on the obverse, the name of the moneyer is provided on the reverse as being a certain Gillys. That the coin was an English product is indicated by the orthography of the inscription, as well as by its style, which has been linked to coins minted in the reigns of Æthelstan's successors, Edmund (939–46) and Eadred (946–55). The coin can perhaps be most closely associated with coins produced in the reign of Eadred by a moneyer also named Gillys, who worked at the very productive Chester mint in the northwest, and was therefore minted after Æthelstan's death.[41] Again, interpretation of the coin has been difficult. It could either represent English recognition of Hywel's status, perhaps designed to be a symbolic gift of some kind, or it could be an example of Hywel trying to enhance his own standing by borrowing from English precedent, not unlike his involvement in the codification of Welsh law (if that can be upheld).[42]

Whatever interpretation is favoured, it is clear that Hywel was a Welsh king possessed of unusual political success. By the end of his reign he ruled over the majority of Wales, which included Deheubarth in the south-west and Gwynedd in the north, but not the kingdoms in the south-east.[43] One notable feature of Welsh chronicle entries for the early tenth century is how devoid they are of domestic incident, of the sort of political intrigue and murder that regularly took place within and between the different kingdoms. It has been suggested that it was only because of the relative political stability within Wales that Hywel would have been able to cross the territories of his fellow Welsh kings, particularly Morgan of Glywysing and Gwent and Tewdwr of Brycheiniog, in order to attend Æthelstan's royal assemblies in England.[44] It also seems that Welsh relations with Æthelstan were relatively peaceful. It is striking, for example, that there is no definitive evidence for Hywel's (or that of other Welsh kings') involvement in the major British-Scandinavian alliance against Æthelstan at *Brunanburh* in 937.[45]

Further observations about the nature of early tenth-century English and Welsh relations can be made thanks to two texts which are very different from each other. The first is a legal document written in Old English and known as the 'Ordinance concerning the *Dunsæte*', which refers to a people who were called the *Dunsæte*—literally, the 'hill-dwellers' (*dun*, 'hill'; *sæte*, 'dwellers, people of a district'). The *Dunsæte* are said to have included both English and Welsh people and to have lived either side of a river, which the text does not explicitly name. It forms one of a group of place-names on the English and Welsh border which incorporate the place-name element *sæte*.[46] The Ordinance describes itself as an 'agreement' between the English *witan* (which could either mean the royal assembly or, more literally, a group of wise men) and the Welsh people, and it offers guidance for what should happen in a variety of different situations—for example, if one person finds that their cattle have been stolen and led across from one territory to another—or for the settlement of disputes more broadly. For a resolution to be reached, the document describes how twelve lawmen, six of them English and six Welsh, were to make decisions together.[47]

The Ordinance bristles with difficulties of interpretation, mainly concerning the precise area of land to which it refers and the date at which it was issued, which is not indicated by the text itself. Towards the close of the document, reference is made to another people who are called the Wentsæte and who are said previously to have 'belonged to the *Dunsæte*', but who are now described as owing dues to the West Saxons. Because the Wentsæte can be identified as people from the kingdom of Gwent, and because the document seems to refer to an area which embraced English and Welsh people and was both close in proximity to Gwent in south-east Wales and over which different authorities, including the West Saxons, at times claimed jurisdiction, the text as a whole is generally thought to refer to a region along the southern border between England and Wales. Most commentators suggest that this could have been the area of Archenfield, just to the south-west of Hereford, and that it involved land on both sides of the River Wye. The lack of an explicit date, or mention of individuals by which the document could be precisely dated, has meant that the Ordinance has been dated to various different periods, mainly on the basis of comparison with other English legal texts and concepts. For a long time the text was thought to relate most naturally to Æthelstan's period of rule, but more recently an argument has been made that it belongs to the late tenth or early eleventh century.[48] Whatever the precise date of the text's original composition, and whatever the exact geographical location to which it refers, it represents an extraordinary survival of the type of everyday practical documentation which must have regulated, or attempted to regulate, routine interactions between those living on the Anglo-Welsh border. If it is to be dated to a period later than Æthelstan's reign, many of its principles may nevertheless have applied also to the early tenth century.

The second text which provides detail about Anglo-Welsh relations in the period takes the form of a prophetic poem entitled *Armes Prydein Vawr* (Great Prophecy of Britain), written by a Welsh author. Like the Ordinance, *Armes Prydein* has proved difficult to date. One of its editors, Sir Ifor Williams, placed it directly in Æthelstan's reign to about the year 930, but others have suggested that it should be dated to a slightly later period in the tenth century, perhaps to the reign of Edmund, Æthelstan's successor.[49] No matter what view one takes about its date of composition, the poem is extraordinary for the vitriolic stance it takes against the English. It foretells how the Welsh, supported by the men of Dublin, the Irish, the men of Cornwall, the men of Strathclyde/Cumbria, and the Bretons, will rise up in battle against 'the foreigners', by which it means the English, bring ruthless destruction on the 'great king' (Old Welsh: *mechteyrn*) and his forces, inflict great shame on them, and ultimately expel them from Britain. In doing so the poet, who may have been a member of the St David's community in south-west Wales, or of the kingdom of Gwynedd in the north,[50] delights in describing the bravery of the Welsh in fulsome terms ('They will rush into battle like a bear from the mountain to avenge the bloodshed of their fellows'), and in gory detail the slaughter they will inflict on the English ('There will be heads split open without brains, women will be widowed, and horses riderless, there will be terrible wailing before the rush of warriors, many wounded by hand').[51] The poet resents English expeditions into Wales, and a repeated cause of fury is the level of tax inflicted on the Welsh by the English and collected by the king's 'stewards' (Old Welsh: *meiryon*). If the poem does belong to the period of Æthelstan's time as king, and if he is in fact the 'great king' alluded to, the complaints about tax recall William of Malmesbury's account of Æthelstan imposing a large annual tribute on the Welsh.[52] At one stage in the poem the 'stewards' sent to collect tax are said to have come from Cirencester, a place-name rendered as Caer Geri in Old Welsh.[53] We saw earlier that Æthelstan had convened a royal assembly in Cirencester in 935 at which he had been keen to display his imperial pretensions, not least by emphasising the *Romanitas* (Romanness) of Cirencester itself. We cannot know how widely spread through tenth-century Wales was the hatred of the English on display in *Armes Prydein*, but the poem provides an indication of how at least one Welsh author experienced English overlordship in the period. And it brings an added dimension to our understanding of how the Welshmen present at Æthelstan's 935 meeting may have felt.

Æthelstan and the North: Strathclyde/Cumbria and Alba

It is difficult to reconstruct the relations of Æthelstan's immediate predecessors with the northern kingdoms of Alt Clut and Pictland (the predecessors of Strathclyde/Cumbria and Alba, respectively). West Saxon kings of the late ninth and early tenth centuries were predominantly focused on areas further south, and sources from northern Britain are scarce. The actions of vikings were a constant source of concern: in addition to viking attacks within England, Alfred and Edward had to contend with the possibility of invasions coming from the north through either Strathclyde/Cumbria or Alba, or a potential coalition of vikings from multiple regions.

Events of the mid-860s are illustrative of the problem. At about the same time that Ívarr is thought to have been leading the 'great army' in England in 866–67, his brothers, Óláf and Auisle, left Ireland and made for Fortriu, where they 'plundered the entire Pictish country and took away hostages from them'.[54] According to the *Chronicle of the Kings of Alba*, Óláf (it does not mention Auisle) remained in Pictland for a period of time, before sailing back to Ireland, where he can be found by 867.[55] By 870 Óláf had returned to northern Britain, this time in the company of Ívarr. Their focus on this occasion was further to the west, on Alt Clut (Dumbarton Rock) in the mouth of the River Clyde, which was attacked and, following a four-month siege, left in ruins. The event had profound repercussions for the then king of Alt Clut, Artgal (d. 872), who seems to have relocated the centre of his kingdom further east and inland. And, during the late ninth and early tenth centuries, the kingdom (now called 'Strathclyde' by contemporaries or the 'land of the Cumbrians' by early English sources, hence Strathclyde/Cumbria) seems to have reconfigured itself and expanded its interests further south, bounded ultimately by the River Eamont.[56]

Despite the deaths of Ívarr in 873 and Óláf in 874 (the latter at the hands of the then king of the Scots, Constantine I), viking attacks nevertheless continued in the north.[57] The *Chronicle of the Kings of Alba* refers to an 875 battle at Dollar, to the east of modern Stirling, which was followed by widespread slaughter of the Scots, and by the vikings spending a year in Pictland.[58] Also in 875 the *Anglo-Saxon Chronicle* reports that the viking leader Hálfdan, the brother of Óláf, having left a base in Mercia, had moved to the River Tyne, from where he led attacks against the Scots and the Strathclyde Britons.[59] Either Hálfdan had come north to avenge his brother's murder, or, in the wake of Óláf's death, he recognised that new opportunities had opened for him.[60] Precious little is known about Alfred's own reaction to viking activities in northern Britain during this time. Passages in the *Historia de Sancto Cuthberto* (History of Saint Cuthbert), which describe a special bond between Alfred and St Cuthbert's community, may at least indicate his cultivation of their support.[61]

In the 880s and early 890s, our sources suggest that viking activity in northern Britain abated, as it did in England.[62] But the reign of Donald, king of the Scots, saw renewed viking attacks, which culminated in the king's murder at their hands in Dunnottar in 900.[63] We have already seen that the 902 expulsion of vikings from Dublin led to their movement eastwards from Ireland, towards the coasts of the Welsh, English, and Scottish kingdoms. The *Fragmentary Annals of Ireland* contain an account of the flight of the viking leader Ingimundr who, having failed to gain a foothold in Anglesey, reached an agreement with Æthelflæd of Mercia that he and his men could inhabit the Chester area (a pact subsequently broken by Ingimundr, who tried to take Chester for himself).[64]

The text has suffered from pseudo-historical embellishments and contains legendary material. But its core details—that vikings were seeking out new settlements in north-western Britain—are corroborated by the evidence of place-names which, roughly from the Wirral northwards into Dumfries and Galloway, show the influence of both Gaelic and Scandinavian linguistic elements.[65] The Scandinavian settlement of this region of the north-west coast may well have been taking place at roughly the same time that the kingdom of Strathclyde/Cumbria was also expanding into similar areas.

During the reign of Donald's successor, Constantine II, vikings continued to attack the kingdom of Alba. An assault in 904 may again have involved the dynasty of Ívarr, since his grandson, another Ívarr, is recorded in Irish annals as being killed.[66] The Cuerdale Hoard, which consists of some seven thousand coins, including those of Arabic, Frankish, and Italian origin, and about eleven hundred non-numismatic silver items, including ingots, arm-rings, bracelets, belt-fittings, and hack silver, was deposited ca. 905 on the southern bank of the River Ribble in Lancashire, near Preston. Now housed in the British Museum, it may have been intended as a payment to a viking force who were tasked with regaining influence in Dublin.[67] Possibly as a result of these growing tensions on the northern and north-western borders of their kingdoms, Edward and his sister, Æthelflæd, are recorded as taking a number of measures to shore up their domestic positions. These included the establishment of peace with those in East Anglia and Northumbria (which included a viking population) in 906, but then also the conducting of war in Northumbria in 909 and at Tettenhall, to the north-west of Wolverhampton, in 910.[68]

We have seen that by 917 two grandsons of Ívarr, Ragnall and Sihtric, had arrived back in Ireland, and Sihtric had reclaimed Dublin.[69] The reestablishment of the dynasty of Ívarr in Dublin increased the threat of attack on Edward's kingdom and on the kingdoms of Strathclyde/Cumbria and Alba. According to the *Fragmentary Annals of Ireland*, it was at about this time that Æthelflæd came to an agreement with those in Alba and Strathclyde/Cumbria that they would provide mutual support if in the future any of the parties suffered a viking attack.[70] As with the text concerning Ingimundr in the *Annals*, there are again problems with this passage, which contains eleventh-century material.[71] But it is nevertheless emblematic of the type of arrangements between neighbouring kingdoms in the north that would have made practical sense in the face of external threats.

Events of 918 showed the importance of joint action. In a battle of that year at Corbridge on the River Tyne, the viking leader Ragnall, having crossed over from Ireland, is said to have fought against the men of Alba and their king, Constantine. According to the *Historia de Sancto Cuthberto*, Constantine was in fact involved at the request of Ealdred of Bamburgh, and together they opposed Ragnall. Owain, then king of Strathclyde/Cumbria, is not known to have been a participant in the battle but the presence of the powerful Ragnall in close proximity would have given him serious cause for concern. The outcome of the battle is recorded differently by surviving sources, which may indicate a degree of success for both sides.[72] By 919 Ragnall had taken control in York, thus repeating the pattern of viking leaders from Dublin claiming power in Northumbria; perhaps his adoption of power there had always been his ultimate aim when he set out from Ireland in 918.

In English territory, Edward reacted swiftly to the potential threat in the north. In 918, having taken control of Mercia after the death of Æthelflæd, he strengthened the burh at Nottingham. In 919 he built a burh in the north-west at Thelwall and had the Manchester burh repaired and staffed with an army, and in 920 he built a second burh in Nottingham, before ordering the construction of another burh further to the north, in Bakewell.[73] After this campaign of burh building, the *Anglo-Saxon Chronicle* describes how Edward was chosen as 'father and lord' by a number of rulers, including Constantine II, king of the Scots, and his people; Ragnall; the lords of Bamburgh; and an unnamed king of the 'Strathclyde Welsh', who may have been Owain, together with 'all the Strathclyde Welsh'.[74] It seems unlikely that Edward, who had so recently taken control of Mercia, would have been able to extend his authority over these northern rulers. It is more likely that version 'A' of the *Anglo-Saxon Chronicle*, which preserves the record, and which was written in support of Edward's regime, was trying to suggest the high levels of his power, no matter the reality. The annal may reflect the fact that in 920 these rulers had come together in order to reach an agreement about their mutual spheres of authority, which must have been in a state of flux since Ragnall's arrival. If the detail of their choosing Edward as their lord can be accepted, it may have represented a pragmatic way for all of the northern parties to reach agreement.[75]

Ragnall died in 921.[76] Perhaps aware of Ragnall's decline, his kinsman, Sihtric, had left Dublin the previous year and landed in England, where he raided Davenport, just to the south of Manchester, the area that Edward had been fortifying.[77] Sihtric would in due course take Ragnall's place in York, while another grandson of Ívarr, a man named Guthfrith, had arrived in Dublin in 921.[78] We will meet Guthfrith again soon.

Following Æthelstan's accession as king in 924, it was imperative that he secure the support of Sihtric and those in York. By 926 he had arranged for a marriage alliance between an unnamed sister of his and Sihtric himself. Although surviving texts provide little information about the nature and extent of Sihtric's own power at York, coins minted in his name, which were in circulation in the east midlands, beyond the traditional confines of the Northumbrian kingdom, suggest that he may have wielded considerable authority.[79]

Sihtric died only a year after his marriage to Æthelstan's sister—an event which, as we have seen, allowed Æthelstan in 927 to add Northumbria to his dominion and for 'England' to be formed.[80] William of Malmesbury preserves detail not found in contemporary sources. As we saw in chapter 2, William relates that Sihtric's brother, Guthfrith, fled to Scotland, and Sihtric's son, Óláf, fled to Ireland. Æthelstan threatened King Constantine II of the Scots and King Owain of Strathclyde/Cumbria with military action, so William tells us, unless Guthfrith were handed over. William states that Constantine and Owain chose to submit to Æthelstan at Dacre, near Eamont Bridge, and Æthelstan was made godfather to Constantine's son, but that Guthfrith launched an ultimately unsuccessful bid to seize York for himself.[81]

When compared to the annal in the *Anglo-Saxon Chronicle* for 927, William's account preserves novel elements whose veracity is not easily ascertained. The first involves the identity of those said to have submitted to Æthelstan; for William this included Owain of Strathclyde/Cumbria, who was not mentioned in the *Anglo-Saxon Chronicle* entry, where an Owain of Gwent is named instead.[82] It is possible either that only one Owain had been present and that the *Anglo-Saxon Chronicle* and William each identify him differently, or that both Owains had been present and that each text simply listed one. It is notable in this connection that William only lists two people as having been present, Owain of Strathclyde/Cumbria and Constantine II, compared to four in the *Chronicle*'s account. It may be that William never intended to provide a full record and that these two kings were named because they feature in the narrative William then provided about the flight of Guthfrith to Scotland. For reasons discussed below, it is entirely plausible that Owain of Strathclyde/Cumbria was present. The second difference in detail is that Guthfrith, the very same man (a descendant of Ívarr) who had established himself in Dublin following the death of Ragnall in 921, launched his own bid for power in York. That Æthelstan had been obliged to deal with a threat from Guthfrith in York is also recorded by an entry in two other late sources: version 'E' of the *Anglo-Saxon Chronicle* for the year 927 and the northern compilation, the *Historia Regum*.[83] The *Annals of Ulster* note plainly that in 927 Guthfrith had left Dublin and that he was back again 'within six months'.[84] In 2007 a substantial viking hoard was found in the valley of the River Nidd. Now known as the 'Vale of York viking hoard', it contains over six hundred coins, as well as jewellery, ingots, hack silver, and other precious artefacts. The items can be traced to many different parts of the viking world, including Afghanistan, continental Europe, Ireland, modern northern Russia, and Scandinavia. The most important point for our present purposes is that the deposition of the hoard has been associated with the disturbed events in York immediately following the meeting at Eamont Bridge. It is impossible to connect Guthfrith specifically with the hoard, but the location in which it was found, near the River Nidd, would have formed one area through which a viking returning to Ireland from York would have travelled.[85]

Because the site of the 927 meeting near Eamont Bridge may well have been at the southern edge of the kingdom of Strathclyde/Cumbria, it is highly likely that the northern Owain had been present. The meeting's location constituted powerful testimony to the strategic significance held by Strathclyde/Cumbria at this period: it was both a landing point for vikings travelling from Ireland to England and an area in which there had already been a degree of Scandinavian settlement. Æthelstan's father, Edward, and his aunt, Æthelflæd, had been building up their defenses in the north-west. Sihtric's death may have provided Æthelstan with the opportunity to demonstrate his own authority in the region. He would surely have wanted the involvement of the then king of Strathclyde/Cumbria. William of Malmesbury's suggestion that Æthelstan, following Guthfrith's flight to Scotland, had asked both Constantine II and Owain for his return raises the possibility that they had been acting in an alliance, or that it might have suited their mutual interests to harbour one of Æthelstan's enemies.

Very little detail survives concerning Æthelstan's actions in the north between 927 and 934. We have seen that, in the south and east of Northumbria, in York and its surroundings, the English king attempted to impose his own governmental structures, introducing coins in his name and using diplomas that had been drafted by his own royal scribe. He also issued legislation in such a way that at least in theory there should be one coinage throughout his newly constituted English kingdom. The reality of Æthelstan's reach may have been rather different, and he may have depended on the loyalty of local secular and ecclesiastical magnates to ensure the success of his rule. And, once he stepped beyond the River Tees, he seems to have entered a zone in which he could no longer dictate the terms on which grants of land were made.[86] Meanwhile, the strategic importance of the north-western area of the kingdom continued, signalled by Æthelstan's gifting of Amounderness, which was situated on the north-west coast and bounded by the Rivers Cocker, Hodder, and Ribble and by the Irish Sea, to the west of modern Preston and near Blackpool. The area itself formed another landing point for vikings crossing the Irish Sea from Dublin. On disembarking they could have picked up the Roman road that begins near Hardhorn and extends to Ribchester, before joining other Roman roads that run east through Skipton and Ilkley to York.[87]

In 934 Æthelstan moved against Constantine and the Scots, and possibly also against Owain of Strathclyde/Cumbria. The *Anglo-Saxon Chronicle* reports, without elaborating further, that he sent an army and a navy to Scotland and inflicted devastation.[88] Thanks to the diploma record, we know that by 7 June of that year Æthelstan and his followers had made it to Nottingham. They then continued north, and the *Historia de Sancto Cuthberto* describes how the king and his 'great army' (*magnum exercitum*) paid a visit to the Cuthbertine community, which later Durham records suggest was then situated in Chester-le-Street. Æthelstan is credited with having made various generous donations of precious objects and of lands.[89] The *Historia Regum* states that, having moved into Alba, Æthelstan's army reached as far north as Dunnottar (*Dunfoeder*) and the mountains of Fortriu (*Wertermorum*), and that his navy made it even further north, to Caithness (*Cathenes*).[90]

Unfortunately, we are not provided with any more detail about Æthelstan's military expedition or why it was undertaken. Were his army and navy acting in unison, despite ending up in different places (Dunnottar and Caithness, respectively)? We have already seen that Æthelstan was in Nottingham on 7 June 934. We also know that, having completed his campaign in Scotland, he was back in England (in Buckingham) by 13 September 934, when he once more issued a grant of land. The large distances involved (the leg between Nottingham and Dunnottar alone is some four hundred miles) and relatively short time frame (of about three months) makes it virtually certain that the army must have been transported part of the way by the navy. A sea route had the added benefit of avoiding the Scottish interior, where the English army would have encountered numerous settlements and key sites. One surviving Roman road that heads in a north-easterly direction, for example, would have passed directly by Scone, which was an important symbolic site for King Constantine.[91] That Æthelstan was acting so far to the north of his kingdom, and penetrating into the kingdom of Alba, demonstrates the scale and ambition of his campaign.

What had prompted Æthelstan into action? Both the 'Worcester Chronicle' and the *Historia Regum*, which relies on the Worcester text for its information, suggest that Constantine had broken the terms of a 'treaty' (*foedus*) that he and Æthelstan had previously agreed, and that, after Æthelstan's military action, Constantine had been compelled to hand over his son as a hostage to Æthelstan.[92] No more detail is provided about, for example, whether or not the agreement near Eamont Bridge in 927 was the one violated by Constantine or whether there had been some subsequent treaty brokered but not recorded in our sources. And there may have been other reasons why Æthelstan intervened militarily. Attention has been drawn to the fact that in the years 933–34 three important individuals died: Edwin, Æthelstan's half-brother (in 933); Guthfrith of the dynasty of Ívarr (in 934); and Ealdred of Bamburgh (in 934).[93] Their removal may have provided Æthelstan with a degree of freedom in the north and west to explore new possibilities. Alternatively, Ealdred's death may have prompted Constantine to pursue his own claims to parts of Northumbria, perhaps mindful of his previous involvement at the 918 battle of Corbridge. If so, this may have been the action from the king of the Scots that the 'Worcester Chronicle' and *Historia Regum* describes as breaking the treaty with Æthelstan.[94]

A further possibility is raised by Symeon of Durham, a twelfth-century historian, in his *Libellus de exordio atque procursu istius hoc est Dunhelmensis Ecclesie* (Tract on the origins and progress of this the Church of Durham). According to this later testimony, Constantine was not Æthelstan's only target in 934, and Owain of Strathclyde/Cumbria was also 'put to flight'.[95] Symeon is the sole source for Owain's involvement in these events of 934, which makes his text difficult to evaluate. Symeon's naming of Constantine and Owain as the joint targets of Æthelstan's aggression in 934 may suggest that they had been acting as partners in opposition to the English king's wishes. A passage of text written by William of Malmesbury, in his account of events in 927, has already raised the possibility that Constantine and Owain had been acting together when harbouring the fugitive Guthfrith. Perhaps the two northern kings were once more allied against the English king. If so, it is possible either that Owain had supported Constantine in the military encounters that took place in Alba, from which he was 'put to flight', or that Æthelstan had conducted a separate campaign within Strathclyde/Cumbria which has not been recorded in surviving sources.[96] Constantine may also have been involved in yet another alliance: it has been pointed out that the king of Scots gave Old Norse names to his son, Illulb (Old Norse: Hildulfr), and to two grandsons, which perhaps suggests that he had been cultivating ties with Scandinavians.[97]

The 'Worcester Chronicle' and *Historia Regum* report that, 'with peace restored' (*paceque redintegrata*), Æthelstan left Scotland and returned home, but they do not offer any further details about what terms of peace may have been agreed.[98] A hint is provided by English royal records: in the 13 September 934 diploma issued at Buckingham noted above, Constantine himself is listed among the witnesses to the transaction. It is the first time that his presence is documented at one of Æthelstan's royal assemblies.[99] For those in attendance on that September day, there could have been no clearer demonstration of Æthelstan's authority than his being able to require the king of the Scots to attend him in a royal assembly so far from the base of his power in the north. Yet Constantine was treated with respect: he is titled *subregulus*, as the Welsh kings had been from 928, and he is allowed to attest immediately after Æthelstan himself. It is much to be regretted that the late manuscript copy of this particular diploma is deficient at this stage: the scribe responsible omitted the names of the remaining witnesses and after Constantine's attestation simply records *cum multis aliis* (with many others). It would be good to know if there had been other *subreguli* present that day—perhaps the Welsh kings who had accompanied Æthelstan at least some of the way and maybe even to war in Scotland itself, and particularly Hywel Dda, who, prior to this, was always the top-ranked of the *subreguli*.

Three months later, on 16 December 934, Æthelstan convened another royal assembly, this time in the south-west of his kingdom in Frome, Somerset. If its witness-list can be accepted as a genuine record of attendance, then it appears that only one *subregulus* was present on this occasion: the Welsh king, Hywel Dda. Perhaps the location of the assembly made it easier for him than for the others to attend. Constantine seems to have returned to Alba for the Christmas period in 934 after what must have been a turbulent summer. By 935 the king of the Scots was once more present at Æthelstan's royal assembly, that held at Cirencester, where he attests in first place, with Owain of Strathclyde/ Cumbria in second place, both of them ranked higher than the three Welsh sub-kings there that day.[100] When Owain had previously been present at a royal assembly in 931, he had been listed as the lowest-ranking *subregulus* behind the three Welsh *subreguli*. For whatever reason, Æthelstan and his advisers deemed it important to recognise these two northern kings, over and above the Welsh kings. Perhaps, given the recent war in Alba and the unprecedented obligation for the king of Scots to attend the English king's assembly, it was all the more important that their high standing was publicly acknowledged so that they were less likely to be insulted. As we have seen, the meeting at Cirencester had been arranged to convey a sense of Æthelstan's *imperium*. We can only imagine how this would have been received by the British kings who witnessed the occasion. Constantine would never again attest an English king's diplomas. Owain would be present for one more of Æthelstan's royal assemblies, on 21 December 935 in Dorchester, at which he is again afforded prominence over the Welsh *subreguli*.[101] The *Anglo-Saxon Chronicle* contains no record for the years 935–36. When it picks up the story again in 937, it inserts a poem which recounts one of the most famous episodes of the early medieval period, the Battle of *Brunanburh*.[102]

Brunanburh

Æthelstan's imperial pretensions and warring actions had created bitter enemies who were keen to reassert themselves. By 937 Óláf Guthfrithson, viking king of Dublin, and Constantine, king of Scots, had joined forces in order to engage Æthelstan in battle. According to an entry in two northern sources, Symeon of Durham's *Libellus de exordio* and the *Historia Regum*, Owain, king of Strathclyde/Cumbria, may also have been involved in their alliance.[103] All three had good reason for their anti-Æthelstan stance. As recently as 935 both Constantine and Owain had been required to attend Æthelstan's royal assemblies. And Óláf may have felt that his own ambitions to rule in northern England were being thwarted by Æthelstan's control and intervention at York. Events within Ireland itself may also have been a factor in Óláf's decision to act. For a number of years, vikings of Limerick in the west had been in competition with vikings of Dublin, in struggles that had also embroiled members of different native Irish dynasties, across various regions of Ireland. Matters had come to a head in 937 when Óláf defeated his Limerick opponent, another Óláf, in an encounter on the River Shannon and imprisoned him.[104] The securing of his position in Ireland in 937 may well have emboldened Óláf to consider military intervention in Æthelstan's England.[105]

For the majority of its account of Æthelstan's reign, the *Anglo-Saxon Chronicle* is relatively exiguous. The seventy-three-lines poem in its annal for 937, which commemorates the Battle of *Brunanburh* that year, stands in stark contrast. Poems are only rarely inserted into the *Anglo-Saxon Chronicle* and, when they are, it is in order to mark events that were of particular significance. The details supplied regarding *Brunanburh* leave no doubt that it was the most important military encounter of Æthelstan's reign, one which threatened everything he had achieved since his accession in 924.

The poem, written by an author whose identity is unknown but who may have been Mercian, is composed in a linguistic style and metre that is traditional, rooted in the customs and rules of heroic Old English verse.[106] It celebrates the way in which Æthelstan, who is described as a 'lord of nobles, dispenser of treasure to men', and his half-brother, Edmund, defeated the alliance that had been joined against them, and stresses that they were the 'sons of Edward'. Numerous arguments have been made concerning its possible date of composition, with some seeing the reign of Æthelstan as its most likely context and others suggesting that the mention of Edmund links it to his reign—that is, the period 939–46.[107] In Old English verse enlivened by dense patterns of alliteration, Æthelstan and Edmund are said to have led men from Mercia and Wessex, to have 'won by the sword's edge undying glory in battle' and to have 'clove the shield-wall, hewed the linden-wood shields with hammered swords'. Soon after the battle began, the poet describes how the English pursued their enemies (who must quickly have turned in flight) for a whole day. According to the poem, five kings and seven of Óláf's earls were killed, in addition to a 'countless host of seamen and Scots'. Constantine is said to have lost his own son in the encounter. The poet declares that neither Óláf nor Constantine had any reason to boast in their actions. Óláf was driven back to Dublin with only a few of his men, and Constantine, whose old age is alluded to in the descriptions 'hoary-haired warrior' and 'grey-haired . . . the old and wily one', fled back to Scotland. Æthelstan and Edmund are then said to have 'returned together to their own country, the land of the West Saxons, exulting in the battle' and to have left the corpses of the felled Scandinavians and Scots to animal scavengers.[108] As noted above, the participation of Owain, king of Strathclyde/Cumbria, in the battle is mentioned only in two northern texts, not in the poem itself. Neither text reports what happened to Owain, and it is possible that he is one of the five kings said by the poet to have been killed.[109]

One famous obstacle to our understanding of the battle is the location in which it is said to have taken place and which has so far eluded certain identification. According to the poem as transmitted in some copies of the *Anglo-Saxon Chronicle*, the battle occurred 'around *Brunanburh*'; in other versions of the *Chronicle*, the place-name is spelled as *Brunnanburh* or as *Brunanbyrig/Brunanbyri*.[110] Etymologically, the place-name *Brunanburh*, which is thought to be the earliest extant version of the name, consists of two elements: *Bruna* or *Brune*, which may either refer to a personal name or to a name for a river, and *burh*, which means 'fortification'. The form spelled *Brunnanburh* could, in its first element, represent a version of the Old English word *burne* (stream, brook, river), in which the letters *u* and *r* have been transposed. If this were true, the place-name would have the meaning of 'fortification by the stream'.[111] Other sources provide different place-names again—for example, *Brunandune* in the *Chronicle* of Æthelweard and *Wendune/Weondune* in Symeon of Durham's *Libellus de exordio* and in the *Historia Regum*. Symeon also suggests that '*Weondune* . . . is called by another name *Æt Brunnanwerc* or *Brunnanbyrig*'.[112] William of Malmesbury, in his history, uses the names *Brunefeld* and *Bruneford*. In the Scottish *Chronicle of the Kings of Alba* the name used is *Duinbrunde*, while in the Welsh *Annales Cambriae* it is *Brune*, and, in the *Annals of Clonmacnoise*, it is described as the *plaines of othlynn*.[113] These further place-names introduce the possibility that the site in question may have had some association with a 'hill' (i.e., the *dun* element in Æthelweard and Symeon),[114] and with a 'field' or area of land suitable for a battle (i.e., the *feld* in William of Malmesbury). The element *weorc* (in Symeon) is synonymous with *burh* and has the same meaning of 'fortification', while the *dun* in *Duinbrunde* appears to be a Gaelic version of the Old English word *burh*.[115] The *Annals of Clonmacnoise* only survive as a seventeenth-century English translation, which means that their term, *plaines of othlynn*, could have been corrupted at a stage in its transmission. Various possible meanings have been suggested, including that it could ultimately refer to an area in the north-west of England known as the Lyme, in Cheshire.[116]

From the poem itself we learn that, in order to reach *Brunanburh*, Óláf had to travel over the Irish Sea, Constantine had to journey south from Scotland, and Æthelstan and Edmund had also left their kingdom in Wessex. When Óláf and his men flee the battle they are said to have 'put out in their studded ships on to *Dingesmere*, to make for Dublin across the deep water'. The meaning and identity of *Dingesmere* has presented another problem: it may be composed of the elements *þing* (meeting, assembly) and *mere* (pond, lake, pool), which, when combined, constituted a place-name to which we will return.[117] Given that the poem describes Constantine as returning to Scotland after the battle, and given that Æthelstan and Edmund are also described as returning to Wessex, it seems most probable that the battle had taken place at some location in the north, presumably within England. Óláf's escape by sea may suggest that it had been close to the coast or to a major river. A passage from *Egils saga*, which refers to a battle on 'Vínheiðr', and which provides extra geographical description, has sometimes also been used in the search for *Brunanburh*.[118]

A location in Northumbria satisfies the broad geographical criteria set out by the poem itself.[119] But was this location in the east or the west? The most logical answer is that it must have been in the west. It seems unthinkable that, in order to reach the battle in the first place, Óláf would have sailed either north, around the top of Scotland, or south, around the coast of England, in order to arrive in the east. A location in the west also satisfies the poem's implication that Óláf and his men were able to flee directly from the battle back to Dublin. As we have seen, generations of vikings based in Dublin had been travelling to and from Britain across the Irish Sea.

That said, the 'Worcester Chronicle' (and the *Historia Regum*, which depends on the 'Worcester Chronicle' at this point) preserves the tradition, not found in the poem, that Óláf came to England for the battle via the River Humber—in other words, in the east.[120] Partly on the basis of this detail, a number of locations in Yorkshire have been suggested for the identity of *Brunanburh*.[121] It would be unwise to rely too closely on the testimony of the 'Worcester Chronicle', which depends on the poem in the *Anglo-Saxon Chronicle* for its account. It has been pointed out that the 'Worcester Chronicle' contains two textual errors. The first involves its claim that Constantine's flight back to Alba involved travel by sea, which does not find support in the poem. The second involves the conflation of Óláf Guthfrithson (described in the poem as 'chief of the Norsemen'), who had been involved at *Brunanburh*, with a subsequent Óláf (Sihtricson) who is recorded in the 'Worcester Chronicle' as becoming king of Northumbria in 941 and who is there erroneously given the title 'king of the Norsemen'.[122] With this confusion of Óláf in mind, it would be understandable why this twelfth-century text inserted a reference to the River Humber, which formed the principal boundary for the Northumbrian kingdom and also a point of entry for various fleets in the period.[123]

Already in the seventeenth century historians were trying to locate *Brunanburh*, and over forty possible locations have now been suggested. Given the parameters put forward in the poem itself—that Óláf came from Ireland and fled back to Dublin as the battle disintegrated around him, that Constantine fled north to Alba at the battle's conclusion, and that Æthelstan and Edmund returned to their own base in Wessex—it is overwhelmingly likely that we should be searching for a location in the north-west of England. In terms of its linguistic derivation, it has been suggested that the only possible modern place-name successor to *Brunanburh* is Bromborough, on the Wirral, an area which also satisfies the various topographical elements of the place-name that have been identified above.[124] For Paul Cavill, and for a number of other historians, Bromborough is the most compelling identification. And Bromborough, and the area of the Wirral in general, certainly fit the historical context: a variety of Scandinavian-influenced place-names on the Wirral

Peninsula suggest that there had been a degree of viking settlement there, and viking artefacts found at Meols on the coastal tip indicate that there were links into the Irish Sea trading network.[125] If Bromborough is correct, Cavill further suggests that *Dingesmere*, from where Óláf and his men are said to have set sail to Dublin, may have lain directly opposite Bromborough, probably in the area of modern Heswall.[126]

When Æthelstan died in 939, Óláf Guthfrithson was able to become king in Northumbria. Because his acquisition of power was therefore only delayed by two years, some historians have downplayed the significance attributed to the 937 battle.[127] The suggestion seems unnecessary. In fact, Æthelstan had managed to uphold his claims to rule across Britain in the face of the fiercest opposition, to be the *rex totius Britanniae* that he had advertised on his coinage. The *Brunanburh* poet himself suggests that there had 'never yet in this island before' been a 'greater slaughter of a host made by the edge of the sword' since the arrival of the Angles and Saxons in the fifth century. This does not seem to have been mere hyperbole since, unusually, the battle is not solely recorded in English sources, but also, as we have seen, in Irish, Scandinavian, Scottish, and Welsh texts. The *Annals of Ulster* describe it as 'a great, lamentable and horrible battle . . . cruelly fought between the Saxons and the Norsemen, in which several thousands of Norsemen, who are uncounted, fell'.[128] Æthelweard, who was writing in the late tenth century, provides vivid testimony for the significance of the occasion in the popular imagination when he describes how 'it is still called the "great battle"'. In Æthelweard's estimation, Æthelstan's success at *Brunanburh* meant that 'the fields of Britain were consolidated into one' and that 'there was peace everywhere'.[129] Æthelstan's defeat of Óláf, Constantine and Owain constituted a critical moment in the early history of England. Had the outcome been reversed, Æthelstan's creation of the English kingdom would have been shattered. The longer the enlarged kingdom endured, the stronger the blueprint that would be provided for future English kings.

6

European Renown

WHEN WILLIAM of Malmesbury composed his account of Æthelstan's reign in the early twelfth century, he was enthusiastic about Æthelstan's standing in continental Europe. 'Kings of other nations', he writes, 'thought themselves fortunate if they could buy his [i.e., Æthelstan's] friendship either by family alliances or by gifts'.[1] Connections between England and Europe were nothing new. Æthelberht (d. 616), the seventh-century king of Kent, for example, had married Bertha, the daughter of the Merovingian king of the Franks, Charibert I (d. 567). And the movement of people to and from Europe was maintained at many different levels of society: the eighth-century Northumbrian scholar, Alcuin, was poached by Charlemagne for his court, and later played a major role in the Carolingian Renaissance, while continental scholars like Grimbald of Saint-Bertin and John the Old Saxon came from Europe to England, where they found a home with King Alfred the Great. Goods as well as people crossed the channel: a famous letter dated 796 from Charlemagne to Offa, king of the Mercians, mentions both the need for traders to be able to move between kingdoms and also a request by Offa for 'black stones' to be sent by Charlemagne in exchange for cloaks.[2] It has been suggested that the 'black stones' were in fact marble columns of black porphyry and that they may ultimately have come from Rome.[3]

At times, marriage alliances could be organised in order to cultivate connections between English and continental kingdoms (although

marriages between the royal family and other English aristocratic families were more usual). Æthelstan's great-grandfather, King Æthelwulf of
Wessex (d. 858), had married Judith, the daughter of Charles the Bald
(d. 877), king of the West Franks. Æthelwulf must have been over fifty
years old at the time, while Judith was about twelve. It is likely that this
particular marriage had been inspired by the mutual benefits an alliance
would bring at a time when both Æthelwulf's and Charles's kingdoms
were being threatened by viking attacks.[4] The *Annals of St-Bertin* record
how in October 856 Æthelwulf, on his way back from a journey to
Rome, was married to Judith in Verberie in northern France where she
was crowned queen by Hincmar, archbishop of Rheims. Æthelwulf is
said to have 'formally conferred on her the title of queen, which was
something not customary before then to him or to his people'.[5] As the
Annals suggest, the marriage was all the more extraordinary because the
king's consort was not usually accorded such a high status in Wessex.
And, in the kingdom of the West Franks, it was unusual for a marriage
to take place outside the close network of Frankish nobles.[6] Remarkably, following Æthelwulf's death little over a year later in January 858,
Judith then married his own son, Æthelbald, an event that shocked
Asser, who described it as being inimical to both pagans and Christians.[7] When Æthelbald himself died within two years, in 860, Judith
undertook another political marriage, this time with Count Baldwin I
of Flanders (d. 879). Their son, the future Count Baldwin II (d. 918),
would go on to marry Ælfthryth, the daughter of King Alfred the Great
(and Æthelstan's aunt) at some point in the period 893–99, thus extending relations between England and Flanders. Flanders itself, which was
located on the North Sea coast and extended beyond the modern region of that name, was the closest continental point of contact with
England. It also contained a major port, Quentovic, which was situated
at the mouth of the River Canche, and which by the ninth century had
long facilitated trade with England. Flanders was, like many other areas
of Europe, coming under significant viking pressure in the mid-ninth
century. And, in 842, Quentovic itself was targeted by vikings in a raid
that resulted in the capture and slaughter of many of its residents.[8] It

seems likely, therefore, that the marriage of Baldwin II and Ælfthryth was once more driven by the need for mutual assistance at a time of heightened external threat.

In order to extend his own influence, Æthelstan made use of marriage alliances to an unprecedented extent. In England his full sister by their mother Ecgwynn, whose identity is not certain, was married in 926 to Sihtric Cáech, the viking leader based in York.[9] The union was intended to secure Northumbria's allegiance at a time when that could not be taken for granted. But it was the marriages of his half-sisters that afforded Æthelstan a continental network of authority far from his base in Wessex, and which witnessed the royal women becoming very influential in their own right. Following the ninth-century collapse of the Carolingian empire, the early tenth century in Europe was in general a time of great political uncertainty and change. As aristocratic families competed for influence and political boundaries were in a state of flux,[10] Æthelstan attempted to take advantage of the political dynamics and to increase his presence on the Continent, arranging for his half-sisters to be married into some of the most important continental dynasties of the day. This tactic had been adopted by Æthelstan's father, Edward, when he arranged for Eadgifu, his daughter by his second wife (who was therefore Æthelstan's half-sister), to be married ca. 919 to Charles the Simple, king of the West Franks. And then, from the mid-920s to about 930, three other of Æthelstan's half-sisters, Eadhild, Eadgyth and Ælfgifu/Eadgifu, were married to Hugh the Great (duke of the Franks), to Otto I (king of the East Franks and later king of Italy and emperor), and to Louis (the brother of King Rudolf II of Burgundy), respectively.[11]

Charles the Simple, who was son of Louis the Stammerer and grandson of Charles the Bald, was in 893 crowned as a rival king to Odo, who had been ruling West Francia since 888. Charles's coronation ignited a civil war. On Odo's death in 898, Charles became the sole king of West Francia,[12] but his reign was plagued by opposing claims for power between various Frankish nobles. Richer of Rheims, writing in the late tenth century, described how, at the very beginning of Charles's reign, the 'lust for wealth' motivated the 'leading men of the realm' into competition with each other.[13] Charles had a number of significant opponents, one

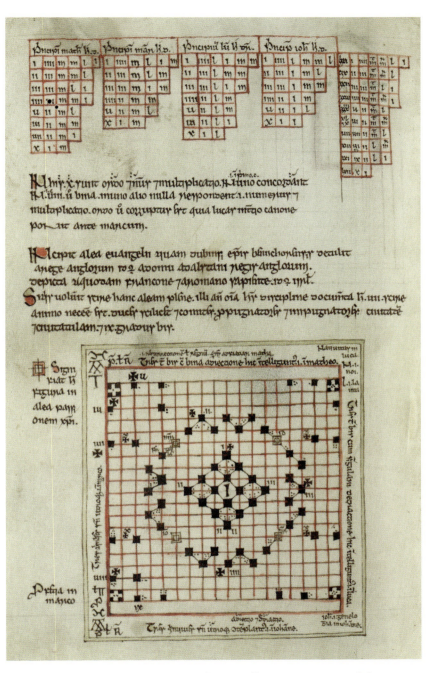

PLATE 17. Fol. 5v of Oxford, Corpus Christi College 122, an image of the game known as *alea euangelii* (gospel dice). Image reproduced by kind permission of the President and Fellows of Corpus Christi College, Oxford.

PLATE 18. A section of Offa's Dyke, from Llanfair Hill to Spring Hill Farm. Image from: https://www.researchgate.net/figure/Drone-photograph-looking -north-over-Offas-Dyke-from-Llanfair-Hill-to-Spring-Hill-Farm_fig2 _338550343.

PLATE 19. A unique coin in the name of Hywel Dda, struck by a moneyer named Gillys. Image © The Trustees of the British Museum.

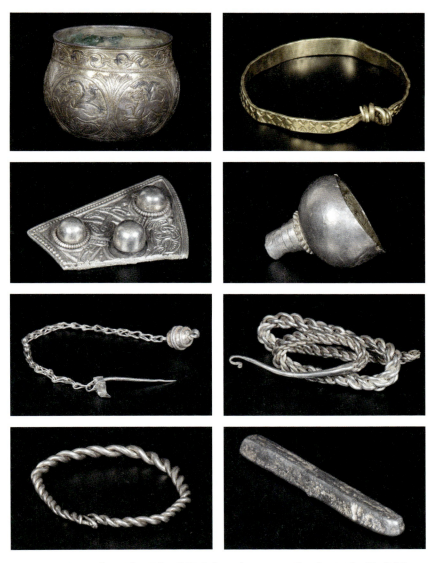

PLATE 20. Items from the Vale of York hoard, preserved today in the York Museum. Image courtesy of York Museums Trust, public domain.

PLATE 21. Fol. 24r of British Library, Cotton MS Tiberius A. ii (the so-called Æthelstan or Coronation Gospels), inscribed with the names of Otto I, king of East Francia, and his mother, Matilda. From the British Library Archive / Bridgeman Images.

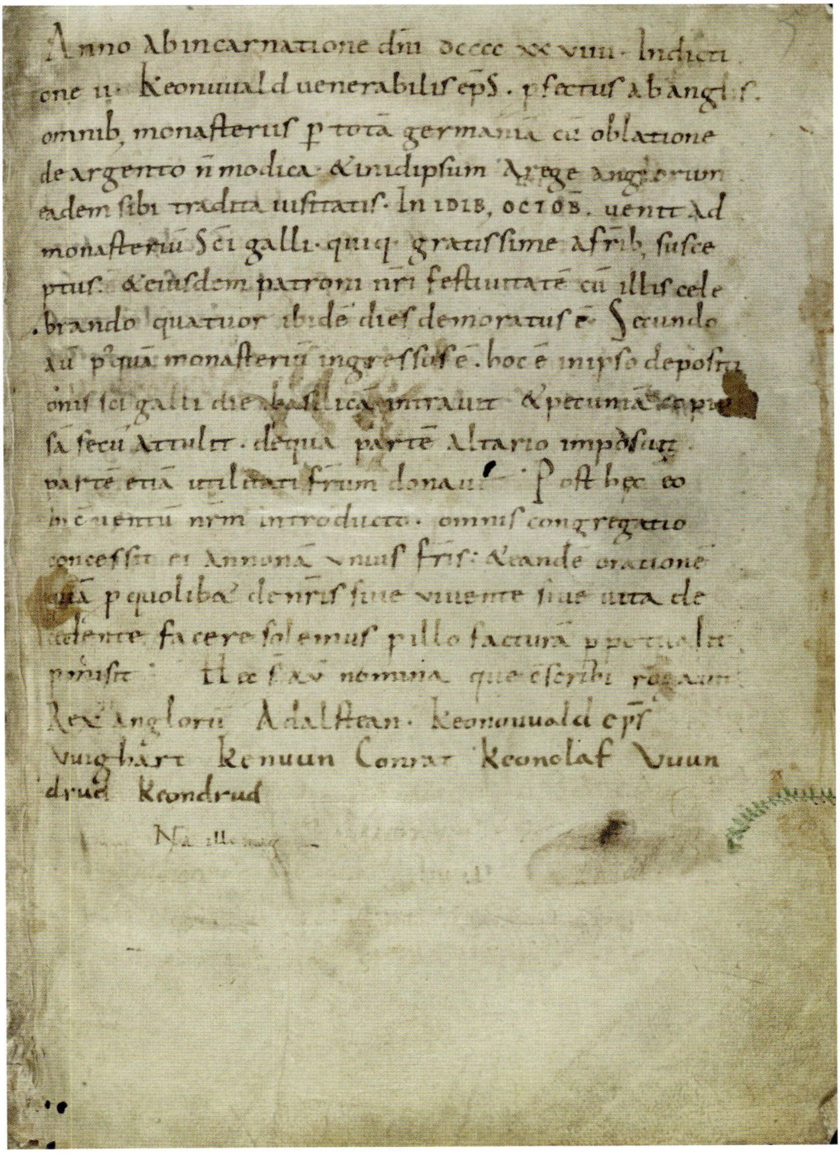

Anno Abincarnatione dñi dcccc xx viiii. Indicti
one iii. Keonuuald uenerabilis epS. pfectus ab angl s.
omnib, monasterus p tota germania cu oblatione
de argento ñ modica. & inidipsum A rege angelorun
eadem sibi tradita iussitatis. In idib, octob. uentt ad
monasteriu Sci galli. quiq gratissime asrib, suscee
ptus. & eiusdem patrom nri festiuitate cu illis cele
brando quatuor ibide dies demoratus e Secundo
au piusq monasterii ingressus e. hoc e inipso depossta
omis sci galli die basilica intrauit & pecunia cpie
sa secu attulit. dequa parte altario imposiut
parte etia unillari frium donauit. Post hec co
bi uentu nrm introducto. omnis congregatio
concessit ei annona & nuis fris: & eande oratione
eua p quolibet denris siue uiuente siue uita de
cedente facere solemus p illo factura p perualit
pmisit. Hee sxv nomina que cscribi rogauit
Rex anglorú Adalstan. Keonuuald epī
Vuigharr Kenuun Connat Keonolaf Vuun
drud Keondrud
        Na illemet

PLATE 22. St Gallen, Stiftsbibliothek, Cod. Sang. 915, page 5, the record of
Bishop Cenwald's visit to St Gallen in 929, accompanying Æthelstan's two
half-sisters.

PLATE 23. Fol. 45r of the Reichenau confraternity book, Zentralbibliothek Zürich, Rh. hist. 27. The names 'Heinricus rex', 'Mahthild regina', 'Otto rex', 'Heinricus', and 'Prun' can be seen towards the top of the column on the far right of the folio.

PLATE 24. Æthelstan's tomb in Malmesbury Abbey. Image courtesy of Fiona Hocken, Operations and Communications Manager, Malmesbury Abbey.

PLATE 25. A York coin in the name of Óláf Guthfrithson bearing the design of a raven. The obverse inscription reads ANLAF CVNVNC (King Óláf). Image reproduced by kind permission of the Classical Numismatic Group, LLC: https://www.cngcoins.com.

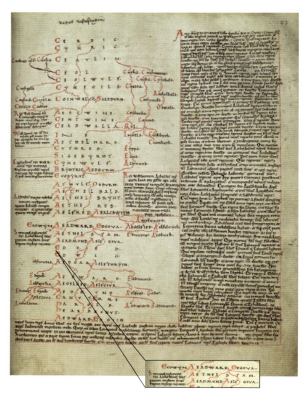

PLATE 26. Part of the West Saxon royal genealogy found towards the front of the 'Worcester Chronicle', page 53 of Oxford, Corpus Christi College 157. Image reproduced by kind permission of the President and Fellows of Corpus Christi College, Oxford.

of whom was Robert, duke of Neustria (a region within the kingdom of West Francia), and brother to the former king, Odo.[14]

Robert tried in numerous ways to displace Charles, at one moment joining forces with Count Baldwin II of Flanders, the very man who had married the West Saxon Ælfthryth, King Alfred's daughter. Matters came to a head in a battle between the two parties on 15 June 923 at Soissons.[15] Although Robert was killed, those on his side nevertheless emerged victorious, and they elected Robert's son-in-law, Radulf, as their new king, a man who was not from the Carolingian line.[16] Charles was later taken captive by Heribert II, count of Vermandois (d. 943), a development which caused his wife, Eadgifu, to take action to guard the safety of their son, Louis. Writing his *Gesta Abbatum Sithiensium* (Deeds of the Abbots of Saint Bertin) in the late tenth century, Folcuin, a monk of the Abbey of Saint-Bertin, describes how she sent Louis back to England, and to the protection of his uncle, King Æthelstan.[17]

With Charles's capture, West Frankish politics had significantly changed. A few years later, in 926, an opportunity presented itself for Æthelstan to exert English influence in north-western Europe once more. William of Malmesbury describes how an envoy named Adelolf, who was the son of Count Baldwin II of Flanders and Ælfthryth, and thus Æthelstan's cousin, arrived in England to request that Hugh the Great, duke of the Franks and count of Paris, be allowed to marry another of Æthelstan's half-sisters, Eadhild. In order to persuade Æthelstan, Adelolf is said to have brought an array of luxury gifts, including exotic spices, precious stones, and horses. Most particularly of all, and clearly aware that relics held special appeal for Æthelstan, Adelolf also brought Constantine the Great's sword, the lance of Charlemagne, Maurice's banner (which had also belonged to Charlemagne), a golden and bejewelled crown, a piece of the cross on which Christ had been crucified, and also a piece of the crown of thorns.[18] William's account needs to be read with caution; not only would he have been motivated to praise Æthelstan, who constituted one of his heroes, but he goes on to reveal that Æthelstan subsequently donated some of the relics to William's own abbey at Malmesbury, which made it particularly important for him to stress their antiquity and genuineness.[19] If it can be accepted that Adelolf had brought gifts of such distinction, they were clearly designed to flatter Æthelstan: to be compared to Charlemagne, and to be reminded of the kingship of Christ himself (via the medium of a fragment of the crown of thorns), sent a powerful message. This, in turn, suggests that Æthelstan's own power was already evident in 926, before he had formed the expanded kingdom of the English. Æthelstan duly agreed for Eadhild to marry Hugh. In doing so he was now able to gain a foothold in the changed political scene in West Francia, since the previous marriage of Eadgifu to Charles, which ended with Charles's imprisonment in 923, no longer gave him the influence he desired.

Eadgifu's own position in the years 923–26 is worth further scrutiny. When she sent her son, Louis, to Æthelstan's protection in 923, it has sometimes been assumed that she accompanied him back to England. But Folcuin, who describes the episode, makes no mention of Eadgifu's departure along with her son.[20] If she had remained in West Francia, it is possible that she, too, had played some part in the marriage of her sister, Eadhild, to Hugh. If so, it would have helped to secure her own status in the wake of her husband's capture, and it would also illustrate the ways in which Æthelstan's half-sisters occupied continental positions of influence that were of benefit to him.[21]

An examination of Eadgifu's later actions makes her political significance clear. Her husband, Charles, died in captivity in Péronne in 929. Radulf had remained as king of West Francia since Charles's defeat at the Battle of Soissons in June 923. As Radulf was childless on his death in 936, the lack of royal heirs thrust Eadgifu to the fore of politics once more. Flodoard of Rheims's *Annals*, Folcuin's *Gesta Abbatum Sithiensium*, and Richer's *Histories* all agree that, at this crucial moment, the West Frankish nobles ultimately looked to England for their new king, where Charles's and Eadgifu's son, Louis, had been living under Æthelstan's protection. Richer's account of what follows is more elaborate than those of Flodoard or Folcuin and reads as if it has been embellished in various ways.[22] Richer describes how Frankish envoys journeyed to England to petition Æthelstan and Louis for Louis's return. According to Richer, Æthelstan was aware of the twists and turns of recent West Frankish politics, and of the duplicity and changing of allegiances of different individuals. He therefore required the envoys to swear an oath as to the veracity of what they said, which they provided. The Frankish party returned home and reported the outcome, whereupon Hugh the Great—and other 'leading men of Gaul', who, according to Folcuin included Heribert II and Arnulf—travelled to Boulogne to await Louis's arrival.[23] Richer again includes extra detail that, having reached the English coast, Æthelstan took the precaution that Oda, the bishop of Ramsbury (later archbishop of Canterbury; d. 958), should first travel ahead to the Continent to secure the oath of the Franks that they would follow through with their promise of making Louis king and that he would be treated properly. Only once this had been secured did Æthelstan permit Louis to cross the channel. Louis was then taken to Laon and crowned king by the archbishop of Rheims, Artald (d. 961), thus becoming Louis IV, king of West Francia. Because he had been brought up at Æthelstan's court, he became known as Louis 'd'Outremer' (Latin: *transmarinus* or *ultramarinus*—literally 'from overseas').[24]

Louis's 936 acquisition of the throne returned his mother, Eadgifu, to political prominence. Louis's own position at the beginning of his reign was weak, and one of his principal opponents was Hugh the Great. Hugh could rely on substantial resources, and, given that he was the son of the king killed by Louis's father at the 923 Battle of Soissons, we might have expected Hugh himself to launch his own bid for the throne. That he did not do so is indicative of his reading of the situation: in 936 the politics were so disturbed that he felt he would be unlikely to receive the support he needed as king.[25] And there is evidence that he profited from his backing of Louis, for he is described in some of Louis's charters as *dux Francorum* (duke of the Franks) or *eximius duxque Francorum egregius* (excellent and outstanding duke of the Franks), a title implying that he had been vested with a high degree of authority by the king.[26] That Eadgifu was able to exert significant influence herself is suggested by Flodoard's annal for 937 which, in saying that 'King Louis withdrew himself from the management of the *princeps* Hugh [the Great] and received his mother [Eadgifu] at Laon', implies that it was Eadgifu's presence which had enabled Louis to move away from Hugh's influence.[27] According to Flodoard, the year 938 saw Louis reclaim properties and fortified sites from various nobles, which augmented his resources and thus strengthened his position. In doing so it is notable that he paid particular attention to the lands of his mother, Eadgifu, by taking back her former possessions of Corbeny, which had been seized by Heribert II of Vermandois, and of Tusey on the River Meuse 'and other *villae* pertaining to it', which had been held by a certain Count Roger. Having narrated this sequence of territorial gains by Louis, Flodoard then immediately describes how Hugh the Great married Hadwig, the sister of the East Frankish king, Otto.[28] The juxtaposition may not be a coincidence: it may imply that, in Flodoard's mind, Louis's seizure of lands led directly to Hugh seeking new alliances and throwing in his lot with the Liudolfings (Otto's family line) east of the Rhine.

From the late ninth century on, after Count Baldwin II married Ælfthryth, the daughter of Alfred the Great, connections between England and Flanders became especially close.[29] Before his death in 899 Alfred had bequeathed to Ælthryth the estates of Wellow (on the Isle of Wight), and Ashton and Chippenham (both of which are in Wiltshire).[30] We have also seen that one of Baldwin's sons, Adelolf, who was Æthelstan's cousin, played a fundamental role in arranging the marriage of Æthelstan's half-sister, Eadhild, to Hugh the Great. When Æthelstan's brother, Edwin, was drowned and his body washed up on shore, Folcuin relates that Adelolf once more intervened and arranged for Edwin to be buried at the abbey of Saint-Bertin with the dignity befitting his status. In the very same chapter of his work, Folcuin suggests that those monks from Saint-Bertin who would not bow to the religious rule imposed on them by their abbot, Gerard, were able to take refuge in England with Æthelstan.[31] When Count Arnulf I of Flanders, the son and successor of Baldwin II, managed to score a victory against his enemy Erluin, count of Montreuil and Ponthieu, by seizing the fortification at Montreuil, the Flanders count looked across the channel to Æthelstan for help and sent Erluin's wife and children to the English king for safekeeping and in order to guarantee his position against Erluin.[32]

Louis IV, king of the West Franks, and Arnulf I, Count of Flanders, seem at various points to have acted in close collaboration. Given that they were cousins, this was, perhaps, to be expected, but their shared interest in maintaining close links with Æthelstan in England was also an important factor. Arnulf had played a significant role in Louis's accession as king in 936, meeting Louis in Boulogne when he landed there after his voyage from England, and the two can subsequently be found together in 938 at Quentovic, where Louis had been renovating the fortifications and port.[33] From Flodoard we learn that in 939 Æthelstan engaged in an unprecedented military intervention in Europe which would involve both Louis and Arnulf. Flodoard relates that Æthelstan had dispatched a fleet of ships in order to help Louis but that, in the event, the fleet laid waste to the coastal regions of Flanders before sailing back to England 'without accomplishing anything of their original mission'.[34] There has been uncertainty concerning Æthelstan's exact purpose in sending his fleet, and the reasons why it ended up ravaging the coast of Flanders rather than providing Louis with assistance. The suggestion has been made that, in focusing their attentions on the Flanders coastline, the naval force had been diverted by Arnulf to do his bidding against his enemy, Erluin. In the immediate aftermath of the coastal ravaging, Arnulf seems to have joined the side of Louis's enemies, perhaps confirming that he had co-opted the force for his own purposes. Whatever the exact circumstances, Æthelstan's mounting of such an expedition is indicative of the strength of his position in England itself, and of the power with which he was able to operate in Europe. It is reminiscent of the way in which he had sent a military force north to the kingdom of Alba in 934.

Two further half-sisters of Æthelstan were deployed in diplomatic marriages with contemporary European rulers, although the identity of one of these sisters (and her husband) has caused great confusion and difficulty. In different sections of his *Gesta Regum Anglorum* (Deeds of the English Kings), William of Malmesbury describes how Henry the Fowler (d. 936), king of the East Franks, in 929 petitioned Æthelstan to arrange a marriage alliance between his son, Otto, and one of the English king's half-sisters. Æthelstan is said to have sent two of his half-sisters to the East Frankish court.[35] As we will see, Bishop Cenwald of Worcester accompanied them on their journey, visiting a variety of German religious houses as they went. The half-sister ultimately selected by Otto was Eadgyth, who was the daughter of Edward the Elder by his second wife, Ælfflæd, and about whom we shall hear more below.

But who was the second sister sent by Æthelstan, and what was her destiny? William's account reveals his own misunderstanding: his text is internally inconsistent and offers different names for the second sister at different points.[36] The matter is further complicated by additional information preserved by two tenth-century authors: the East Frankish female writer, Hrotsvitha of Gandersheim, and the English secular author, the Ealdorman Æthelweard. Their work corroborates some aspects of William's versions but also introduces further difficulties.[37] Because it is impossible to resolve the textual discrepancies with certainty, they are discussed separately in appendix II. The important point to note for our present purposes is that the second sister sent by Æthelstan to the East Frankish court could either have been named Ælfgifu, born to Edward's second wife, or she might be identified with Eadgifu, a daughter of Edward's third wife. It has also proved problematic to know to whom this second sister was eventually married. Our sources broadly agree that the man in question was based near the Alps, and the most compelling suggestion hitherto made is that he should be equated with Louis, the brother of Rudolf II, king of Burgundy (912–37) and of Italy (922–26).[38]

With this marriage of Ælfgifu/Eadgifu into the Burgundian line, Æthelstan had extended English influence yet further and into another powerful ruling family, a prudent tactic given the unpredictability of early tenth-century continental politics. The reign of Rudolf II had been characterised, on the one hand, by Magyar raids from Hungary and, on the other hand, by the king's desire to expand the area of his kingdom, with success in Italy coming in 922.[39] Rudolf II's death in 937 precipitated a crisis. Although his son, Conrad, succeeded him, Conrad's young age made his position vulnerable, to the extent that Otto I removed him into the safety of his East Frankish court in 938.[40] And Hugh, count of Arles, attempted to intrude himself at this crucial moment by marrying Rudolf II's widow and then by arranging for his son to marry Rudolf II's daughter. Not long afterwards, in 938, the West Frankish king, Louis IV, can be found in Breisach, a town in modern

Germany, but which in the tenth century was situated in a liminal area between Burgundy and East Francia. It looks as if Louis IV also had interests in Burgundy. It is striking that, thanks to his policy of creating strategic marriage alliances with continental rulers, Æthelstan was closely connected to the unfolding politics in Burgundy in the late 930s, both through Eadgifu (the mother of Louis IV) and through Ælfgifu/Eadgifu, the wife of Rudolf II's brother.[41]

We should return now to the marriage of Eadgyth to Otto, who had been selected by the East Frankish prince above her sister, Ælfgifu/Eadgifu. According to Hrotsvitha, it was Otto's father, Henry the Fowler, who sought out a bride for his son and deliberately looked beyond the confines of his own kingdom in doing so. Hrotsvitha says that 'he [i.e., Henry] sent duly experienced representatives to the charming [*deliciosa*] land of the nation of the Angles' and that the messengers took suitable gifts with them in order to win the hand of Eadgyth specifically.[42] An important factor for Hrotsvitha was that Eadgyth was of noble descent: she makes much of the fact that, while Æthelstan himself had been born to 'an ignoble consort', Eadgyth came from a line of 'great monarchs' that supposedly stretched all the way back to the seventh-century Northumbrian king Oswald.[43] Oswald was a very particular figure for Hrotsvitha to mention. The king had been one of Bede's heroes in his *Ecclesiastical History*, an example of a king who had managed to combine his religious duties with his secular role and was one of the principal champions of early Christianity. Following Oswald's death in battle against the heathen King Penda of Mercia in 642, in which his body had been dismembered, veneration of Oswald quickly spread across Britain and Europe. Evidence of this is to be found in the fact that a number of different religious institutions claim to hold his relics. His head is today said to rest alongside the remains of St Cuthbert in Durham Cathedral, but appeals concerning the possession of his head (or parts of his skull) have also been made by various places in Europe, including Echternach in Luxembourg, Hildersheim in Germany, Schaffhausen and Zug in Switzerland, and Utrecht in the Netherlands. We know that Bede's work was being read in East Francia, suggesting that, by providing Eadgyth with lineage going back to Oswald, Hrotsvitha intended the link to have a wide impact.[44] Alternatively, it is possible that connections between Eadgyth and Oswald may have been pressed by the English party in the marriage allegiance, since the cult of Oswald had been supported by Æthelred and Æthelflæd of Mercia.[45]

In order to secure the marriage alliance, Hrotsvitha stresses the importance of the giving of gifts between the different political parties. Such exchanges were important in the early medieval period, both for the ceremony and ritual involved in the occasions and in order to secure good will and prove the authenticity of each party's intentions. Henry's ambassadors are said to have taken gifts with them in their journey to England, along with official correspondence for Æthelstan to read, while Æthelstan, in return, is supposed to have brought together many precious objects that he could dispatch back to East Francia. Two manuscripts surviving today may have been just the kind of precious items exchanged between Æthelstan and Henry. The so-called Gandersheim Gospels, a manuscript originally composed in Metz in the mid-ninth century, but which from the early eleventh century was in the possession of Gandersheim, has, on the recto of its folio 168, an important and difficult-to-decipher inscription at the foot of that page. Written in a form of English script—'Anglo-Saxon square minuscule'—it says, simply,

> + eadgifu regina: -   æþelstan rex angulsaxonum
> 7 mercianorum: -

The inscription raises a number of questions including when, where, and under what circumstances a scribe who wrote an English script form added these words to a continental manuscript. There is also a question about the identity of Eadgifu, who, from the placement of her name, seems in this context to be afforded prominence over Æthelstan.[46] The royal style attached to Æthelstan's name, which implies rulership over Wessex and Mercia but not over Northumbria as well, does not replicate any form that can be found in the king's diplomas. And the Eadgifu named could relate to one of three possible women: Æthelstan's step-mother, the third wife of Edward the Elder; Æthelstan's half-sister who married Charles the Simple, king of the West Franks; or another half-sister of Æthelstan who may have married Louis, brother of Rudolf II, king of Burgundy, depending on her exact identity.

The identity of Eadgifu is not certain because we cannot recover the circumstances in which the inscription was added to the manuscript. If the inscription had been added in England, for example, we might link it to the period of time that Louis, the son of Charles the Simple and Eadgifu, spent at Æthelstan's court when his father was imprisoned in 923. There could have been a number of reasons why the name of Louis's mother was then entered into the manuscript, and the manuscript itself could subsequently have returned to the Continent when Louis became king of West Francia in 936. Alternatively, if the inscription had been added to the manuscript by an Englishman visiting the Continent, one possible interpretation is that the scribe belonged to the group led by Cenwald which in 929 visited various German monasteries on its way to the East Frankish court, where Otto would select a bride from one of two of Æthelstan's half-sisters. A difficulty with this elucidation is that the Eadgifu of the inscription is titled *regina* (queen), which is not appropriate for that particular half-sister.[47] Another plausible scenario would be to suggest that this manuscript might have been one of the very gifts given by Æthelstan to Otto (mentioned by Hrotsvitha) as part of the marriage negotiations, who may then have given it to Gandersheim, where his niece, Gerberga, was following a religious life and later became abbess. If that were true, then the Eadgifu mentioned would be more likely to be Æthelstan's step-mother, for reasons that will be described below.

Cotton Tiberius A. ii, known as the Æthelstan or Coronation Gospels, is a manuscript preserved today in the British Library. It was originally written in Belgium in the late ninth or possibly early tenth century, and, having come into Æthelstan's possession, was subsequently given by him to the community of Christ Church, Canterbury.[48] On the recto of its twenty-fourth folio, inserted after the opening of the Gospel of St Matthew, is the following inscription:

+ ODDA REX

+ MIHTHILD MATER REGIS

The people named are Otto I, king of East Francia, and his mother, Matilda. The inscription may be dated to the period between 936, the date when Otto became king, and 968, the date of Matilda's death.

Could the manuscript have originally been given as a gift by the Liudolf-ings to Æthelstan as part of the exchange of precious items described by Hrotsvitha in the marriage negotiations? If so, the names of Otto and Matilda could have been added at some subsequent stage, to commem-orate their connection with the manuscript, perhaps even to mark the moment in 936 when Otto was elevated to the throne, thus thrusting his English wife, Eadgyth, to the fore of East Frankish politics. If the manu-script had been given as part of the marriage negotiations, the Gander-sheim Gospels may have constituted a gift in the other direction, from the English court to their contemporaries in East Francia. That might make it more likely that the Eadgifu named in the Gandersheim Gos-pels would be Æthelstan's step-mother, to mirror the inscription given here—of king and mother—in Cotton Tiberius A. ii. Again, though, the lack of any further detail beyond the mere inscription in the manu-script makes it impossible to be sure of the circumstances in which it had originally been donated. It could equally well have been a gift made by Otto to England long after the negotiations for Eadgyth's hand had taken place.[49]

Whatever messages and gifts were given to Æthelstan in 929, they evidently met with success. Hrotsvitha reports that, although the East Frankish ambassadors had specifically targeted Eadgyth, Æthelstan ac-tually sent back two sisters for Otto to choose from, one of whom is called *Adiva* by Hrotsvitha.[50] Extraordinarily, we can reconstruct a little detail about the journey which took the two sisters to Otto in the first place, although they themselves are not explicitly mentioned. Towards the front of the oldest capitulary to have survived from St Gallen (in modern Switzerland) can be found a record of a visit to the abbey there in October 929 by Bishop Cenwald of Worcester. It states that, before Cenwald arrived at St Gallen on 15 October, he had visited 'all the mon-asteries throughout Germany' and that he had taken with him a large amount of silver given to him by Æthelstan, presumably to make pious offerings as he went, and possibly also so that he could acquire items like manuscripts and relics that would have appealed to Æthelstan. He remained with the monks at St Gallen for four days, and on 16 October, he made a substantial monetary donation to the abbey, and also directly to the monks for their own use. The quid pro quo for this donation was that the monks would remember a number of individuals in their prayers, who are then listed at the end, and include King Æthelstan, Bishop Cenwald, Wigheard, Coenwynn, Coenred, Coenlaf, Wynthryth, and Coenthryth. It was not uncommon in the early medieval period for those from the same family to be given names that begin with the same first element (known as a prototheme), so it is possible that some of those recorded, whose names have the first element *Coen-*, were related to Cenwald.[51]

It was perhaps on the same occasion that a list of names, which begins with that of King Æthelstan, was entered into another St Gallen manuscript, its confraternity book. The list contains thirty names in total, which, in addition to Æthelstan, included the archbishop of Canterbury, Wulfhelm; seven bishops who were actively presiding over their respective sees in England; and two abbots, one of whom, Cynath, was the abbot of Evesham whom we have already met.[52] Some or all of those named may have been accompanying Cenwald on his journey in 929. Another entry in the confraternity book of the Reichenau community, some thirty-five miles to the north-west of St Gallen—which mentions King Æthelstan and Archbishop Wulfhelm, and which seems to have been written at the request of Wigheard, the same individual noted in the St Gallen capitulary—suggests that Cenwald and his party may, on the same trip, have visited the German monastery there.[53]

By the time he reached St Gallen and Reichenau, which are situated towards the eastern fringes of Burgundy, it is possible that Cenwald was by then engaged in discussions concerning marriage into the Burgundian line.[54] Although the records are brief, they provide moving commemoration of a party of tenth-century English men and women traversing central Europe on an important diplomatic mission. We can imagine that Cenwald and his companions witnessed the names being inserted into the precious manuscripts of St Gallen and Reichenau and that the accompanying ceremony impressed on them the genuineness of the continental monks' spiritual care for their English counterparts.

Once Eadgyth had been chosen as Otto's bride, the marriage itself occurred in late 929 or early 930.[55] The union brought benefits to both sides. With his accession in 919, Henry the Fowler was the first of the Li-udolfings to be made king of East Francia, and, since the royal line was not long established, it was especially vulnerable to challenge. The creation of a tie with the English royal house, which stretched back to the sixth century, and which, as we have seen, had already been expanded in several directions into continental ruling dynasties, therefore lent authority to Henry's and Otto's positions. At just the time that the marriage was being concluded, the tenth-century East Frankish historian, Widukind of Corvey, records how Henry was beset both by external threats from the Magyars of Hungary and by internal strife generated by nobles who were on the lookout for ways to enhance their own status and wealth.[56] For Æthelstan, meanwhile, the marriage of Eadgyth represented the cementing of ties with one further ruling family on the Continent. This would have brought with it attendant political prestige, and also the solidification of a network of his half-sisters in Europe, on whom he could call as and when needed. As we will see, Otto turned out to be a king of the same mould as Æthelstan, a ruler of great strength and ambition.[57]

At about the time of Otto's marriage to Eadgyth in 929 or 930, an entry was made in the Reichenau confraternity book in which the name of Otto is listed and he is given the title *rex* (king). Listed alongside him is his father, Henry, who is identically titled, and also his mother, Matilda. Otto's younger brothers, Henry and Brun, are also present, but they are not supplied with a royal style.[58] It is possible that the wedding plans and the succession plans were both part of Henry's attempt to secure the future of the Liudolfing royal house. If this were the case, though, it is nevertheless striking that subsequent diplomas issued by Henry make no allusion to Otto's future kingly status.[59]

After their marriage, nothing is heard of Otto and Eadgyth until 936, when the health of King Henry worsened. At this moment, so Widukind tells us, the king announces his intention that Otto should be his successor, confirms it by the means of a written will, and seeks to ensure a smooth transition by apportioning some of his estates to his other sons. Henry died on 2 July 936 and was buried in the church at Quedlinburg.[60] After Henry's death, Otto was anointed king. Hrotsvitha, writing in the late tenth century, compares Otto to the biblical King David.[61] Significantly, Otto's crowning took place at Aachen, the site that Charlemagne himself had used as his principal residence, where he held his royal court and where he had founded the palace chapel in which he was later buried. This must have sent a very powerful message to contemporaries concerning the type of king Otto aspired to be—one who sought to gain imperial status in the same way that Charlemagne had done, and to extend his territorial possessions. When Widukind describes the occasion, he makes an explicit connection between Otto's imperial pretensions and Aachen, saying that Aachen was situated close to 'Jülich, so called from Julius Caesar its founder' (even if the reference to Caesar is misleading).[62] What role did Eadgyth play in these early moments of Otto's new reign? Hrotsvitha and Widukind are silent on the matter, but the early eleventh-century historian Thietmar of Merseburg states that, after his own crowning, Otto then 'ordered the consecration of his wife, Eadgyth.'[63]

One dynamic that emerges following Eadgyth's arrival in East Francia is a seeming rivalry with her mother-in-law, Matilda, whose preference was that Henry, her younger son, and not Otto, her elder son, should succeed their father as king. Before he died, Henry the Fowler may have foreseen this very issue. In September 929, just before Eadgyth formally married into the family, Henry granted Matilda some landed possessions in Quedlinburg, Pöhlde, Nordhausen, Grone and Duderstadt, and it has been argued that this was perhaps a way of stabilising her position: it seems unlikely that she had been crowned queen during the reign of her husband, and she was about to be faced with the presence of a queen from an ancient and noble family line.[64] The diploma recording this grant contains a clause which specifies Otto's own agreement to the grant; no other diploma hitherto issued by Henry had noted Otto's involvement in this way, suggesting that it had been important for all concerned that Otto publicly agreed to the grant.[65] The ebb and flow of the two women's power is revealed also in their appearances in diplomas: as Eadgyth becomes queen in 936, she begins to be present in ways unprecedented for her, at the same time as Matilda, who had previously been a more frequent intervenor, can only be found present in one diploma from that point onwards. When Eadgyth died early in 946, Matilda once more reappears in the diploma record.[66]

Otto and Eadgyth had two children together, a boy, Liudolf, and a girl, Liudgard. Like their parents, they were also married off in ways that sought to extend East Frankish influence and stability. In 947 Liudolf married Ida, the daughter of Duke Herman I of Swabia, and, at about the same time in 947, Liudgard became the wife of Conrad the Red, the Duke of Lotharingia.[67] Otto's reign was at times very turbulent: he had to suppress challenges that came both from members of his family and from those in different parts of his East Frankish kingdom. Eadgyth lived through these episodes with her husband. In a long entry for 939, Adalbert of Magdeburg, a tenth-century author who added a continuation to the *Chronicle* of Regino of Prüm, describes in detail how Otto was at times faced by the opposition of his brother, Henry, who had allied with Dukes Eberhard of Franconia and Giselbert of Lotharingia, and also that of Louis IV, the West Frankish king. Otto reacted with strength and besieged both Chèvremont, which belonged to Giselbert, and Breisach, which had been in Eberhard's hands. While these violent and dangerous events were taking place, and the outcome must have been far from clear, Adalbert remarks that Queen Eadgyth had been removed from the centre of action and was staying at the Lorsch monastery.[68]

It is difficult to reconstruct much more about Eadgyth's actions as queen. Thietmar describes how she encouraged Otto to found a monastery at Magdeburg, which had been given to her as part of her dowry and which would later be elevated in status to an archbishopric, while other texts suggest she may have been instrumental in calming any tensions between Otto and his mother, Matilda.[69] Attention has been drawn to a passage of text in the *Life of St Dunstan* by the author known only by an initial, B., who was writing about an incident involving the hero of his text, Dunstan, and Æthelstan's successor as king, Edmund (d. 946). In the passage in question Dunstan, having been threatened with exile from England, sought the help of ambassadors from the 'eastern kingdom' (*regnum orientis*). One suggestion is that this might refer to the kingdom of East Francia, and therefore that Eadgyth's presence there could have had the effect of attracting English political dissidents into her protection.[70] While it is no doubt true that Æthelstan's half-sisters in Europe could have provided safe havens for people ostracised from England, in this specific example it is difficult to understand exactly what B. meant when referring to an 'eastern kingdom', which, in addition to East Francia, could equally well have implied Byzantium.[71]

Eadgyth died of unknown causes on 26 January, 946, at the age of about thirty-six. Both Widukind and Hrotsvitha stress the grief felt by all at her passing, with Hrotsvitha noting that she had loved the East Frankish people with a 'motherly kindness'. Widukind adds the intriguing statement that, following Eadgyth's death, Otto learned to read for the first time: perhaps he had been motivated by her scholarly example, or perhaps her absence made such a skill all the more necessary.[72] She was buried in the new monastery that she and Otto had founded at Magdeburg. By 1510 Eadgyth's remains had been translated into Magdeburg Cathedral. And, in 2008, when archaeologists opened her tomb, they found a lead box inscribed in Latin, part of which reads EDIT REGINE CINERES HIC SARCOPHAGUS HABET (This sarcophagus contains the ashes of Queen Eadgyth). More than ashes, the box housed a selection of human bones. Further archaeological investigation revealed that they belonged to a female of thirty to forty years of age, and, from analysis of the teeth in her upper jaw, it seemed that this female had not grown up in the vicinity of Magdeburg but could actually be traced to a chalky area of Wessex, that she had been a rider of horses, and that she regularly consumed fish.[73] The coincidence of her age on her death and her place of origin was sufficient to equate the remains with Eadgyth herself. On her death, Otto is said to have declared that, when he died, their son, Liudolf, would succeed as king.[74] But events transpired rather differently: in 951 Otto remarried, this time to Adelaide, the daughter of Rudolf II of Burgundy, and widow of Lothar (d. 950), king of Italy. Otto's own status would be enhanced in 962 when he was anointed emperor by Pope John XII. And it was Otto's and Adelaide's son, also named Otto, who would go on to succeed his father as king and latterly as emperor, too.

In addition to the creation of alliances via strategic marriages, Æthelstan can be shown to have offered refuge at his court to various continental figures. We have already seen that he did so in the case of Louis d'Outremer (later Louis IV) and when Arnulf of Flanders asked for his aid in taking in the wife and children of his enemy, Erluin. He created links between Brittany and Norway in similar fashion. In the early tenth century, Brittany found itself the object of serious viking attack, with the result that many were killed or driven from their homes and Brittany's independence was ceded to viking control.[75] The *Chronicle of Nantes*, which has survived only in fifteenth-century form, but which was written originally in the mid-eleventh century, provides the detail that the count of Poher, a man named Matuedoi, was one of those who, together with other Bretons, fled overseas in order to seek out Æthelstan's protection in England.[76] He took with him his son, Alan, who would later be given the memorable epithet of Barbetorte ('Crooked Beard'). The *Chronicle* adds that Æthelstan 'had lifted him [i.e., Alan] from the holy font'—in other words, Æthelstan had stood sponsor at Alan's baptism and therefore become his godfather. There was precedent for kings making use of baptismal ceremonies in order to enmesh others in a ritualised and thus more formal relationship. King Alfred had taken this action with respect to the viking leader, Guthrum, who, following his own baptism, was afterwards renamed Æthelstan.[77] Æthelstan's creation of Alan as his godson thus established a more enduring bond between them and meant that Alan recognised that Æthelstan was the superior—in political, spiritual, and moral terms—of the two. The *Chronicle of Nantes* describes Alan as being an especially strong individual, so much so that he hunted with wooden rather than iron weapons. In characterising Alan like this, the author draws attention to his upbringing at Æthelstan's court in such a way that implies— whether consciously or not—that it had in part been Æthelstan's example and guidance that had made him so hardy.[78] In 936 Alan and other Bretons who had sheltered in England sailed across the channel, and, with Æthelstan's support, ultimately reclaimed their territory from viking control.[79] The extent and nature of Æthelstan's support is not specified. That Alan's time in England had been formative is suggested by Breton coins of the 940s, which use their English equivalents as models.[80] The details of Æthelstan and Alan bring to mind another occasion on which the English king had attempted to intervene militarily in Europe.

A number of Scandinavian sources make a connection between Æthelstan's court and a young Hákon 'inn góði' ('the Good') Haraldsson, the son of Harald hárfagri ('Finehair'), who was king of Norway until about 931/2. Hákon later became king of Norway (ca. 933/4–ca. 960). The sources include two in Latin which belong roughly to the middle or end of the twelfth century: a text written by Theodricus Monachus entitled *Historia de Antiquitate Regum Norwagensium* (Ancient History of the Norwegian Kings, written sometime between 1177 and 1188); and the *Historia Norwegiae* (History of Norway), which has been ascribed various dates from the mid-twelfth century to the early thirteenth century.[81] There are in addition three vernacular saga texts, the *Ágrip af Nóregs konunga sögum* (Summary of the Histories of the Kings of Norway), of the 1190s; *Fagrskinna* (Fair Vellum), of about 1220; and *Heimskringla* (Disc of the World), which was probably compiled by Snorri Sturluson in 1230–35.[82] The comparatively late date of all of the sources (chronologically far distant from the events of the early tenth century that they describe), and the generic form of the sagas (which include much legendary material, factual error, and invented dialogue), mean that they present numerous challenges of understanding. So difficult has interpretation of the material been that even the bare dates of the reigns of the various kings of the tenth century have been much debated, and the sagas assume—wrongly—that Æthelstan himself reigned into the late 940s.[83] But, with careful examination, and where the sources agree on common elements of detail, we might be permitted to find some of their contents relatively reliable.[84]

All of the sources agree that Hákon was sent by his father, Harald, to Æthelstan in England, where he became the king's 'foster son', and from where one of the vernacular sobriquets applied to Hákon—'Aðalsteinsfóstri' (literally, 'foster son of Æthelstan')—is derived. Theodricus suggests that he had been sent specifically so that he could learn from English ways.[85]

Both *Fagrskinna* and *Heimskringla* include a more elaborate story of
the way in which King Harald and Æthelstan became linked in a political
relationship involving Harald's son, Hákon. The core details are similar
in both. Æthelstan is supposed to have sent messengers to Harald in
Norway who, when they came before the Norwegian king, presented
him with a precious sword together with a bejewelled scabbard. As soon
as the king grasped the sword, the messengers declared that this action
demonstrated that Harald had accepted that he had a subservient position to Æthelstan. Recognising that he had been tricked, Harald decided to respond in kind. He later asked one of his trusted men to take
his son, Hákon, to Æthelstan in England. They travelled to London, and
Hákon was placed on Æthelstan's lap. The very act of placing the child on
the king's lap, and the king's acceptance of this gesture, bound Æthelstan
in a formal relationship as Hákon's foster father. Both sagas relate that
the person involved in raising another's child is of a lower status. The
purpose of these stories was to demonstrate that, despite both kings
trying to assert their own superiority over the other, they were actually
equal in status.[86]

To what extent can the details in these later Scandinavian sources be
accepted? It is certainly feasible that Hákon was brought up at the court
of King Æthelstan as his foster son, both because the sources agree and
because we know that Æthelstan had acted in a similar way for others
from different parts of Europe—notably, with Alan of Brittany and
Louis d'Outremer. As for the details in *Fagrskinna* and *Heimskringla*
concerning the deceptive gift and countergift of a sword and of Hákon
between Æthelstan and Harald, there is much that has simply been invented.[87] But the very fostering of Hákon indicates that, although no
tenth-century English source recalls the detail, there were diplomatic
relations between Æthelstan's England and Harald's Norway. And this
may find corroboration in the later work of William of Malmesbury, but
in a different form. William states that, because of Æthelstan's preeminent status, a number of European kings sought out his friendship,
including Harald himself, who is said to have sent a 'ship with gilded
beak and a scarlet sail, the inside of which was hung round with a close-
set row of gilded shields'.[88] The names of Harald's envoys who travelled

to meet Æthelstan are given as Helgrim and Osfrith. It is difficult to verify the details provided by William, although it is possible that there are kernels of truth within it. There are records of other ships being conveyed as diplomatic gifts: in the mid-eleventh century, for example, an English noble by the name of Godwine, who was himself of Scandinavian heritage, sought to win over the then king of England, Edward the Confessor, by giving him a ship which is described in elaborate terms.[89] And the creation of a relationship between Æthelstan in England and Harald in Norway would have made sense for both parties: for Æthelstan it represented the support of a powerful Scandinavian ruler at a time when he was under threat of viking raids, while for Harald it meant the expansion of his own diplomatic network when his position was under a degree of pressure from Danish kings.[90]

Having been raised at King Æthelstan's court, Hákon, as we have seen, went on to become king of Norway by ca. 933/34. According to one tradition Hákon had been called back to Norway in order to challenge the rule of his elder brother, named Eiríkr, which was renowned for its brutality.[91] But an alternative historiographical tradition gives more agency to Æthelstan: that it was specifically as a result of the English king's prompting that, following Harald's death, Hákon went back to Norway.[92] *Heimskringla* even goes so far as to suggest that Æthelstan provided Hákon with a force of men and ships in order to facilitate his return to Norway. The veracity of the statement cannot be straightforwardly accepted, not least because none of the other Scandinavian sources make the same claim. But could Æthelstan have been offering military help to Hákon for his return to Norway in the same way that he had previously done with King Louis? Once established as king, Hákon's reign is characterised in the sagas by a number of features, which included his attempts to introduce Christianity to a still-pagan Norwegian society; his holding of large assemblies to make decisions (including the creation of an assembly for western Norway known as the Gulating); his organisation of ship levies for the defence of Norway (Old Norse: *leiðangr*); and that he established various laws. As ever with the sagas, there are difficulties in accepting these details. Some have interpreted the *leiðangr*, for example, as likely to belong to a later period than the tenth century and only to parts of Norway.[93] Even so, it is striking that these features closely match many of Æthelstan's own priorities as king. The English king was renowned for his support of the church, his holding of large meetings of the royal *witan*, his ability to harness military force via the use of the *fyrd* (a system that enabled English kings to assemble military forces and which had been particularly important in the reign of King Alfred), and his actions as a law-maker. Perhaps Æthelstan's example had influenced Hákon.[94]

William of Malmesbury had been justified in his boast about Æthelstan's renown on a European stage. No previous English king had either sought or effected such a wide influence into continental and Scandinavian Europe as he managed. Æthelstan's actions also demonstrate how closely connected England and the Continent were in the early tenth century. It was thanks to travellers moving back and forth across the channel, the exchanges of correspondence, and the necessities of trade that Æthelstan would have known how and when to intervene in the ways that we have seen. By the end of his reign he had ensured that, no matter how the political situation on the Continent evolved, he and his family were placed on a firm footing for their own ambitions to be realised.

7

Death and Legacy

ON 27 OCTOBER 939 Æthelstan died, at the age of about forty-five. The *Anglo-Saxon Chronicle*, using the date of his coronation (4 September 925) as its starting point rather than the year in which he came to power (924), states that he had ruled for fourteen years and ten weeks. A late tenth-century regnal list gives a more specific calculation of fourteen years, seven weeks, and three days.[1] According to version 'D' of the *Anglo-Saxon Chronicle*, he died at Gloucester, although no more details about the circumstances are provided.[2] Worcester and Malmesbury historians record that his body was subsequently taken to Malmesbury, where it was buried underneath the altar of St Mary.[3] William of Malmesbury suggests that Æthelstan's burial there had been according to the king's own wishes, which he had declared in 937 when arranging for the burial (also at Malmesbury) of his cousins, Ælfwine and Æthelwine, who had been killed at the Battle of *Brunanburh*.[4] Æthelstan's father, Edward, and grandfather, Alfred, had been buried at the New Minster, Winchester, which had been built at their command and under their supervision, as had his half-brother, Ælfweard; his uncle, Æthelweard; and his grandmother, Ealhswith.[5] Æthelstan's choice of a different burial site is therefore noteworthy. Perhaps he wanted to dissociate himself from Winchester, which had been hostile to his becoming king in the first place. Perhaps he wanted to favour the Malmesbury brethren because of his devotion to St Aldhelm (a devotion highlighted by William of Malmesbury) and the decision had nothing to do with his feelings about Winchester. Perhaps a decision had been taken for the

burial of subsequent kings of the West Saxon line to be spread between
a variety of churches so that the West Saxon royal line was remembered
more widely than just in Winchester itself. Or, perhaps, because
Malmesbury was situated close to the border between Mercia and Wessex, the location sent a final message that he had been king for all the
English people, not just for the West Saxons.[6] During his life Æthelstan
is said to have been generous to those at Malmesbury Abbey, to have
provided them with a plentiful supply of relics and lands. After his death
the Malmesbury community stood to gain from his burial in their
church, since the presence of his remains had the potential to attract
pilgrims from whom financial offerings could be expected. William
himself refers to the fame conferred on Malmesbury by Æthelstan's
choice to be buried there, and inserts a small poem to mark his death:

> Here lies one honoured by the world and grieved by his land:
> Path of rectitude, thunderbolt of justice, model of purity.
> His spirit has gone to heaven, its covering of flesh dissolved:
> An urn receives those triumphant relics.
> The sun had lit up Scorpio with its twelfth dawn
> When he struck down the king with his tail.[7]

The early medieval Malmesbury site is known to have comprised a number of churches, but none of their physical remains has so far been uncovered.[8] The location of Æthelstan's original burial is also lost, but a
tomb from the late fourteenth or early fifteenth century, constructed in
order to generate enthusiasm for his cult, can be found in the current
abbey. It bears a stone replica of a crowned Æthelstan dressed in late
medieval garb.[9]

The death of such a powerful individual opened new opportunities,
with the result that the political situation rapidly changed. As we have
seen, Æthelstan had remained unmarried throughout his life and produced no known heirs. Edmund, his half-brother, and the person who
had fought alongside him at *Brunanburh*, therefore became king at the
age of eighteen in a succession that seems not to have been contested.
The relative ease of the transition in power may imply that Edmund's
accession had been agreed in advance. Some of Edmund's diplomas

dated 940 style him 'king of the English'.[10] But the English kingdom bequeathed to him by Æthelstan quickly proved difficult to hold together. On the basis of the patchy and incompatible sources that survive, it has proved challenging to reconstruct the details and bare chronology of Northumbrian history following Æthelstan's death and into the 940s. A number of different scenarios have been proposed.[11] According to one reading of the evidence, Óláf Guthfrithson, the very person defeated by Æthelstan at *Brunanburh*, set sail from Dublin already in 939, presumably after receiving news of Æthelstan's death, and arrived soon afterwards in Northumbria in 939 or 940.[12] At York, Óláf marked his arrival by the minting of an extraordinary series of coins known as the 'Raven type'. If a raven is indeed the bird depicted, it may form an allusion to the pagan god Odin, who is associated in Old Norse legend with the bird.[13] Óláf's new set of coins constituted a conspicuous change from the English coins previously used at York, revealed not only by the imagery just described, but also by its inscription ANLAF CVNVNC, a combination of the Old English name 'Óláf' and the Old Norse word for 'king', and also by the weight of the coin, which was deliberately lowered from the English standard.[14] As well as taking control in York, Óláf seems to have extended his rule into the east midlands. In doing so, he reversed many of the territorial gains previously made by Æthelstan and his father, Edward, and became the first viking to resume authority in northern and midland England since Sihtric (d. 927). Óláf did not rule in Northumbria for long, as he died ca. 941.[15] But a pattern, of alternating viking and English rule at York had been set, and would endure until about 954, when York would receive its last viking ruler.[16]

How, then, do we assess Æthelstan's rule, and what kind of person had he been? There can be no doubting his achievements in being the first king to have brought together a kingdom recognisable as 'England'. His royal scribe, 'Æthelstan A', was fully justified in proclaiming in elaborate terms Æthelstan's new-found levels of power. Having been brought up in Mercia, away from the centre of power in Wessex, and having witnessed his father's struggles in trying to shore up parts of the midlands and wrest control from the hands of viking settlers, he may quickly have realised that his main chance of political success lay in forcibly bringing together all of the English kingdoms under his control. In this regard he may have been influenced by the example of his grandfather, Alfred, who had successfully won over Mercia, and, in joining it with Wessex, had for the first time created a 'kingdom of the Anglo-Saxons'. Æthelstan's 'England', as we have seen, comprised people from a variety of ethnic and cultural backgrounds. And, despite the advances he made in modes of governance—revealed by his use of diplomas, laws, and coins—there were complications in how he asserted his rule at the limits of his authority, especially once he stepped beyond the River Tees in Northumbria. In one respect, though, Æthelstan's formation of an English kingdom was aided by a sense of common identity that can be evidenced as early as the eighth century. When the great Northumbrian, Bede, wrote his *Ecclesiastical History* in 731, he opened by dedicating it to the then king of Northumbria, Ceolwulf. The king, Bede tells us, had 'asked to see the "History of the English Church and People"' (*Historiam gentis Anglorum ecclesiasticam*), which Bede had recently completed.[17] It is striking that Bede could refer to a history of one people—explicitly the English people (*gens Anglorum*)—at a time when the political reality involved an 'England' comprising a number of individual and warring kingdoms. This was an idea that may have come to Bede through the letters of Pope Gregory the Great, who had initiated the Roman Christian mission to England. And Bede had good reason to perpetuate the concept: as a Jarrow monk who wanted above all to foster the idea of one church that adhered to Roman customs, he was also keen to promote the idea of the 'church of the English' (*ecclesia Anglorum*). Political stability brought with it benefits for the church and the establishment of Christianity. But in fostering ideas of a *gens* and *ecclesia* of the English, he conveyed a powerful notion of a Germanic people who, despite their differences, could recognise a shared identity. This early sense of an 'English' identity has been labelled 'precocious' by modern historians.[18] When Alfred created his 'kingdom of the Anglo-Saxons' by joining Wessex and Mercia, and when he was also sponsoring an educational reform that placed a special emphasis on the use of the English vernacular, Bede's text provided inspiration and was one of the texts selected for translation from Latin into Old English. It is perhaps no surprise, then, that it was during the reign of Alfred that we detect a growing sense of what it meant to be a member of the 'English' people, the *Angelcynn* in Old English. When Alfred was negotiating terms with viking Guthrum, for example, he states that he was doing so in conjunction with the *witan* 'of all the English race' (*ealles Angelcynnes witan*). Seen in the context of Alfred's creation of the 'kingdom of the Anglo-Saxons', and the notion of 'Englishness' that had circulated since the early eighth century, and then of Edward's accession to the 'kingdom of the Anglo-Saxons' and his great efforts to secure Mercia and to gain recognition of northern rulers in 920, Æthelstan's formation of the English kingdom becomes easier to understand. Of course, quite what it meant to be a member of the *gens Anglorum* would have signified different things to different people: we cannot expect someone in York, so recently ruled by descendants of the family of Ívarr, to have had the same outlook as someone in Winchester, Wessex's political centre. The same holds true today. And although Æthelstan formed one English kingdom, we have seen that the polity was in reality precarious and there were cracks beneath the surface. Æthelstan's triumph involved his gaining recognition as the first 'king of England' and his being the first ruler who gave the *gens Anglorum* a kingdom whose political and geographical shape could be recognised literally as a 'land of the English', the *Engla lond* in Old English: England.

In addition to his creation of the 'kingdom of the Anglo-Saxons', Alfred had also seen the merit in winning over the Welsh, and Æthelstan, too, had wider British ambitions. As we have seen, he implemented a policy that resulted in the regular attendance of Welsh kings at his royal assemblies, and, following a military campaign in Alba in 934, he was able to command the presence of the king of the Scots and the king of the Strathclyde Britons as well. The royal assembly he held at Cirencester in 935, at which were present three Welsh kings and the kings of Alba and of Strathclyde/Cumbria, made deliberate use of the Roman origins of the site, evident in the physical remains all around them. In some ways he was at the height of his power that day: no king before him had united the different English kingdoms, less still compelled the presence of such an array of British kings to a royal assembly in England. It was fitting that Æthelstan and his advisers stressed connections with the Roman past. In doing so they conveyed a sense of the king's *imperium*, which they would make explicit in the inscriptions used on his coins and diplomas regularly issued from the centre of his power.

Æthelstan may also have had another example in mind. He had a keen understanding of the politics of contemporary Europe, to the extent that, as we have seen, he formulated a considered policy to win over rulers in different parts of the European continent and made use of his numerous half-sisters as part of strategic marriage alliances. Ambassadors from the Continent, in approaching Æthelstan in England, brought gifts that made connections with the great European emperor of the late eighth and early ninth centuries, Charlemagne.[19] Charlemagne had come closer than anyone else to reestablishing the geographical bounds of the old Roman Empire in western Europe, and he had provided a centralised and sophisticated means of administering those extended territories. Æthelstan could not claim to have won the levels of power that Charlemagne had earlier achieved. But there were similarities both in the way that Æthelstan joined together formerly independent territories and in the means by which he sought to govern them.[20] The English king and his advisers certainly had a good understanding of the power of political propaganda, of presenting him as if he were a Charlemagne-like figure. From the evidence of his diplomas, his coins and his law codes, we form the clear impression of a king with unprecedented political *auctoritas* (authority) and one who was keen to publicize his elevated standing as widely as possible. Not only was he the 'first king of England', but he was the 'king of all Britain', too. A measure of the success of this message is provided by the reverence with which a text from outside of England, the *Annals of Ulster*, registered his death: he was characterised as the 'pillar of the dignity of the western world'.[21]

From the perspective of some eleven hundred years after his period as king, and working from the patchy, jaundiced, and stereotypical nature of the surviving sources, it is notoriously difficult to know anything about Æthelstan the man. According to the only description we have of him, preserved in the pages of William of Malmesbury, he was slim, fair-haired, and of average height. In temperament, we are told that he was able to adjust his disposition according to need: for nobles he was 'serious in consideration of his own position', while for those of humbler background he 'laid aside the haughty air of royalty and was mild and affable'.[22] These descriptions are so generic as to be almost worthless. But I think we can say a little more about the type of person the first king of England must have been. His meteoric rise from a position of some uncertainty to rulership over a newly formed 'England', and also parts of Britain, must mean that he was a man of peculiar ambition and drive. In order to achieve his aims, amid a contemporary scene that was riven with political intrigue and external threats, he was ruthless in his actions, epitomised by his Scottish war of 934, his slaughter of the alliance that rose against him at *Brunanburh* in 937, and his 939 military intervention on the Continent. Murmurs that he may have been involved in the death of his brother, Edwin, are credible. It is striking that, earlier in the same passage by William of Malmesbury which offers a description of Æthelstan, the twelfth-century historian comments that Æthelstan was able to unite England simply by the 'terror' (*terrore*) of his name. Although William's comment may have been inspired by literary conventions,[23] those in tenth-century Wales were in no doubt about the brutality of English rule: Welsh inhabitants had been so affected by the English that, as shown in the poem *Armes Prydein Vawr*, they dreamed in the most bloodthirsty terms of the multiple ways in which they could cast off English rule and bring about the slaughter of the English people. In apparent contrast to his ruthlessness, Æthelstan was also an enthusiastic patron of the arts: intellectual life flourished under his protection, and scholars from across Europe sought out his court as a place where learning would be encouraged. So, too, did the church prosper. Numerous establishments were favoured with gifts of land and precious objects, and he enabled interactions with the Continent in such a way that manuscripts concerning various aspects of Christian worship, and continental clerics, made their way to England. In this sense, the image of Æthelstan in the earliest surviving contemporary manuscript portrait of an English king, in which he is shown with bowed head in front of St Cuthbert, seems realistic.

It is true that Æthelstan's creation of the English kingdom did not outlast his own death. In this respect, his achievements have been found wanting by some historians who have (rightly) pointed out that any advance towards 'England' was tied to the rule and actions of one person. Recent assessments have suggested that in fact the creation of England proper should be credited to one of Æthelstan's successors, Edgar *pacificus* ('the peaceable'), who became king of the English in 959 and ruled until 975. It was only under Edgar that an administrative system of shires that embraced the whole of the English kingdom was firmly established and likewise a single system of coinage.[24] But just because the English kingdom broke down after Æthelstan's death in 939, and because systems of administration were not as widespread or as enduring as they would later be, does not mean that we should deprive Æthelstan of the accolade of being the 'first king of England'. In fact, he had been so ahead of his time that it would have been more surprising if his political achievements had endured. He had clearly shown what could be achieved and provided a political framework for future kings, such as Edgar himself, for which he deserves to be more widely known.[25] The year 927, when Æthelstan first formed England, should be as recognisable as 1066, the date when England was undone. Perhaps it says something about our collective outlook as a nation that we have historically focussed on England's conquest rather than its formation.

Soon after his death, writers and historians of the late tenth century onwards were quick to recognise the significance of Æthelstan's reign. For the layman Æthelweard, who composed a Latin translation of the *Anglo-Saxon Chronicle* towards the end of the tenth century, Æthelstan was both 'very mighty' (*robustissimus*) and had 'enjoyed the crown of empire' (*imperii functus fuerat stefos*). It is striking that Æthelweard deploys the word *imperium* and that, in mentioning 'the crown', he uses a Grecism, *stephos/stefos*, which is otherwise unattested in English texts of the pre-1066 period: this was partly the result of the style in which Æthelweard wrote his text, but it also indicated his desire to stress the unique power that Æthelstan had achieved. As a result of Æthelstan's victory at *Brunanburh*, so Æthelweard reports, England became a place of plenty and of peace and security.[26]

Following the Norman Conquest of 1066, Anglo-Norman historians of the late eleventh and early twelfth centuries sought to understand Britain's earlier history. Numerous centres of learning were hard at work, of which one was the religious community at Worcester. Worcester had been unusual in having a bishop—Wulfstan II—whose episcopal tenure stretched across the turbulent events of 1066. Wulfstan commissioned an ambitious historical enterprise. Two monks, Florence and John, and possibly more, shared responsibility for the composition of a major chronicle. Extraordinarily, the autograph manuscript of this chronicle, dating from the 1130s to 1140s, survives to this day, housed in the library of Corpus Christi College, Oxford. Even a cursory glance at the manuscript, which is monumental in proportions and handsomely written, conveys something of the aspirations of the Worcester monks in their writing of history.

Before the chronicle proper begins, a series of preliminary texts can be found, which have not been printed in a modern edition and which include items such as episcopal lists and royal genealogies. They comprise an 'historian's tool-box', as one commentator has recently noted, a way for the Worcester monks to determine the core facts of English history.[27] On page 53 of the manuscript a genealogy of the West Saxon kings can be found. All the great names are there, including those of Alfred and his wife, Ealhswith, and then of Edward and his various wives, including his first, Ecgwynn. When the genealogy reaches the name of Æthelstan its author, unable to pass him over without further comment, inserts a summary entry just to the left. Translated from Latin, it reads, 'the vigorous and glorious King Æthelstan was the first of the kings of the English who ruled alone throughout the entirety of England'. For those writing history immediately after the Anglo-Saxon period there was no doubting Æthelstan's importance as the 'first king of England'.

———

Although the significance of Æthelstan's reign was recognised by his contemporaries, and by those in the early twelfth century who were the first to explicate the history of pre-Conquest England, his name is not today as readily recognisable as that of two other early medieval English kings: his grandfather, Alfred the Great, and one of his successors, Æthelred 'the Unready'. This can partly be explained by the fact that, unlike Alfred, Æthelstan seems not to have had the benefit of a contemporary biography composed in his favour. Alfred had Asser to sing his merits, and, while Æthelstan certainly profited from the grandiose expressions of his power articulated by his royal scribe, 'Æthelstan A', he seemingly did not commission an extended narrative that would have provided an account of his life and deeds—or, at least, none that now survives. The relatively slender overview in the work of William of Malmesbury is the most that has come down to us. Æthelred, meanwhile, is primarily known because he ultimately failed to protect the English kingdom from viking attack, with the result that the line of West Saxon kings was interrupted and the Danish Cnut became king in 1016. It is clear that Æthelred suffered in his reign from poor advice, which gained him the Old English epithet, *unræd*, which literally means 'bad counsel'. Over time, *unræd* morphed into its more famous version, 'the Unready': it is a mistranslation and misunderstanding of the Old English original, but it was a short-hand description of Æthelred that stuck and cemented his notoriety.[28] We might think that Æthelstan's status as the 'first king of England' and his actions at *Brunanburh* would have guaranteed his perpetual renown. That was certainly the view of the author Geffrei Gaimar, who, when he came to provide an Anglo-Norman history of England towards the middle of the twelfth century, commented that 'so many were killed' at *Brunanburh* 'that people will, I think, speak of it for evermore'.[29]

Gaimar's prediction was in one respect accurate: there is a large body of scholarly works which investigates many different aspects of Æthelstan's life and reign, and of the texts and artefacts that were produced in the early tenth century. The year 2024, which celebrated the eleven hundredth anniversary of Æthelstan's first becoming king, saw a degree of wider interest which included the holding of a carnival and an archaeological dig near Malmesbury Abbey, the latter resulting in the discovery of early medieval human remains in the grounds of the adjacent

Old Bell Hotel.[30] But, for whatever reason, Æthelstan has not benefited from as much popular attention as his life merits.[31] One possible explanation is tied to Alfred. When Anglo-Norman historians of the early to mid-twelfth century composed their accounts of pre-Conquest history, they had recourse to many of the sources on which we rely today—particularly the narrative backbone provided by different versions of the *Anglo-Saxon Chronicle*. In looking at the annals for Alfred's reign, which were composed at Alfred's court, they would have found a triumphalist overview designed to propound Alfred's successes to a wide audience, even for battles in which Alfred had lost to vikings. Read carefully, the annals betray the limits of Alfred's authority: when he takes London in 886, for example, it is said that 'all the English people that were not under subjection to the Danes submitted to him'.[32] The Danelaw is deliberately excluded from Alfred's hegemony. But the positive slant of the annals, particularly when compared to their poor equivalents for Æthelstan's reign, had the potential to influence readers. In about 1125, close to the time when the Worcester historians were composing their genealogies, another writer, Orderic Vitalis, had formed an alternative view. For Orderic, it was Alfred who was 'the first king to hold sway over all of England'.[33] As it turned out, it was an assessment that would prove enduring, and it is Alfred, not Æthelstan, who has lived on in the popular imagination, helped by the anointing of him as 'the Great'.[34] William of Malmesbury, in those verses he said he found in an 'ancient volume', had described Æthelstan as *Magnus*—'the Great'—but it was an appellation that did not persist.[35] Æthelstan, then, is a victim of historiography, all the more reason why he should now occupy our full attention.

GLOSSARY OF TECHNICAL
TERMS AND TITLES

ætheling An Old English term which has the literal meaning 'of noble family' and which, by the tenth century, was applied to those considered 'throne-worthy'.

burh A fortified stronghold, which later took on administrative functions and which often contained a mint.

Danelaw A term which refers to areas of the east midlands, East Anglia, and parts of Northumbria, in which there had been Scandinavian settlement and in which Scandinavian laws in part held force.

diploma A form of document in which a grantor, most often the king, grants land and associated rights to a beneficiary. By the early tenth century, a diploma was often bilingual in form, written mostly in Latin, but with a boundary clause that could be in the vernacular Old English.

ealdorman A royal official in charge of an administrative district known as a shire.

moneyer The person responsible for producing the king's coinage.

ordeal A physical test prescribed in law for determining a person's guilt/innocence.

reeve A land-owning official in a position of power. The reeve had various responsibilities, including the enforcement of the king's laws.

royal assembly A gathering presided over by the king and attended by important secular and ecclesiastical dignitaries; sometimes referred to by the Old English term *witan*, which means literally 'wise men'. Royal assemblies provided the fora for the issuing of royal diplomas and law codes.

subregulus A term (roughly meaning 'sub-king') in the diplomas of 'Æthelstan A' applied to the kings from the Welsh kingdoms, from Alba and from Strathclyde/Cumbria, who attended Æthelstan's royal assemblies.

thegn A land-owning noble who held a position in the localities (with a variety of responsibilities).

tithe A tax owed to the church, comprising one-tenth of livestock and crops.

Adelolf (d. 933) — Count of Boulogne. Son of Baldwin II, cousin of Æthelstan.

Ælfflæd — Second consort of King Edward the Elder (married ca. 899). Pronounced 'Aelf-flad'.

Ælfgifu — Daughter of Edward the Elder and Ælfflæd; may have married Louis of Burgundy. Pronounced 'Alv-yi-voo'. *On the difficulties of her identification, see Appendix II in the present volume.*

Ælfweard (d. 2 August 924) — Son of Edward the Elder and Ælfflæd; Æthelstan's half-brother.

Æthelflæd (d. 12 June 918) — 'Lady of the Mercians', consort of Æthelred, ealdorman of the Mercians, and daughter of King Alfred the Great. Æthelstan's aunt. Pronounced 'Ath-el-flad'.

Æthelred (d. 911) — Ealdorman of the Mercians, and husband of Æthelflæd, 'lady of the Mercians'.

'Æthelstan A' — Royal scribe working for the king, known by this anonymous title, who was responsible for diplomas written in the years 928–35.

Æthelweard (d. ca. 998) — Ealdorman 'of the western provinces' who, between 975 and 983, wrote a Latin translation of the *Anglo-Saxon Chronicle* known as the *Chronicon Æthelweardi* (Chronicle of Æthelweard).

Æthelwold (d. 902)	Cousin of King Edward the Elder who challenged for the throne.
Æthelwulf (d. 13 January 858)	King of the West Saxons 839–58, father of King Alfred the Great, and thus Æthelstan's great-grandfather.
Alan Barbetorte ('Crooked Beard'; d. 952)	Duke of Brittany.
Alfred the Great (d. 26 October 899)	King of the West Saxons 871–ca. 886; king of the Anglo-Saxons ca. 886–899. Æthelstan's grandfather.
Arnulf I (d. 965)	Count of Flanders. Son of Baldwin II of Flanders and Ælfthryth, Æthelstan's aunt.
Asser (d. 908 or 909)	A Welsh monk from St David's in the kingdom of Dyfed in south-west Wales who became a member of King Alfred's court and wrote an account (known as a *vita*) of the king's life.
Baldwin II (d. 918)	Count of Flanders, married to Ælfthryth, the daughter of King Alfred, and thus Æthelstan's aunt.
Cenwald	Bishop of Worcester 928 or 929 to 957, who played a pivotal role in the marriage negotiations between Æthelstan's half-sister, Eadgyth, and Otto I. Pronounced 'Ken-wald'.
Charles I ('the Great'; d. 814)	King of the Franks 768–814; king of the Lombards 774–814; and emperor 800–14.
Charles the Simple (d. 929)	King of West Francia 898–923.
Constantine II (d. 952)	King of Alba 900–ca. 943.
Cynath	An abbot active in Æthelstan's reign whose name may associate him with Pictish or Gaelic territory.

Eadgifu (d. ca. 966/7)	Third consort of King Edward the Elder (married ca. 919). Pronounced 'Ey-ahd-yee-voo'.
Eadgifu (d. in or after 951)	Daughter of Edward the Elder and Ælfflæd, consort of Charles the Simple, king of the West Franks. Half-sister of Æthelstan.
Eadgifu	Daughter of Edward the Elder and Eadgifu, may have married Louis of Burgundy. Half-sister of Æthelstan. *On the difficulties of her identification, see Appendix II in the present volume.*
Eadgyth (d. 946)	Daughter of Edward the Elder and Ælfflæd, consort of Otto I, king of East Francia and emperor. Half-sister of Æthelstan. Pronounced 'Ay-ahd-geeth'.
Eadhild (d. in or before 937)	Daughter of Edward the Elder and Ælfflæd, consort of Hugh the Great, duke of the Franks. Half-sister of Æthelstan.
Ealdred	Ruler in Northumbria who submitted to Edward the Elder in 920 and to Æthelstan in 927. Son of Eadwulf.
Ealhswith (d. 902)	Consort of King Alfred the Great. Pronounced 'Alch-swith'.
Ecgwynn	First consort of King Edward the Elder. Æthelstan's mother. Pronounced 'Edge-win'.
Edward the Elder (d. 17 July 924)	King of the Anglo-Saxons 26 October 899–17 July 924. Son of Alfred the Great; Æthelstan's father.
Edwin	Æthelstan's half-brother who drowned at sea under mysterious circumstances in 933.
Flodoard (d. 966)	Member of the West Frankish church of Rheims responsible for writing a set of *Annals* and the *History of the Church of Rheims*.

Folcuin (d. 16 September 990)	Monk of Saint-Bertin in Saint-Omer, France, who wrote the *Gesta Abbatum Sithiensium* (Deeds of the Abbots of Saint Bertin), in 961 or 962.
Frithestan (d. 932 × 933)	Bishop of Winchester, and sometime opponent of Æthelstan.
Gislebert (d. 939)	Duke in Lotharingia.
Guthrum (d. 890)	Viking leader, defeated by King Alfred the Great at the 878 Battle of Edington. He came to terms with Alfred, became king of East Anglia and, having been baptised, was given a baptismal name of 'Æthelstan'.
Hæsten (fl. 882–93)	Viking leader of the late ninth century. Pronounced 'Hay-sten'.
Hákon Haraldsson	Son of Harald Finehair; king of Norway ca. 933 or 934 to ca. 960.
Hálfdan (d. 877)	One of viking leaders of 'great army' in England. The brother of Ívarr.
Henry the Fowler (d. 936)	*Dux* in Saxony, king of East Francia 919–36.
Heribert II (d. 943)	Count of Vermandois.
Hrotsvitha	Member of Gandersheim Abbey, first German female poet, and historian.
Hugh the Great (d. 956)	Duke of Francia 936–56; he married Æthelstan's half-sister, Eadhild.
Hywel Dda ('the Good'; d. 949 or 950)	King in Wales, ruler of Deheubarth from 903 or 904 and latterly in Gwynedd from 942 or 943.
Idwal Foel ab Anarawd (d. 942)	King of Gwynedd 916–42.
Ingimundr	Viking leader of the early tenth century who raided Anglesey and is then said to have settled in and around Chester.

Israel the Grammarian	Breton scholar connected with Æthelstan's court.
Ívarr (d. 873)	Viking leader whose descendants exerted much influence in Dublin and York. Described as 'king of the Norsemen of all Ireland and Britain' in the *Annals of Ulster*.
Louis IV (d'Outremer)	King of West Francia 936–54. Son of Charles the Simple and Eadgifu, half-sister of Æthelstan.
Matuedoi	Count of Poher.
Morgan ab Owain (also Morgan Hen, 'the Old'; d. 974)	King of Glywysing and Gwent (later known as Morgannwg).
Óláf Guthfrithson (d. 941)	King of Dublin and York. Grandson of Ívarr.
Óláf Sihtricson (Cuarán, 'of the Sandal'; d. 981)	King of Dublin and York.
Otto I ('the Great'; d. 973)	King of East Francia 936–73, king of Italy 962–73, and emperor 962–73.
Owain ap Hywel (d. ca. 930)	King of Glywysing and Gwent (later known as Morgannwg).
Owain ap Dyfnwal (fl. 934)	King of Strathclyde/Cumbria.
Peter	Possible author of 'Carta dirige Gressus.'
Ragnall I (d. 920)	King of York. Grandson of Ívarr.
Regino of Prüm (d. ca. 915)	Abbot of Prüm; author of a chronicle.
Richer of Rheims	Monk of Saint-Rémi at Rheims; author of a history of the West Frankish kings covering the period 888–ca. 998.
Sihtric Cáech (the 'One-Eyed'; d. 927)	King of York. Grandson of Ívarr. He married Æthelstan's unnamed sister.

Tewdwr ab Elise	King of Brycheiniog.
Thietmar of Merseburg (d. 1 Dec. 1018)	Bishop of Merseburg, and chronicler.
Widukind of Corvey	East Frankish historian.
William Longsword (d. 942)	Duke of Normandy 927–42.
William of Malmesbury (d. in or after 1142)	Monk and scholar, author of the *Gesta Regum Anglorum* (Deeds of the English Kings) and the *Gesta Pontificum Anglorum* (Deeds of the English Bishops).
Wulfstan I (d. 955 or 956)	Archbishop of York.

CHRONOLOGY OF PRINCIPAL EVENTS

Note that the order of the events listed for any given year does not necessarily replicate the original order in which they occurred.

894 Possibly the year in which Æthelstan was born; English kingdoms are besieged by viking attacks.

899 Death of King Alfred the Great (26 October); accession of Edward the Elder, Æthelstan's father.

900 Edward the Elder is consecrated king (8 June).

918 Death of Æthelflæd, 'lady of the Mercians', Æthelstan's aunt.

919 The viking Ragnall, of the dynasty of Ívarr, is recognised as king in York; marriage of Eadgifu, Æthelstan's half-sister, to Charles the Simple.

920 Sihtric Cáech, brother of Ragnall, departs Dublin and makes for England, attacking Davenport, south of Manchester.

921 Ragnall dies; Guthfrith arrives in Dublin; Sihtric Cáech recognised as king in York.

924 Death of Edward the Elder (17 July); Æthelstan becomes 'king of the Anglo-Saxons and of the Danes'.

925 Æthelstan consecrated king at Kingston-upon-Thames (4 September).

926 Æthelstan meets Sihtric Cáech at Tamworth in Mercia (30 January) and arranges a marriage alliance between Sihtric and his unnamed full sister.

927 Death of Sihtric Cáech; Æthelstan becomes 'king of the English', having taken control of Northumbria; Æthelstan receives the submission of various rulers at a ceremony near Eamont Bridge (12 July).

929   Bishop Cenwald leads party to the East Frankish court, as a result of which Æthelstan's half-sister, Eadgyth, marries Otto I in 929/30.

933   Death of Edwin, half-brother of Æthelstan, under mysterious circumstances.

934   Æthelstan goes to war against the Scots in Alba and penetrates far into their kingdom; death of viking Guthfrith of the dynasty of Ívarr, and of Ealdred of Bamburgh.

936   Otto becomes king of East Francia; Æthelstan is in York, from where he receives a delegation of Franks who seek the return of Louis d'Outremer.

937   The Battle of *Brunanburh* is fought. Æthelstan and the *ætheling* Edmund overcome an alliance comprising Óláf Guthfrithson, king of Dublin; Constantine II, king of Alba; and Owain, king of Strathclyde/Cumbria.

939   According to Flodoard of Rheims, Æthelstan sends a fleet to intervene in continental affairs; Æthelstan dies at Gloucester (27 October) and is subsequently buried at the abbey of Malmesbury.

Æthelstan's Diplomas

WHAT FOLLOWS BELOW is a list in chronological order of the (wholly or partially) genuine diplomas issued in the name of King Æthelstan. It is adapted from a lecture handout prepared by Professor Simon Keynes. The diplomas by the royal scribe 'Æthelstan A' can be divided into four separate groups on the basis of their style and formulation, as indicated in the list. By convention, diplomas are cited according to their so-called 'S' number, which refers to their entries in P. H. Sawyer, *Anglo-Saxon Charters: An Annotated List and Bibliography*, Royal Historical Society Guides and Handbooks 8 (London: Offices of the Royal Historical Society, 1968). Sawyer's catalogue can also be accessed online as the 'Electronic Sawyer', managed by Cambridge University Library: https:// esawyer.lib.cam.ac.uk/about/index.html. Where a diploma has been edited in the British Academy series 'Anglo-Saxon Charters', its place in the relevant volume/archive is indicated in parentheses afterwards, using the following abbreviations (a practice adopted throughout the present volume):

Abing   *Charters of Abingdon Abbey*, ed. S. E. Kelly, Anglo-Saxon Charters 7–8 (Oxford: Oxford University Press, 2000–2001).

Bark   *Charters of Barking Abbey and Waltham Holy Cross*, ed. S. E. Kelly, Anglo-Saxon Charters 20 (Oxford: Oxford University Press, 2021).

Burt *Charters of Burton Abbey*, ed. P. H. Sawyer, Anglo-Saxon
    Charters 2 (Oxford: Oxford University Press, 1979).

CantCC *Charters of Christ Church, Canterbury*, ed. N. Brooks and
    S. E. Kelly, Anglo-Saxon Charters 17–18 (Oxford:
    Oxford University Press, 2013).

CantStA *Charters of St Augustine's Abbey, Canterbury*, ed. S. E.
    Kelly, Anglo-Saxon Charters 4 (Oxford: Oxford Univer-
    sity Press, 1995).

Glast *Charters of Glastonbury Abbey*, ed. S. E. Kelly, Anglo-Saxon
    Charters 15 (Oxford: Oxford University Press, 2012).

Malm *Charters of Malmesbury Abbey*, ed. S. E. Kelly, Anglo-
    Saxon Charters 11 (Oxford: Oxford University Press,
    2005).

North *Charters of Northern Houses*, ed. D. A. Woodman,
    Anglo-Saxon Charters 16 (Oxford: Oxford University
    Press, 2012).

Sel   *Charters of Selsey*, ed. S. E. Kelly, Anglo-Saxon Charters
    6 (Oxford: Oxford University Press, 1998).

Shaft *Charters of Shaftesbury Abbey*, ed. S. E. Kelly, Anglo-
    Saxon Charters 5 (Oxford: Oxford University Press,
    1995).

Sherb *Charters of Sherborne*, ed. M. A. O'Donovan, Anglo-
    Saxon Charters 3 (Oxford: Oxford University Press,
    1988).

WinchNM *Charters of the New Minster, Winchester*, ed. S. Miller,
    Anglo-Saxon Charters 9 (Oxford: Oxford University
    Press, 2001).

WinchOM *Charters of the Old Minster, Winchester*, ed. A. R. Rumble
    (in preparation).

Diplomas of 925–926

S 395 (*Burt* 2): 925.
S 394 (*CantStA* 26): 4 September 925.
S 397 (*Burt* 3): 926.
S 396 (*Abing* 21): 926.

Diplomas of 928 (by 'Æthelstan A')

S 400 (*WinchOM* 57): 16 April 928.
S 399 (*Glast* 23): 16 April 928.

Diplomas of 930 (by 'Æthelstan A')

S 403 (*Sel* 17): 3 April 930.
S 405: 29 April 930.

Diplomas of 931–933 (by 'Æthelstan A')

S 412 (*WinchOM* 58): 23 March 931.
S 413 (*Abing* 23): 20 June 931.
S 1604 (*Abing* 24): 15 July 931.
S 416 (*WinchOM* 59): 12 November 931.
S 417 (*WinchOM* 60): 30 August 932.
S 418a (*Bark* 4): 9 November 932.
S 418 (*WinchNM* 10): 24 December 932.
S 419 (*Shaft* 8): 24 December 932.
S 379 (*WinchNM* 8): 11 January 933.
S 422 (*Sherb* 7): 26 January 933.
S 423 (*Sherb* 8): 26 January 933.

Diplomas of 934–935 (by 'Æthelstan A')

S 425 (*CantCC* 106): 28 May 934.
S 407 (*North* 1): 7 June 934.
S 426 (*Glast* 24): 13 September 934.
S 434 (*Malm* 26): 21 December 935.
S 458: 935?

Diplomas of 935–939

S 430 (*WinchOM* 63): 935.
S 429 (*Shaft* 9): 935.

S 431 (*Glast* 25): 936 (for 935?).

S 438: 937.

S 432: 937.

S 437: 937.

S 411 (*Abing* 29): 937?

S 441 (*WinchOM* 66): 938.

S 442 (*Glast* 26): 938.

S 440 (*WinchOM* 65): 938.

S 448 (*Abing* 30): 939.

S 449 (*WinchOM* 70): 939.

S 447 (*CantCC* 107): 939.

S 446 (*WinchOM* 69): 939.

S 445 (*Shaft* 10): 939.

The Identity of Æthelstan's Half-Sister, Sent to East Francia in 929

IN CHAPTER 6 we saw that Æthelstan sent two of his half-sisters to the East Frankish court, in order that one could be selected as a bride for Otto (d. 973), the son of the then German king, Henry the Fowler (d. 936). Eadgyth (Æthelstan's daughter by his second wife, Ælfflæd) ultimately became Otto's consort in 929 or 930, but the identity of the other sister, who herself married into the Burgundian royal house, has caused great confusion and difficulty since none of the surviving sources preserve details that fully support each other. It is worth setting out the evidence here, even if it cannot be completely resolved. It is most probable that her name would have been either Ælfgifu, or Eadgifu.

A complexity, as we will see, involves the possible names provided by our sources, which are very similar to each other: Ealdgyth, Ælfgifu and Eadgifu. William of Malmesbury betrays his own confusion by providing discrepant details in the different parts of his text. In one instance he says that an 'Ealdgyth', as well as Eadgyth, were sent to Henry, and that Eadgyth became Otto's wife, while Ealdgyth was married to 'a certain duke near the Alps'.[1] On another occasion he notes that Eadgyth and (this time) an Ælfgifu, whom he describes as being two of six daughters of Edward by his second wife, Ælfflæd, had been sent. He again says that the sister who was not chosen by Otto was given to an

Alpine duke, but this time he suggests that it was Ælfgifu (rather than Eadgyth) who had married Otto, which we know to be incorrect. William goes on to say that Edward had two other daughters by his third wife, Eadgifu, one named Eadburh and another (confusingly) with the same name as her mother, Eadgifu. This latter Eadgifu is said by William to have married Louis of Aquitaine; and Eadburh became a nun in Winchester.[2]

Further information is provided by two other sources, the late tenth-century *Chronicle*, written by the ealdorman Æthelweard, and Hrotsvitha's poetical text, the *Gesta Ottonis* (Deeds of Otto), composed in the period 965–68.[3] Æthelweard addresses the prologue of his *Chronicle* to his relative named Matilda, who was the abbess of Essen. Æthelweard explains that while Matilda was descended from the line of King Alfred, he was descended from that of Alfred's brother, Æthelred, making them distant cousins. Matilda was also herself the granddaughter of Otto and Eadgyth, and Æthelweard explains that Æthelstan had sent two of his half-sisters for Otto to choose from and that Otto had selected Eadgyth, 'from whom you [i.e. Matilda] spring in the first place'. Although he does not name the other sister, he adds the detail that she married a king near the Alps. He hopes that Matilda might be able to supply him with the further information about the second sister's identity, both because of her own family connection and because she is the more likely, given her residence in Europe, to have the detail to hand.[4] Æthelweard confirms, then, that it was Eadgyth who had married Otto, and, while he could not identify the second sister's name, he also says that she married an Alpine ruler, whom he terms a king.

When Hrotsvitha composed her poetical piece celebrating Otto, she, too, described how Otto gained an English wife. According to Hrotsvitha, ambassadors had been sent to Æthelstan to request Eadgyth's hand. Hrotsvitha goes on to describe the nobility of Eadgyth's lineage and also says that she was sent to Otto along with her sister, whom Hrotsvitha names as *Adiva*, a rendering of the Old English name, 'Eadgifu'.[5] Hrotsvitha gives no further detail about this particular sister's next steps and to whom she would be married. In William of Malmesbury's narrative, the only Eadgifu that this could refer to is the one he describes as being matched with Louis of Aquitaine (and not as having been sent to Otto).

How, if at all, can these discrepant details be resolved? It has been suggested that William of Malmesbury, when looking back at records from the period, mistakenly created an extra daughter for Edward the Elder, either by Edward's second wife, Ælfflæd, or by his third wife, Eadgifu.[6] As we have seen, Hrotsvitha names the thus far unidentified sister as 'Eadgifu' (*Adiva*), which would make her the daughter of Edward's third wife, also named Eadgifu. There are two reasons why this identification has been doubted: firstly, because Eadgifu would have been very young at the time of the marriage (about ten or eleven); and secondly, because the three sisters we know to have been married to European rulers were all full sisters and shared Ælfflæd as their mother. In one part of his account, William implies that the unidentified sister was also a daughter of Ælfflæd.[7] The arguments are important but not conclusive: we have seen that Æthelwulf had married a very young bride in Judith, and we know that Æthelstan's full sister by his mother Ecgwynn, had been married to Sihtric, the viking leader at York. Given that Æthelweard, who was writing in the late tenth century, was unable to recover the name of the sister concerned, it is possible that William, when writing in the early twelfth century, also had no further detail about the matter.[8]

If we put aside Hrotsvitha's identification of the second sister as 'Eadgifu' for one moment, and if we assume that William was correct to say that the sister was the daughter of Ælfflæd, then William seems to give her two different names, on one occasion calling her 'Ealdgyth' and on another 'Ælfgifu'.[9] Because William mentions the name of the unidentified sister in conjunction with the Eadgyth who was married to Otto, the name 'Ealdgyth' might represent a simple misreading and miscopying by William, with the result that 'Ælfgifu' should be the preferred name of this second sister. In sum, we may be dealing with an extra daughter of Edward by his second wife, probably named Ælfgifu, or with an extra daughter by his third wife, named Eadgifu.

NOTES

Introduction

1. For the location of the meeting, see chapter 2 of the present volume.

2. For the identity of the poet, see chapter 2 of the present volume.

3. For this view, see Edmonds, 'The Emergence and Transformation of Medieval Cumbria'. Scholars have not been in agreement about whether or not 'Strathclyde' and 'the land of the Cumbrians' should be thought of as one kingdom, nor about the suggestion that the kingdom was expanding southwards in the late ninth and early tenth centuries. For a useful summary of all of the complex material, with details of further references, see Edmonds, 'The Expansion of the Kingdom of Strathclyde'. For a history of the kingdom, see, for example, Phythian-Adams, *Land of the Cumbrians*; and Clarkson, *Strathclyde and the Anglo-Saxons*.

4. Woolf, 'Scotland', 251–52. Dál Riata included parts of the western seaboard of modern Scotland (roughly in the region of Argyll) and of Northern Ireland (roughly in County Antrim). Pictavia, or Pictland, was the area north of the Firth of Forth in which the people known as the Picts lived.

5. Woolf, *From Pictland to Alba 789–1070*; McGuigan, *Máel Coluim III 'Canmore'*, 20–93.

6. Lloyd, *A History of Wales*; Charles-Edwards, *Wales and the Britons*; Edwards, *Life in Early Medieval Wales*, 262–63.

7. Downham, *Viking Kings*, 12. For overviews of Irish history of the period, see, for example, Byrne, *Irish Kings and High-Kings*; Ó Cróinín, *Early Medieval Ireland*; E. Breathnach, 'Ireland, c. 900–c. 1000'; and Charles-Edwards, *Early Christian Ireland*.

8. Smyth, *Scandinavian York and Dublin*; Downham, *Viking Kings*.

9. For a recent biography of Charlemagne, and the importance of calling him Charles, see Nelson, *King and Emperor*, 7. Because it is more familiar to the modern reader, the name Charlemagne is used in this book.

10. For the complexities in describing the geographical extent of West Francia, see Dunbabin, 'West Francia: The Kingdom', 372–74. See also Firnhaber-Baker, *House of Lilies*.

11. Barraclough, *The Crucible of Europe*; McKitterick, *The Frankish Kingdoms*; Wickham, *The Inheritance of Rome*.

12. Crawford, *Daily Life in Anglo-Saxon England*, 74.

13. Thomov, 'Four Scandinavian Ship Graffiti'.

14. Ortenberg, 'Archbishop Sigeric's Journey to Rome in 990'.

15. For a recent account of the use of maps, including in the ancient world, see Caputo, *Tracks on the Ocean*.

16. Keynes, 'Manuscripts of the *Anglo-Saxon Chronicle*'. This is not the only model of transmission that has been suggested for this highly complex set of manuscripts. Brooks, 'Why Is the *Anglo-Saxon Chronicle* about Kings?', has suggested that, rather than the *Chronicle* being updated in the different localities across the kingdom, there may have been a central court copy that was consulted on different occasions and that these versions then formed the basis for the extant copies 'A'–'G'.

17. For the 'northern recension', its contents, and the extent to which it does contain a northern orientation, see Stafford, *After Alfred*, 106–34.

18. For a very important elucidation of the different evolutionary stages of the *Chronicle* from the late ninth to the mid-tenth century, see Stafford, *After Alfred*, 52–105.

19. In versions 'B' and 'C' they have been inserted as a block, whereas in version 'D' a degree of integration with existing annals has been attempted.

20. Stafford, *After Alfred*, 64–77, suggests that these Mercian annals ran in 'parallel' to Edward's 'court annals' of the same years (68).

21. The annals from 934 until the death of King Edmund in 946 form a block; see Stafford, *After Alfred*, 90–93.

22. WM, *GR*, ii.132 (ed. and trans. Mynors, Thomson and Winterbottom, 210–11), slightly adapted here.

23. WM, *GR*, ii.138 (ed. and trans. Mynors, Thomson and Winterbottom, 224–25).

24. For the idiosyncratic Latin style of the tenth century, known to scholars as hermeneutic Latin, see Lapidge, 'The Hermeneutic Style'.

25. For a positive interpretation, see Wood, 'The Making of King Aethelstan's Empire', 265–67; WM, *GR*, vol. 2, *Introduction and Commentary*, Thomson, 116–18; and Foot, *Æthelstan*, 251–28. For a more sceptical view, see Lapidge, 'Some Latin Poems', 50–59; and Dumville, *Wessex and England from Alfred to Edgar*, 142–43.

26. Roach, *Kingship and Consent*.

27. For the complexities of witness lists as a form of evidence, see chapter 3 of the present volume.

28. Diplomas of the second group, which were issued in the years 928–35, can themselves be sub-divided into four further groups. For a list of Æthelstan's diplomas which sets out all of these groups, see appendix I of the present volume.

29. Keynes, 'Royal Government and the Written Word'; and Roach, 'Law Codes and Legal Norms'.

30. I am grateful to Professor Rory Naismith for drawing my attention to the recent discovery of an Æthelstan coin from Lydford.

31. For the importance of such an outside perspective, but for the sixteenth and seventeenth centuries, see Jackson, *Devil-Land*.

32. Hudson, 'The Scottish Chronicle'.

33. *Libri vitae* contained the names of people who had some sort of special connection with the religious community in question. They often later attracted records and notes of other kinds too.

34. For further discussion, see Naismith, 'The Anglo-Saxons'.

35. In 2021, Æthelstan topped a Twitter poll conducted by Tom Holland to discover the identity of England's greatest ever monarch: https://x.com/theresthistory/status/14612735349

82934533?s=46&t=lievV3-mghPnx8wJdNWNVw. See also Holland, *Athelstan: The Making of England*; and Hill, *The Age of Æthelstan*.

Chapter One

1. English territory was not the only target. For viking attacks in Britain more widely, see chapter 5 of the present volume. See also Keynes, 'The Vikings in England'.

2. *ASC*, s.a. 870. Edmund died on 20 November 869. Because this part of the *Anglo-Saxon Chronicle* begins its years in September, the death of Edmund is noted in its annal for 870. For the detail that Edmund's resistance was only brief, see *The Chronicle of Æthelweard*, IV.2 (ed. and trans. Campbell, 36). Edmund, later known as Edmund the Martyr, was quickly culted. A shrine in his memory survives today in Bury St Edmunds; see Young, *In Search of England's Lost King*.

3. For the coins of Æthelred and Oswald, see Naismith, *MEC*, 147, 164.

4. *ASC*, s.a. 873.

5. We now know that there must have been several thousand vikings at Torksey in an island camp that stretched over an area of about fifty-five hectares and that, as well as housing those involved in fighting, there were also those responsible for crafts of various kinds, and possibly women and children too. See Hadley et al., 'The Winter Camp of the Viking Great Army'.

6. *ASC*, s.a. 874.

7. *ASC*, s.a. 877. Interpretation of the levels of power and status held by Ceolwulf II has changed recently thanks to study of the so-called 'Two Emperors' coins; on this, see Naismith, *MEC*, 169.

8. *ASC*, s.a. 866 and 867.

9. Ívarr is named as a leader of the viking army; see *The Chronicle of Æthelweard*, IV.2 (ed. and trans. Campbell, 35). For the identification of Ívarr, see Downham, *Viking Kings*, 63.

10. *ASC*, s.a. 875 and 876.

11. Downham, *Viking Kings*. For York and Dublin, see also Smyth, *Scandinavian York and Dublin*.

12. On Ealdred, see chapter 2 of the present volume. On the rulers of Bamburgh, see Keynes, 'Bamburgh'; and McGuigan, 'Bamburgh and the Northern English Realm', 95–150.

13. *ASC*, s.a. 871. Despite the *Anglo-Saxon Chronicle* suggesting there were nine battles, only six battles are in fact noted for 871; see Keynes and Lapidge, *Alfred the Great*, 243–44n78. On the prominence of war in the period, see Abels, 'Warfare in Early Medieval Britain'. I am very grateful to Richard Abels for sharing with me the manuscript of his chapter in advance of publication.

14. *ASC*, s.a. 871.

15. *ASC*, s.a. 876, 877 and 878.

16. Keynes and Lapidge, *Alfred the Great*, 248n103.

17. Asser, chap. 56 (trans. Keynes and Lapidge, 84–85).

18. Abrams, 'Edward the Elder's Danelaw'.

19. See Coupland, 'The Vikings in Francia and Anglo-Saxon England'.

20. The passage can be found in the preface to an Old English translation of Gregory the Great's *Pastoral Care*; see Keynes and Lapidge, *Alfred the Great*, 125.

21. See S 344 (*CantCC* 93), discussed in Brooks, *The Early History of the Church of Canterbury*, 171–72. See also *Charters of Christ Church Canterbury, Part 2*, ed. Brooks and Kelly, 793–99.

22. Asser, chap. 77 (trans. Keynes and Lapidge, 92–93).

23. Molyneaux, 'The *Old English Bede*'.

24. Keynes and Lapidge, *Alfred the Great*, 126.

25. Keynes and Lapidge, *Alfred the Great*, 203–6.

26. The scale of the literary resurgence under Alfred has been much debated. See, for example, Lapidge, 'Latin Learning in Ninth-Century England'; and Godden, 'The Alfredian Project'.

27. See Keynes, 'King Alfred and the Mercians'.

28. Naismith, *MEC*, 170–71.

29. *ASC*, s.a. 886.

30. For Alfred, the 'kingdom of the Anglo-Saxons', and ideas concerning the 'English', see Keynes, 'England, *c.* 900–1016', 459; Keynes, 'Edward, King of the Anglo-Saxons'; Foot, 'The Making of *Angelcynn*'; and Pratt, *The Political Thought of King Alfred the Great*, 6–7, 105–7.

31. For the text of the treaty itself, see 'The Treaty between Alfred and Guthrum, (886–890)', in Whitelock, *EHD*, 416–17 (no. 34). For further discussion, see Kershaw, 'The Alfred-Guthrum Treaty', at 46–47 for the possible date of the treaty.

32. On the draft form of Asser's *Life of Alfred*, see Kirby, 'Asser and His Life of King Alfred'.

33. For the positive spin of the Alfredian annals, see Keynes, 'A Tale of Two Kings'.

34. See Keynes and Lapidge, *Alfred the Great*, 41–42. Asser himself was from the community of St David's in south-western Wales. Asser's intended audience has been debated. For the idea that it was a piece of flattery aimed at Alfred and his immediate circle, see Campbell, 'Asser's Life of King Alfred'. For further discussion, see Scharer, 'The Writing of History'. Smyth, *King Alfred the Great*, has argued that Asser's *Life* was a forgery, though it is a view that has not gained acceptance.

35. See further below, chapter 5 of the present volume.

36. *The Chronicle of Æthelweard*, IV.3 (ed. and trans. Campbell, 49).

37. A later tradition from Bury St Edmunds calls the daughter 'Edith', who, it is suggested, may be synonymous with an Edith of Polesworth; see Thacker, 'Dynastic Monasteries and Family Cults', 257–58. But the identification is not certain: because Edward and his second wife, Ælfflæd, would also have a daughter, who was certainly named Eadgyth (Edith), it has been judged unlikely that two of his daughters would have had the same name; see Yorke, *Nunneries and the Anglo-Saxon Royal Houses*, 77–78.

38. For Hrotsvitha's Latin text, see Hrotsvitha of Gandersheim, *Gesta Ottonis*, line 80 (ed. Berschin, *Opera omnia*, 278); and the translation in Hill, *Medieval Monarchy in Action*, 122.

39. WM, *GR*, ii.126.1 (ed. and trans. Mynors, Thomson, and Winterbottom, 198–99).

40. WM, *GR*, ii.131.2 (ed. and trans. Mynors, Thomson, and Winterbottom, 206–7).

41. See chapter 7 of the present volume.

42. A passage in the *Vita S. Dvnstani* mentions that Dunstan, who later become the archbishop of Canterbury and who belonged to a powerful family, was related to Æthelstan, and it has been suggested that his connection may have been through Æthelstan's mother, Ecgwynn;

see B., *Vita S. Dvnstani*, chap. 10 (ed. and trans. Winterbottom and Lapidge, 34–35), where Dunstan is said to have been related to a rich woman named Æthelflæd who was 'of royal stock'. For the suggestion that Ecgwynn provided the connection, see Yorke, 'Æthelwold and the Politics of the Tenth Century', 66–67, 69–70.

43. For the difficulty in identifying one of the daughters, see chapter 6 and appendix II of the present volume.

44. WM, *GR*, ii.138 (ed. and trans. Mynors, Thomson, and Winterbottom, 224–25); and see WM, *GR*, vol. 2, *Commentary*, Thomson, 127.

45. WM, *GR*, ii.139.1–3 (ed. and trans. Mynors, Thomson, and Winterbottom, 224–27). It is possible that the story involving Ecgwynn gained momentum in and around 924, when Æthelstan first became king, given what was, as we will see, a disputed succession. See also Foot, *Æthelstan*, 30–31, which asserts that it was very unlikely that Ecgwynn was anything other than of noble stock.

46. WM, *GR*, ii.133.1–2 (ed. and trans. Mynors, Thomson, and Winterbottom, 210–11).The number thirty carried symbolic significance, since this was the age at which Jesus is said to have begun his ministry.

47. *ASC*, s.a. 851. For the possible burial of Æthelstan, king of Kent, Essex, Surrey and Sussex, in the Old Minster, Winchester, see Yorke, 'Royal Burial in Winchester', 65.

48. See also Kershaw, 'The Alfred-Guthrum Treaty', 51.

49. *The Chronicle of Æthelweard*, IV.3 (ed. and trans. Campbell, 51).

50. For childhood in the early medieval period, see Crawford, *Childhood in Anglo-Saxon England*.

51. Hamerow, 'Anglo-Saxon Timber Buildings', 136–43.

52. For more about these sites, see Rahtz, 'Buildings and Rural Settlement', 65–68; Rahtz, 'Cheddar'; and Gittos, 'Yeavering'.

53. WM, *GR*, ii.133.2 (ed. and trans. Mynors, Thomson, and Winterbottom, 210–11).

54. See Keynes and Lapidge, *Alfred the Great*, 232n19. See also Nelson, 'The Problem of King Alfred's Royal Anointing'. For discussion of an acrostic poem previously connected to this occasion, see chapter 4 of the present volume.

55. For Alfred's reburial in the New Minster, Winchester, see chapter 7 of the present volume.

56. *ASC* ABC, s.a. 900.

57. *ASC* C, s.a. 900. On the coins of 'Alvvaldus', see Naismith, *MEC*, 293.

58. *ASC* ABCD, s.a. 903.

59. Keynes, 'Edward, King of the Anglo-Saxons', 48–49. For the suggestion that Edward may not have been consecrated at Kingston, see Foot, *Æthelstan*, 74n46.

60. Keynes, 'England, *c.* 900–1016', 463–64; Keynes, 'Edward, King of the Anglo-Saxons'.

61. S 363 (*Malm* 24). It is the only occasion on which Ælfflæd was listed in Edward's surviving diplomas.

62. WM, *GR*, ii.126.1–2 (ed. and trans. Mynors, Thomson, and Winterbottom, 198–201).For the death of Æthelhelm, see *ASC*, s.a. 897. For the identification of Ælfflæd's father, see Yorke, 'Æthelwold and the Politics of the Tenth Century', 70; cf. Sharp, 'The West Saxon Tradition'.

63. S 365 (*WinchNM* 4); and S 366 (*WinchNM* 5).

64. WM, *GR*, ii.133.2 (ed. and trans. Mynors, Thomson, and Winterbottom, 210–11).

65. See chapter 2 in the present volume. See also Foot, *Æthelstan*, 34–37.

66. WM, *GR*, ii.133.3–4 (ed. and trans. Mynors, Thomson, and Winterbottom, 211–13). The account in William's text is confused: it variously refers to the fact that Æthelstan was educated at the orders of his grandfather, Alfred, his father, Edward, or his aunt and uncle, Æthelflæd and Æthelred.

67. On this passage in William's text, including comments about its possible literary allusions, see Wood, '"Stand Strong against the Monsters"', 197–99.

68. Asser, chap. 75 (trans. Keynes and Lapidge, 90–91).

69. See *Asser's Life of King Alfred*, ed. Stevenson, 300; and Keynes and Lapidge, *Alfred the Great*, 257n148.

70. See chapters 3 and 4 in the present volume. In the prose preface to the translation of Gregory's *Pastoral Care*, it is remarked that once the young had been trained to read Old English, 'thereafter one may instruct in Latin those whom one wishes to teach further and wishes to advance to holy orders'; Keynes and Lapidge, *Alfred the Great*, 126.

71. See *Anglo-Saxon Conversations*, ed. Gwara and Porter.

72. WM, *GR*, ii.132.1 (ed. and trans. Mynors, Thomson, and Winterbottom, 210–11).

73. This is a large subject in secondary literature. For a useful starting point, see Hadley and Richards, *Cultures in Contact*.

74. As ruler of Mercia, Æthelflæd seems to have had a degree of authority over parts of Wales, and she is described in 916 as leading an army to the royal residence at Llangorse Lake in Wales, which she destroyed and from where she took captive some prominent Welsh individuals, including the queen; *MR*, s.a. 916. See also Charles-Edwards, *Wales and the Britons*, 504, 506.

75. *ASC*, s.a. 917; *MR*, s.a. 917.

76. *ASC*, s.a. 918; *MR*, s.a. 918.

77. *ASC*, s.a. 918.

78. *MR*, s.a. 919.

79. For the battle of Corbridge, see *HSC*, section 22 (ed. and trans. Johnson South, 60–61), and chapter 5 of the present volume.

80. Woolf, *From Pictland to Alba*, 142–44; Downham, *Viking Kings*, 91–95.

81. *ASC* A, s.a. 920.

82. See chapter 2 of the present volume.

83. Davidson, 'The (Non)submission of the Northern Kings', 200–211. See also Foot, *Æthelstan*, 14–17.

84. For Eadgifu and Charles the Simple, see WM, *GR*, ii.112.1 and ii.126.1–2 (ed. and trans. Mynors, Thomson, and Winterbottom, 170–71 and 198–201 respectively); and Nelson, 'Eadgifu'.

85. WM, *GR*, ii.126.2 (ed. and trans. Mynors, Thomson, and Winterbottom, 200–201).

86. Stafford, 'Eadgifu'.

87. *AU*, 920.5. For Guthfrith's control of Dublin, see *AU*, 921.5.

88. *HR*, s.a. 920.

89. For the death of Ragnall, see *AU*, 921.4.

90. Naismith, *MEC*, 302. See also Blackburn, 'Currency under the Vikings'.

91. See Downham, *Viking Kings*, 97–99.

Chapter Two

1. *ASC* BCD, s.a. 924; JW, *Chron.*, s.a. 924 (ed. Darlington and McGurk, trans. Bray and McGurk, 384–85); WM, *GR*, ii.133.1 (ed. and trans. Mynors, Thomson, and Winterbottom, 210–11). For doubt about William's testimony concerning the rebellion in Chester, see Downham, *Viking Kings*, 99.

2. The *'Liber Vitae' of the New Minster and Hyde Abbey*, ed. Keynes, 17–18, 81.

3. For Edmund's age in 939, see *ASC* ABCD, s.a. 940.

4. *ASC* AEF, s.a. 924.

5. London, British Library, Stowe MS 944, fol. 9v: 'Aeðeluuerdus scilicet atque Aelfuuerdus haud dispari gloria, in sepulturae consortio secuti sunt, quorum unus clito, alter uero regalibus infulis redimitus, inmatura ambo morte preuenti sunt' (Æthelweard and Ælfweard, not at all dissimilar in glory, followed in the association of their burial, one of whom was an *ætheling*, the other crowned by a royal crown, [but] both were forestalled by an early death).

6. The *Textus Roffensis* is housed today in Rochester Cathedral Library, MS A.3.5, with the detail concerning Ælfweard on fol. 8v. Online images can be found here at *Textus Roffensis*, University of Manchester, n.d., https://luna.manchester.ac.uk/luna/servlet/media/book /showBook/Man4MedievalVC~4~4~990378~142729, accessed 10 October 2024.

7. *MR*, s.a. 924.

8. A formal division of the kingdom did take place later in 957, which indicates that it would have been one option available to Edward and his successors: see Keynes, 'England, *c.* 900–1016', 477–79.

9. *ASC* D, s.a. 924.

10. WM, *GR*, ii.140 (ed. and trans. Mynors, Thomson, and Winterbottom, 228–29). For the different stages in which William completed his work, which has resulted in the survival of different versions of his text, see Thomson in WM, *GR*, vol. 2, *Introduction and Commentary*, xvii–xxxv.

11. For other possible reasons why Æthelstan remained unmarried, including theories about his sexuality, see Foot, *Æthelstan*, 59–61. For the possibility that Æthelstan had been married, but the details were nowhere recorded, see Firth, *Early English Queens*, 93–94.

12. *Liber Eliensis*, iii.50 (ed. Blake, 292), translated in *Liber Eliensis: A History of the Isle of Ely from the Seventh Century to the Twelfth*, iii.50 (trans. Fairweather, 356).

13. S 395 (*Burt* 2)—on which see also below, chapter 3 of the present volume. The bishops who attest the diploma are Ælfwine (Ælle) of Lichfield, Wynsige of Dorchester, Wilferth of Worcester and Edgar of Hereford: see Keynes, *An Atlas of Attestations in Anglo-Saxon Charters*, table XXXVII.

14. S 397 (*Burt* 3) records a grant of land in Hope and Ashford, Derbyshire, and S 395 (*Burt* 2) comprises a grant of land at *Hwituntune*, which may be Whittington in Derbyshire, or the place of the same name in Staffordshire.

15. See S 397 (*Burt* 3); and S 396 (*Abing* 21).

16. Alfred is said to have been motivated by the supposed ignoble status of Æthelstan's mother, Ecgwynn, and by his own jealousy. See WM, *GR*, ii.131.1–2 and ii.137.1–2 (ed. and trans. Mynors, Thomson, and Winterbottom, 206–7 and 222–23). See also above, chapter 1 of the present volume.

17. On the *Schola Anglorum/Schola Saxonum*, see the introduction to the present volume.

18. For this textual relationship, see *Charters of Malmesbury Abbey*, ed. Kelly, 218.

19. In addition to S 395 (*Burt* 2), see S 394 (*CantStA* 26), S 397 (*Burt* 3) and S 396 (*Abing* 21).

20. *The 'Liber Vitae' of the New Minster and Hyde Abbey*, ed. Keynes, 21, notes that Æthelstan's name nevertheless does appear in royal genealogies elsewhere in the manuscript.

21. See Plenderleith, Hohler, and Freyhan, 'The Stole and the Maniples'.

22. For Æthelstan's journey north in 934, see below, chapter 5 of the present volume.

23. For the list of Æthelstan's gifts to St Cuthbert's community, see *HSC*, section 26 (ed. and trans. Johnson South, 64–65, with commentary on 109). For discussion of this passage, see Keynes, 'King Athelstan's Books', 177–78 and n172, who suggests that the entry in the *Historia* may not represent an original record of gifts made by Æthelstan in 934. This may have the implication that some of the gifts listed, including the vestments, need not be associated with the visit in 934 and could actually have been donated to the community by someone other than Æthelstan. Caution is therefore needed in the recreation of the circumstances in which these items of liturgical dress came north. For the embroideries, see Coatsworth, 'The Embroideries from the Tomb of St Cuthbert'.

24. S 1417 (*WinchNM* 9).

25. *The 'Liber Vitae' of the New Minster and Hyde Abbey*, ed. Keynes, 21; cf. *Charters of the New Minster, Winchester*, ed. Miller, 52–53.

26. For a discussion of the witnesses listed, see *The 'Liber Vitae' of the New Minster and Hyde Abbey*, ed. Keynes, 20–21.

27. For the derivation of *clito(n)* and a study of the status of the *ætheling*, see Dumville, 'The Ætheling', 10.

28. Yorke, 'Æthelwold and the Politics of the Tenth Century', 72, notes (relying on Dumville, 'The Ætheling') that *cliton* had been used by Frithegod in the tenth century as a variant term for *rex* (king).

29. The manuscript in question is London, British Library, Royal 1. B. vii, on which see Gneuss and Lapidge, *Anglo-Saxon Manuscripts*, 366–67 (no. 445). For a translation of the manumission, see *Select English Historical Documents*, no. xix (ed. and trans. Harmer, 63); and Keynes, 'King Athelstan's Books', 185–89 at 185n201.

30. Keynes, 'King Athelstan's Books', 187.

31. Larson, *The King's Household in England*, 192–93.

32. For reeves and Æthelstan's laws, see below, chapter 3 of the present volume.

33. In a forthcoming edition of manumissions, Dr David Pelteret suggests that, on the basis of the patterns of attestations, Eanstan is most likely to have been a provost in a religious community rather than someone in secular office. I am grateful to Dr Pelteret for sending me his manuscript in advance of publication.

34. The list itself seems to have been divided into parts. For further comment about the nature of these parts and what they might represent, see *Charters of the New Minster*, ed. Miller, 51–54 (no. 9); *The 'Liber Vitae' of the New Minster and Hyde Abbey*, ed. Keynes, 20–21; and Foot, *Æthelstan*, 65–66.

35. See chapter 1 of the present volume.

36. S 396 (*Abing* 21).

37. II As. 3.2 and II As. 10 (ed. and trans. Attenborough, 130–31, 132–33).

38. Larson, *The King's Household in England*, 131–32.

39. Larson, *The King's Household in England*, 125–32. For King Eadred's will, see *Select English Historical Documents*, no. 21 (ed. and trans. Harmer, 34–35, 64–65); and see also Whitelock, *EHD*, 554–56 (no. 107). For the status of the individuals who held these positions, and their close relationship to the king, see Gautier, 'Butlers and Dish-Bearers'.

40. For the office of the *cancellarius*, see Keynes, *The Diplomas of King Æthelred 'the Unready'*, 145–53.

41. S 454 (*Malm* 48) is a forged diploma in the name of Æthelstan which describes a certain Wolsinus as being the *cancellarius* and Odo as his *thesaurarius* (treasurer). For the suggestion that these titles reflect post-Conquest usage, see *Charters of Malmesbury*, ed. Kelly, 292–93. For further discussion, see Foot, *Æthelstan*, 67–68.

42. It was supposedly at Æthelstan's court that Dunstan had learned how Edmund of East Anglia had been martyred in the ninth century; see the opening of the *Passio S. Eadmundi*, edited by Winterbottom in *Three Lives of English Saints*, 67; and the discussion in Foot, *Æthelstan*, 69–70. For the early medieval court in general, see Cubitt (ed.), *Court Culture in the Early Middle Ages*.

43. Both Adelard and the 'Worcester Chronicle' state that Æthelstan was consecrated by Archbishop Æthelhelm, a detail not found in tenth-century sources. See Adelard of Ghent, *Lectiones in Depositione S. Dunstani*, III (ed. and trans. Winterbottom and Lapidge, 118–19); and JW, *Chron.*, s.a. 924 (ed. Darlington and McGurk, trans. Bray and McGurk, 384–85).

44. See above, chapter 1 of the present volume.

45. See above, chapter 1 of the present volume. For the 838 meeting at Kingston, see S 1438 (*CantCC* 69); Keynes, 'Kingston-upon-Thames'; and Woolf, *From Pictland to Alba*, 136–37. For London in the early medieval period, see Naismith, *Citadel of the Saxons*.

46. Pratt, 'The Making of the Second English Coronation *Ordo*'. See also *English Coronation 'Ordines'*, ed. Pratt, 18–20, 27–37 (for West Frankish influence) and 26, 37–40 (for the possible date of the 'A' version of the 'Second Coronation *Ordo*').

47. *English Coronation 'Ordines'*, ed. Pratt, 172–73. On the unique style of crown worn by Æthelstan, see Foot, *Æthelstan*, 216–23, esp. 222–23. For further discussion of what the *Ordo* implied about a king's legal duties, see Lambert, *Law and Order*, 205–7.

48. For Æthelstan's royal titles in 926, see S 396 (*Abing* 21); and S 397 (*Burt* 3).

49. See above, chapter 1 of the present volume.

50. *ASC* D, s.a. 926.

51. The terms of an early eleventh century Kentish marriage agreement demonstrate what was involved, as does a legal tract concerning marriage: see Whitelock, *EHD*, 596–97 (no. 130), and 467–68 (no. 50), respectively. For discussion, see Cardwell, '*Be wifmannes beweddunge*: Betrothals and Weddings in Anglo-Saxon England'.

52. WM, *GR* ii.126.1 (ed. and trans. Mynors, Thomson, and Winterbottom, 198–99).

53. See the introduction to the present volume.

54. New discoveries of coins that may have been minted in the north midlands raise important questions about political authority in this disputed area, however, and may suggest that

Sihtric's authority stretched further south than previously thought. See, for example, G. Williams, 'Roriva Castr: A New Danelaw Mint of the 920s'.

55. Woolf, *From Pictland to Alba*, 149–50, who at 149 makes important observations about the possible northern orientation of the 'D' annal for 926, which may explain its willingness to recognise Sihtric as 'king'. The 926 annal in 'D' could either have been drawn from northern material or represent a continuation of the *Mercian Register*: see *The Anglo-Saxon Chronicle: A Collaborative Edition*, ed. Cubbin, xxxi. See also Sharp, 'The West Saxon Tradition', 79–88; and Foot, *Æthelstan*, 18.

56. For the establishment of a burh at Tamworth by Æthelflæd, see *MR*, s.a. 913.

57. *The Annals of Flodoard of Reims*, s.a. 926 (8E) (ed. and trans. Fanning and Bachrach, 16). For the Latin text, see *Les Annales de Flodoard*, ed. Lauer, 36.

58. WM, *GR*, ii.135.3–6 (ed. and trans. Mynors, Thomson, and Winterbottom, 218–21).

59. WM, *GR*, ii.135.6 (ed. and trans. Mynors, Thomson, and Winterbottom, 220–21).

60. For the marriage of Eadgifu to Charles the Simple, see chapter 1 of the present volume. For the suggestion that Eadgifu had been involved in the negotiations that led to Eadhild's marriage to Hugh, see Nelson, 'Eadgifu'.

61. *ASC* D, s.a. 926 (*recte* 927). For the date of 'D', see *The Anglo-Saxon Chronicle: A Collaborative Edition*, ed. Cubbin, lxxviii–lxxix; and Gneuss and Lapidge, *Anglo-Saxon Manuscripts*, 296–97 (no. 372).

62. See Lapidge, 'Some Latin Poems', 79n140.

63. On Guthfrith and Dublin in 921, see chapter 1 of the present volume. On the events of 927, see *AU*, 927.

64. WM, *GR*, ii.134.2–4 (ed. and trans. Mynors, Thomson, and Winterbottom, 214–15). In another passage concerning events immediately after the death of Sihtric, William suggests that Æthelstan subdued Northumbria 'after driving out a certain Ealdwulf who was in revolt'; WM, *GR*, ii.131.3 (ed. and trans. Mynors, Thomson, and Winterbottom, 206–7). The 'Worcester Chronicle' contains similar detail when it says that Æthelstan 'expelled Ealdred, Eadwulf's son, from the royal town which is called Bamburgh in the English tongue'; JW, *Chron.*, s.a. 926 (ed. Darlington and McGurk, trans. Bray and McGurk, 386–87). As Darlington and McGurk note, in JW, *Chron.*, vol. 2, 387n6, these details may have arisen from a misunderstanding of the Old English annal in the *Anglo-Saxon Chronicle*; cf. Foot, *Æthelstan*, 19.

65. Lapidge, 'Some Latin Poems', 77.

66. Stevenson, 'A Latin Poem'. For the Carolingian poem, see *Poetae Latini aevi Carolini*, MGH 1, ed. Dümmler, 399–400 (no. IV). The identity of the poet depends on one's reading of a line in the last stanza of the poem. According to Lapidge, 'Some Latin Poems', 78, the line in question reads 'per Petri preconia' (through the announcements of Peter), but, on the basis of close comparison with the ninth-century Carolingian poem which forms its exemplar, this reading has been challenged. See Zacher, 'Multilingualism at the Court of King Æthelstan', 94–96, who suggests instead that the crucial line should read 'perpeti praeconio' (with perpetual announcement). For further discussion about 'Carta, dirige gressus', including its authorship, see Bobrycki, 'Breaking and Making Tradition'.

67. Foot, *Æthelstan*, 112.

68. Stanzas 3–5 of the poem read,

Quos iam regit cum ista	Whom he now rules with this
perfecta Saxonia:	Saxon-land [i.e. England] (now) made whole:
uiuit rex Æþelstanus	King Æthelstan lives
per facta gloriosus!	glorious through his deeds!

Ille, Sictric defuncto,	He, with Sihtric having died,
armat tum in prelio	in such circumstances arms for battle
Saxonum exercitum	the army of the English
per totum Bryttanium.	throughout all Britain.

Constantinus rex Scottorum	Constantine, king of the Scots,
aduolat Bryttanium:	hastens to Britain:
Saxonum regem saluando,	by supporting the king of the English
fidelis seruitio.	[he is] loyal in his service.

The Latin text and English translation are taken (almost) verbatim from Lapidge, 'Some Latin Poems', 77–78.

69. If the poet was indeed named Peter, he could be the same Peter who was named in the New Minster lease. See Lapidge, 'Some Latin Poems', 81.

70. McKitterick, *Charlemagne*; and Nelson, *King and Emperor*.

71. Naismith, *MEC*, 187.

72. For the example of Mercia, and the different zones of authority within it, see Baxter, *The Earls of Mercia*, 61–124. For the division of the kingdom in 957, see *ASC* C, s.a. 957.

73. For the River Eamont as the boundary between Strathclyde/Cumbria and Northumbria, see below, chapter 5 of the present volume.

74. Woolf, *From Pictland to Alba*, 151–52.

75. Bede, *Ecclesiastical History*, iv.32 (ed. and trans. Colgrave and Mynors, 446–47). Woolf, *From Pictland to Alba*, 152, also raises the possibility that 'Dacre . . . was the old name of the Eamont'.

76. This is a suggestion I owe to Professor Rory Naismith.

77. Downham, *Viking Kings*, 100–101, 150–51.

78. WM, *GR*, ii.134.5 (ed. and trans. Mynors, Thomson, and Winterbottom, 214–15). See also Thomson in WM, *GR*, vol. 2, *Introduction and Commentary*, 121.

79. For all of these details, see WM, *GR*, ii.134.5–7 (ed. and trans. Mynors, Thomson, and Winterbottom, 214–17).

80. See below, chapter 5 of the present volume.

81. See appendix I of the present volume.

82. For Æthelstan's gifts of relics to Exeter, and for his establishment of St Germans, see below, chapter 4 of the present volume. For English views of their British neighbours in the twelfth century, see Gillingham, 'The Beginnings of English Imperialism'. For Æthelstan and Exeter, see Orme, *Exeter Cathedral*, 6–12; Insley, 'Athelstan, Charters and the English in Cornwall'; and Insley, 'Kings and Lords in Tenth-Century Cornwall', who, at 10–12, discusses the various terms used in the early medieval period to refer to the Cornish.

83. WM, *GR*, ii.112.2, ii.126.2, and ii.135.1–2 (ed. and trans. Mynors, Thomson, and Winterbottom, 170–71, 198–201, and 216–19 respectively). The date of the marriage is suggested by the East

Frankish historian Widukind of Corvey; see Wood, 'The Three Books of the Deeds of the Saxons', 215 and 270n314.

84. See chapter 6 of the present volume.

85. See chapter 3 of the present volume.

86. For Dunstan and Æthelwold, see chapter 4 of the present volume. For the Latin style of Æthelstan's diplomas, see Woodman, '"Æthelstan A" and the Rhetoric of Rule'. For the background to the development of that style of language, see Gretsch, *The Intellectual Foundations of the English Benedictine Reform*, 332–83. For hermeneutic Latin and the late tenth-century reform, see Stephenson, *The Politics of Language*, 68–101.

87. For Foot, *Æthelstan*, 42, the labelling of Edwin as *rex* was an error on Folcuin's part. Foot draws attention to other errors in this part of Folcuin, including that Æthelstan is named as still being king in 944.

88. Folcuin, *Gesta abbatum S. Bertini Sithiensium*, c. 107 (ed. Holder-Egger, 629); translated in Whitelock, *EHD*, 346–47 (no. 26).

89. WM, *GR*, ii.139.3 (ed. and trans. Mynors, Thomson, and Winterbottom, 226–27).

90. *HR*, s.a. 933; Henry of Huntingdon, *Historia Anglorum*, v.18 (ed. and trans. Greenway, 310–11); *ASC* E, s.a. 933.

91. *ASC* A, s.a. 934.

92. See chapter 5 of the present volume.

93. For a discussion of these documents, see chapter 3 of the present volume.

94. For early tenth-century multilingualism, see Zacher, 'Multilingualism at the Court of King Æthelstan', 77–103.

95. This may be one reason why the coverage of Domesday Book (composed ca. 1086) does not extend into modern Durham and Northumbria.

96. Woodman, 'Charters, Northumbria and the Unification of England'.

97. *AU*, 913.1; *HSC*, section 24 (ed. and trans. Johnson South, 62–63).

98. On Ealdred and Bamburgh, see Hudson, 'Ealdred'; and Rollason, *Northumbria*, 263, 266–69. On Bamburgh more broadly in this period, see the excellent account by McGuigan, 'Bamburgh and the Northern English Realm', 95–150.

99. S 426 (*Glast* 24), and below, chapter 5 of the present volume.

100. For the tenth-century poem *Armes Prydein Vawr*, which shows the bitterness of Welsh feelings towards the English, see below, chapter 5 of the present volume.

Chapter Three

1. Other terms included the Old English *gemot* or, in Latin, the *conuentus*: see Roach, *Kingship and Consent*, 20–21.

2. For an edition of all early medieval writs and a history of the origins of the document, see *Anglo-Saxon Writs*, ed. Harmer.

3. For an account of the loss of medieval manuscripts in general, see Bartlett, *History in Flames*.

4. See the introduction and appendix I of the present volume.

5. On attendance at the royal assembly and the difficulty of using witness-lists, see Roach, *Kingship and Consent*, 27–44, esp. 32–34, and 39 (for the diplomas of 'Æthelstan A').

6. Keynes, 'Welsh Kings', 87–88; Roach, *Kingship and Consent*, 34, 42.

7. For the importance of the 'solemn assembly' in the early medieval period, see Bobrycki, *The Crowd in the Early Middle Ages*, 112–16.

8. See Stafford, 'Ealdorman'; Stafford, 'Reeve'; and Keynes, 'Thegn'.

9. Hill, 'The Shiring of Mercia—Again'; Molyneaux, *The Formation of the English Kingdom*, 155–72.

10. See Keynes, 'Hundreds'; Keynes, 'Shires'; and Miller, 'Wapentakes'.

11. Molyneaux, *The Formation of the English Kingdom*, 141–55.

12. See, for example, Roberts, 'Bishops, Canon Law and Governance'; and Cubitt, 'Bishops and Councils in Late Saxon England'.

13. For further analysis of the ecclesiastical attestations in Æthelstan's diplomas, see chapter 4 of the present volume.

14. For the estimated size of the royal assemblies, see Roach, *Kingship and Consent*, 43.

15. For the attestations of the sub-kings, see below, chapter 5 of the present volume, and Keynes, *An Atlas of Attestations in Anglo-Saxon Charters*, table XXXVI. For the 'alliterative' diplomas, possibly produced by Bishop Cenwald, see Keynes, 'King Athelstan's Books', 153–59; and *Charters of Burton Abbey*, ed. Sawyer, xlvii–xlix. For Cenwald in the reign of Æthelstan, see below, chapters 4 and 6 of the present volume.

16. The bishops are discussed in chapter 4 of the present volume.

17. Roach, *Kingship and Consent*, 33 (and for the idea that the lists may in part reflect the 'personal choice' of 'Æthelstan A').

18. Stenton, *Anglo-Saxon England*, 349–53; Maddicott, *The Origins of the English Parliament*, 1–56.

19. See Keynes, *An Atlas of Attestations in Anglo-Saxon Charters*, table XXXVIII; and Fellows Jensen, *Scandinavian Personal Names*.

20. Diplomas from the reign of King Edgar allow for more definitive conclusions to be drawn about an Anglo-Scandinavian ruling class in the Danelaw; see Abrams, 'King Edgar and the Men of the Danelaw'. The attestations of some of these individuals from after the reign of Æthelstan may confirm that their interests were tied to the north; see Roach, *Kingship and Consent*, 38–39.

21. Whitelock, 'The Dealings of the Kings of England', discusses the difficulties in locating some of those secular men with Scandinavian names listed in Æthelstan's diplomas.

22. For the idea of a diplomatic 'mainstream', see Keynes, 'Church Councils'.

23. Neither set of diplomas contains witness-lists as comprehensive as those of 'Æthelstan A'.

24. See Roach, *Kingship and Consent*, 37–38.

25. See below, chapter 4 of the present volume; Keynes, 'Wulfstan I'; and *Charters of Northern Houses*, ed. Woodman, 51–55.

26. The nature of the diplomas that they do attest, which show a greater connection with the midlands and north of the kingdom—for example, by granting land in the midlands, or being preserved in midland and northern archives—suggests that the Scandinavian-influenced names were perhaps included in witness-lists of diplomas where their local interests were more obviously affected. See Abrams, 'King Edgar and the Men of the Danelaw'; Roach, *Kingship and Consent*, 38–39; and *Charters of Northern Houses*, ed. Woodman, 110–15.

27. Roach, *Kingship and Consent*, 38–39.

28. See Keynes, *An Atlas of Attestations in Anglo-Saxon Charters*, table XXXVIII.

29. See Byrhtferth of Ramsey, *Vita S. Oswaldi*, iii.14, in Byrhtferth of Ramsey: *The Lives of St Oswald and St Ecgwine*, ed. and trans. Lapidge, 84–85. On the career of Æthelstan 'Half-King', see Hart, 'Athelstan "Half King" and His Family'.

30. S 442 (*Glast* 26).

31. See Roach, *Kingship and Consent*, 35–36.

32. For the Battle of *Brunanburh*, see below, chapter 5 of the present volume.

33. We do, however, have a number of scribal memoranda attached to the side of single-sheet diplomas, which may have constituted a register of those present at the meeting which could later be written up in neat form as a witness-list. See S 163 (*CantCC* 40), a diploma of King Coenwulf of Mercia dated 808, and S 293 (*CantCC* 73), a diploma of King Æthelwulf of Wessex dated 843.

34. Keynes, *The Diplomas of King Æthelred 'the Unready'*, 176–86; Roach, 'Penitential Discourse'.

35. Barrow, 'Demonstrative Behaviour and Political Communication'; Insley, 'Charters, Ritual and Late Tenth-Century English Kingship'.

36. *The Life of Bishop Wilfrid*, chap. XVII (ed. and trans. Colgrave, 36–37). For the blurring of boundaries between charters and hagiography, see Woodman, 'Hagiography and Charters in Early Northumbria'.

37. Wormald, *The Making of English Law*, 438; Roach, *Kingship and Consent*, 53–71.

38. The matter is controversial. For a full discussion, with appropriate references, see the fundamental work of Keynes, 'Church Councils'.

39. *ASC*, s.a. 1085, discussed in Roach, *Kingship and Consent*, 71–72.

40. II As. 20 (ed. and trans. Attenborough, 136–39); cf. the second law code of Edward the Elder, chap. 8, in *The Laws of the Earliest English Kings*, ed. and trans. Attenborough, 120–21.

41. See appendix 1 of the present volume.

42. For analysis of the year 956, see Keynes, *The Diplomas of King Æthelred 'the Unready'*, 48–69.

43. See the careful discussion in Roach, *Kingship and Consent*, 71–76 and 243, table 4. And cf. Foot, *Æthelstan*, 131–32, which compares English practise to that in Francia.

44. This is a point made in Roach, *Kingship and Consent*, 75.

45. For his Mercian upbringing and the initial West Saxon reaction to Æthelstan, see above, chapters 1 and 2 of the present volume.

46. S 400 (*WinchOM* 57); S 399 (*Glast* 23). See also WM, *GR*, ii.134.56–57 (ed. and trans. Mynors, Thomson and Winterbottom, 216–17).

47. S 416.

48. Surviving records show that some places had previously been used as assembly sites, while others were new; Roach, *Kingship and Consent*, 57–63, 239–40.

49. Roach, *Kingship and Consent*, 62–63. For the royal vill, see Sawyer, 'The Royal *Tun* in Pre-Conquest England', 289–99 (with a list of vills). For the *feorm*, see Faith, 'Feorm'. For a new interpretation of the *feorm*, with the suggestion that it may in origin have been a reference to a feast rather than a tax in kind, see Lambert and Leggett, 'Food and Power in Early Medieval England'.

50. S 407 (*North* 1); *HSC*, section 26 (ed. and trans. Johnson South, 64–65).

51. Foot, *Æthelstan*, 87, draws attention to the fact that 934 was also the first year in which Æthelstan held a royal assembly in Winchester itself, an event which she connects to the death of his brother, Edwin, in 933, which may have removed a party opposed to the king.

52. S 426 (*Glast* 24); and S 427.

53. For the young Louis at Æthelstan's court, see chapter 6 of the present volume.

54. William of Malmesbury records a separate occasion when Æthelstan was at York and received Norwegian ambassadors named Helgrim and Osfrith; see WM, *GR*, ii.135.1 (ed. and trans. Mynors, Thomson, and Winterbottom, 216–17).

55. See below, chapter 5 of the present volume.

56. The diplomas from Burton Abbey are S 395 (*Burt* 2) and S 397 (*Burt* 3); the diploma from St Augustine's Abbey is S 394 (*CantStA* 26); and the diploma from Abingdon Abbey is S 396 (*Abing* 21).

57. S 397 (*Burt* 3) and S 396 (*Abing* 21).

58. S 395 (*Burt* 2).

59. For Æthelstan's royal styles, see Keynes, 'England, *c.* 900–1016'.

60. Bede suggests that one hide of land was the equivalent needed to support one household. This area of land increased as time progressed; see Faith, 'Hide'.

61. Some royal diplomas show this division of parts with boundary clauses that have clearly been inserted by a different scribe to that of the main text and added after the main text had been written, while other diplomas were composed in one sitting. For so-called single- and two-stage production, and what this suggests about the production of royal diplomas, see Keynes, 'Church Councils', 71–92.

62. The bounds are discussed in Gurney, 'Yttingaford and the Tenth-Century Bounds of Chalgrave and Linslade'. For the importance of Watling Street in forming a boundary between the kingdoms of Wessex and Mercia, see the introduction to the present volume.

63. S 397 (*Burt* 3) and S 396 (*Abing* 21).

64. *Charters of Abingdon Abbey, Part 1*, ed. Kelly, 90–91. The attestation of Ælfwine (Ælle) so low in the witness-lists of S 397 and S 396 may make it unlikely that 'Æthelstan A' was the draftsman of these documents.

65. S 394 (*CantStA* 26).

66. *Charters of St Augustine's Abbey, Canterbury, and Minster-in-Thanet*, ed. Kelly, 100–103.

67. See appendix I of the present volume.

68. S 416 and S 425 (*CantCC* 106) respectively.

69. For S 416, see Plate 13.

70. The script is titled 'Phase II Square Minuscule'; see Dumville, 'English Square Minuscule Script'.

71. See Plate 13.

72. S 425 (*CantCC* 106).

73. The indiction was in origin an imperial tax cycle of fifteen years, which began in the year 312; Cheney, *A Handbook of Dates*, 2–4.

74. The comparison is made in Stevenson, 'The Anglo-Saxon Chancery'; for the description of the 'Æthelstan A' diplomas being akin to a 'pyrotechnic display', see 33. For the Latin style of

the diplomas of 'Æthelstan A', see Woodman, '"Æthelstan A" and the Rhetoric of Rule'; and Smith, *Land and Book*, 37–47, 175–81.

75. For the state of literacy in the ninth century, see the introduction to the present volume. The ninth-century Mercian diplomas which invoke Aldhelm include S 193, S 197 (*Pet 8*), S 210 and S 225 (*Abing 20*). For discussion, see Snook, *The Anglo-Saxon Chancery*, 33–36.

76. Snook, *The Anglo-Saxon Chancery*, 107–11.

77. The script is Phase II Square Minuscule.

78. See Plate 14.

79. Kaster, 'Gloss, Glosses, Latin'.

80. For the 'performative' aspects of Frankish diplomas, see Koziol, *The Politics of Memory and Identity in Carolingian Royal Diplomas*.

81. Keynes, 'The West Saxon Charters of King Æthelwulf and His Sons'.

82. The existence of a so-called chancery is the subject of significant scholarly debate. See, for example, Drögereit, 'Gab es eine Angelsächsische Königskanzlei?'; Chaplais, 'The Royal Anglo-Saxon "Chancery" of the Tenth Century Revisited'; *Charters of Abingdon Abbey, Part 1*, ed. Kelly, lxxix–lxxxiv; and Keynes, 'Church Councils'.

83. For the British dimensions of Æthelstan's reign, see chapter 5 of the present volume.

84. Of course, not all diplomas would have been produced in the same way, and there is extensive scholarly discussion about the circumstances in which diplomas may have been composed. For an overview, with further references, see Keynes, 'Church Councils'.

85. On the significance of the use of Old English in law-making, see Foot, *Æthelstan*, 136. Æthelstan's coronation had stressed the expectation that he would uphold justice; see chapter 2 of the present volume. On the role of the early medieval king as an arbiter of justice, see, for example, Fouracre, 'Carolingian Justice'.

86. See Wormald, *The Making of English Law*, 119–25; Pratt, *The Political Thought of King Alfred the Great*, 222–32; Hudson, *The Oxford History of the Laws of England*, 24; and Lambert, *Law and Order*, 164–65, which stresses the 'profoundly ideological intent' of Alfred's *domboc* (164).

87. For the difficulty in discerning precisely how early medieval laws were used in practice, see P. Wormald, '*Lex scripta* and *verbum regis*'. For explication of the ways in which laws were implemented, see Keynes, 'Royal Government and the Written Word'. For laws in the later tenth and early eleventh centuries, see C. Cubitt, '"As the Lawbook Teaches"'.

88. For what Æthelstan's laws can tell us about the operation of law in the early tenth century, see Roach, 'Law Codes and Legal Norms', 465–86. For the suggestion that Æthelstan's legislative activity followed from his formation of the English kingdom, see D. Pratt, 'Written Law and the Communication of Authority'. See also Lambert, *Law and Order*, 163–201, which suggests that the laws of Æthelstan provide evidence for substantive changes to legal processes in the tenth century when compared to the early Anglo-Saxon period—changes which were emblematic of the growing power of kings.

89. Here they are referred to as the 'first code of Æthelstan', 'Æthelstan's second code', and so on.

90. Wormald, *The Making of English Law*, 439–40.

91. Wormald, *The Making of English Law*, 367–68 and 373–74, respectively. On the ordeal in general, see Bartlett, *Trial by Fire and Water*.

92. Archbishop Wulfstan II, the celebrated legislator of the late tenth and early eleventh centuries, may have been responsible for some of the contents of Æthelstan's first code; see Wormald, *The Making of English Law*, 295.

93. I As. (ed. and trans. Attenborough, 122–23).

94. Ivarsen, 'Æthelstan, Wulfstan and a Revised History of Tithes in England'.

95. In the *ASC*, s.a. 855, Æthelwulf is said to have made this donation via the issuing of diplomas. For his so-called 'Decimation Charters', see *Charters of Malmesbury Abbey*, ed. Kelly, 65–91; and Keynes, 'The West Saxon Charters of King Æthelwulf and His Sons', 1109–49. For further discussion, see Ivarsen, 'Æthelstan, Wulfstan and a Revised History of Tithes in England', 247.

96. See Wormald, *The Making of English Law*, 436, map. See also Lavelle, 'Why Grateley?'.

97. Wormald, *The Making of English Law*, 294; Foot, *Æthelstan*, 152–53; Roach, 'Law Codes and Legal Norms', 468.

98. For the issue of theft in early medieval England, see Lambert, 'Theft, Homicide and Crime in Late Anglo-Saxon Law'; and Lambert, *Law and Order*, 172–81.

99. For clauses related to theft, see, for example, II As. 1, 3.1–2, 6.2–3, 7, 8, 11 (ed. and trans. Attenborough, 126–35).

100. For the injunction concerning witchcraft, see II As. 6 (ed. and trans. Attenborough, 130–31).

101. Pratt, 'Written Law and the Communication of Authority'.

102. Lambert, *Law and Order*, 152–56.

103. See *The Laws of the Earliest English Kings*, ed. Attenborough, 208.

104. II As. 20 (ed. and trans. Attenborough, 136–39).

105. II As. 20.3 (ed. and trans. Attenborough, 136–37).

106. For the role of reeves in law, for the ways in which laws were conveyed from royal assemblies to the localities, and for the issue of disobedience in a legal context, see Lambert, *Law and Order*, 127–28, 141–47, and 213–14, respectively. The enforcement of law in the localities must have involved a range of people beyond the reeves, including local lords (thegns) of various kinds; Lambert, *Law and Order*, 238–43, 274–83. For the importance of hundreds in such matters, see Lambert, *Law and Order*, 245–50.

107. II As. 25 (ed. and trans. Attenborough, 140–41). Early medieval English society was stratified according to rank, from the lowest, the slaves (*ceorls*) to the more elevated ranks of royal official, such as reeves or ealdormen. Each rank was given a monetary value known as that person's wergeld.

108. II As. 25 (ed. and trans. Attenborough, 140–41).

109. *Ordal* (ed. and trans. Attenborough, 170–73). For further discussion, see Lambert, *Law and Order*, 255–58.

110. Those parts of the 'Æthelstan A' diplomas which call for liturgical observances are discussed in chapter 4 of the present volume.

111. V As. 1.3–4 (ed. and trans. Attenborough, 154–55).

112. V As. prologue (ed. and trans. Attenborough, 152–53).

113. See Keynes, 'Royal Government', 226–57.

114. For what Æthelstan's third code reveals about the operation of law in his reign, see Keynes, 'Royal Government', 238–39; and Roach, 'Law Codes and Legal Norms', 469–72.

115. III As. 3 (ed. and trans. Attenborough, 144–45). For the suggestion that Æthelstan offered this amnesty before increasing the severity of the punishment for theft, see Lambert, *Law and Order*, 175–77.

116. III As. epilogue (ed. and trans. Attenborough, 146–47).

117. Keynes, 'Royal Government', 239; Roach, 'Law Codes and Legal Norms', 472–74.

118. IV As. 2 (ed. and trans. Attenborough, 146–47).

119. IV As. 3.2 (ed. and trans. Attenborough, 146–49).

120. IV As. 6 (ed. and trans. Attenborough, 148–51).

121. IV As. 6.4–7 (ed. and trans. Attenborough, 150–51).

122. On the composite form of Æthelstan's sixth law code, see Wormald, *The Making of English Law*, 297–98. See also Keynes, 'Royal Government', 239–40; and Roach, 'Law Codes and Legal Norms', 474–76.

123. For an overview of early English gilds, and a comparison with similar Carolingian bodies, see Naismith, 'Gilds, States and Societies in the Early Middle Ages'.

124. VI As. 7 (ed. and trans. Attenborough, 162–63). One responsibility could involve the use of violence in the context of feud; see Lambert, *Law and Order*, 224–30.

125. VI As. 7.6 (ed. and trans. Attenborough, 164–65).

126. VI As. 12 (ed. and trans. Attenborough, 168–69). See also Wormald, *The Making of English Law*, 298, 440; and Lambert, *Law and Order*, 177.

127. Naismith, 'Gilds, States and Societies', 660.

128. VI As. 8.9 (ed. and trans. Attenborough, 166–67).

129. Wormald, *The Making of English Law*, 298–300. For the requirement of charitable acts to be undertaken by various different people/institutions that can be found in parts of Æthelstan's laws and diplomas, see Keynes, 'Royal Government', 236n42, 237n48; Wormald, *The Making of English Law*, 302; and Ivarsen, 'Æthelstan, Wulfstan and a Revised History of Tithes in England', 244.

130. Metcalf, 'The Monetary History of England'. On the difficulties of estimating the size of the early medieval coinage, see Sawyer, *The Wealth of Anglo-Saxon England*, 115–26.

131. See the 796 letter of Charlemagne to Offa, in Whitelock, *EHD*, 848–49 (no. 197).

132. Blackburn, 'Two New Halfpennies'. For medieval money in general, see Naismith, *Making Money in the Early Middle Ages*.

133. For the suggestion that the laws about money may originally date to an earlier period, see Blackburn, 'Mints, Burhs and the Grately Code'; Wormald, *The Making of English Law*, 294, 440; and Foot, *Æthelstan*, 152–53 (which also cites the work of Blackburn).

134. II As. 14 (ed. and trans. Attenborough, 134–35).

135. On the burh and *port* of Æthelstan's (and Edward's) laws, see Molyneaux, *The Formation of the English Kingdom*, 106–9.

136. For an overview of coinage of the early tenth century, which is very complex, see Blunt, 'The Coinage of Athelstan'; Blunt, Stewart, and Lyon, *Coinage in Tenth-Century England*, 108–13; and Naismith, *MEC*, 174–210, esp. 201–4, and, for the regional structure of the tenth-century coinage, 185–89.

137. Blunt, Stewart, and Lyon, *Coinage in Tenth-Century England*, 110. The 2007 discovery of the Vale of York hoard significantly increased the number of these coins that survived with the

image of a church inscribed on them; see Williams, 'The Coins from the Vale of York Viking Hoard'.

138. Blunt, 'Four Italian Coins Imitating Anglo-Saxon Types'.

139. In Northumbria, the Circumscription coins came after those with the design of a church on their reverse.

140. For all of these details, see Naismith, *MEC*, 202–3. For the style REX SAXORUM, see Blunt, 'The Coinage of Athelstan', 115.

141. The manuscript in question is Cambridge, Corpus Christi College 183, on which see above, chapter 2 of the present volume. For Æthelstan's style of crown, see Foot, *Æthelstan*, 216–23.

142. Naismith, *MEC*, 202.

143. Blunt, 'The Coinage of Athelstan', 114–16; Molyneaux, *The Formation of the English Kingdom*, 126–41; Foot, *Æthelstan*, 151–57.

144. This point is made very effectively in Naismith, 'Prelude to Reform'.

145. In one rare surviving example, a coin of Louis the Child (899–911), king of East Francia, has simply had an Æthelstan inscription imprinted on top of an existing legend; Blunt, 'A Penny of the English King Athelstan'. For the evidence of hoards and single finds and what they can tell us about the circulation of Æthelstan's coinage, see Naismith, *MEC*, 188–89.

146. Naismith, *MEC*, 191, table 15.

147. II As. 14.2 (ed. and trans. Attenborough, 134–35).

148. See Hill, 'Athelstan's Urban Reforms'.

149. See Naismith, 'Prelude to Reform', 71–72, table 3.6; and Blunt, 'The Coinage', 78–9, 101–4.

150. For Regnald, see Smart, '"Not the Oldest Known List"', 309–10.

151. For these names and their derivations, see Smart, 'Economic Migrants?'.

152. See chapter 6 of the present volume.

153. See Wickham, *The Inheritance of Rome*, 467, and, for the Carolingian period itself, 375–404. See also Wood, 'The Making of King Aethelstan's Empire'; and Wood, '"Stand Strong against the Monsters"'.

154. Wickham, *The Inheritance of Rome*, 460–61.

155. The classic account is Campbell, *The Anglo-Saxon State*; the quotation herein is on 10.

156. Davies, 'The Medieval State'; Baxter, 'The Limits of the Anglo-Saxon State'.

157. Foot, 'The Historiography of the Anglo-Saxon "Nation-State"'. For the later medieval period, see Burt and Partington, *Arise, England*.

158. For this extract from the *Institutes of Polity*, see Swanton, *Anglo-Saxon Prose*, 213.

Chapter Four

1. Augustine's Bible is known by the classmark Cambridge, Corpus Christi College, MS 286, which can be viewed online at 'Cambridge, Corpus Christi College, MS 286: Gospels of St Augustine', Parker Library on the Web, Stanford University Libraries, n.d.,: https://parker.stanford .edu/parker/catalog/mk707wk3350, accessed 10 October 2024. For an overview of early Christianity in England, on which there is a vast literature, see Blair, *The Church in Anglo-Saxon Society*,

8–290. See also Meens, 'A Background to Augustine's Mission'. For Bede's early plans, see Bede, *Ecclesiastical History*, i.29 (ed. and trans. Colgrave and Mynors, 104–7).

2. Blair, *The Church in Anglo-Saxon Society*.

3. *ASC* DE, s.a. 793.

4. *The Chronicle of Æthelweard*, IV.3 (ed. and trans. Campbell, 51), reports for the year 895 that the viking king Guthfrith was buried in York Minster itself. For the epigraphic evidence suggestive of Scandinavian foundation of churches, see Parsons, 'The Inscriptions of Viking-Age York'. See also Blair, *The Church in Anglo-Saxon Society*, 291–92; and Barrow, 'Survival and Mutation'.

5. See the prose preface to the translation of Gregory's *Pastoral Care* in Keynes and Lapidge, *Alfred the Great*, 125.

6. For an overview of this period of Alfred's reign, see Keynes and Lapidge, *Alfred the Great*, 23–41. For the revival of the divine office in England under Alfred, see Billett, *The Divine Office in Anglo-Saxon England*, 133–48, a reference I owe to Professor Catherine Cubitt. Despite Alfred's positive actions, questions have been raised about the extent of his commitment to the church. A letter from Pope John VIII to England implied that Alfred had neglected his ecclesiastical responsibilities. For the letter, see Whitelock, *EHD*, 881–83 (no. 222). For further discussion, see Thacker, 'Dynastic Monasteries and Family Cults', 251–53; and Cubitt, 'The Institutional Church', 386.

7. This was similar to Alfred's reputation regarding the church—on which, see Thacker, 'Dynastic Monasteries and Family Cults', 252–53.

8. Thacker, 'Dynastic Monasteries and Family Cults', 253–54; Rumble, 'Edward the Elder'. On Edward and the New Minster, see *The 'Liber Vitae' of the New Minster and Hyde Abbey Winchester*, ed. Keynes, 16–19.

9. Thacker, 'Dynastic Monasteries and Family Cults', 255–56. For the foundation of St Oswald's in Gloucester, see C. Heighway, 'Gloucester and the New Minster of St Oswald'.

10. *English Coronation 'Ordines'*, ed. Pratt, 146–47. For the likely original date of the second coronation *Ordo*, see the summary of scholarship in *English Coronation 'Ordines'*, ed. Pratt, 37–40. See also chapter 2 of the present volume.

11. S 395 (*Burt* 2).

12. The contents of BL Cotton Tiberius A. ii were rearranged in the seventeenth century, with the result that the poem can now be found on fol. 15r and the prose inscription on fol. 15v. See also Lapidge, 'Some Latin Poems', 81–85, and esp. 83 for the detail that the poem was copied in the hand of a continental scribe; and Keynes, 'King Athelstan's Books', 147–53.

13. S 394 (*CantStA* 26).

14. *Charters of St Augustine's Abbey, Canterbury, and Minster-in-Thanet*, ed. Kelly, cix–cx.

15. S 405; S 394 (*CantStA* 26).

16. S 419 (*Shaft* 8) and S 429 (*Shaft* 9) are diplomas for Shaftesbury, S 422 (*Sherb* 7) and S 423 (*Sherb* 8) are for Sherborne, S 432 is for Athelney and S 438 is for St Mary's, Wilton.

17. Blair, *The Church in Anglo-Saxon Society*, 341–48.

18. S 412; S 418a (*Bark* 4).

19. S 403 (*Sel* 17); S 405.

20. An exception to this pattern is S 425 (*CantCC* 106), in which a group of thegns are given unusual prominence immediately after the episcopal attestations, probably because the scribe

was working from a memorandum and trying to fit a large number of thegns onto the space provided by the single sheet; *Charters of Christ Church, Canterbury, Part 2*, ed. Brooks and Kelly, 868, 872.

21. The pattern of abbatial attestations is set out in Keynes, *An Atlas of Attestations in Anglo-Saxon Charters*, table XXXVII.

22. For discussion of witness-lists, see chapter 3 of the present volume.

23. See S 394 (*CantStA* 26) and S 395 (*Burt* 2), respectively.

24. For all of these details, and the suggestion that the name 'Cynath' may in origin be Pictish or Gaelic, see Dumville, 'A Pictish or Gaelic Ecclesiastic in Mercia?'

25. For Cynath and Evesham, see Robinson, *The Times of Saint Dunstan*, 36–40. On Cynath's career, see *Charters of Abingdon Abbey, Part 1*, ed. Kelly, 98.

26. S 404 (*Abing* 22). For a discussion of its complicated textual features, see *Charters of Abingdon Abbey, Part 1*, ed. Kelly, 94–99. On the journey to Germany, see below, chapter 6 of the present volume.

27. See S 448 (*Abing* 30); S 446 (*WinchOM* 69); and S 449 (*WinchOM* 70), respectively.

28. Dumville, *Wessex and England*, 177–78.

29. *Charters of Abingdon Abbey, Part 1*, ed. Kelly, 128.

30. WM, GR, ii.217 (ed. and trans. Mynors, Thomson, and Winterbottom, 400–403).

31. Liebermann, *Die heiligen Englands*, 15–16 (II. 33); Rollason, 'Lists of Saints' Resting-Places'. For the cult of Eadburh, see Braswell, 'Saint Edburga of Winchester'. For an overview of Eadburh's life, see Yorke, 'Eadburh'. For the suggestion that Æthelstan's grant of land to his half-sister, Eadburh—which was witnessed also by the *æthelings* Edmund and Eadred—may have constituted an attempt to settle their succession, see Roach, *Kingship and Consent*, 40–41, 93.

32. S 432.

33. S 449 (*WinchOM* 70).

34. S 422 (*Sherb* 7); S 423 (*Sherb* 8); S 379 (*WinchNM* 8).

35. S 419 (*Shaft* 8).

36. S 418 (*WinchNM* 10).

37. For further discussion of these five diplomas, see *Charters of the New Minster, Winchester*, ed. Miller, 58.

38. For the biblical background to such matters, see Ivarsen, 'Æthelstan, Wulfstan and a Revised History of Tithes in England', 242–45.

39. ASC E, s.a. 933; Folcuin, *Gesta abbatum S. Bertini Sithiensium*, chap. 107 (ed. Holder-Egger, 629); translated in Whitelock, *EHD*, 346–47 (no. 26). See also chapter 2 of the present volume.

40. See chapter 2 of the present volume.

41. WM, GR, ii.139.3–5 (ed. and trans. Mynors, Thomson, and Winterbottom, 226–27).

42. William of Malmesbury himself says he is not sure whether or not to trust the details in his account of Edwin's death given how warmly Æthelstan treated his other siblings; see WM, GR, ii.140 (ed. and trans. Mynors, Thomson, and Winterbottom, 228–29).

43. Wormald, *The Making of English Law*, 307–8; Roach, 'Public Rites and Public Wrongs', 199n81 (where the work of Wormald is also cited).

44. WM, GP, ii.85 and ii.93 (ed. and trans. Winterbottom, 292–93 and 312–13, respectively).

45. For Milton's dedication, see F. Arnold-Foster, *Studies in Church Dedications*, 2:188, 2:256–57; Yorke, *Wessex in the Early Middle Ages*, 209.

46. For Radbod's letter, see WM, *GP*, v.249 (ed. and trans. Winterbottom, 596–99).

47. S 391, dated 843 (for 934).

48. British Library, Additional 56488.

49. S 884, dated 995, now preserved in the Somerset Record Office in Taunton: DD/SAS PR 502.

50. S 455, edited in Bates, *Two Cartularies*, 38–40, where the views of W. H. Stevenson about the document's authenticity are printed.

51. There are, however, those who suggest that this is a suspicious feature of the diploma. See the discussion in Jenkins and Owen, 'The Welsh Marginalia', 65 (and n122). See also Edwards, *The Charters of the Early West Saxon Kingdom*, 207.

52. The translation is taken from Bates, *Two Cartularies*, 38.

53. See chapter 3 of the present volume.

54. See Tinti, 'The Archiepiscopal Pallium', 307–42; and Tinti, 'England and the Papacy'.

55. Brooks, *The Early History of the Church of Canterbury*, 216–17. For journeys to Rome to collect the pallium, see the comments of Stafford, 'Charles the Bald, Judith and England', 142 and n23.

56. See chapter 3 of the present volume.

57. *Charters of Northern Houses*, ed. Woodman, 47–48. On Hrothweard, see Rollason, Gore, and Fellows-Jensen, *Sources for York History*, 70.

58. Keynes, 'Wulfstan I', 512–13; *Charters of Northern Houses*, ed. Woodman, 51–55.

59. For the manumission involving Eadhelm, see chapter 2 of the present volume.

60. For discussion of this list of names, on which the present detail is based, see Barker, 'Two Lost Documents of King Athelstan', 138–41. See also *The Durham 'Liber Vitae'*, ed. D. Rollason and L. Rollason, 1:92.

61. The circumstances in which Oda was chosen as bishop are related in Byrhtferth's *Life of Saint Oswald* in a passage which may also suggest that he had been part of Æthelstan's close circle; see Byrhtferth of Ramsey, *The Lives of St Oswald and St Ecgwine*, i.5 (ed. and trans. Lapidge, 22–23). The matter is complicated by Byrhtferth's disregard for detail. See Lapidge, 'Byrhtferth and Oswald', 66–68; and Foot, *Æthelstan*, 97–98.

62. S 394 (*CantStA* 26).

63. For Ælfheah 'the Bald' and Dunstan, see *The Early Lives of St Dunstan*, 7.2 (ed. and trans. Winterbottom and Lapidge, 26–27). For discussion, see Robinson, *The Times of Saint Dunstan*, 82–83; and Foot, *Æthelstan*, 97.

64. McGuigan, 'Cuthbert's Relics', suggests that Durham house traditions concerning Chester-le-Street need not be accurate, and he draws attention to the importance of the Old English text, 'On the Resting-Places of the Saints', which locates Cuthbert's community at Norham.

65. See chapter 2 of the present volume.

66. S 395 (*Burt* 2) and S 394 (*CantStA* 26) for Lichfield, and S 397 (*Burt* 3) and S 396 (*Abing* 21) for London.

67. See Foot, *Æthelstan*, 98.

68. Keynes, *An Atlas of Attestations in Anglo-Saxon Charters*, table XXXVII.

69. See above, chapters 2 and 3 of the present volume.

70. The most fully developed argument in favour of this identification can be found in Snook, *The Anglo-Saxon Chancery*, 107–10.

71. S 401.

72. For the latter possibility, see McGuigan, 'Cuthbert's Relics', 156. For an overview of the effects of the Scandinavian settlement on the church and Christianity, see Abrams, 'Conversion and Assimilation'. From the time of Oswald onwards, some archbishops of York simultaneously held the archbishopric and the Worcester church. Is it possible that Worcester records / house traditions therefore preserve more precise details about the relationship of these four bishops to York? For other connections between York and Worcester diplomas, see *Charters of Northern Houses*, ed. Woodman, 91–92.

73. *Charters of Barking Abbey and Waltham Holy Cross*, ed. Kelly, 166.

74. For the suggestion that the Benedict of the diploma witness-lists can be equated with a Benedict named in an inscription in BL Cotton Otho B. ix, where he is described as *Euernensicus* (i.e., an Irishman), see Keynes, 'King Athelstan's Books', 172–73. I am very grateful to Dr Oliver Padel and Dr Ben Guy for their suggestions and guidance about the name-form, 'Mancant', and to whom I owe the suggestion that it derives from the Brittonic Maucant. I am also grateful to Dr Fran Colman for her guidance. On the unusual Old English name, 'Buga', who is listed as a bishop without a known see in S 400 (*WinchOM* 57), see Colman, 'On the Moneyers' Names Buga and Boia on Anglo-Saxon Coins'.

75. 'Mancant' can be found attesting S 417 and S 418a (*Bark* 4). Compare Foot, *Æthelstan*, 107.

76. For Cenwald's mission to the East Frankish court, see below, chapter 6.

77. On the difficulty of handling witness-lists as evidence, and the specific challenges of the diplomas of 'Æthelstan A', which are so different in terms of their style and formulation, see above, chapter 3.

78. See chapter 3 of the present volume.

79. See WM, *GR*, ii.129 (ed. and trans. Mynors, Thomson, and Winterbottom, 204–5) and WM, *GP*, ii.80. 3 (ed. and trans. Winterbottom, 280–81). And see O'Donovan, 'An Interim Revision of Episcopal Dates for the Province of Canterbury', 109–10.

80. See chapter 5 of the present volume. For comments about Cornish distinctiveness, see, for example, Insley, 'Charters and Episcopal Scriptoria in the Anglo-Saxon South-West', 178–79.

81. Kenstec is said to have been based at a place called, in Cornish, *Dinuurrin*, which has been equated with Bodmin; see Olson, *Early Monasteries*, 51–56. For the possibility that the Sherborne church had some pastoral responsibility for parts of Cornwall, see Insley, 'Languages of Boundaries and Boundaries of Language in Cornish Charters', 349.

82. S 1296—on which, see Napier and Stevenson, *The Crawford Collection*, 18–19 (no. VII), and also 102–10; and Whitelock, *EHD*, 892–94 (no. 229).

83. Olson, *Early Monasteries*, 60–66. Bishops of Cornwall were also at times associated with St Petroc's, Padstow, before in 1050 the bishoprics of Devon and Cornwall were combined into one at Exeter; see Keynes, 'Appendix II: Archbishops and Bishops', 550–53.

84. S 450 is dated to 943 in the diploma's dating clause, which must be an error if the diploma is a grant in the name of Æthelstan. For the possibility that some diplomatic elements belong to a date later in the tenth century than Æthelstan's reign, see Olson, *Early Monasteries*, 79n123.

85. Olson, *Early Monasteries*, 78–84; Insley, 'Languages of Boundaries and Boundaries of Language in Cornish Charters', 361–64.

86. S 1207.

87. Padel, 'Two New Pre-Conquest Charters for Cornwall', 20, 22.

88. Brett, with Edmonds, and Russell, *Brittany and the Atlantic Archipelago*, 278–79.

89. No 'Maenchi' attests any of Æthelsan's diplomas as an ealdorman; see Keynes, *An Atlas of Attestations in Anglo-Saxon Charters*, table XXXVIII.

90. Both of these ideas are suggested in Padel, 'Two New Pre-Conquest Charters', 22–23. See also Insley, 'Athelstan, Charters and the English in Cornwall', 20, where he suggests that the part of the charter which mentions Æthelstan may have been an interpolation.

91. For scepticism about these house traditions, and the suggestion that the Cuthbertine community may actually have moved instead to Norham, see McGuigan, 'Cuthbert's Relics'.

92. See chapter 3 of the present volume.

93. *HSC*, sections 26–27 (ed. and trans. Johnson South, 64–67).

94. *HSC*, section 16 (ed. and trans. Johnson South, 54–57). For discussion, see Simpson, 'The King Alfred / St Cuthbert Episode'.

95. For the veneration of Cuthbert in the south of England, see Rollason, 'St Cuthbert and Wessex'; and Foot, *Æthelstan*, 208.

96. *MR*, s.a. 909.

97. Oswald's head would later be placed in Cuthbert's coffin. For these details about Oswald's death and the treatment of his relics, see Bede, *Ecclesiastical History*, iii.9, iii.11, and iii.12, and iii.11 for the quotation (ed. and trans. Colgrave and Mynors, 240–45, 244–51, and 250–53 respectively). See also Thacker, '*Membra Disjecta*', 97–127.

98. This seems to have been recognised by William of Malmesbury, who states, 'Æthelflæd and her husband Æthelred had built a well-provisioned monastery . . . and they had transferred there from Bardney the remains of King Oswald, all Mercia being under their sway'; WM, *GP*, iv.155. 3 (ed. and trans. Winterbottom, 446–47).

99. For the Latin text, see Hrotsvitha of Gandersheim, *Gesta Ottonis*, lines 95–96 (ed. Berschin, *Opera omnia*, 279), and the translation in Hill, *Medieval Monarchy in Action*, 123.

100. See Foot, *Æthelstan*, 207. For Oswald and Cynegils, see Bede, *Ecclesiastical History*, iii.7 (ed. and trans. Colgrave and Mynors, 232–37).

101. See Foot, *Æthelstan*, 206–7, where she also draws attention to the prominence given to Cynegils in a list of West Saxon kings in the New Minster *Liber vitae*. A charter which only survives in a copy of the early fourteenth century also preserves the detail that Æthelstan favoured St Oswald's, Gloucester. See Hare, 'The Documentary Evidence for the History of St Oswald's, Gloucester'.

102. See below, chapter 6 of the present volume.

103. Robinson, *The Times of Saint Dunstan*, 74–75; Dumville, *Wessex and England*, 155.

104. For an overview of the 'successor states', see Wickham, *The Inheritance of Rome*, 427–52.

105. See chapter 6 of the present volume.

106. The letter can be found in WM, *GP*, v.249 (ed. and trans. Winterbottom, 596–99), and in additions to WM, *GR*, 138B (ed. and trans. Mynors, Thomson, and Winterbottom, 820–23).

107. The letter is edited, translated, and fully discussed in Brett, 'A Breton Pilgrim in England'; the text and translation of the letter are at 57–60.

108. Dumville, *Wessex and England*, 200–201.

109. This record, said to have been taken from a manuscript now lost, is printed in Dugdale, *Monasticon Anglicanum*, ed. Caley, Ellis and Bandinel, 2:349–50. See also Dumville, *Wessex and England*, 157; and Brett, with Edmonds and Russell, *Brittany and the Atlantic Archipelago*, 183.

110. For a text, a translation, and discussion of the Exeter relic list, see Conner, *Anglo-Saxon Exeter*, 171–87. For discussion of the same evidence, see Brett, 'A Breton Pilgrim', 46–47. See also Rollason, 'Relic-Cults as an Instrument of Royal Policy', 94; and Smith, 'Eleventh-Century Relic Collections and the Holy Land'.

111. Brett, 'A Breton Pilgrim', 47.

112. See Keynes, 'King Athelstan's Books', 198–99. See also chapter 6 of the present volume.

113. S 1417 (*WinchNM* 9). See also chapter 2 of the present volume.

114. Godescealc is named as a recipient of a spurious diploma of King Æthelstan in S 409 (*Abing* 25) and is listed among the witnesses of another Abingdon forgery, S 410 (*Abing* 26). For further discussion, see *Charters of Abingdon Abbey, Part 1*, ed. Kelly, ccix, ccxii–ccxiii; and *Historia Ecclesiae Abbendonensis*, ed. Hudson, xcv, clxxi.

115. For Theodred's will, see Whitelock, *EHD*, 553–54 (no. 106). On Theodred and other Germans in England, see Wood, 'The Making of King Aethelstan's Empire', 261–63; and *Charters of St Paul's, London*, ed. Kelly, 116–18.

116. WM, *GP*, v.249 (ed. and trans. Winterbottom, 598–99).

117. On Æthelstan as a collector of relics, see Robinson, *The Times of Saint Dunstan*, 71–80.

118. For the quotation from the Old English relic list at Exeter, see Conner, *Anglo-Saxon Exeter*, 177. For the account of theft by Æthelstan's representatives, see Geary, *Furta Sacra*, 59–60; and Brett, with Edmonds and Russell, *Brittany and the Atlantic Archipelago*, 210.

119. WM, *GR*, ii.135.4–6 (ed. and trans. Mynors, Thomson, and Winterbottom, 218–21). For a full discussion of this gift of relics, and the degree to which it might have been invented by William of Malmesbury, see Foot, *Æthelstan*, 192–98.

120. For the religious policies adopted by Charlemagne, and how they relate to royal power, see McKitterick, *Charlemagne*, 292–380. For a recent assessment of the Carolingian 'renaissance', see Westwell, Rembold, and Van Rhijn, *Rethinking the Carolingian Reforms*. For Charlemagne's legacy, see, for example, Gabriele, *An Empire of Memory*.

121. See, however, the comments of Foot, *Æthelstan*, 194–95, on the ways in which William might have embellished details, and on competing Ottonian claims to similar relics.

122. WM, *GR*, ii.135.6 (ed. and trans. Mynors, Thomson, and Winterbottom, 220–21). For Æthelstan's burial at Malmesbury, see chapter 7 of the present volume.

123. See the full discussion in Foot, *Æthelstan*, 198–203, and esp. 199–200 for Winchester's claims to relics previously owned by Æthelstan.

124. Keynes, 'King Athelstan's Books', 150, 156–59. See also Stevenson, 'The Irish Contribution to Anglo-Latin Hermeneutic Prose'; and Woodman, '"Æthelstan A" and the Rhetoric of Rule'.

125. See chapter 2 of the present volume.

126. Keynes, 'King Athelstan's Books', 174, 180; Karkov, *The Ruler Portraits of Anglo-Saxon England*, 55–60; and Foot, *Æthelstan*, 120–21.

127. Rollason, 'St Cuthbert and Wessex'.

128. British Library, Cotton Otho B. ix, another gift from Æthelstan to St Cuthbert's community, was badly damaged in the 1731 fire of Sir Robert Cotton's library at Ashburnham House which, we know from catalogues and descriptions of the library, decimated many manuscripts that contained important texts from the early medieval period. Cotton Otho B. ix is thought to have contained another portrait of Æthelstan, perhaps by the same artist who was responsible for the image in Cambridge, Corpus Christi College 183; see Keynes, 'Athelstan's Books', 173–74. For a wonderful account of the circle of antiquaries who took an interest in early England, see De Hamel, *The Posthumous Papers of the Manuscripts Club*.

129. See Keynes, 'King Athelstan's Books', 181; and Simpson, 'The King Alfred / St Cuthbert Episode', 403–4.

130. For online images of the manuscript, see 'Gospels of MacDurnan', Lambeth Palace Library, n.d., https://images.lambethpalacelibrary.org.uk/luna/servlet/detail/LPLIBLPL~17 ~17~2738~100757?sort=creator%2Ctype%2Cdate%2Ctitle&qvq=q:macdurnan%20gospels.

131. For text and translation, see Keynes, 'Athelstan's Books', 153 and n52. The word division and punctuation of the original manuscript has been preserved in the transcription given here, but not the abbreviations, which have been expanded.

132. For an account of Mael Brigte's career and the positions he held, see Dumville, 'Mael Brigte mac Tornáin, Pluralist Coarb'. For the 913 entry in the *Annals of Ulster*, see *AU*, 913.

133. Keynes, 'King Athelstan's Books', 156–59; Foot, *Æthelstan*, 106–7.

134. *Charters of the New Minster*, ed. Miller, 53.

135. For all of these details, see Keynes, 'King Athelstan's Books', 170–73. For Benedict's attestation to a diploma, see S 413 (*Abing* 23).

136. See Lapidge, 'Israel the Grammarian', 89.

137. For the suggestion that the name 'Israel' may refer to the presence of a Jew at Æthelstan's court rather than the Breton scholar of that name, see Wasserstein, 'The First Jew in England'.

138. See Murray, *History of Board Games Other Than Chess*, 61–62, for this specific game. I am grateful to Dr Irving Finkel of the British Museum for his guidance on this matter.

139. Robinson, *The Times of Saint Dunstan*, 171–81.

140. For a full discussion of Israel's career, see Lapidge, 'Israel the Grammarian'; Wood, '"Stand Strong against the Monsters"', 192–217; and Wood, 'A Carolingian Scholar in the Court of King Æthelstan'.

141. Woodman, '"Æthelstan A" and the Rhetoric of Rule', 217–48. For the links between a Greek litany included in a dossier of texts compiled by Israel and a litany copied into British Library, Cotton Galba A. xviii, the so-called 'Æthelstan Psalter', see Lapidge, 'Israel the Grammarian', 101–3.

142. Bayless, '*Alea*, *Tæfl*, and Related Games'.

143. For a full discussion of poems composed during Æthelstan's reign, see Lapidge, 'Some Latin Poems', 49–86.

144. The Latin text and English translation are from Gallagher, 'Latin Acrostic Poetry in Anglo-Saxon England', 255. A slightly alternative version can be found in Lapidge, 'Some Latin Poems', 60–61.

145. For all of these details, see Lapidge, 'Some Latin Poems', 60–71. The manuscript in which the poem has been copied (on fol. 78v) is Oxford, Bodleian Library, Rawlinson C. 697, which is thought originally to have been written in north-eastern France in the late ninth century; Gneuss and Lapidge, *Anglo-Saxon Manuscripts*, 506 (no. 661). It contains copies of Aldhelm's *Enigmata* (Riddles), Aldhelm's verse treatise on virginity, and the *Psychomachia* of Prudentius.

146. See Lapidge, 'Some Latin Poems'; and Gallagher, 'Latin Acrostic Poetry'.

147. For the occasion in question, described as a ceremony in which Æthelstan was 'knighted', see chapter 1 of the present volume. For this interpretation of when the poem was written, see Lapidge, 'Some Latin Poems', 61–69.

148. Wieland, 'A New Look at the Poem "Archalis clamare triumuir"'; Gallagher, 'Latin Acrostic Poetry', 260–62. For very interesting comments about the different name puzzles that she detects in the poem, see Zacher, 'Multilingualism at the Court of King Æthelstan', 86–91.

149. For a recent edition of the poetry of Egill, see *Poetry in Sagas of Icelanders, Part 1*, ed. Ross, Gade and Wills, 152–391.

150. *Egils Saga*, chaps. 50–55 (trans. and ed. Fell, 74–86).

151. See below, chapter 5 of the present volume.

152. *Egils Saga*, chaps. 54–55 (trans. and ed. Fell, 81–85).

153. *Egils Saga*, ed. Fell, xvi; Jesch, 'Skaldic Verse', 315.

154. See Jesch, 'Skaldic Verse', 315–17, 320.

155. The translation is taken from Jesch, 'Skaldic Verse', 316. Compare *Egils Saga*, ed. Fell, 86 (and 187n6 for further explanation). For Egill as a poet, see, for example, Larrington, 'Egill's Longer Poems'.

156. For possible links between *Beowulf*, the most famous of all early English poems, and the period of Æthelstan's reign, see Foot, *Æthelstan*, 115–17.

157. See, for example, Cubitt, 'The Tenth-Century Benedictine Reform in England'.

158. For the possible date of composition, see Wulfstan of Winchester, *Life of St Æthelwold*, ed. Lapidge and Winterbottom, xv–xvi, xcix–c.

159. Wulfstan of Winchester, *Life of St Æthelwold*, chap. 7 (ed. and trans. Lapidge and Winterbottom, 10–11).

160. On Æthelwold's possible attestations, see Wulfstan of Winchester, *Life of St Æthelwold*, ed. Lapidge and Winterbottom, xliii. See also Yorke, 'Æthelwold and the Politics of the Tenth Century', 68–69.

161. Wulfstan of Winchester, *Life of St Æthelwold*, chaps. 7–8 (ed. and trans. Lapidge and Winterbottom, 10–13).

162. Wulfstan of Winchester, *Life of St Æthelwold*, chap. 9 (ed. and trans. Lapidge and Winterbottom, 14–15).

163. For the date of Adelard's work, see *The Early Lives of St Dunstan*, ed. Winterbottom and Lapidge, cxxv.

164. For B.'s version of Dunstan's career, see *The Early Lives of St Dunstan*, chap. 5 and chap. 7.2–3 (ed. and trans. Winterbottom and Lapidge, 16–19 and 26–27), and, for Adelard's version, see Adelard of Ghent, *Lectiones in Depositione S. Dunstani*, III (ed. and trans. Winterbottom and Lapidge, *The Early Lives of St Dunstan*, 116–19).

165. Brooks, 'The Career of St Dunstan', 4. Compare Lapidge, 'Dunstan [St Dunstan]', which, while acknowledging that Adelard's account should not be straightforwardly accepted, also

suggests that Æthelhelm's previous role as bishop of Wells, a see close to Glastonbury, might make his relationship to Dunstan credible. For there being no attestation by Dunstan in Æthelstan's diplomas, see *The Early Lives of St Dunstan*, ed. Winterbottom and Lapidge, xviii.

166. See *The Early Lives of St Dunstan*, chaps. 7.2, 21.3, and 10.1–3 (ed. and trans. Winterbottom and Lapidge, 26–27, 68–69, and 34–35). On the possible identity of the *matrona* with Æthelflæd, see Lapidge, 'Dunstan [St Dunstan]'.

167. Lapidge, 'Dunstan [St Dunstan]'.

168. Brooks, 'The Career of St Dunstan', 5–7. If Dunstan was related in some way to Æthelflæd, and therefore ultimately to the royal line, it has been suggested that the connection would have been through Æthelstan's mother, Ecgwynn; see Yorke, 'Æthewold and the Politics of the Tenth Century', 66–67, and, for discussion of the term *neptis* used to describe Æthelflæd's relationship to Æthelstan, 66n14.

169. For Ælfheah's tonsure, see *The Early Lives of St Dunstan*, ed. and trans. Winterbottom and Lapidge, 26n77. For further discussion, see Blair, *The Church in Anglo-Saxon Society*, 348–50.

170. For Æthelwold's sending of the monk, Osgar, to Fleury, the supposed home of the remains of Benedict of Nursia (d. 547), see Wulfstan of Winchester, *Life of St Æthelwold*, chap. 14 (ed. and trans. Lapidge and Winterbottom, 24–27). For Æthelwold and Dunstan at Æthelstan's court, see also Foot, *Æthelstan*, 107–10.

Chapter Five

1. *ASC* D, s.a. 926 (*recte* 927).

2. Wormald, *The Making of English Law*, 445.

3. For the use of 'Albion' in Æthelstan's diplomas, see Crick, 'Edgar, Albion and Insular Dominion', 161–62, which notes that the diplomas in question do not survive as contemporary copies. For an example of the use of 'Albion' in a royal style, see S 411 (*Abing* 29), discussed in *Charters of Abingdon Abbey, Part I*, ed. Kelly, 123.

4. Naismith, *MEC*, 202–3. For the claims of tenth-century English kings to rule in Britain, see Molyneaux, 'Why Were Some Tenth-Century English Kings Presented as Rulers of Britain?'

5. For Britain's complex political composition, see the introduction to the present volume.

6. *ASC*, s.a. 830. For Egbert's actions in Wales, see Lloyd, *A History of Wales from the Earliest Times to the Edwardian Conquest*, 325; and Charles-Edwards, *Wales and the Britons*, 475.

7. *ASC*, s.a. 853.

8. *AU*, 877.3. Charles-Edwards, *Wales and the Britons*, 487, discusses the possibility that 'dark foreigners' could also have been motivated to attack Rhodri because of his earlier killing of one of their leaders, Orm, in 856, or because, having taken control of Mercia, they were now pursuing a Mercian claim to rule over parts of Wales.

9. Asser, chaps. 79–80 (trans. Keynes and Lapidge, 93–96). Anarawd probably threw in his lot with Alfred in the period 888–92; see Charles-Edwards, *Wales and the Britons*, 494; cf. Keynes and Lapidge, *Alfred the Great*, 263n183.

10. For the date of Hyfaidd's death, see Charles-Edwards, *Wales and the Britons*, 495n127, and, for the joint actions of Anarawd and the Mercians, 495–96.

11. For 913–14, see *AU*, 913.5, 914.4.

12. *ASC*, s.a. 914. Cyfeilliog was bishop of an area known as Ergyng, in the west of modern Herefordshire; see Charles-Edwards, *Wales and the Britons*, 506.

13. *AU*, 917.2, 917.4.

14. *MR*, s.a. 914, 915. For Æthelflæd's burhs, see Blake and Sargent, '"For the Protection of All the People"'.

15. *ASC* A, s.a. 918.

16. Charles-Edwards, *Wales and the Britons*, 504.

17. For Edward's purchase of Cyfeilliog's freedom, see *ASC*, s.a. 914. For Æthelflæd's actions in Brycheiniog, see *MR*, s.a. 916. For further discussion of the position of Gwent and Brychein-iog, see Charles-Edwards, *Wales and the Britons*, 505–6, and, for Mercian interest in Brycheiniog in 916 and for the Merfynions and Dyfed, 507–8.

18. Charles-Edwards, *Wales and the Britons*, 513.

19. WM, *GR*, ii.131.3 (ed. and trans. Mynors, Thomson, and Winterbottom, 206–7).

20. WM, *GR*, ii.134.5–6 (ed. and trans. Mynors, Thomson, and Winterbottom, 214–17).

21. See chapter 3 of the present volume; Roach, *Kingship and Consent*, 32–34 and 39 for the diplomas of 'Æthelstan A'; and Keynes, 'Welsh Kings', 87–88. For the attendance of King An-arawd of Gwynedd at King Alfred's court, see Maund, *The Welsh Kings*, 44; and Lloyd, *A History of Wales*, 328.

22. According to Charles-Edwards, *Wales and the Britons*, 516, Gwriad was a relative of Hywel Dda and possibly king of Powys or Ceredigion, but other suggestions have been made as well. For a summary, see Keynes, 'Welsh Kings', 89n78. For further discussion, see Halloran, 'Welsh Kings at the English Court', 300–302.

23. Kirby, 'Hywel Dda: Anglophil?', 4.

24. The subscriptions of the sub-kings are tabulated in Keynes, *An Atlas of Attestations in Anglo-Saxon Charters*, table XXXVI. The evidence is discussed in Keynes, 'Welsh Kings', 89–90. For Hywel's trip to Rome, see *AC*, s.a. 928.

25. *Charters of Northern Houses*, ed. Woodman, 86–97.

26. Keynes, 'Welsh Kings', 91.

27. See Keynes, 'Welsh Kings', 91–92.

28. *Charters of St Paul's, London*, ed. Kelly, 158–60.

29. See Keynes, 'Welsh Kings', 92.

30. Keynes, 'Welsh Kings', 96–104. For the 'alliterative' charters, which have been linked with Bishop Cenwald of Worcester, see *Charters of Burton Abbey*, ed. Sawyer, xlvii–xlix; and Keynes, 'Koenwald', 273–75.

31. Keynes, 'Welsh Kings', 90.

32. See, most famously, Lloyd, *A History of Wales*, 333–43. For a different interpretation, see Kirby, 'Hywel Dda: Anglophil?'. For further discussion, see Charles-Edwards, *Wales and the Britons*, 326–27, 510–19; and Thomas, 'The Context of the Hywel Dda Penny'.

33. Cheney, *A Handbook of Dates for Students of British History*, 200.

34. *AC*, s.a. 928 (B and C texts). In 854 the *AC* record that Cyngen ap Cadell, king of Powys, died in Rome.

35. Thomas, 'Three Welsh Kings and Rome', 571–73.

36. See above, chapter 2 of the present volume.

37. For the positive interpretation of Hywel's motivations, see Lloyd, *A History of Wales*, 336–37. For the less positive view, see Kirby, 'Hywel Dda: Anglophil?', 6–7.

38. *The Law of Hywel Dda*, ed. Jenkins, xi–xxvi, 1.

39. See Charles-Edwards, *The Welsh Laws*, 83–86.

40. For a summary discussion of the Old Welsh technical terms and their Old English equivalents, with appropriate bibliographical references, see Keynes, 'Welsh Kings', 115–17. For the possible influence of Irish law on the laws of Wales, see Charles-Edwards, *Welsh Laws*, 86. See also Kirby, 'Hywel Dda: Anglophil?', 10–12.

41. Blunt, 'The Cabinet of the Marquess of Ailesbury and the Penny of Hywel Dda', 119. Thomas, 'The Context of the Hywel Dda Penny', 88, suggests that 'on a numismatic and histori-cal basis, its [i.e. the coin's] production can therefore be ascribed to the period 939 × 950'.

42. See Keynes, 'Welsh Kings', 108–9; Thomas, 'The Context of the Hywel Dda Penny'; and Naismith, *MEC*, 311–12.

43. Thornton, 'Hywel Dda [Hywel Dda ap Cadell]'. For the suggestion that Hywel's position in Wales was augmented by his relations both with Æthelflæd of Mercia and Æthelstan, see Thomas, 'Three Welsh Kings', 570–73.

44. Charles-Edwards, *Wales and the Britons*, 518–19.

45. For a possible Welsh reaction to the anti-Æthelstan allegiance at *Brunanburh*, see Breeze, 'The Battle of Brunanburh and Welsh Tradition'.

46. Lewis, 'Welsh Territories and Welsh Identities', 140–42.

47. The text of the 'Ordinance concerning the *Dunsæte*' can be found in *Die Gesetze der Angelsachsen*, ed. Liebermann, 1:374–79. For a translation, see Noble, *Offa's Dyke Reviewed*, 105–9.

48. For a date in Æthelstan's reign, see, for example, Fordham, 'Peacekeeping and Order on the Anglo-Welsh Frontier'. For a later date, see Molyneaux, 'The *Ordinance Concerning the Dun-sæte* and the Anglo-Welsh Frontier'.

49. *Armes Prydein: The Prophecy of Britain*, ed. Williams, xvii–xx. For arguments for a later date, see Dumville, 'Brittany and *Armes Prydein*'; Tolstoy, 'When and Where was *Armes Prydein* Composed?'; and Breeze, '*Armes Prydein*, Hywel Dda, and the Reign of Edmund of Wessex', which, at 210–15, includes a further translation of *Armes Prydein*.

50. *Armes Prydein: The Prophecy of Britain*, ed. Williams, xxiv–xxvi, proposes that the poet was from St David's, while Tolstoy, 'When and Where', suggests a Gwynedd origin. See also Charles-Edwards, *Wales and the Britons*, 519–35.

51. *Armes Prydein: The Prophecy of Britain*, ed. Williams, 8–11 (lines 113–14, 117–20 respectively).

52. WM, *GR*, ii.134.5–7 (ed. and trans. Mynors, Thomson, and Winterbottom, 214–17). That Æthelstan was indeed the 'Great King' alluded to by the poet, and held to be a tyrant, is sug-gested in *Armes Prydein: The Prophecy of Britain*, ed. Williams, xii–xx. For further discussion, including detail about the transmission of the poem, see Thomas and Callander, 'Reading Asser'. The exact date of the poem has important implications for the way in which it is under-stood, either as calling the Welsh to arms in advance of the Battle of *Brunanburh* (and possibly as a critique of the relationship of Hywel Dda with Æthelstan), or, if it post-dates *Brunanburh*,

as a reflection that the Welsh would be needed for any chance of success against the English. For further discussion, with accompanying references, see Thomas and Callander, 'Reading Asser', 116–17.

53. On this form of place-name, see Thomas and Callander, 'Reading Asser', 137–39.

54. *AU*, 866.1. For Ívarr and the 'great army', see chapter 1 of the present volume.

55. Textual complications in the *Chronicle of the Kings of Alba* have given rise to a number of interpretations concerning the length of time Óláf spent in Pictland, which may have been from 1 January to 17 March 866. See Hudson, 'The Scottish Chronicle', 148–49 (Latin text) and 153–54 (English translation). Smyth, *Scandinavian Kings in the British Isles*, 143–49, suggested an alternative view, that Óláf remained in Pictland until 869; this is discussed in Woolf, *From Pictland to Alba*, 106–9. For Óláf's presence in Ireland in 867, see Downham, *Viking Kings*, 139–40.

56. There has been scholarly disagreement about whether or not the names 'Strathclyde' and 'land of the Cumbrians' represent two separate kingdoms or whether they should be thought of as synonymous with each other, in which case 'Cumbrian' may have been the term used by the English to refer to the inhabitants of Strathclyde. There has also been disagreement about the possible expansion of the Strathclyde kingdom in the late ninth and early tenth centuries, a theory which is based on the interpretation of Brittonic place-names in the area south of the Solway Firth. For some historians, a number of the place-names could represent not expansion by the Strathclyde kingdom in the late ninth/early tenth centuries but the survival under pre-867 Northumbrian rule of British communities and then their reassertion following the collapse of Northumbrian power in the area. For a useful summary of all of the complex material, with further references, see Edmonds, 'The Expansion of the Kingdom of Strathclyde'; Edmonds, 'The Emergence and Transformation of Medieval Cumbria'; and Clarkson, *Strathclyde and the Anglo-Saxons*, 63–69 (with a useful map of the Brittonic place-names on 68). For the suggestion that some Brittonic place-names represent a reassertion of existing Brittonic-speaking communities, see, for example, Phythian-Adams, *Land of the Cumbrians*, 47–106.

57. The power of Ívarr is recognised by the title allotted to him in Irish annals on his death of 'king of the Norsemen of all Ireland and Britain'; see *AU*, 873.3. For the murder of Óláf by Constantine, see Hudson, 'The Scottish Chronicle', 148 (Latin text) and 154 (English translation).

58. Hudson, 'Scottish Chronicle', 148–49 (Latin text) and 154 (English translation). Woolf, *From Pictland to Alba*, 111–12, suggests that the *Chronicle of the Kings of Alba*, in its reference to the battle at Dollar and the slaughter 'as far as Atholl', might have been combining two originally separate events into one. The *Annals of Ulster* record an encounter in 875 between the 'Picts' and the 'dark foreigners' which resulted in a loss for the Picts; see *AU*, 875.3.

59. *ASC*, s.a. 875.

60. *AU*, 875.4, records the death of Óláf's son, 'Oistín', at the hands of a man who may be identified as Hálfdan himself; see Woolf, *From Pictland to Alba*, 112–13; cf. Downham, *Viking Kings*, 143–44.

61. See *HSC*, sections 14–19a (ed. and trans. Johnson South, 52–59). For issues concerning the status of some of these passages, see Simpson, 'The King Alfred / St Cuthbert Episode'. Constantine I, king of the Picts, tried to solidify his own position by marrying his sister, Mael Muire, to two successive Irish high-kings, Aed Finnliath (d. 879) and Flann Sinna (d. 916).

Constantine was also implicated in the murder of King Artgal in 872. Constantine subsequently married a second (unnamed) sister to Artgal's son and successor, Rhun. For the death of Artgal, see *AU*, 872.5. Clarkson, *Strathclyde and the Anglo-Saxons*, 50–52, discusses the possible reasons why Artgal was killed. See also Woolf, *From Pictland to Alba*, 110–11.

62. Downham, *Viking Kings*, 145.

63. Hudson, 'Scottish Chronicle', 149 (Latin text) and 155 (English translation).

64. *The Fragmentary Annals of Ireland*, ed. Radner, 166–69. On Ingimundr, see Wainwright, 'Ingimund's Invasion'.

65. Fellows-Jensen, 'Scandinavian Place-Names'; Griffiths, 'Settlement and Acculturation in the Irish Sea Region'; Watson, 'Viking-Age Amounderness'.

66. Hudson, 'Scottish Chronicle', 149–50 (Latin) and 155 (English translation). For the identification of the 904 battle site, see Woolf, *From Pictland to Alba*, 130. *AU*, 904.4, provides the detail of Ívarr's death.

67. Graham-Campbell, 'Some Archaeological Reflections on the Cuerdale Hoard'. And see Downham, *Viking Kings*, 83–84, which also cites the work of Graham-Campbell.

68. See *ASC*, s.a. 906, 909, and 910. The names of some of the viking kings killed at Tettenhall may suggest that Edward was dealing with further members of the dynasty of Ívarr; see Downham, *Viking Kings*, 87, which relies on Dumville, 'Old Dubliners and New Dubliners in Ireland and Britain', 88–89.

69. *AU*, 917.2, 917.4.

70. *Fragmentary Annals of Ireland*, ed. Radner, 180–83; Clarkson, *Strathclyde and the Anglo-Saxons*, 59–63.

71. Downham, 'The Good, the Bad and the Ugly'; Downham, *Viking Kings*, 164. For further discussion, see Clarkson, *Strathclyde and the Anglo-Saxons*, 59–63.

72. For accounts of the battle, see *AU*, 918.4; Hudson, 'Scottish Chronicle', 150 (Latin) and 157 (English translation); and *HSC*, section 22 (ed. and trans. Johnson South, 60–61). Another encounter at Corbridge is mentioned in section 24 of the *HSC*, which has prompted much discussion among historians, particularly over the number of battles at Corbridge that took place (one or two) and the date(s) at which they happened. For discussion of this material, and the view that there was only one battle of Corbridge dated 918, see Downham, *Viking Kings*, 91–95.

73. All of these details are provided by annals 918–20 in the *ASC* and the *Mercian Register*.

74. *ASC*, s.a. 920.

75. Woolf, *From Pictland to Alba*, 145–47; Clarkson, *Strathclyde and the Anglo-Saxons*, 70–74; Davidson, 'The (Non)submission of the Northern Kings'.

76. *AU*, 921.4.

77. Sihtric's attack on Davenport is recorded in *HR*, s.a. 920.

78. *AU*, 921.5.

79. For the possibility that the unnamed sister should be identified with Edith of Polesworth, and for the extension of Sihtric's power into the east midlands, see chapter 2 of the present volume.

80. *ASC* D, s.a. 927.

81. See WM, *GR*, ii.134.2 (ed. and trans. Mynors, Thomson, and Winterbottom, 214–15), and chapter 2 of the present volume.

82. For William's detail that the submission took place at Dacre, see chapter 2 of the present volume.

83. *ASC* E, s.a. 927 and *HR*, s.a. 927.

84. *AU*, 927.3.

85. Williams, 'The Coins from the Vale of York Viking Hoard'.

86. Above, chapters 2 and 3 of the present volume.

87. For this grant of land, see S 407 (*North* 1); chapter 2 of the present volume; and Woodman, 'Charters, Northumbria and the Unification of England', 35–51.

88. *ASC*, s.a. 934.

89. *HSC*, section 26 (ed. and trans. Johnson South, 64–65).

90. *HR*, s.a. 934. For the identification of *Wertermorum* with the 'mountains of Fortriu', see Woolf, *From Pictland to Alba*, 161.

91. Margary, *Roman Roads in Britain*, 493–95. The *Chronicle of the Kings of Alba* preserves the detail of an important ritual occasion enacted at Scone between Constantine and a bishop named Cellach; see Hudson, 'Scottish Chronicle', 150 (Latin) and 156 (English translation). The significance of this episode in representing the authority being invested in Constantine's kingship is stressed in Woolf, *From Pictland to Alba*, 134–37. For Æthelstan's war in Scotland, see Woolf, *From Pictland to Alba*, 165–66.

92. JW, *Chron.*, s.a. 934 (ed. Darlington and McGurk, trans. Bray and McGurk, 388–91); *HR*, s.a. 934. For the relationship between the 'Worcester Chronicle' and the *Historia Regum*, see Woodman, 'Annals 848 to 1118 in the *Historia Regum*'.

93. For Edwin's death, see above, chapter 2 of the present volume. For the death of Guthfrith, see *AU*, 934.1. A late source known as the *Annals of Clonmacnoise* refer to the death of a certain 'Adulf m^cEtulfe', who it is suggested is synonymous with Ealdred of Bamburgh. See *The Annals of Clonmacnoise*, ed. Murphy, s.a. 928 (*recte* 934). For a discussion of his possible identity, see Woolf, *From Pictland to Alba*, 163–64.

94. These suggestions rely on the excellent and more extended analysis in Woolf, *From Pictland to Alba*, 161–65.

95. Symeon of Durham, *Libellus de Exordio*, ii.18 (ed. and trans. Rollason, 136–37).

96. Clarkson, *Strathclyde and the Anglo-Saxons*, 80–84.

97. Downham, *Vikings Kings*, 150–51.

98. JW, *Chron.*, s.a. 934 (ed. Darlington and McGurk, trans. Bray and McGurk, 390–91); *HR*, s.a. 934.

99. S 426 (*Glast* 24).

100. S 1792 (*LondStP* 11).

101. S 434 (*Malm* 26).

102. For the poem's place in tenth-century annals of the *Anglo-Saxon Chronicle*, see Stafford, *After Alfred*, 86.

103. Symeon of Durham, *Libellus de Exordio*, ii.18 (ed. and trans. Rollason, 138–39); *HR*, s.a. 937. It would be interesting to know more about the reaction of Wulfstan I, archbishop of York (whose allegiance Æthelstan had tried hard to secure in 934), to events of 937. After 935 Wulfstan I disappears from the witness-lists of diplomas. He can later be found acting on the side of Óláf Guthfrithson. See Whitelock, 'The Dealings of the Kings of England'; and Keynes, 'Wulfstan I'.

104. See *Annala Rioghachta Eireann*, s.a. 935 (= 937) (ed. and trans. O'Donovan, 2:632–33).

105. Downham, *Viking Kings*, 35–42, at 41.

106. *The Battle of Brunanburh*, ed. Campbell, 16–42. For the possibility that the poet was Mercian, see Stafford, *After Alfred*, 89n28, 91. For poets in early medieval England, see Thornbury, *Becoming a Poet in Anglo-Saxon England*.

107. For an overview, see Foot, *Æthelstan*, 112–15, which locates the poem in Æthelstan's reign. Walker, 'A Context for *Brunanburh*', cited also by Foot, *Æthelstan*, suggests the poem might more naturally belong to the reign of Edmund. For comparisons of the poem to skaldic poetry, see Townend, 'Pre-Cnut Praise Poetry'. The poem's textual allusions to other parts of the *Anglo-Saxon Chronicle* have suggested to Stafford, *After Alfred*, 91–92 (where the work of Townend is also quoted), that the poem was composed specifically for inclusion with the other annals, rather than being intended as a separate, stand-alone piece.

108. For all of the quoted text, see *ASC*, s.a. 937.

109. *The Battle of Brunanburh*, ed. Campbell, 48, 54.

110. For a very helpful overview of all aspects relating to the place-name *Brunanburh*, see Cavill, 'The Place-Name Debate'. See also Livingston, *Never Greater Slaughter*.

111. For all of these possibilities, see *The Battle of Brunanburh*, ed. Campbell, 60–62; and Cavill, 'The Place-Name Debate', 331.

112. Symeon of Durham, *Libellus de Exordio*, ii.18 (ed. and trans. Rollason, 138–39). See also *HR*, s.a. 937.

113. Hudson, 'Scottish Chronicle', 150; *AC*, s.a. 937; *The Annals of Clonmacnoise*, s.a. 931 (= 937) (ed. Murphy, 151). For a list of all extant spellings and versions of the place-name, see Cavill, 'The Place-Name Debate', 329–30.

114. Cavill, 'The Place-Name Debate', 333, explains that *dun* has the broad meaning of 'hill' but that it comes to have a special meaning when applied to an early medieval settlement site.

115. Cavill, 'The Place-Name Debate', 333–35.

116. Cavill, 'The Place-Name Debate', 346–47.

117. Cavill, 'The Place-Name Debate', 336–37; cf. *The Battle of Brunanburh*, ed. Campbell, 115.

118. For comments about the extent to which *Egils saga* can be used in this connection, see, for example, *The Battle of Brunanburh*, ed. Campbell, 68–78. Compare Cavill, 'The Place-Name Debate', 336.

119. In his account, William of Malmesbury suggests that Óláf had travelled quite far into England before the battle itself, although what this actually means is unclear, and the passage in general contains error and legendary material: WM, *GR*, ii.131.4–7 (ed. and trans. Mynors, Thomson, and Winterbottom, 206–9).

120. JW, *Chron.*, s.a. 937 (ed. Darlington and McGurk, trans. Bray and McGurk, 392–93).

121. Wood, 'Searching for Brunanburh'. For a critique of Wood's hypothesis, see Cavill, 'The Battle of Brunanburh'.

122. JW, *Chron.*, s.a. 941 (ed. Darlington and McGurk, trans. Bray and McGurk, 394–95).

123. This argument depends on Cavill, 'The Place-Name Debate', 338–39, which, on the basis of another entry in the 'Worcester Chronicle', further suggests that it was a habit of the chronicler to note the entry of a fleet through the River Humber. For the addition of such clarifying remarks being a feature of the work of John of Worcester, see JW, *Chron.*, vol. 4, *Chronicula*, ed. McGurk and Woodman, xxvii.

124. For the linguistic derivation, see Dodgson, 'The Background of Brunanburh'; and Cavill, 'The Place-Name Debate', 344–47.

125. For the place-name evidence, see, for example, Dodgson, 'The Background of Brunanburh'. For the artefacts from Meols, see Griffiths, Philpott, and Egan, *Meols*, 58–77.

126. Cavill, 'The Place-Name Debate', 346–47.

127. Downham, *Viking Kings*, 105.

128. *AU*, 937.6. For a possible Welsh allusion to the battle, see Breeze, 'The Battle of Brunanburh and Welsh Tradition', 479–82.

129. *The Chronicle of Æthelweard*, IV.5 (ed. and trans. Campbell, 54).

Chapter Six

1. WM, *GR*, ii.135.1 (ed. and trans. Mynors, Thomson, and Winterbottom, 216–17).

2. Whitelock, *EHD*, 848–49 (no. 197).

3. Peacock, 'Charlemagne's Black Stones'.

4. See Firth, *Early English Queens*, 21.

5. *The Annals of St-Bertin*, s.a. 856 (trans. Nelson, 83).

6. Stafford, 'Charles the Bald, Judith and England', 139–53.

7. Asser, chap. 17 (trans. Keynes and Lapidge, 73).

8. *The Annals of St-Bertin*, s.a. 842 (trans. Nelson, 53). For these events, see Grierson, 'The Relations between England and Flanders'.

9. See chapter 2 of the present volume.

10. See the introduction to the present volume.

11. On Ælfgifu/Eadgifu, see appendix II of the present volume. For what continental rulers stood to gain from their association with Æthelstan, see Ortenberg, '"The King from Overseas"'. See also Foot, 'Dynastic Strategies'.

12. On the complex continental politics of the period, see Nelson, 'The Frankish Kingdoms', 262–72.

13. Richer of Saint-Rémi, *Histories*, 1.4 (ed. and trans. Lake, 14–15); with the Latin text in *Richer von Saint-Remi, Historiae*, ed. Hoffmann, 39.

14. For 'Neustria' and its eastern counterpart, 'Austrasia', see McKitterick, *The Frankish Kingdoms*, 17–19.

15. *The Annals of Flodoard*, s.a. 923 (5D) (trans. Fanning and Bachrach, 8) with the Latin text in *Les annales*, ed. Lauer, 13.

16. Those in the so-called 'southern principalities' of West Francia viewed Radulf as a usurper; see Zimmermann, 'Western Francia', 429.

17. See Folcuin, *Gesta Abbatum S. Bertini Sithiensium*, chap. 101 (ed. Holder-Egger, 625–26), for the detail concerning Eadgifu and Louis.

18. WM, *GR*, ii.135.3–6 (ed. and trans. Mynors, Thomson, and Winterbottom, 218–21). On these gifts, see Loomis, 'The Holy Relics of Charlemagne and King Athelstan'.

19. WM, *GR*, ii.135.6 (ed. and trans. Mynors, Thomson, and Winterbottom, 220–21).

20. This point is stressed in Nelson, 'Eadgifu'. See also MacLean, 'Making a Difference', 173.

21. Nelson, 'Eadgifu'.

22. Richer of Saint-Rémi, *Histories*, 2.1–4 (ed. and trans. Lake, 158–71); with Latin text in *Richer von Saint-Remi, Historiae*, ed. Hoffmann, 97–101.

23. Richer of Saint-Rémi, *Histories*, 2.3 (ed. and trans. Lake, 166–67); with Latin text in *Richer von Saint-Remi, Historiae*, ed. Hoffmann, 99. In his text, Folcuin writes *Adalolfus*, which Grierson, 'The Relations between England and Flanders', 88n4, shows to be an error for Arnulfus.

24. McKitterick, *The Frankish Kingdoms*, 315.

25. McKitterick, *The Frankish Kingdoms*, 314–15.

26. See, for example, *Recueil des actes de Louis IV*, nos. I and IV (ed. Lauer, 1–3, 8–13); and, on which, see McKitterick, *The Frankish Kingdoms*, 315.

27. *The Annals of Flodoard*, s.a. 937 (19B) (trans. Fanning and Bachrach, 29); with the Latin text in *Les Annales*, ed. Lauer, 65.

28. For Eadgifu's ownership of Tusey and Corbeny, see MacLean, 'Making a Difference', 181–85. For Flodoard, see *The Annals of Flodoard*, s.a. 938 (20A) (trans. Fanning and Bachrach, 30), with the Latin text in *Les Annales*, ed. Lauer, 69; and cf. Richer of Saint-Rémi, *Histories* 2.6 (ed. and trans. Lake, 174–5), with the Latin text in *Richer von Saint-Remi, Historiae*, ed. Hoffmann, 102

29. Bates, 'West Francia', 410–11.

30. For the relevant part of Alfred's will, see Keynes and Lapidge, *Alfred the Great*, 177 (and notes on 321).

31. Folcuin, *Gesta Abbatum S. Bertini Sithiensium*, chap. 107 (ed. Holder-Egger, 629). I am very grateful to Dr Fraser McNair for sending me his translation of Folcuin's *Gesta* in advance of publication. For England and Flanders in this period, see Grierson, 'The Relations between England and Flanders', 71–112.

32. *The Annals of Flodoard*, s.a. 939 (21B) (trans. Fanning and Bachrach, 31), with the Latin text in *Les annales*, ed. Lauer, 71–72.

33. *The Annals of Flodoard*, s.a. 938 (20A) (trans. Fanning and Bachrach, 30), with the Latin text in *Les annales*, ed. Lauer, 68–69. For the identification of Flodoard's *Guisum* in this annal with Quentovic, see Grierson, 'The Relations between England and Flanders', 79n3. For Louis IV, Arnulf and Æthelstan, see Grierson, 'The Relations between England and Flanders', 79, 88–89; and MacLean, 'Making a Difference', 175–78.

34. *The Annals of Flodoard*, s.a. 939 (21D) (trans. Fanning and Bachrach, 31–32), with the Latin text in *Les annales*, ed. Lauer, 73. It has been suggested that a handful of Æthelstan's surviving diplomas of 939, including one in which he grants land at Droxford on the River Meon in Hampshire to another of his sisters, Eadburh, may have represented the king's preparations for this naval expedition. Eadburh herself was a nun at Winchester; see MacLean, 'Making a Difference', 177–78. The diploma granting land at Droxford is S 446. For further discussion of this document, see above, chapter 4 of the present volume. For Eadburh, see WM, *GR*, ii.126.3, ii.217 and ii.219 (ed. and trans. Mynors, Thomson, and Winterbottom, 200–201, 400–403, and 404–5).

35. WM, *GR*, ii.112.2, ii.126.2, and ii.135.1 (ed. and trans. Mynors, Thomson, and Winterbottom, 170–71, 200–201 and 216–17).

36. See WM, *GR*, ii.112.2 and ii.126.1–3 (ed. and trans. Mynors, Thomson, and Winterbottom, 170–71 and 198–201).

37. See Hrotsvitha of Gandersheim, *Gesta Ottonis*, line 112 (ed. Berschin, 279), translated in Hill, *Medieval Monarchy in Action*, 123. See also the prologue in *The Chronicle of Æthelweard* (ed. and trans. Campbell, 1–2).

38. See the useful summary of the position in MacLean, 'Making a Difference', 168n4. For the suggestion that this marriage between an English princess and Louis, the brother of Rudolf II of Burgundian, helped intrude Ottonian influence into Burgundy, see Reuter, 'The Ottonians and Wessex', 83–85, which also draws attention to the name given to the son of Louis and the English princess, which may have suggested a degree of ambition that he could succeed to the Burgundian throne.

39. For all of these details, and the different regions of Burgundy and their geographical limits, see Bouchard, 'Burgundy and Provence'.

40. Bouchard, 'Burgundy and Provence', 341.

41. If Louis IV was pushing a claim to Burgundy, he may have relied on the familial bonds between his mother, Eadgifu, and her sister, Ælfgifu/Eadgifu; see MacLean, 'Making a Difference', 179–80.

42. See Hrotsvitha of Gandersheim, *Gesta Ottonis*, lines 75–77 (ed. Berschin, 278), translated in Hill, *Medieval Monarchy in Action*, 122.

43. Hrotsvitha of Gandersheim, *Gesta Ottonis*, lines 80 and 95–97 (ed. Berschin, 278–79), translated in Hill, *Medieval Monarchy in Action*, 122–23.

44. For claims to possession of Oswald's head, see Bailey, 'St Oswald's Heads', 201–3. For Widukind of Corvey's reading of Bede, see Widukind of Corvey, *Res gestae Saxonicae*, i.8 (ed. Hirsch and Lohmann, 10), translated in Widukind of Corvey, *Deeds of the Saxons*, trans. B. S. Bachrach and D. S. Bachrach, 12 (and n46 for his reading of Bede). See also Wood, 'The Three Books of the Deeds of the Saxons', 167 (and n48). For echoes of Bede in Hrotsvitha's text, see Zeydel, 'The Authenticity of Hrotsvitha's Works', 53.

45. See chapter 4 of the present volume.

46. The inscription is fully discussed in Keynes, 'King Athelstan's Books', 189–93, on which the present discussion relies.

47. Otto ultimately selected Eadgyth as his bride, and the remaining half-sister, who, as we have seen, may have been named Ælfgifu or Eadgifu, married Louis, the brother of Rudolf II of Burgundy, and thus not himself a king.

48. Gneuss and Lapidge, *Anglo-Saxon Manuscripts*, 284–85 (no. 362).

49. See the comprehensive discussion in Keynes, 'King Athelstan's Books'.

50. On the identity of *Adiva*, see appendix II of the present volume.

51. For the text, a translation, and commentary on this record, including the suggestion that some of these names may represent Cenwald's relatives, see Keynes, 'King Athelstan's Books', 198–200. The St Gallen capitulary is St Gallen, Stiftsbibliothek 915, which can be seen at 'Cod. Sang. 915: Capitulary', E-codices, n.d., https://www.e-codices.unifr.ch/en/list/one/csg/0915 /#details, accessed on 10 October 2024.

52. On Cynath, see chapter 4 of the present volume.

53. The St Gallen confraternity book is St Gallen, Stiftsarchiv, Cod. C 3 B 55, where the list of names occurs on p. 77. The Reichenau confraternity book is Zürich, Zentralbibliothek, Rh. hist. 27, which can be seen at 'Ms. Rh. hist. 27: Codex of Fraternisation', E-codices, https://www.e

-codices.unifr.ch/en/list/one/zbz/Ms-Rh-hist0027, accessed on 10 October 2024. Keynes, 'King Athelstan's Books', 198–200, prints and discusses the relevant entries from these manuscripts.

54. Keynes, 'King Athelstan's Books', 199n4.

55. For the date, see Keynes, 'King Athelstan's Books', 148 (and n28).

56. Widukind of Corvey, *Res gestae Saxonicae*, i.31–32, i.36 and i.38 (ed. Hirsch and Lohmann, 43–45, 51–54, and 55–57), translated in Widukind of Corvey, *Deeds of the Saxons*, trans. B. S. Bachrach and D. S. Bachrach, 44–46, 50–54, 54–57. These disturbances were noted also in Thietmar of Merseburg's *Chronicon*, which relies in part on the work of Widukind; see, for example, *The Chronicon of Thietmar of Merseburg*, i.15 (trans. Warner in *Ottonian Germany*, 79). For further discussion of the political context, see Reuter, 'The Ottonians and Wessex', 76–77.

57. For comparisons between East Francia and England of the time, see Reuter, 'The Making of England and Germany'.

58. Becher, *Otto der Große*, 97.

59. Full discussion of these matters can be found in Reuter, 'The Ottonians and Wessex', 79–81.

60. Widukind of Corvey, *Res gestae Saxonicae*, i.41 (ed. Hirsch and Lohmann, 60–61), translated in Widukind of Corvey, *Deeds of the Saxons*, trans. B. S. Bachrach and D. S. Bachrach, 58–59.

61. See, for example, Hrotsvitha of Gandersheim, *Gesta Ottonis*, lines 139–40 (ed. Berschin, 280), translated in Hill, *Medieval Monarchy in Action*, 124. For the possible reasons why Hrotsvitha made the comparison with David, see Althoff, 'Saxony and the Elbe Slavs in the Tenth Century', 290.

62. Widukind of Corvey, *Res gestae Saxonicae*, ii.1 (ed. Hirsch and Lohmann, 63), translated in Widukind of Corvey, *Deeds of the Saxons*, trans. B. S. Bachrach and D. S. Bachrach, 62. For Otto's position at the beginning of his reign, see Reuter, 'The Ottonians and Wessex', 85–86.

63. *The Chronicon of Thietmar of Merseburg*, ii.1 (trans. Warner in *Ottonian Germany*, 90). See also Reuter, 'The Ottonians and Wessex', 87.

64. Reuter, 'The Ottonians and Wessex', 86–87.

65. DDH I 20. For further discussion, see Schmid, 'Die Thronfolge Ottos des Großen'; Reuter, 'The Ottonians and Wessex', 79–80; and Roach, 'D O I. 1—Eine Fälschung der frühen Salierzeit?'. I am grateful to Professor Levi Roach for sharing his article with me in advance of its publication.

66. Reuter, 'The Ottonians and Wessex', 88–89.

67. See Müller-Mertens, 'The Ottonians as Kings and Emperors', 246. Liudolf would later rebel against his father and cause him numerous problems.

68. See *Adalbert's Continuation*, s.a. 939, in *History and Politics in late Carolingian and Ottonian Europe*, trans. MacLean, 243–45.

69. *The Chronicon of Thietmar of Merseburg*, ii.3 and ii.20 (trans. Warner in *Ottonian Germany*, 91–92 and 106–7). Two diplomas of Otto I note that Magdeburg had been given to Eadgyth as part of her dower: D O I 14 and D O I 15. See Di Giovanni, 'Matilde, Edgith e Adelaide', a reference I owe to Professor Levi Roach. For the hagiographical works that explain Eadgyth's role in urging peace between Otto and Matilda, see Reuter, 'The Ottonians and Wessex', 90, and nn82–83.

70. Reuter, 'The Ottonians and Wessex', 92–93.

71. B., *Vita S. Dvnstani*, chap. 13.7 (ed. and trans. Winterbottom and Lapidge, 46–47, and n137).

72. For Eadgyth's death, see Widukind, *Res gestae Saxonicae*, ii.41 (ed. Hirsch and Lohmann, 99–100), translated in Widukind of Corvey, *Deeds of the Saxons*, trans. B. S. Bachrach and D. S. Bachrach, 97; and Hrotsvitha of Gandersheim, *Gesta Ottonis*, lines 395–404 (ed. Berschin, 289), translated in Hill, *Medieval Monarchy in Action*, 129. For the statement concerning Otto's learning to read and write, see Widukind of Corvey, *Res gestae Saxonicae*, ii.37 (ed. Hirsch and Lohmann, 96), translated in Widukind of Corvey, *Deeds of the Saxons*, trans. B. S. Bachrach and D. S. Bachrach, 93. For the possibility that Eadgyth may have been made a cult figure after her death, see Corbet, *Les saints ottoniens*, 46–50, a reference I owe to Professor Levi Roach.

73. See 'Bones Confirmed as Those of Saxon Princess Eadgyth', press release, University of Bristol, 17 June 2010, https://www.bristol.ac.uk/news/2010/7073.html. See also Davies, *Ædgyth of Wessex*, 190–94.

74. Widukind of Corvey, *Res gestae Saxonicae*, iii.1 (ed. Hirsch and Lohmann, 104), translated in Widukind of Corvey, *Deeds of the Saxons*, trans. B. S. Bachrach and D. S. Bachrach, 99–100; and *The Chronicon of Thietmar of Merseburg*, ii.4 (trans. Warner in *Ottonian Germany*, 92). For the suggestion that Otto may have considered a further marriage alliance with England, see Reuter, 'The Ottonians and Wessex', 94.

75. *The Annals of Flodoard*, s.a. 919 (1), 921 (3G), 931 (13H) (trans. Fanning and Bachrach, 3, 5, 21); with the Latin text in *Les annales*, ed. Lauer, 1, 6, 50. For Brittany in this period, see Brett, Edmonds, and Russell, *Brittany and the Atlantic Archipelago*, 180–90.

76. For the suggestion that Matuedoi and Alan may have arrived in England during the reign of Edward the Elder, see Foot, *Æthelstan*, 53. For Alan's time in England, see Quaghebeur, 'Alain de Bretagne'.

77. See the *Chronicle of Nantes*, chap. 27, in Whitelock, *EHD*, 345 (no. 25). For Alfred and Guthrum, see *ASC*, s.a. 878.

78. *Chronicle of Nantes*, chap. 29, in Whitelock, *EHD*, 345–46 (no. 25).

79. *The Annals of Flodoard*, s.a. 936 (18A) (trans. Fanning and Bachrach, 28); with Latin text in *Les annales*, ed. Lauer, 63.

80. Naismith, 'A Pair of Tenth-Century Pennies'; Brett, Edmonds, and Russell, *Brittany and the Atlantic Archipelago*, 189.

81. See *Theodrici Monachi Historia de Antiquitate Regum Norwagensium*, ed. Storm, translated in Theodoricus Monachus, *Historia de Antiquitate Regum Norwagiensium*, trans. D. MacDougall and I. MacDougall; and *Historia Norwegiæ*, ed. Storm, 71–124, translated in *A History of Norway*, trans. Kunin.

82. *Ágrip af Nóregs konunga sögum*, ed. Einarsson; *Ágrip af Nóregskonungasǫgum*, ed. Driscoll; *Fagrskinna: A Catalogue of the Kings of Norway*, trans. Finaly; Snorri Sturluson, *Heimskringla*, trans. Finlay and Faulkes.

83. I follow the approximate dates suggested in Bagge, *From Viking Stronghold to Christian Kingdom*, 389–90. For the difficulties in dating the end of Harald's reign and the beginning of Hákon's reign, see Bagge, *From Viking Stronghold to Christian Kingdom*, 25–26 and n14.

84. For expert analysis of these sources (on which the present discussion relies) and what they mean for both Hákon and Æthelstan, see Page, 'The Audience of Beowulf'; and Williams, 'Hákon Aðalsteins fóstri'.

85. Theodoricus Monachus, *Historia de Antiquitate Regum Norwagiensium*, chap. 2 (trans. D. MacDougall and I. MacDougall, 5).

86. *Fagrskinna*, chap. 4 (trans. Finlay, 52–54); and Snorri Sturluson, *Heimskringla*, chaps. 38–39 (trans. Finlay and Faulkes, 84–85).

87. See also the discussion in Foot, *Æthelstan*, 52–55, which, at 54nn86–87, cites Fjalldal, *Anglo-Saxon England in Icelandic Medieval Texts*, 34–36.

88. WM, *GR*, ii.135.1 (ed. and trans. Mynors, Thomson, and Winterbottom, 216–17).

89. Keynes and Love, 'Earl Godwine's Ship'.

90. Bagge, *From Viking Stronghold to Christian Kingdom*, 25–26. For the suggestion that Helgrim and Osfrith may have travelled to England in order to arrange for Hákon to be fostered by Æthelstan, see Foot, *Æthelstan*, 54–55.

91. See Theodoricus Monachus, *Historia de Antiquitate Regum Norwagiensium*, chap. 2 (trans. D. MacDougall and I. MacDougall, 5); *A History of Norway*, trans. Kunin and ed. Phelpstead, 15; and *Ágrip af Nóregskonungasǫgum*, trans. Driscoll, 9.

92. *Fagrskinna*, chap. 7 (trans. Finlay, 56); Snorri Sturluson, *Heimskringla*, chaps. 38–39 (trans. Finlay and Faulkes, 84–85).

93. Others have noted that, although there is nothing that can certainly link the *leiðangr* to Hákon, his reign may have necessitated the development of a naval levy because of the many defences he had to mount against the attacks of Eiríkr's sons; see Jones, *A History of the Vikings*, 121; Malmros, 'Leiðangr'; and Bagge, *From Viking Stronghold to Christian Kingdom*, 72–75. For the Gulating, see Bagge, *From Viking Stronghold to Christian Kingdom*, 179–80. That there may well have been attempts to Christianise Norway in this period may be revealed by archaeological excavations on the island of Veøy which have produced evidence of Christian graveyards; see Williams, 'Hákon Aðalsteins fóstri', 116–17, and references cited therein.

94. See Page, 'The Audience of Beowulf'; Williams, 'Hákon Aðalsteins fóstri'; and Hnefill Aðalsteinsson, 'A Piece of Horse-Liver and the Ratification of Law'. Of course, the influence was in both directions, as attested by place-names formed in full or in part from Old Norse words, elements of Scandinavian influence in early English laws, and the poetry practised at the English court, which was reminiscent of Scandinavian skaldic poetry and of which *The Battle of Brunanburh* forms an example; see Townend, 'Pre-Cnut Praise Poetry in Viking Age England'; and Townend, 'What Happened to York Viking Poetry?'

Chapter Seven

1. *The Anglo-Saxon Chronicle: A Revised Translation*, Whitelock, Douglas, and Tucker, 70n6.

2. *ASC* D, s.a. 939.

3. JW, *Chron.*, s.a. 940 (ed. Darlington and McGurk, trans. Bray and McGurk, 394–95); WM, *GR*, ii.140 (ed. and trans. Mynors, Thomson, and Winterbottom, 228–29); WM, *GP*, v.246.4 (ed. and trans. Winterbottom, 594–95).

4. WM, *GR*, ii.135.6 (ed. and trans. Mynors, Thomson, and Winterbottom, 220–21); WM, *GP*, v.246.2 (ed. and trans. Winterbottom, 592–93).

5. *The 'Liber Vitae' of the New Minster and Hyde Abbey, Winchester*, ed. Keynes, 81.

6. For the hostility to Æthelstan from Winchester, see chapter 2 of the present volume. For further discussion of the burial site, see Marafioti, *The King's Body*, 54–64.

7. WM, *GP*, v.246.5 (ed. and trans. Winterbottom, 594–95). For the poem's literary models, see Wood, '"Stand Strong against the Monsters"', 195–96.

8. WM, *GP*, vol. 2, *Introduction and Commentary*, app. B, Thomson, 330–33; McAleavy, *Malmesbury Abbey*, 23. For a bone mount with distinctive acanthus-leaf decoration, see Hart et al., 'A Medieval Monastic Cemetery'.

9. McAleavy, *Malmesbury Abbey*, 195–96.

10. See, for example, S 459 (*Shaft* 11); and S 460 (*Abing* 31). For the reign of Edmund, see, for example, Williams, 'Edmund I'; and Blanchard and Riedel, *The Reigns of Edmund, Eadred and Eadwig*.

11. Beaven, 'King Edmund I and the Danes of York'; Woolf, 'Erik Bloodaxe Revisited'; Downham, 'The Chronology of the Last Scandinavian Kings'.

12. Downham, 'The Chronology of the Last Scandinavian Kings', 30, 32.

13. For the other possible interpretations of the bird depicted, and discussion of the coin type in general, see Naismith, *MEC*, 299. See also Blackburn, 'The Coinage of Scandinavian York', 336.

14. Naismith, *MEC*, 299.

15. *HR*, s.a. 941.

16. For a recent account of these years of Northumbrian history, see McGuigan, 'Going North'.

17. Bede, *Ecclesiastical History of the English People*, preface (ed. and trans. Colgrave and Mynors, 2–3).

18. The classic study of such matters is Wormald, 'Bede, the *Bretwaldas* and the Origins of the *Gens Anglorum*'. See also Foot, 'The Making of *Angelcynn*'; and Keynes, 'Edward, King of the Anglo-Saxons'.

19. WM, *GR*, ii.135.3–6 (ed. and trans. Mynors, Thomson, and Winterbottom, 218–21).

20. Wickham, *The Inheritance of Rome*, 453–71; Wood, 'The Making of King Aethelstan's Empire', 250–72.

21. *AU*, 939.6.

22. WM, *GR*, ii.134.4–5 (ed. and trans. Mynors, Thomson, and Winterbottom, 214–15).

23. Maguinness, 'Some Methods of the Latin Panegyrists', 56–57. For a similar description (of a different ruler) in the mid-twelfth century, see *The History of Alfred of Beverley*, ed. Slevin and trans. Lockyer, 40.

24. See, for example, Molyneaux, *The Formation of the English Kingdom*.

25. Edgar can be shown to have emulated Æthelstan's approach to kingship in various ways. For an overview of his reign, see Scragg, *Edgar, King of the English*.

26. *The Chronicle of Æthelweard*, IV.5 (ed. and trans. Campbell, 54).

27. Kelly, 'Worcester's Own History', 121.

28. Roach, *Æthelred the Unready*.

29. Geffrei Gaimar, *Estoire des Engleis | History of the English* (ed. and trans. Short, 192–93).

30. On the human remains found, see S. Parker, 'Thousand-Year-Old Skeletons Found in Hotel Garden', BBC, 6 July 2024, https://www.bbc.co.uk/news/articles/cnk4xekngdgo. For other events held in Malmesbury, see 'Athelstan 1100', home page, n.d., https://www.athelstan1100.co.uk, accessed 10 July 2025. See also 'Athelstan Museum, Malmesbury', home page, https://www.athelstanmuseum.org.uk, accessed 10 July 2025.

31. For Æthelstan beyond the medieval period, see Foot, *Æthelstan*, 227–50. Æthelstan does feature in the fictional books written by Bernard Cornwell in his series 'The Last Kingdom'.

32. *ASC*, s.a. 886.

33. See Orderic Vitalis, *The Ecclesiastical History of Orderic Vitalis*, iv.ii.202 (ed. and trans. Chibnall, 2:240–41); quoted and discussed in Firth, 'What's in a Name?', 1–32.

34. Keynes, 'The Cult of King Alfred the Great'.

35. See WM, *GR*, ii.133.3 (ed. and trans. Mynors, Thomson, and Winterbottom, 210–11). Wood, 'The Making of King Aethelstan's Empire', 272, draws attention to the same description.

Appendix II

1. WM, *GR*, ii.112.2 (ed. and trans. Mynors, Thomson, and Winterbottom, 170–71).

2. WM, *GR*, ii.126.1–3 (ed. and trans. Mynors, Thomson, and Winterbottom, 198–201).

3. See *The Chronicle of Æthelweard* (ed. and trans. Campbell); and Hrotsvitha of Gandersheim, *Gesta Ottonis* (ed. Berschin, ix, for the date of composition; and 276–305, for the *Gesta Ottonis* itself).

4. *The Chronicle of Æthelweard*, prologue (ed. and trans. Campbell, 1–2).

5. The details about *Adiva* can be found in Hrotsvitha of Gandersheim, *Gesta Ottonis*, line 112 (ed. Berschin, 279).

6. Hlawitschka, 'Die verwandtschaftlchen Verbindungen'; Foot, *Æthelstan*, 64–67. See also the very useful discussion in MacLean, 'Making a Difference'.

7. WM, *GR*, ii.126.2 (ed. and trans. Mynors, Thomson, and Winterbottom, 198–201).

8. Keynes, 'King Athelstan's Books', 191n232.

9. In the second instance William actually calls her 'Eadgyth' and suggests that it was an 'Ælfgifu' who married Otto. Given that is patently an error, it seems as if William has accidentally transposed the names.

BIBLIOGRAPHY

Frequently Cited Sources and Abbreviations

AC   *Annales Cambriae, A. D. 682–954: Texts A–C in Parallel*, ed. and trans. D. N. Dumville, Basic Texts for Brittonic History 1 (Cambridge: Department of Anglo-Saxon, Norse and Celtic, University of Cambridge, 2002).

[I–VI] As.   Law Codes of Æthelstan, e.g. II As. 14. See under *The Laws of the Earliest English Kings*, ed. F. L. Attenborough (Cambridge: Cambridge University Press, 1922).

ASC   *Anglo-Saxon Chronicle.* Cited by manuscript version and by year.

Asser   Asser, *Life of King Alfred*, in *Alfred the Great: Asser's "Life of King Alfred" and Other Contemporary Sources*, trans. S. Keynes and M. Lapidge (Harmondsworth, UK: Penguin, 1983).

AU   *The Annals of Ulster to A.D. 1131*, ed. S. Mac Airt and G. Mac Niocaill (Dublin: Dublin Institute for Advanced Studies, 1983).

DDH I   Diplomas of Henry I, king of East Francia, in *Diplomata: Die Urkunden Konrad I., Heinrich I. und Otto I*, ed. T. Sickel, MGH Diplomata regum 1 (Hanover, Germany: Hahn, 1879–84).

D O I   Diplomas of Otto I, king of East Francia, in *Diplomata: Die Urkunden Konrad I., Heinrich I. und Otto I*, ed. T. Sickel, MGH Diplomata regum 1 (Hanover, Germany: Hahn, 1879–84).

Foot, *Æthelstan*   S. Foot, *Æthelstan: The First King of England* (New Haven, CT: Yale University Press, 2011).

HR   *Historia Regum*, part of which is edited and translated in *Byrhtferth of Ramsey, Historia Regum*, ed. and trans. M. Lapidge (Oxford: Clarendon Press, 2022).

HSC   *Historia de Sancto Cuthberto: A History of St Cuthbert and a Record of his Patrimony*, ed. T. Johnson South (Woodbridge: D. S. Brewer, 2002).

JW, *Chron.*   John of Worcester, *The Chronicle of John of Worcester*: vol. 2, *The Annals from 450 to 1066*, ed. R. R. Darlington and P. McGurk, trans. J. Bray and P. McGurk (Oxford: Clarendon Press, 1995); vol. 3, *The Annals from 1067 to*

1140, ed. and trans. P. McGurk (Oxford: Clarendon Press, 1998); vol. 4, *Chronicula*, ed. and trans. P. McGurk and D. A. Woodman (Oxford: Clarendon Press, 2024).

MGH   Monumenta Germaniae Historica

    SS   Scriptores in folio

    SRG   Scriptores rerum Germanicarum

    MR   *Mercian Register* (see the introduction to the present volume).

Naismith, *MEC*   R. Naismith, *Medieval European Coinage, with a Catalogue of the Coins in the Fitzwilliam Museum, Cambridge*, vol. 8, *Britain and Ireland, c. 400–1066* (Cambridge: Cambridge University Press, 2017).

ODNB   *Oxford Dictionary of National Biography*, online ed., ed. David Cannadine et al., n.d., https://www.oxforddnb.com.

S   P. H. Sawyer, *Anglo-Saxon Charters: An Annotated List and Bibliography*, Royal Historical Society Guides and Handbooks 8 (London: Offices of the Royal Historical Society, 1968). And see https://esawyer.lib.cam.ac.uk /about/index.html. For the way in which diplomas are cited, see further appendix I.

s.a.   *sub anno*

WBEASE   *The Wiley Blackwell Encyclopedia of Anglo-Saxon England*, ed. M. Lapidge, J. Blair, S. Keynes, and D. Scragg, 2nd ed. (Chichester, UK: Wiley Blackwell, 2014).

Whitelock, *EHD*   *English Historical Documents*, vol. 1, *c. 500–1042*, 2nd ed., ed. D. Whitelock (London: Routledge, 1979).

WM, *GP*   William of Malmesbury, *Gesta Pontificum Anglorum*: vol. 1, *Text and Translation*, ed. and trans. M. Winterbottom with R. M. Thomson (Oxford: Clarendon Press, 2007); vol. 2, *Introduction and Commentary*, by R. M. Thomson (Oxford: Clarendon Press, 2007).

WM, *GR*   William of Malmesbury, *Gesta Regum Anglorum*: vol. 1, ed. and trans. R. A. B. Mynors, R. M. Thomson, and M. Winterbottom (Oxford: Clarendon Press, 1998); vol. 2, *General Introduction and Commentary*, by R. M. Thomson (Oxford: Clarendon Press, 2003).

Primary Sources

Adelard of Ghent, *Lectiones in Depositione S. Dunstani*, in *The Early Lives of St Dunstan*, ed. and trans. M. Winterbottom and M. Lapidge (Oxford: Clarendon Press, 2012), 112–45.

Ágrip af Nóregs konunga sögum: Fagrskinna—Noregs konunga tal, ed. B. Einarsson, Íslenzk Fornrit 19 (Reykjavik, Iceland: Hið Íslenzka Fornritafélag, 1984).

Ágrip af Nóregskonungasǫgum: A Twelfth-Century Synoptic History of the Kings of Norway, 2nd ed., ed. and trans. M. J. Driscoll, Viking Society for Northern Research Text Series 10 (London: Viking Society for Northern Research, 2008).

The Anglo-Saxon Chronicle: A Collaborative Edition, Volume 6, MS D, ed. G. P. Cubbin (Cambridge: D. S. Brewer, 1996).

The Anglo-Saxon Chronicle: A Revised Translation, ed. D. Whitelock, with D. C. Douglas, and S. I. Tucker (London: Eyre and Spottiswoode, 1961).

Anglo-Saxon Conversations: The Colloquies of Ælfric Bata, ed. S. Gwara and D. W. Porter (Woodbridge, UK: Boydell, 1997).

Anglo-Saxon Writs, ed. F. E. Harmer (Manchester, UK: Manchester University Press, 1952).

Annala Rioghachta Eireann: Annals of the Kingdom of Ireland by the Four Masters from the Earliest Period to the Year 1616, ed. and trans. J. O'Donovan, 7 vols. (Dublin: Hodges, Smith, 1856).

Les Annales de Flodoard, ed. P. Lauer (Paris: Alphonse Picard et Fils, 1905).

The Annals of Clonmacnoise, ed. D. Murphy (Dublin: Royal Society of Antiquaries of Ireland, 1896).

The Annals of Flodoard of Reims, 919–966, ed. and trans. S. Fanning and B. S. Bachrach (Toronto: University of Toronto Press, 2011).

The Annals of St-Bertin, trans. J. L. Nelson (Manchester, UK: Manchester University Press, 1991).

Armes Prydein: The Prophecy of Britain from the Book of Taliesin, ed. I. Williams, with English version by R. Bromwich (Dublin: Dublin Institute for Advanced Studies, 1982).

Asser's Life of King Alfred, Together with the Annals of Saint Neots Erroneously Ascribed to Asser, ed. W. H. Stevenson (Oxford: Clarendon Press, 1959).

B., *Vita S. Dvnstani*, in *The Early Lives of St Dunstan*, ed. and trans. M. Winterbottom and M. Lapidge (Oxford: Clarendon Press, 2012), 1–109.

The Battle of Brunanburh, ed. A. Campbell (London: Heinemann, 1938).

Bede, *Ecclesiastical History of the English People*, rev. ed., ed. and trans. B. Colgrave and R. A. B. Mynors (Oxford: Clarendon Press, 1991).

Byrhtferth of Ramsey, *The Lives of St Oswald and St Ecgwine*, ed. and trans. M. Lapidge (Oxford: Clarendon Press, 2009).

Charters of Abingdon Abbey, Part 1, ed. S. E. Kelly, Anglo-Saxon Charters 7 (Oxford: Oxford University Press, 2000).

Charters of Barking Abbey and Waltham Holy Cross, ed. S. E. Kelly, Anglo-Saxon Charters 20 (Oxford: Oxford University Press, 2021).

Charters of Burton Abbey, ed. P. H. Sawyer, Anglo-Saxon Charters 2 (Oxford: Oxford University Press, 1979).

Charters of Christ Church Canterbury, Part 1, ed. N. P. Brooks and S. E. Kelly, Anglo-Saxon Charters 17 (Oxford: Oxford University Press, 2013).

Charters of Christ Church Canterbury, Part 2, ed. N. P. Brooks and S. E. Kelly, Anglo-Saxon Charters 18 (Oxford: Oxford University Press, 2013).

Charters of Malmesbury Abbey, ed. S. E. Kelly, Anglo-Saxon Charters 11 (Oxford: Oxford University Press, 2005).

Charters of Northern Houses, ed. D. A. Woodman, Anglo-Saxon Charters 16 (Oxford: Oxford University Press, 2012).

Charters of St Augustine's Abbey, Canterbury, and Minster-in-Thanet, ed. S. E. Kelly, Anglo-Saxon Charters 4 (Oxford: Oxford University Press, 1995).

Charters of St Paul's, London, ed. S. E. Kelly, Anglo-Saxon Charters 10 (Oxford: Oxford University Press, 2004).

Charters of the New Minster, Winchester, ed. S. Miller, Anglo-Saxon Charters 9 (Oxford: Oxford University Press, 2001).

The Chronicle of Æthelweard, ed. and trans. A. Campbell (London: Thomas Nelson and Sons, 1962).

Die Gesetze der Angelsachsen, ed. F. Liebermann, 3 vols. (Halle: Max Niemeyer, 1903–16).

The Durham 'Liber Vitae', vol. 1, *Introductory Essays, Edition, Commentary on the Edition and Indexes*, ed. D. Rollason and L. Rollason (London: British Library, 2007).

The Early Lives of St Dunstan, ed. and trans. M. Winterbottom and M. Lapidge (Oxford: Clarendon Press, 2012).

Egils saga, trans. and ed. C. Fell with J. Lucas (London: Dent, 1975).

English Coronation 'Ordines' in the Ninth and Early Tenth Centuries, ed. and trans. D. Pratt, Henry Bradshaw Society 125 (London: Henry Bradshaw Society, 2023).

Fagrskinna: A Catalogue of the Kings of Norway; A Translation with Introduction and Notes, trans. A. Finlay (Leiden, Netherlands: Brill, 2004).

Folcuin, *Gesta abbatum S. Bertini Sithiensium*, ed. O. Holder-Egger, MGH SS xiii (Hanover, Germany: Hahn, 1881), 600–635.

The Fragmentary Annals of Ireland, ed. J. N. Radner (Dublin: Dublin Institute for Advanced Studies, 1978).

Geffrei Gaimar, *Estoire des Engleis | History of the English*, ed. and trans. I. Short (Oxford: Oxford University Press, 2009).

Henry of Huntingdon, *Historia Anglorum: The History of the English People*, ed. and trans. D. Greenway (Oxford: Clarendon Press, 1996).

Historia Ecclesiae Abbendonensis: The History of the Church of Abingdon, ed. and trans. J. Hudson (Oxford: Clarendon Press, 2007).

Historia Norwegiæ, in *Monumenta Historica Norvegiæ: Latinske Kildeskrifter til Norges Historie i Middelalderen*, ed. G. Storm (Kristiania, Sweden: Trykt hos A.W. Brøgger, 1880), 71–124.

History and Politics in Late Carolingian and Ottonian Europe: The Chronicle of Regino of Prüm and Adalbert of Magdeburg, trans. S. MacLean (Manchester, UK: Manchester University Press, 2009).

The History of Alfred of Beverley, ed. J. P. T. Slevin, trans. L. Lockyer, Boydell Medieval Texts 3 (Woodbridge, UK: Boydell, 2023).

A History of Norway and the Passion and Miracles of the Blessed Óláfr, trans. D. Kunin and ed. C. Phelpstead, Viking Society for Northern Research Text Series 13 (London: Viking Society for Northern Research, 2001).

Hrotsvitha of Gandersheim, *Gesta Ottonis*, in *Hrotsvit Opera omnia*, ed. W. Berschin (Munich: K. G. Saur, 2001), 271–305.

Hudson, B. T., 'The Scottish Chronicle', *Scottish Historical Review* 77 (1998): 129–61.

The Law of Hywel Dda: Law Texts from Medieval Wales, ed. and trans. D. Jenkins (Llandysul, UK: Gomer, 1986).

The Laws of the Earliest English Kings, ed. F. L. Attenborough (Cambridge: Cambridge University Press, 1922).

Liber Eliensis, ed. E. O. Blake, Camden Third Series 92 (London: Offices of the Royal Historical Society, 1962).

Liber Eliensis: A History of the Isle of Ely from the Seventh Century to the Twelfth, trans. J. Fairweather (Woodbridge, UK: Boydell, 2005).

The 'Liber Vitae' of the New Minster and Hyde Abbey, Winchester, ed. S. Keynes, Early English Manuscripts in Facsimile 26 (Copenhagen: Rosenkilde og Bagger, 1996).

The Life of Bishop Wilfrid by Eddius Stephanus, ed. and trans. B. Colgrave (Cambridge: Cambridge University Press, 1927).

Ottonian Germany: The Chronicon of Thietmar of Merseburg, trans. D. A. Warner (Manchester, UK: Manchester University Press, 2001).

Orderic Vitalis, The Ecclesiastical History of Orderic Vitalis, ed. and trans. M. Chibnall, 6 vols. (Oxford: Clarendon Press, 1969–80).

Poetae Latini aevi Carolini, ed. E. Dümmler, MGH 1 (Berlin: Apud Weidmannos, 1881).

Poetry in Sagas of Icelanders, Part 1, ed. M. C. Ross, K. E. Gade, and T. Wills (Turnhout, Belgium: Brepols, 2022).

Recueil des actes de Louis IV, roi de France 936–954, ed. P. Lauer (Paris: Imprimerie Nationale, 1914).

Richer of Saint-Rémi, Histories, vol. 1, Books 1–2, ed. and trans. J. Lake (Cambridge, MA: Harvard University Press, 2011).

Richer von Saint-Remi, Historiae, ed. H. Hoffmann, MGH SS 38 (Hanover, Germany: Hahn, 2000).

Select English Historical Documents of the Ninth and Tenth Centuries, ed. F. E. Harmer (Cambridge: Cambridge University Press, 1914).

Snorri Sturluson, Heimskringla, vol. 1, The Beginnings to Óláfr Tryggvason, translated by A. Finlay and A. Faulkes, Viking Society for Northern Research, 2nd ed. (London: Viking Society for Northern Research, 2016).

Symeon of Durham, Libellus de Exordio atque Procursu istius hoc est Dunhelmensis Ecclesie: Tract on the Origins and Progress of This the Church of Durham, ed. and trans. D. W. Rollason (Oxford: Clarendon Press, 2000).

Theodrici Monachi Historia de Antiquitate Regum Norwagensium, in Monumenta Historica Norvegiæ: Latinske Kildeskrifter til Norges Historie i Middelalderen, ed. G. Storm (Kristiania, Sweden: Trykt hos A.W. Brøgger, 1880), 2–68.

Theodoricus Monachus, Historia de Antiquitate Regum Norwagiensium: An Account of the Ancient History of the Norwegian Kings, trans. D. and I. MacDougall, with an introduction by P. Foote, Viking Society for Northern Research Text Series 11 (London: Viking Society for Northern Research, 1998).

Three Lives of English Saints, ed. M. Winterbottom (Toronto: Pontifical Institute of Mediaeval Studies, 1972).

Widukind of Corvey, Deeds of the Saxons, trans. B. S. Bachrach and D. S. Bachrach (Washington, DC: Catholic University of America Press, 2014).

Widukind of Corvey, Res gestae Saxonicae, ed. P. Hirsch and H.-E. Lohmann, Die Sachsengeschichte des Widukind von Korvie, 5th ed., MGH SRG (Hanover, Germany: Hahn, 1935).

Wulfstan of Winchester, Life of St Æthelwold, ed. and trans. M. Lapidge and M. Winterbottom (Oxford: Clarendon Press, 2004).

Secondary Sources

Abels, R., 'Warfare in Early Medieval Britain, c. 400–c. 1100', in The New Cambridge History of Britain, vol. 1, c. 410–c. 1100, ed. F. Edmonds and R. Naismith (Cambridge: Cambridge University Press, forthcoming).

Abrams, L., 'Conversion and Assimilation', in *Cultures in Contact: Scandinavian Settlement in England in the Ninth and Tenth Centuries*, ed. D. M. Hadley and J. D. Richards (Turnhout, Belgium: 2000), 135–53.

Abrams, L., 'Edward the Elder's Danelaw', in *Edward the Elder, 899–924*, ed. N. J. Higham and D. H. Hill (Abingdon, UK: Routledge 2001), 128–43.

Abrams, L., 'King Edgar and the Men of the Danelaw', in *Edgar, King of the English, 959–975*, ed. D. Scragg (Woodbridge, UK: Boydell, 2008), 171–91.

Althoff, G., 'Saxony and the Elbe Slavs in the Tenth Century', in *The New Cambridge Medieval History*, vol. 3, *c. 900–c. 1024*, ed. T. Reuter (Cambridge: Cambridge University Press, 1999), 267–92.

Arnold-Foster, F., *Studies in Church Dedications*, 3 vols. (London: Skeffington and Son, 1899).

Bagge, S., *From Viking Stronghold to Christian Kingdom: State Formation in Norway, c. 900–1350* (Copenhagen: Museum Tusculanum Press, 2010).

Bailey, R. N., 'St Oswald's Heads', in *Oswald: Northumbrian King to European Saint*, ed. C. Stancliffe and E. Cambridge (Stamford, UK: Paul Watkins, 1995), 195–209.

Barker, E. E., 'Two Lost Documents of King Athelstan', *Anglo-Saxon England* 6 (1977): 137–43.

Barraclough, G., *The Crucible of Europe: The Ninth and Tenth Centuries in European History* (Berkeley: University of California Press, 1976).

Barrow, J., 'Demonstrative Behaviour and Political Communication in Later Anglo-Saxon England', *Anglo-Saxon England* 36 (2007): 127–50.

Barrow, J., 'Survival and Mutation: Ecclesiastical Institutions in the Danelaw in the Ninth and Tenth Centuries', in *Cultures in Contact: Scandinavian Settlement in England in the Ninth and Tenth Centuries*, ed. D. M. Hadley and J. D. Richards (Turnhout, Belgium: Brepols, 2000), 155–76.

Bartlett, R., *History in Flames: The Destruction and Survival of Medieval Manuscripts* (Cambridge: Cambridge University Press, 2024).

Bartlett, R., *Trial by Fire and Water: The Medieval Judicial Ordeal* (Oxford: Clarendon Press, 1986).

Bates, D., 'West Francia: The Northern Principalities', in *The New Cambridge Medieval History*, vol. 3, *c. 900–c. 1024*, ed. T. Reuter (Cambridge: Cambridge University Press, 1999), 398–419.

Bates, E. H., *Two Cartularies of the Benedictine Abbeys of Muchelney and Athelney in the County of Somerset*, Somerset Record Society 14 (London: Harrison and Sons, 1899).

Battiscombe, C. F., *The Relics of Saint Cuthbert: Studies by Various Authors Collected and Edited with an Historical Introduction* (Oxford: Oxford University Press, 1956).

Baxter, S., *The Earls of Mercia: Lordship and Power in Late Anglo-Saxon England* (Oxford: Oxford University Press, 2007).

Baxter, S., 'The Limits of the Anglo-Saxon State', in *Der frühmittelalterliche Staat—europäische Perspektiven*, ed. W. Pohl and V. Wieser (Vienna: Verlag der Österreichischen Akademie der Wissenschaften, 2009), 503–13.

Bayless, M., '*Alea, Tæfl*, and Related Games: Vocabulary and Context', in *Latin Learning and English Lore: Studies in Anglo-Saxon Literature for Michael Lapidge*, vol. 2, ed. K. O'Brien O'Keeffe and A. Orchard (Toronto: University of Toronto Press, 2005), 9–27.

Beaven, M. L. R., 'King Edmund I and the Danes of York', *English Historical Review* 33, no. 129 (1918): 1–9.

Becher, M., *Otto der Große, Kaiser und Reich: Eine Biographie* (Munich: C. H. Beck, 2012).

Bhreathnach, E., 'Ireland, c. 900–c. 1000', in *A Companion to the Early Middle Ages: Britain and Ireland c. 500–c. 1100*, ed. P. Stafford (Chichester, UK: Blackwell, 2009), 268–84.

Billett, J. D., *The Divine Office in Anglo-Saxon England, 597–c. 1000* (Woodbridge, UK: Boydell, 2014).

Blackburn, M., 'The Coinage of Scandinavian York', in *Aspects of Anglo-Scandinavian York*, ed. R. A. Hall, The Archaeology of York 8, fasc. 4 (York, UK: Archaeological Trust, 2004), 325–49.

Blackburn, M., 'Currency under the Vikings. Part 2: The Two Scandinavian Kingdoms of the Danelaw, c. 895–954', in *Viking Coinage and Currency in the British Isles*, British Numismatic Society Special Publication 7 (London: Spink, 2011), 32–57.

Blackburn, M., 'Mints, Burhs and the Grately Code, Cap. 14.2', in *The Defence of Wessex*, ed. D. Hill and A. Rumble (Manchester, UK: Manchester University Press, 1996), 160–75.

Blackburn, M., 'Two New Halfpennies of Edward the Elder and Athelstan', *British Numismatic Journal* 63 (1993): 123–25.

Blair, J., *The Church in Anglo-Saxon Society* (Oxford: Oxford University Press, 2005).

Blake, M., and Sargent, A., '"For the Protection of All the People": Æthelflæd and Her Burhs in Northwest Mercia', *Midland History* 43, no. 2 (2018): 120–54.

Blanchard, M. E., and Riedel, C., *The Reigns of Edmund, Eadred and Eadwig, 939–959* (Woodbridge, UK: Boydell, 2024).

Blunt, C. E., 'The Cabinet of the Marquess of Ailesbury and the Penny of Hywel Dda', *British Numismatic Journal* 52 (1982): 117–22.

Blunt, C. E., 'The Coinage of Athelstan, King of England 924–939', *British Numismatic Journal* 42 (1974): 35–160.

Blunt, C. E., 'Four Italian Coins Imitating Anglo-Saxon Types', *British Numismatic Journal* 25 (1945–48): 282–85.

Blunt, C. E., 'A Penny of the English King Athelstan Overstruck on a Cologne Denier', in *Lagom: Festschrift für Peter Berghaus zum 60. Geburtstag am 20. November 1979*, ed. T. Fischer and P. Ilisch (Münster, West Germany: Numismatischer Verlag der Münzenhandlung Dombrowski, 1981), 119–21.

Blunt, C. E., Stewart, B. H. I. H., and Lyon, C. S. S., *Coinage in Tenth-Century England, from Edward the Elder to Edgar's Reform* (Oxford: Oxford University Press, 1989).

Bobrycki, S., 'Breaking and Making Tradition: Æthelstan, 'Abd Al-Rahman III and Their Panegyrists', in *Every Inch a King: Comparative Studies on Kings and Kingship in the Ancient and Medieval Worlds*, ed. L. Mitchell and C. Melville (Leiden, Netherlands: Brill, 2013), 245–67.

Bobrycki, S., *The Crowd in the Early Middle Ages* (Princeton, NJ: Princeton University Press, 2024).

Bouchard, C. B., 'Burgundy and Provence, 879–1032', in *The New Cambridge Medieval History*, vol. 3, *c. 900–c. 1024*, ed. T. Reuter (Cambridge: Cambridge University Press, 1999), 328–45.

Braswell, L., 'Saint Edburga of Winchester: A Study of Her Cult, A.D. 950–1500, with an Edition of the Fourteenth-Century Middle English and Latin Lives', *Mediaeval Studies* 33 (1971): 292–333.

Breeze, A., '*Armes Prydein*, Hywel Dda, and the Reign of Edmund of Wessex', *Études Celtiques* 33 (1997): 209–22.

Breeze, A., 'The Battle of Brunanburh and Welsh Tradition', *Neophilologus* 83, no. 3 (1999): 479–82.

Brett, C., 'A Breton Pilgrim in England in the Reign of King Æthelstan', in *France and the British Isles in the Middle Ages and Renaissance: Essays by Members of Girton College, Cambridge, in Memory of Ruth Morgan*, ed. G. Jondorf and D. N. Dumville (Woodbridge, UK: Boydell, 1991), 43–70.

Brett, C., with Edmonds, F., and Russell, P., *Brittany and the Atlantic Archipelago, 450–1200: Contact, Myth and History* (Cambridge: Cambridge University Press, 2022).

Brooks, N., 'The Career of St Dunstan', in *St Dunstan: His Life, Times and Cult*, ed. N. Ramsay, M. Sparks, and T. Tatton-Brown (Woodbridge, UK: Boydell, 1992), 1–23.

Brooks, N., *The Early History of the Church of Canterbury: Christ Church from 597 to 1066* (Leicester, UK: Leicester University Press, 1984).

Brooks, N. P., 'Why Is the *Anglo-Saxon Chronicle* about Kings?', *Anglo-Saxon England* 39 (2011): 43–70.

Burt, C., and Partington, R., *Arise, England: Six Kings and the Making of the English State* (London: Faber and Faber, 2024).

Byrne, F. J., *Irish Kings and High-Kings* (London: Batsford, 1973).

Campbell, J., *The Anglo-Saxon State* (London: Hambledon and London, 2000).

Campbell, J., 'Asser's Life of King Alfred', in *The Inheritance of Historiography, 350–900*, ed. C. Holdsworth and T. P. Wiseman (Exeter, UK: University of Exeter Press, 1986), 115–35.

Caputo, S., *Tracks on the Ocean: A History of Trailblazing, Maps and Maritime Travel* (London: Profile Books, 2024).

Cardwell, S., '*Be wifmannes beweddunge*: Betrothals and Weddings in Anglo-Saxon England', *Anglo-Saxon England* 48 (2022): 1–26.

Cavill, P., 'The Battle of Brunanburh: The Yorkshire Hypothesis', *English Studies* 104, no. 1 (2023): 19–38.

Cavill, P., 'The Place-Name Debate', in *The Battle of Brunanburh: A Casebook*, ed. M. Livingston (Exeter, UK: University of Exeter Press, 2011), 327–49.

Chaplais, P., 'The Royal Anglo-Saxon "Chancery" of the Tenth Century Revisited', in *Studies in Medieval History Presented to R. H. C. Davis*, ed. H. Mayr-Harting and R. I. Moore (London: Hambledon, 1985), 41–51.

Charles-Edwards, T. M., *Early Christian Ireland* (Cambridge: Cambridge University Press, 2000).

Charles-Edwards, T. M., *Wales and the Britons, 350–1064* (Oxford: Oxford University Press, 2014).

Charles-Edwards, T. M., *The Welsh Laws* (Cardiff, UK: University of Wales Press, 1989).

Cheney, C. R., *A Handbook of Dates for Students of British History*, rev. ed., rev. M. Jones (Cambridge: Cambridge University Press, 2004).

Clarkson, T., *Strathclyde and the Anglo-Saxons in the Viking Age* (Edinburgh: John Donald, 2014).

Coatsworth, E., 'The Embroideries from the Tomb of St Cuthbert', in *Edward the Elder, 899–924*, ed. N. J. Higham and D. H. Hill (Abingdon, UK: Routledge, 2001), 292–306.

Colman, F., 'On the Moneyers' Names Buga and Boia on Anglo-Saxon Coins', *Nomina* 34 (2011): 91–120.

Conner, P. W., *Anglo-Saxon Exeter: A Tenth-Century Cultural History* (Woodbridge, UK: Boydell, 1993).

Corbet, P., *Les saints ottoniens: Sainteté dynastique, sainteté royale et sainteté féminine autour de l'an mil* (Sigmaringen, West Germany: Jan Thorbecke Verlag, 1986).

Coupland, S., 'The Vikings in Francia and Anglo-Saxon England to 911', in *The New Cambridge Medieval History*, vol. 2, *c. 700–c. 900*, ed. R. McKitterick (Cambridge: Cambridge University Press, 1995), 190–201.

Crawford, S., *Childhood in Anglo-Saxon England*, 2nd ed. (Cheltenham, UK: History Press, 2024).

Crawford, S., *Daily Life in Anglo-Saxon England* (Oxford: Greenwood, 2009).

Crick, J., 'Edgar, Albion and Insular Dominion', in *Edgar, King of the English, 959–975*, ed. D. Scragg (Woodbridge, UK: , Boydell, 2008), 158–70.

Cubitt, C., '"As the Lawbook Teaches": Reeves, Lawbooks and Urban Life in the Anonymous Old English Legend of the Seven Sleepers', *English Historical Review* 124 (2009): 1021–49.

Cubitt, C., 'Bishops and Councils in Late Saxon England: The Intersection of Secular and Ecclesiastical Law', in *Recht und Gericht in Kirche und Welt um 900*, ed. W. Hartmann and A. Grabowsky (Munich: Oldenbourg, 2007), 151–67.

Cubitt, C. R. E. (ed.), *Court Culture in the Early Middle Ages, The Proceedings of the First Alcuin Conference* (Turnhout, Belgium: Brepols, 2003).

Cubitt, C., 'The Institutional Church', in *A Companion to the Early Middle Ages: Britain and Ireland c. 500–c. 1100*, ed. P. Stafford (Chichester, UK: Wiley-Blackwell, 2009), 376–94.

Cubitt, C., 'The Tenth-Century Benedictine Reform in England', *Early Medieval Europe* 6, no. 1 (1997): 77–94.

Davidson, M., 'The (Non)submission of the Northern Kings in 920', in *Edward the Elder, 899–924*, ed. N. J. Higham and D. H. Hill (Abingdon, UK: Routledge, 2001), 200–211.

Davies, M. E., *Ædgyth of Wessex: The Anglo-Saxon Queen of Germany* (MiddelstedtFD, 2016).

Davies, R., 'The Medieval State: The Tyranny of a Concept', *Journal of Historical Sociology* 16, no. 2 (2003): 280–300.

De Hamel, C., *The Posthumous Papers of the Manuscripts Club* (London: Penguin, 2022).

Di Giovanni, I., 'Matilde, Edgith e Adelaide: Scontri generazionali e dotari delle regine in Germania', *Reti Medievali Rivista* 13, no. 2 (2012): 1–43.

Dodgson, J. McN., 'The Background of Brunanburh', *Saga-Book of the Viking Society* 14 (1957): 303–16.

Downham, C., 'The Chronology of the Last Scandinavian Kings of York, AD 937–954', *Northern History* 40 (2003): 25–51.

Downham, C., 'The Good, the Bad and the Ugly: Portrayals of Vikings in the "Fragmentary Annals of Ireland"', in *The Medieval Chronicle III: Proceedings of the 3rd International Conference on the Medieval Chronicle, Doorn/Utrecht 12–17 July 2002*, ed. E. Kooper (Amsterdam: Rodopi, 2004), 27–39.

Downham, C., *Viking Kings of Britain and Ireland: The Dynasty of Ívarr to A.D. 1014* (Edinburgh: Dunedin Academic Press, 2007).

Drögereit, R., 'Gab es eine Angelsächsische Königskanzlei?', *Archiv für Urkundenforschung* 13 (1935): 335–436.

Dugdale, W., *Monasticon Anglicanum: A History of the Abbies and Other Monasteries, Hospitals, Frieries, and Cathedral and Collegiate Churches, with Their Dependencies, in England and Wales*, ed. J. Caley, H. Ellis, and B. Bandinel, 6 vols. in 8 (London: Longman & Co., Lackington & Co., and Joseph Harding, 1817–30).

Dumville, D. N., 'The Ætheling: A Study in Anglo-Saxon Constitutional History', *Anglo-Saxon England* 8 (1979): 1–33.

Dumville, D. N., 'Brittany and *Armes Prydein*', *Études Celtiques* 20 (1983): 145–59.

Dumville, D. N., 'English Square Minuscule Script: The Background and Earliest Phases', *Anglo-Saxon England* 16 (1987): 147–79.

Dumville, D. N., 'Mael Brigte mac Tornáin, Pluralist Coarb (†927)', *Journal of Celtic Studies* 4 (2004): 97–116.

Dumville, D. N., 'Old Dubliners and New Dubliners in Ireland and Britain: A Viking-Age Story', *Medieval Dublin* 6 (2004): 78–93.

Dumville, D. N., 'A Pictish or Gaelic Ecclesiastic in Mercia?', *Scottish Gaelic Studies* 21 (2003): 1–8.

Dumville, D. N., *Wessex and England from Alfred to Edgar: Six Essays on Political, Cultural and Ecclesiastical Revival* (Woodbridge, UK: Boydell, 1992).

Dunbabin, J., 'West Francia: The Kingdom', in *The New Cambridge Medieval History*, vol. 3, *c. 900–c. 1024*, ed. T. Reuter (Cambridge: Cambridge University Press, 1999), 372–97.

Edmonds, F., 'The Emergence and Transformation of Medieval Cumbria', *Scottish Historical Review* 93, no. 2 (2014): 195–216.

Edmonds, F., 'The Expansion of the Kingdom of Strathclyde', *Early Medieval Europe* 23 (2015): 43–66.

Edwards, H., *The Charters of the Early West Saxon Kingdom*, BAR British Series 198 (Oxford: British Archaeological Reports, 1988).

Edwards, N., *Life in Early Medieval Wales* (Oxford: Oxford University Press, 2023).

Faith, R., 'Feorm', in *WBEASE*, 186–87.

Faith, R., 'Hide', in *WBEASE*, 243–44.

Fellows Jensen, G., *Scandinavian Personal Names in Lincolnshire and Yorkshire*, Navnestudier 7 (Copenhagen: Akademisk Forlag, 1968).

Fellows-Jensen, G., 'Scandinavian Place-Names of the Irish Sea Province', in *Viking Treasure from the North-West: The Cuerdale Hoard in Its Context*, ed. J. Graham-Campbell (Liverpool: National Museums and Galleries on Merseyside, 1992), 31–42.

Firnhaber-Baker, J., *House of Lilies: The Dynasty That Made Medieval France* (London: Allen Lane, 2024).

Firth, M., *Early English Queens, 850–1000*, Potestas Reginae (Abingdon, UK: Routledge, 2024).

Firth, M., 'What's in a Name? Tracing the Origins of Alfred's "the Great"', *English Historical Review* 139, no. 596 (2024): 1–32.

Fjalldal, M., *Anglo-Saxon England in Icelandic Medieval Texts* (Toronto: University of Toronto Press, 2005).

Foot, S., 'Dynastic Strategies: The West Saxon Royal Family in Europe', in *England and the Continent in the Tenth Century: Studies in Honour of Wilhelm Levison (1876–1947)*, ed. D. Rollason, C. Leyser, and H. Williams (Turnhout, Belgium: Brepols, 2010), 237–53.

Foot, S., 'The Historiography of the Anglo-Saxon "Nation-State"', in *Power and the Nation in European History*, ed. L. Scales and O. Zimmer (Cambridge: Cambridge University Press, 2005), 125–42.

Foot, S., 'The Making of *Angelcynn*: English Identity before the Norman Conquest', *Transactions of the Royal Historical Society* 6 (1996): 25–49.

Fordham, M., 'Peacekeeping and Order on the Anglo-Welsh Frontier in the Early Tenth Century', *Midland History* 32 (2007): 1–18.

Fouracre, P., 'Carolingian Justice: The Rhetoric of Improvement and Contexts of Abuse', in *Frankish History: Studies in the Construction of Power* (Farnham, UK: Ashgate, 2013), 771–803.

Gabriele, M., *An Empire of Memory: The Legend of Charlemagne, the Franks, and Jerusalem before the First Crusade* (Oxford: Oxford University Press, 2011).

Gallagher, R., 'Latin Acrostic Poetry in Anglo-Saxon England: Reassessing the Contribution of John the Old Saxon', *Medium Ævum* 86, no. 2 (2017): 249–74.

Gautier, A., 'Butlers and Dish-Bearers in Anglo-Saxon Courts: Household Officers at the Royal Table', *Historical Research* 90, no. 248 (2017): 269–95.

Geary, P. J., *Furta Sacra: Thefts of Relics in the Central Middle Ages* (Princeton, NJ: Princeton University Press, 1978).

Gillingham, J., 'The Beginnings of English Imperialism', *Journal of Historical Sociology* 5, no. 4 (1992): 392–409.

Gittos, H., 'Yeavering', in *WBEASE*, 517–18.

Gneuss, H., and Lapidge, M., *Anglo-Saxon Manuscripts: A Bibliographical Handlist of Manuscripts and Manuscript Fragments Written or Owned in England up to 1100* (Toronto: University of Toronto Press, 2014).

Godden, M., 'The Alfredian Project and Its Aftermath: Rethinking the Literary History of the Ninth and Tenth Centuries', *Proceedings of the British Academy* 162 (2009): 93–122.

Graham-Campbell, J., 'Some Archaeological Reflections on the Cuerdale Hoard', in *Coinage in Ninth-Century Northumbria: The Tenth Oxford Symposium on Coinage and Monetary History*, ed. D. M. Metcalf, BAR British Series 180 (Oxford: British Archaeological Reports, 1987), 329–54.

Gretsch, M., *The Intellectual Foundations of the English Benedictine Reform*, Cambridge Studies in Anglo-Saxon England 25 (Cambridge: Cambridge University Press, 1999).

Grierson, P., 'The Relations between England and Flanders before the Norman Conquest', *Transactions of the Royal Historical Society* 23 (1941): 71–112.

Griffiths, D., 'Settlement and Acculturation in the Irish Sea Region', in *Land, Sea and Home: Proceedings of a Conference on Viking-Period Settlement, at Cardiff, July 2001*, ed. J. Hines, A. Lane, and M. Redknap, Society for Medieval Archaeology Monograph 20 (Leeds, UK: Maney, 2004), 125–38.

Griffiths, D., Philpott, R. A., and Egan, G., *Meols: The Archaeology of the North Wirral Coast; Discoveries and Observations in the 19th and 20th Centuries, with a Catalogue of Collections* (Oxford: Oxford University School of Archaeology, 2007).

Gurney, F. G., 'Yttingaford and the Tenth-Century Bounds of Chalgrave and Linslade', *Bedfordshire Historical Record Society* 5 (1920): 163–79.

Hadley, D., and Richards, J. D., *Cultures in Contact: Scandinavian Settlement in England in the Ninth and Tenth Centuries* (Turnhout, Belgium: Brepols, 2000).

Hadley, D. M., Richards, J. D., Brown, H., Craig-Atkins, E., Mahoney-Swales, D., Perry, G., Stein, S., and Woods, A., 'The Winter Camp of the Viking Great Army, AD 872–3, Torksey, Lincolnshire', *Antiquaries Journal* 96 (2016): 23–67.

Halloran, K., 'Welsh Kings at the English Court, 928–956', *Welsh History Review* 25, no. 3 (2011): 297–313.

Hamerow, H., 'Anglo-Saxon Timber Buildings and Their Social Context', in *The Oxford Handbook of Anglo-Saxon Archaeology*, ed. H. Hamerow, D. A. Hinton, and S. Crawford (Oxford: Oxford University Press, 2011), 128–55.

Hare, M., 'The Documentary Evidence for the History of St Oswald's, Gloucester to 1086 AD', in *The Golden Minster: The Anglo-Saxon Minster and Later Medieval Priory of St Oswald at Gloucester*, ed. C. Heighway and R. Bryant, CBA Research Report 117 (York, UK: Council for British Archaeology, 1999), 33–45.

Hart, C., 'Athelstan "Half King" and His Family', in *The Danelaw* (London: Hambledon, 1992), 569–604.

Hart, J., Holbrook, N., Henderson, D., Hinton, D. A., Ives, R., McSloy, E. R., and Warman, S., 'A Medieval Monastic Cemetery within the Precinct of Malmesbury Abbey: Excavations at the Old Cinema Site, Market Cross', *Wiltshire Archaeological and Natural History Magazine* 104 (2011): 166–92.

Heighway, C., 'Gloucester and the New Minster of St Oswald', in *Edward the Elder, 899–924*, ed. N. J. Higham and D. H. Hill (Abingdon, UK: Routledge, 2001), 102–11.

Hill, B. H., *Medieval Monarchy in Action: The German Empire from Henry I to Henry IV* (London: George Allen and Unwin, 1972).

Hill, D., 'Athelstan's Urban Reforms', in *Anglo-Saxon Studies in Archaeology and History*, vol. 11, ed. D. Griffiths (Oxford: Oxford University School of Archaeology, 2000), 173–86.

Hill, D., 'The Shiring of Mercia—Again', in *Edward the Elder, 899–924*, ed. N. J. Higham and D. H. Hill (Abingdon, UK: Routledge, 2001), 144–59.

Hill, P., *The Age of Æthelstan: Britain's Forgotten History* (Stroud, UK: Tempus, 2004).

Hlawitschka, E., 'Die verwandtschaftlichen Verbindungen zwischen dem hochburgundischen und dem niederburgundischen Königshaus. Zugleich ein Beitrag zur Geschichte Burgunds in der 1. Hälfte des 10. Jahrhunderts', in *Grundwissenschaften und Geschichte: Festschrift für Peter Acht*, ed. W. Schlögl and P. Herde (Kallmünz, West Germany: Verlag Michael Lassleben, 1976), 28–57.

Hnefill Aðalsteinsson, J., 'A Piece of Horse-Liver and the Ratification of Law' in *A Piece of Horse Liver: Myth, Ritual and Folklore in Old Icelandic Sources*, trans. T. Gunnell and J. Turville-Petre (Reykjavik: Iceland University Press, 1998), 57–80.

Holland, T., *Athelstan: The Making of England* (London: Allen Lane, 2016).

Hudson, B. T., 'Ealdred (d. 933?)', in *ODNB*.

Hudson, J., *The Oxford History of the Laws of England: 871–1216* (Oxford: Oxford University Press, 2012).

Insley, C., 'Athelstan, Charters and the English in Cornwall', in *Charters and Charter Scholarship in Britain and Ireland*, ed. M. T. Flanagan and J. A. Green (Basingstoke and New York, UK: Palgrave Macmillan, 2005), 15–31.

Insley, C., 'Charters and Episcopal Scriptoria in the Anglo-Saxon South-West', *Early Medieval Europe* 7 (1998): 173–97.

Insley, C., 'Charters, Ritual and Late Tenth-Century English Kingship', in *Gender and Historiography: Studies in the Earlier Middle Ages in Honour of Pauline Stafford*, ed. J. L. Nelson, S. Reynolds, and S. M. Johns (London: Institute of Historical Research, 2012), 75–89.

Insley, C., 'Kings and Lords in Tenth-Century Cornwall', *History* 98, no. 329 (2013): 2–22.

Insley, C., 'Languages of Boundaries and Boundaries of Language in Cornish Charters', in *The Languages of Early Medieval Charters: Latin, Germanic Vernaculars, and the Written Word*, ed. R. Gallagher, E. Roberts, and F. Tinti (Leiden, Netherlands: Brill, 2021), 342–77.

Ivarsen, I., 'Æthelstan, Wulfstan and a Revised History of Tithes in England', *Early Medieval Europe* 29, no. 2 (2021): 225–52.

Jackson, C., *Devil-Land: England under Siege, 1588–1688* (London: Allen Lane, 2021).

Jenkins, D., and Owen, M. E., 'The Welsh Marginalia in the Lichfield Gospels: Part 1', *Cambridge Medieval Celtic Studies* 5 (1983): 37–66.

Jesch, J., 'Skaldic Verse in Scandinavian England', in *Vikings and the Danelaw: Selected Papers from the Proceedings of the Thirteenth Viking Congress, Nottingham and York, 21–30 August 1997*, ed. J. Graham-Campbell, R. A. Hall, J. Jesch, and D. Parsons (Oxford: Oxbow Books, 2001), 313–25.

Jones, G., *A History of the Vikings* (Oxford: Oxford University Press, 2001).

Karkov, C. E., *The Ruler Portraits of Anglo-Saxon England* (Woodbridge, UK: Boydell, 2004).

Kaster, R. A., 'Gloss, Glosses, Latin', in *Oxford Classical Dictionary*, 4th ed., ed. S. Hornblower and A. Spawforth (Oxford: Oxford University Press, 2012).

Kelly, S., 'Worcester's Own History: An Account of the Foundation of the See and a Summary of Benefactions, AD 680–1093', in *Constructing History across the Norman Conquest: Worcester, c. 1050–c. 1150*, ed. F. Tinti and D. A. Woodman (Woodbridge, UK: York Medieval Press, 2022), 121–49.

Kershaw, P., 'The Alfred-Guthrum Treaty: Scripting Accommodation and Interaction in Viking Age England', in *Cultures in Contact: Scandinavian Settlement in England*, ed. D. Hadley and J. D. Richards (Turnhout, Belgium: Brepols, 2000), 43–64.

Keynes, S., 'Appendix II: Archbishops and Bishops, 597–1066', in *WBEASE*, 539–66.

Keynes, S., *An Atlas of Attestations in Anglo-Saxon Charters, c. 670–1066* (Cambridge: Department of Anglo-Saxon, Norse and Celtic, University of Cambridge, 2002).

Keynes, S., 'Bamburgh', in *WBEASE*, 56.

Keynes, S., 'Church Councils, Royal Assemblies and Anglo-Saxon Royal Diplomas', in *Kingship, Legislation and Power in Anglo-Saxon England*, ed. G. R. Owen-Crocker and B. W. Schneider (Woodbridge, UK: Boydell, 2013), 17–182.

Keynes, S., 'The Cult of King Alfred the Great', *Anglo-Saxon England* 28 (1999): 225–356.

Keynes, S., *The Diplomas of King Æthelred 'the Unready', 978–1016: A Study in Their Use as Historical Evidence* (Cambridge: Cambridge University Press, 1980).

Keynes, S., 'Edward, King of the Anglo-Saxons', in *Edward the Elder, 899–924*, ed. N. J. Higham and D. H. Hill (Abingdon, UK: Routledge, 2001), 40–66.

Keynes, S., 'England, c. 900–1016', in *The New Cambridge Medieval History*, vol. 3, c. 900–c. 1024, ed. T. Reuter (Cambridge: Cambridge University Press, 1999), 456–84.

Keynes, S., 'King Alfred and the Mercians', in *Kings, Currency and Alliances: The History and Coinage of Southern England in the Ninth Century*, ed. M. A. S. Blackburn and D. N. Dumville (Woodbridge, UK: Boydell, 1998), 1–45.

Keynes, S., 'King Athelstan's Books', in *Learning and Literature in Anglo-Saxon England: Studies Presented to Peter Clemoes*, ed. M. Lapidge and H. Gneuss (Cambridge: Cambridge University Press, 1985), 143–201.

Keynes, 'Kingston-upon-Thames', in *WBEASE*, 277.

Keynes, S., 'Koenwald', in *WBEASE*, 279–80.

Keynes, S., 'Manuscripts of the Anglo-Saxon Chronicle', in *The Cambridge History of the Book in Britain*, vol. 1, *c. 400–1100*, ed. R. Gameson (Cambridge: Cambridge University Press, 2011), 537–52.

Keynes, S., 'Royal Government and the Written Word in Late Anglo-Saxon England', in *The Uses of Literacy in Early Medieval Europe*, ed. R. McKitterick (Cambridge: Cambridge University Press, 1998), 226–57.

Keynes, S., 'Shire', in *WBEASE*, 434–35.

Keynes, S., 'A Tale of Two Kings: Alfred the Great and Æthelred the Unready', *Transactions of the Royal Historical Society* 36 (1986): 195–217.

Keynes, S., 'Thegn', in *WBEASE*, 459–61.

Keynes, S., 'The Vikings in England, c. 790–1016', in *The Oxford Illustrated History of the Vikings*, ed. P. H. Sawyer (Oxford: Oxford University Press, 1997), 48–82.

Keynes, S., 'The West Saxon Charters of King Æthelwulf and His Sons', *English Historical Review* 109 (1994): 1109–49.

Keynes, S., 'Welsh Kings at Anglo-Saxon Royal Assemblies (928–55)', *Haskins Society Journal* 26 (2014): 69–122.

Keynes, S., 'Wulfstan I', in *WBEASE*, 512–13.

Keynes, S. and Lapidge, M., *Alfred the Great: Asser's "Life of King Alfred" and Other Contemporary Sources* (Harmondsworth, UK: Penguin, 1983).

Keynes, S., and Love, R., 'Earl Godwine's Ship', *Anglo-Saxon England* 38 (2010): 185–223.

Kirby, D. P., 'Asser and His Life of King Alfred', *Studia Celtica* 6 (1971): 12–35.

Kirby, D. P., 'Hywel Dda: Anglophil?', *Welsh Historical Review* 8 (1976): 1–13.

Koziol, G., *The Politics of Memory and Identity in Carolingian Royal Diplomas: The West Frankish Kingdom (840–987)*, Utrecht Studies in Medieval Literacy 19 (Turnhout, Belgium: Brepols, 2012).

Lambert, T., *Law and Order in Anglo-Saxon England* (Oxford: Oxford University Press, 2017).

Lambert, T., 'Theft, Homicide and Crime in Late Anglo-Saxon Law', *Past and Present* 214 (2012): 3–43.

Lambert, T., and Leggett, S., 'Food and Power in Early Medieval England: Rethinking *Feorm*', *Anglo-Saxon England* 49 (2020): 107–53.

Lapidge, M., 'Byrhtferth and Oswald', in *St Oswald of Worcester: Life and Influence*, ed. N. Brooks and C. Cubitt (London: Leicester University Press, 1996), 64–83.

Lapidge, M., 'Dunstan [St Dunstan] (d. 988)', in *ODNB*.

Lapidge, M., 'The Hermeneutic Style in Tenth-Century Anglo-Latin Literature', in his *Anglo-Latin Literature, 900–1066* (London: Hambledon, 1993), 105–49.

Lapidge, M., 'Israel the Grammarian', in his *Anglo-Latin Literature, 900–1066* (London: Hambledon, 1993), 87–104.

Lapidge, M., 'Latin Learning in Ninth-Century England', in his *Anglo-Latin Literature, 600–899* (London: Hambledon, 1996), 409–54.

Lapidge, M., 'Some Latin Poems as Evidence for the Reign of Athelstan', in his *Anglo-Latin Literature, 900–1066* (London: Hambledon, 1993), 49–86.

Larrington, C., 'Egill's Longer Poems: *Arinbjarnarkviða* and *Sonatorrek*', in *Introductory Essays on Egils Saga and Njáls Saga*, ed. J. Hines and D. Slay (London: Viking Society for Northern Research, 1992), 49–63.

Larson, L. M., *The King's Household in England before the Norman Conquest* (St. Clair Shores, MI: Scholarly Press, 1969).

Lavelle, R., 'Why Grateley? Reflections on Anglo-Saxon Kingship in a Hampshire Landscape', *Proceedings of the Hampshire Field Club Archaeological Society* 60 (2005): 154–69.

Lewis, C. P., 'Welsh Territories and Welsh Identities in Late Anglo-Saxon England', in *Britons in Anglo-Saxon England*, ed. N. Higham (Woodbridge, UK: Boydell, 2007), 130–43.

Liebermann, F., *Die heiligen Englands* (Hanover, Germany: Hahn, 1889).

Livingston, M., *Never Greater Slaughter: Brunanburh and the Birth of England* (Oxford: Osprey, 2021).

Lloyd, J. E., *A History of Wales from the Earliest Times to the Edwardian Conquest*, vol. 1 (London: Longmans, Green, 1911).

Loomis, L. H., 'The Holy Relics of Charlemagne and King Athelstan: The Lances of Longinus and St Mauricius', *Speculum* 25, no. 4 (1950): 437–56.

MacLean, S., 'Making a Difference in Tenth-Century Politics: King Athelstan's Sisters and Frankish Queenship', in *Frankland: The Franks and the World of the Early Middle Ages, Essays in Honour of Dame Jinty Nelson*, ed. P. Fouracre and D. Ganz (Manchester, UK: Manchester University Press, 2008), 167–90.

Maddicott, J. R., *The Origins of the English Parliament, 924–1327* (Oxford: Oxford University Press, 2011).

Maguinness, W. S., 'Some Methods of the Latin Panegyrists', *Hermathena* 22, no. 47 (1932): 42–61.

Malmros, R., 'Leiðangr', in *Medieval Scandinavia: An Encyclopedia*, ed. P. Pulsiano (New York: Garland, 1993), 389–90.

Marafioti, N., *The King's Body: Burial and Succession in Late Anglo-Saxon England* (Toronto: University of Toronto Press, 2014).

Margary, I. D., *Roman Roads in Britain*, 3rd ed. (London: John Baker, 1973).

Maund, K., *The Welsh Kings: The Medieval Rulers of Wales* (Stroud, UK: Tempus, 2000).

McAleavy, T., *Malmesbury Abbey 670–1539: Patronage, Scholarship and Scandal* (Woodbridge, UK: Boydell, 2023).

McGuigan, N., 'Bamburgh and the Northern English Realm: Understanding the Dominion of Uhtred', in *The Battle of Carham: A Thousand Years On*, ed. N. McGuigan and A. Woolf (Edinburgh: John Donald, 2018), 95–150.

McGuigan, N., 'Cuthbert's Relics and the Origins of the Diocese of Durham', *Anglo-Saxon England* 48 (2019): 121–62.

McGuigan, N., 'Going North: Revisiting the End of Northern Independence', in *The Reigns of Edmund, Eadred and Eadwig, 939–959*, ed. M. E. Blanchard and C. Riedel (Woodbridge, UK: Boydell, 2024), 121–49.

McGuigan, N., *Máel Coluim III 'Canmore'* (Edinburgh: John Donald, 2021).

McKitterick, R., *Charlemagne: The Formation of a European Identity* (Cambridge: Cambridge University Press, 2008).

McKitterick, R., *The Frankish Kingdoms under the Carolingians, 751–987* (London: Longman, 1983).

Meens, R. 'A Background to Augustine's Mission to Anglo-Saxon England', *Anglo-Saxon England* 23 (1994): 5–17.

Metcalf, D. M., 'The Monetary History of England in the Tenth Century Viewed in the Perspective of the Eleventh Century', in *Anglo-Saxon Monetary History: Essays in Memory of Michael Dolley*, ed. M. A. S. Blackburn (Leicester, UK: Leicester University Press, 1986), 133–57.

Miller, S., 'Hundreds', in *WBEASE*, 249.

Miller, S., 'Wapentakes', in *WBEASE*, 488.

Molyneaux, G., *The Formation of the English Kingdom in the Tenth Century* (Oxford: Oxford University Press, 2015).

Molyneaux, G., 'The *Old English Bede*: English Ideology or Christian Instruction?', *English Historical Review* 124, no. 511 (2009): 1289–1323.

Molyneaux, G., 'The *Ordinance Concerning the Dunsæte* and the Anglo-Welsh Frontier in the Late Tenth and Eleventh Centuries', *Anglo-Saxon England* 40 (2012): 249–72.

Molyneaux, G., 'Why Were Some Tenth-Century English Kings Presented as Rulers of Britain?', *Transactions of the Royal Historical Society*, sixth ser., 21 (2011): 59–91.

Müller-Mertens, E., 'The Ottonians as Kings and Emperors', in *The New Cambridge Medieval History*, vol. 3, *c. 900–c. 1024*, ed. T. Reuter (Cambridge: Cambridge University Press, 1999), 233–66.

Murray, H. J. R., *A History of Board-Games Other Than Chess* (Oxford: Oxford University Press, 1951).

Naismith, R., 'The Anglo-Saxons: Myth and History', *Early Medieval England and Its Neighbours* 51 (2025), forthcoming.

Naismith, R., *Citadel of the Saxons: The Rise of Early London* (London: I. B. Tauris, 2019).

Naismith, R., 'Gilds, States and Societies in the Early Middle Ages', *Early Medieval Europe* 28, no. 4 (2020): 627–62.

Naismith, R., *Making Money in the Early Middle Ages* (Princeton, NJ: Princeton University Press, 2023).

Naismith, R., 'A Pair of Tenth-Century Pennies Found on the Banks of the Loire', *Numismatic Chronicle* 174 (2014): 223–25.

Naismith, R., 'Prelude to Reform: Tenth-Century English Coinage in Perspective', in *Early Medieval Monetary History: Studies in Memory of Mark Blackburn*, ed. R. Naismith, M. Allen, and E. Screen (Farnham, UK: Ashgate, 2014), 39–83.

Napier, A. S., and Stevenson, W. H., *The Crawford Collection of Early Charters and Documents Now in the Bodleian Library* (Oxford: Oxford University Press, 1895).

Nelson, J. L., 'Eadgifu (d. in or after 951)', in *ODNB*.

Nelson, J. L., 'The Frankish Kingdoms, 814–898: The West', in *The New Cambridge Medieval History*, vol. 2, *c. 700–c. 900*, ed. R. McKitterick (Cambridge: Cambridge University Press, 1995), 110–41.

Nelson, J. L., *King and Emperor: A New Life of Charlemagne* (London: Allen Lane, 2019).

Nelson, J. L., 'The Problem of King Alfred's Royal Anointing', *Journal of Ecclesiastical History* 18 (1967): 145–63.

Noble, F., *Offa's Dyke Reviewed*, ed. M. Gelling, BAR British Series 114 (Oxford: British Archaeological Reports, 1983).

Ó Cróinín, D., *Early Medieval Ireland 400–1200* (London: Longman, 1995).

O'Donovan, M. A., 'An Interim Revision of Episcopal Dates for the Province of Canterbury, 850–950: Part II', *Anglo-Saxon England* 2 (1974): 91–113.

Olson, L., *Early Monasteries in Cornwall* (Woodbridge, UK: Boydell, 1989).

Orme, N., *Exeter Cathedral: The First Thousand Years, 400–1550* (Exeter, UK: Impress Books, 2009).

Ortenberg, V., 'Archbishop Sigeric's Journey to Rome in 990', *Anglo-Saxon England* 19 (1990): 197–246.

Ortenberg, V., '"The King from Overseas": Why did Æthelstan Matter in Tenth-Century Continental Affairs?', in *England and the Continent in the Tenth Century: Studies in Honour of Wilhelm Levison (1876–1947)*, ed. D. Rollason, C. Leyser, and H. Williams (Turnhout, Belgium: Brepols, 2010), 211–36.

Padel, O. J., 'Two New Pre-Conquest Charters for Cornwall', *Cornish Studies* 6 (1979): 20–27.

Page, R. I., 'The Audience of Beowulf and the Vikings', in *The Dating of Beowulf*, ed. C. Chase (Toronto: University of Toronto Press, 1997), 113–22.

Parsons, D. N., 'The Inscriptions of Viking-Age York', in *Aspects of Anglo-Scandinavian York*, ed. R. A. Hall, The Archaeology of York 8, fasc. 4 (York, UK: York Archaeological Trust, 2004), 350–56.

Peacock, D. P. S., 'Charlemagne's Black Stones: The Re-use of Roman Columns in Early Medieval Europe', *Antiquity* 71, no. 273 (1997): 709–15.

Phythian-Adams, C., *Land of the Cumbrians: A Study in British Provincial Origins, A.D. 400–1200* (Aldershot, UK: Scolar, 1996).

Plenderleith, E., Hohler, C., and Freyhan, R., 'The Stole and the Maniples', in *The Relics of Saint Cuthbert: Studies by Various Authors Collected and Edited with an Historical Introduction*, ed. C. F. Battiscombe (Oxford: Oxford University Press, 1956), 375–432.

Pratt, D., 'The Making of the Second English Coronation *Ordo*', *Anglo-Saxon England* 46 (2017): 147–258.

Pratt, D., *The Political Thought of King Alfred the Great* (Cambridge: Cambridge University Press, 2007).

Pratt, D., 'Written Law and the Communication of Authority in 10th-Century England', in *England and the Continent in the 10th Century: Studies in Honour of Wilhelm Levison (1876–1947)*, ed. D. Rollason, C. Leyser, and H. Williams (Turnhout, Belgium: Brepols, 2010), 331–50.

Quaghebeur, J., 'Alain de Bretagne, l'exil d'un prince', in *Multi-disciplinary Approaches to Medieval Brittany, 450–1200*, ed. C. Brett, P. Russell, and F. Edmonds (Turnhout, Belgium: Brepols, 2023), 109–40.

Rahtz, P., 'Buildings and Rural Settlement', in *The Archaeology of Anglo-Saxon England*, ed. D. M. Wilson (Cambridge: Cambridge University Press, 1981), 49–98.

Rahtz, P., 'Cheddar', in *WBEASE*, 103.

Reuter, T., 'The Making of England and Germany, 850–1050: Points of Comparison and Difference', in *Medieval Europeans, Studies in Ethnic Identity and National Perspectives in Medieval Europe*, ed. A. P. Smyth (London: Macmillan, 1998), 53–70.

Reuter, T., 'The Ottonians and Wessex', in *Communications and Power in Medieval Europe: The Carolingian and Ottonian Centuries*, ed. T. Reuter (London: Hambledon, 1994), 73–104.

Roach, L., *Æthelred the Unready* (New Haven, CT: Yale University Press, 2016).

Roach, L., 'D O I. 1—Eine Fälschung der frühen Salierzeit?', *Archiv für Diplomatik* 70 (2024): 19–50.

Roach, L., *Kingship and Consent in Anglo-Saxon England, 871–978* (Cambridge: Cambridge University Press, 2013).

Roach, L., 'Law Codes and Legal Norms in Later Anglo-Saxon England', *Historical Research* 86, no. 233 (2013): 465–86.

Roach, L., 'Penitential Discourse in the Diplomas of King Æthelred "the Unready"', *Journal of Ecclesiastical History* 64 (2013): 258–76.

Roach, L., 'Public Rites and Public Wrongs: Ritual Aspects of Diplomas in Tenth- and Eleventh-Century England', *Early Medieval Europe* 19, no. 2 (2011): 182–203.

Roberts, E., 'Bishops, Canon Law and Governance in Tenth-Century England: The *Constitutiones* of Oda of Canterbury', *Journal of Ecclesiastical History* online, October 8, 2024, https://www.cambridge.org/core/journals/journal-of-ecclesiastical-history/article/bishops-canon-law-and-governance-in-tenthcentury-england-the-constitutiones-of-oda-of-canterbury/4EC376ABE0BD945DDF36D34C451AE0CE.

Robinson, J. A., *The Times of Saint Dunstan: The Ford Lectures Delivered in the University of Oxford in the Michaelmas Term, 1922* (Oxford: Oxford University Press, 1923).

Rollason, D. W., 'Lists of Saints' Resting-Places in Anglo-Saxon England', *Anglo-Saxon England* 7 (1978): 61–93.

Rollason, D. W., *Northumbria, 500–1100: Creation and Destruction of a Kingdom* (Cambridge: Cambridge University Press, 2003).

Rollason, D. W., 'Relic-Cults as an Instrument of Royal Policy, c. 900–c. 1050', *Anglo-Saxon England* 15 (1986): 91–103.

Rollason, D. W., 'St Cuthbert and Wessex: The Evidence of Cambridge, Corpus Christi College MS 183', in *St Cuthbert, His Cult and His Community to A.D. 1200*, ed. G. Bonner, D. Rollason, and C. Stancliffe (Woodbridge, UK: Boydell, 1989), 413–24.

Rollason, D. W., Gore, D., and Fellows-Jensen, G., *Sources for York History to AD 1100*, The Archaeology of York 1 (York, UK: York Archaeological Trust, 1998).

Rumble, A. R., 'Edward the Elder and the Churches of Winchester and Wessex', in *Edward the Elder, 899–924*, ed. N. J. Higham and D. H. Hill (Abingdon, UK: Routledge, 2001), 230–47.

Sawyer, P., 'The Last Scandinavian Kings of York', *Northern History* 31 (1995): 39–44.

Sawyer, P., 'The Royal *Tun* in Pre-Conquest England', in *Ideal and Reality in Frankish and Anglo-Saxon Society: Studies Presented to J. M. Wallace-Hadrill*, ed. P. Wormald, D. Bullough, and R. Collins (Oxford: Basil Blackwell, 1983), 273–99.

Sawyer, P., *The Wealth of Anglo-Saxon England* (Oxford: Oxford University Press, 2013).

Scharer, A., 'The Writing of History at King Alfred's Court', *Early Medieval Europe* 5, no. 2 (1996): 177–206.

Schmid, K., 'Die Thronfolge Ottos des Großen', in *Zeitschrift der Savigny-Stiftung für Rechtsgeschichte* 81 (1964): 80–163.

Scragg, D. (ed.), *Edgar, King of the English, 959–975* (Woodbridge, UK: Boydell, 2008).

Sharp, S., 'The West Saxon Tradition of Dynastic Marriage: With Special Reference to Edward the Elder', in *Edward the Elder, 899–924*, ed. N. J. Higham and D. H. Hill (Abingdon, UK: Routledge, 2001), 79–88.

Simpson, L., 'The King Alfred / St Cuthbert Episode in the *Historia de Sancto Cuthberto*: Its Significance for Mid-Tenth-Century English History', in *St Cuthbert, His Cult and His Community to AD 1200*, ed. G. Bonner, D. Rollason, and C. Stancliffe (Woodbridge, UK: Boydell, 1989), 397–411.

Smart, V., 'Economic Migrants? Continental Moneyers' Names on the Tenth-Century English Coinage', *Nomina* 32 (2009): 113–56.

Smart, V., '"Not the Oldest Known List": Scandinavian Moneyers' Names on the Tenth-Century English Coinage', in *Coinage and History in the North Sea World, c. AD 500–1250: Essays in Honour of Marion Archibald*, ed. B. Cook and G. Williams (Leiden, Netherlands: Brill, 2006), 297–324.

Smith, J. M. J., 'Eleventh-Century Relic Collections and the Holy Land', in *Natural Materials of the Holy Land and the Visual Translation of Place, 500–1500*, ed. R. Bartal, N. Bodner, and B. Kuhnel (Abingdon, UK: Routledge, 2017), 19–35.

Smith, S. T., *Land and Book: Literature and Land Tenure in Anglo-Saxon England* (Toronto: University of Toronto Press, 2012).

Smyth, A. P., *King Alfred the Great* (Oxford: Oxford University Press, 1995).

Smyth, A. P., *Scandinavian Kings in the British Isles* (Oxford: Oxford University Press, 1977).

Smyth, A. P., *Scandinavian York and Dublin: The History and Archaeology of Two Related Viking Kingdoms*, 2 vols. (Dublin: Templekieran, 1975–79).

Snook, B., *The Anglo-Saxon Chancery: The History, Language and Production of Anglo-Saxon Charters from Alfred to Edgar* (Woodbridge, UK: Boydell, 2015).

Stafford, P., *After Alfred: Anglo-Saxon Chronicles and Chroniclers, 900–1150* (Oxford: Oxford University Press, 2020).

Stafford, P., 'Charles the Bald, Judith and England', in *Charles the Bald: Court and Kingdom*, ed. M. T. Gibson and J. L. Nelson, 2nd rev. ed. (Aldershot, UK: Variorum, 1990), 139–53.

Stafford, P., 'Eadgifu (b. in or before 904, d. in or after 966)', in *ODNB*.

Stafford, P., 'Ealdorman', in *WBEASE*, 156–57.

Stafford, P., 'Reeve', in *WBEASE*, 397–98.

Stenton, F. M., *Anglo-Saxon England*, 3rd ed. (Oxford: Oxford University Press, 1971).

Stephenson, R., *The Politics of Language: Byrhtferth, Ælfric, and the Multilingual Identity of the Benedictine Reform* (Toronto: University of Toronto Press, 2015).

Stevenson, J., 'The Irish Contribution to Anglo-Latin Hermeneutic Prose', in *Ogma: Essays in Celtic Studies in Honour of Próinséas Ní Chatháin*, ed. M. Richter and J-M. Picard (Dublin: Four Courts, 2002), 268–82.

Stevenson, W. H., 'A Latin Poem Addressed to King Athelstan', *English Historical Review* 26, no. 103 (1911): 482–87.

Stevenson, W. H., 'The Anglo-Saxon Chancery', Sanders Lectures in Bibliography, Cambridge University, 1898, accessed on a Robinson College, Cambridge website: https://dk.robinson.cam.ac.uk/sites/default/files/files/Stevenson%202011.pdf.

Swanton, M., *Anglo-Saxon Prose* (Gloucester, UK: Choir Press, 2016).

Thacker, A., 'Dynastic Monasteries and Family Cults', in *Edward the Elder, 899–924*, ed. N. J. Higham and D. H. Hill (Abingdon, UK: Routledge, 2001), 248–63.

Thacker, A., '*Membra Disjecta*: The Division of the Body and the Diffusion of the Cult', in *Oswald: Northumbrian King to European Saint*, ed. C. Stancliffe and E. Cambridge (Stamford, UK: Paul Watkins, 1995), 97–127.

Thomas, R., 'The Context of the Hywel Dda Penny', in *Interpreting Early Medieval Coinage: Essays in Memory of Stewart Lyon*, ed. M. Allen, R. Naismith, and H. Pagan, British Numismatic Society Special Publication 15 (London: British Numismatic Society, 2022), 87–98.

Thomas, R., 'Three Welsh Kings and Rome: Royal Pilgrimage, Overlordship, and Anglo-Welsh Relations in the Early Middle Ages', *Early Medieval Europe* 28, no. 4 (2020): 560–91.

Thomas, R., and Callander, D., 'Reading Asser in Early Medieval Wales: The Evidence of *Armes Prydein Vawr*', *Anglo-Saxon England* 46 (2017): 115–45.

Thomov, T., 'Four Scandinavian Ship Graffiti from Hagia Sophia', *Byzantine and Modern Greek Studies* 38, no. 2 (2014): 168–84.

Thornbury, E. V., *Becoming a Poet in Anglo-Saxon England* (Cambridge: Cambridge University Press, 2014).

Thornton, D. E., 'Hywel Dda [Hywel Dda ap Cadell]', in *ODNB*.

Tinti, F., 'The Archiepiscopal Pallium in Late Anglo-Saxon England', in *England and Rome in the Early Middle Ages: Pilgrimage, Art, and Politics*, ed. F. Tinti (Turnhout, Belgium: Brepols, 2014), 307–42.

Tinti, F., 'England and the Papacy in the Tenth Century', in *England and the Continent in the Tenth Century: Studies in Honour of Wilhelm Levison (1876–1947)*, ed. D. Rollason, C. Leyser, and H. Williams (Turnhout, Belgium: Brepols, 2010), 163–84.

Tolstoy, N., 'When and Where Was *Armes Prydein* Composed?', *Studia Celtica* 42 (2008): 145–49.

Townend, M., 'Pre-Cnut Praise Poetry in Viking Age England', *Review of English Studies*, n.s., 51, no. 203 (2000): 349–70.

Townend, M., 'What Happened to York Viking Poetry? Memory, Tradition and the Transmission of Skaldic Verse', *Saga-Book* 27 (2003): 48–90.

Wainwright, F. T., 'Ingimund's Invasion', in *Scandinavian England: Collected Papers* (Chichester, UK: Phillimore, 1975), 131–61.

Walker, S., 'A Context for *Brunanburh*', in *Warriors and Churchmen*, ed. T. Reuter (London: Hambledon, 1992), 21–39.

Wasserstein, D. J., 'The First Jew in England: "The Game of the Evangel" and a Hiberno-Latin Contribution to Anglo-Saxon History', in *Ogma: Essays in Celtic Studies in Honour of Próinséas Ní Chatháin*, ed. M. Richter and J.-M. Picard (Dublin: Four Courts, 2002), 283–88.

Watson, R., 'Viking-Age Amounderness: A Reconsideration', in *Place-Names, Language and the Anglo-Saxon Landscape*, ed. N. J. Higham and M. J. Ryan, Publications of the Manchester Centre for Anglo-Saxon Studies 10 (Woodbridge, UK: Boydell, 2011), 125–41.

Westwell, A., Rembold, I., and Van Rhijn, C., *Rethinking the Carolingian Reforms* (Manchester, UK: Manchester University Press, 2023).

Whitelock, D., 'The Dealings of the Kings of England with Northumbria in the Tenth and Eleventh Centuries', in her *History, Law and Literature in 10th–11th Century England* (London: Variorum, 1981), 70–88 (no. III).

Wickham, C., *The Inheritance of Rome: Illuminating the Dark Ages 400–1000* (New York: Penguin, 2009).

Wieland, G. R., 'A New Look at the Poem "Archalis clamare triumuir"', in *Insignis Sophiae Arcator: Medieval Latin Studies in Honour of Michael Herren on His 65th Birthday*, ed. G. R. Wieland, C. Ruff, and R. G. Arthur, Publications of the Journal of Medieval Latin 6 (Turnhout, Belgium: Brepols, 2006), 178–92.

Williams, A., 'Edmund I (920/21–946)' in *ODNB*.

Williams, G., 'The Coins from the Vale of York Viking Hoard: Preliminary Report', *British Numismatic Journal* 78 (2008): 228–34.

Williams, G., 'Hákon Aðalsteins fóstri: Aspects of Anglo-Saxon Kingship in Tenth-Century Norway', in *The North Sea World in the Middle Ages: Studies in the Cultural History of North-Western Europe*, ed. T. M. Liszka and L. E. M. Walker (Dublin: Four Courts, 2001), 108–26.

Williams, G., 'Roriva Castr: A New Danelaw Mint of the 920s', in *Scripta varia numismatico Tuukka Talvio sexagenario dedicate*, ed. O. Järvinen, Suomen Numismaattinen Yhdistyksen Julkaisuja 6 (Helsinki: Suomen Numismaattinen Yhdistys, 2008), 41–47.

Wood, M., 'A Carolingian Scholar in the Court of King Æthelstan', in *England and the Continent in the Tenth Century: Studies in Honour of Wilhelm Levison (1876–1947)*, ed. D. Rollason, C. Leyser, and H. Williams (Turnhout, Belgium: Brepols, 2010), 135–62.

Wood, M., 'The Making of King Aethelstan's Empire: An English Charlemagne', in *Ideal and Reality in Frankish and Anglo-Saxon Society: Studies Presented to J. M. Wallace-Hadrill*, ed. P. Wormald, D. Bullough, and R. Collins (Oxford: Basil Blackwell, 1983), 250–72.

Wood, M., 'Searching for Brunanburh: The Yorkshire Context of the "Great War" of 937', *Yorkshire Archaeological Journal* 85, no. 1 (2013): 138–59.

Wood, M., '"Stand Strong against the Monsters": Kingship and Learning in the Empire of King Æthelstan', in *Lay Intellectuals in the Carolingian World*, ed. P. Wormald and J. L. Nelson (Cambridge: Cambridge University Press, 2007), 192–217.

Wood, R. F., 'The Three Books of the Deeds of the Saxons, by Widukind of Corvey, Translated with Introduction, Notes and Bibliography' (PhD thesis, University of California–Los Angeles, 1949).

Woodman, D. A., '"Æthelstan A" and the Rhetoric of Rule', *Anglo-Saxon England* 42 (2013): 217–48.

Woodman, D. A., 'Annals 848 to 1118 in the *Historia Regum*', in *The Battle of Carham: A Thousand Years On*, ed. N. McGuigan and A. Woolf (Edinburgh: John Donald, 2018), 202–30.

Woodman, D. A., 'Charters, Northumbria and the Unification of England in the Tenth and Eleventh Centuries', *Northern History* 52, no. 1 (2015): 35–51.

Woodman, D. A., 'Hagiography and Charters in Early Northumbria', in *Writing, Kingship and Power in Anglo-Saxon England*, ed. R. Naismith and D. A. Woodman (Cambridge: Cambridge University Press, 2017), 52–70.

Woolf, A., 'Erik Bloodaxe Revisited', *Northern History* 34, no. 1 (1998): 189–93.

Woolf, A., *From Pictland to Alba 789–1070*, New Edinburgh History of Scotland 2 (Edinburgh: Edinburgh University Press, 2008).

Woolf, A., 'Scotland', in *A Companion to the Early Middle Ages: Britain and Ireland c. 500–c. 1100*, ed. P. Stafford (Chichester, UK: Wiley-Blackwell, 2009), 251–67.

Wormald, P., 'Bede, the *Bretwaldas* and the Origins of the *Gens Anglorum*', in *The Times of Bede: Studies in Early English Christian Society and Its Historian*, ed. P. Wormald and S. Baxter (Oxford: Blackwell, 2006), 106–34.

Wormald, P., '*Lex scripta* and *verbum regis*: Legislation and Germanic Kingship from Euric to Cnut', in *Legal Culture in the Early Medieval West: Law as Text, Image and Experience* (London: Hambledon, 1999), 1–43.

Wormald, P., *The Making of English Law: King Alfred to the Twelfth Century*, vol. 1, *Legislation and Its Limits* (Oxford: Blackwell, 1999).

Yorke, B., 'Æthelwold and the Politics of the Tenth Century', in *Bishop Æthelwold: His Career and Influence*, ed. B. Yorke (Woodbridge, UK: Boydell, 1988), 65–88.

Yorke, B., 'Eadburh [St Eadburh, Eadburga]', in *ODNB*.

Yorke, B., *Nunneries and the Anglo-Saxon Royal Houses* (London: Continuum, 2003).

Yorke, B., 'Royal Burial in Winchester: Context and Significance', in *Early Medieval Winchester: Communities, Authority and Power in an Urban Space, c. 800–c. 1200*, ed. R. Lavelle, S. Roffey, and K. Weikert (Oxford: Oxbow Books, 2021), 59–80.

Yorke, B., *Wessex in the Early Middle Ages* (Leicester, UK: Leicester University Press, 1995).

Young, F., *In Search of England's Lost King* (London: I. B. Tauris, 2018).

Zacher, S., 'Multilingualism at the Court of King Æthelstan: Latin Praise Poetry and *The Battle of Brunanburh*', in *Conceptualizing Multilingualism in Medieval England, c. 800–c. 1250*, ed. E. M. Tyler (Turnhout, Belgium: 2011), 77–103.

Zeydel, E. H., 'The Authenticity of Hrotsvitha's Works', *Modern Language Notes* 61 (1946): 50–55.

Zimmermann, M., 'Western Francia: The Southern Principalities', in *The New Cambridge Medieval History*, vol. 3, *c. 900–c. 1024*, ed. T. Reuter (Cambridge: Cambridge University Press, 1999), 420–55.

INDEX

Page numbers in italic indicate maps.

Whittlebury, 99
Widukind of Corvey, 18, 192, 193, 195
Wigferth, 49
Wigred, 125
William of Malmesbury, 12–13, 29, 30, 34, 41,
    59, 166–67, 227–29; on Æthelstan, 32–33,
    35, 44–46, 60, 135, 168, 178, 181–82, 198–99,
    207, 210, 211; on Battle of *Brunanburh*, 174;
    on Brittany, 132–33; on death of Edwin,
    63, 118–19; on Eadburh, 117; on Edward
    the Elder, 43; on Malmesbury Abbey,
    202; on marriage alliances, 53–54, 185–86;
    on Sihtric, 55; on Welsh kings, 152, 154
Wilton, 22, 41, 114
Wiltshire, 23, 34, 41, 47, 85, 116–19, 127, 155, 184
Winchester, 10, 31, 33, 43, 45–49, 58, 64, 92,
    105, 111, 114, 117, 123, 124, 127, 136, 139, 144,
    155, 201–2, 205, 228; bishop of, 46, 88, 122,
    125, 126, 145; royal palace in, 2
witness-lists, 71–76, 114–15, 123–25, 154, 157
Wolverhampton, 164
women: land grants to, 116–17; in law code,
    98; royal, influence of, 180

Worcester, 25, 61, 110, 116, 123–26, 139, 145,
    185, 190, 201, 209, 211
'Worcester Chronicle', plate 26, 43, 169–71,
    176, 209
word-play, 87
writs, 70
Wroxeter, 9, 83
Wulfgar, 76
Wulfhelm, 50, 91, 92, 100, 118, 121, 191
Wulfhere, 121
Wulfstan I, 65, 66, 76, 79, 122
Wulfstan II, 92, 108, 209
Wulfstan of Winchester, 144
Wulfswith, 116
Wye River, 60, 154, 160

Yeavering, 31
York, 4, 6, 14, 16, 21, 22, 38–42, 52–55, 57–59,
    64–66, 68, 69, 74, 76, 79, 81, 102, 103, 106,
    108, 110, 121–26, 131, 148, 150, 156, 165–68,
    172, 180, 203, 205, 229; Óláf Guthfrithson
    in, 203; see in, 109, 121–23
Ystrad Tywi, 5, 150